Reality's Dark Light

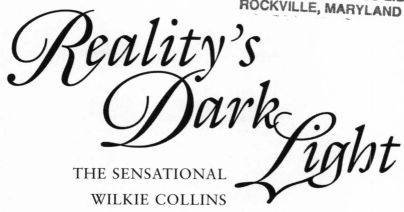

Reality's Dark Light

THE SENSATIONAL
WILKIE COLLINS

Edited by

Maria K. Bachman
and
Don Richard Cox

Tennessee Studies in Literature Volume 41

THE UNIVERSITY OF TENNESSEE PRESS
Knoxville

Tennessee Studies in Literature, a distinguished series sponsored by the Department of English at the University of Tennessee, Knoxville, began publication in 1956. Beginning in 1984, with volume 27, TSL evolved from a series of annual volumes of miscellaneous essays into a series of occasional volumes, each one dealing with a specific theme, period, or genre, for which the editor of that volume has invited contributions from leading scholars in the field.

Inquiries concerning this series should be addressed to the Editorial Board, Tennessee Studies in Literature, Department of English, The University of Tennessee, Knoxville, Tennessee 37996-0430. Those desiring to purchase additional copies of this issue or copies of back issues should address The University of Tennessee Press, Suite 110 Conference Center, Knoxville, Tennessee 36996-4108.

Frontispiece. Wilkie Collins. Caricature by Frederick Waddy, 1872. *Once a Week,* 24 Feb. 1872.

This book is printed on acid-free paper.

LIBRARY OF CONGRESS CATALOGING-IN-PUBLICATION DATA

Reality's dark light: the sensational Wilkie Collins/edited by Maria K. Bachman and Don Richard Cox.— 1st ed.
    p. cm.— (Tennessee studies in literature; v. 41)
Includes bibliographical references and index.
ISBN 1-57233-274-3 (cl. alk. paper)

1. Collins, Wilkie, 1824–1889—Criticism and interpretation.
2. Detective and mystery stories, English—History and criticism.
3. Psychological fiction, English—History and criticism.
4. Sensationalism in literature.
I. Bachman, Maria K., 1963–
II. Cox, Don Richard.
III. Series.

PR4497.R43 2003
823'.8—dc21   2003006421

Contents

Illustrations

Acknowledgments

W E WOULD LIKE TO THANK THE UNIVERSITY OF TENNESSEE'S JOHN C. HODGES BETTER ENGLISH FUND FOR ITS SUPPORT OF THIS volume. We are also greatly indebted to the University of Tennessee library's interlibrary loan department for its invaluable assistance. Finally, we would especially like to express our sincere thanks to Casey Cothran, our extraordinarily efficient and enthusiastic research assistant.

Introduction
The Real Wilkie Collins

———◦◦◦———

Fancy and Imagination, Grace and Beauty, all those
qualities which are to the work of Art what scent and
colour are to the flower, can only grow towards heaven
by taking root in earth. Is not the noblest poetry of
prose fiction the poetry of every-day truth?

   Directing my characters and my story, then, towards
the light of Reality wherever I could find it, I have
not hesitated to violate some of the conventionalities
of sentimental fiction.

—Wilkie Collins
Letter of Dedication to *Basil*, 1852

T THE TIME WILKIE COLLINS ISSUED HIS
STATEMENT IN *BASIL* (1852) CALLING FOR
TRUTH AND REALITY IN FICTION, THE TERM
sensation novel did not exist, and thus he felt no
need to defend the genre.[1] But Collins did believe
he was attempting something new and different
in *Basil,* and he felt obliged to justify his approach
and distinguish it from what he dismissed as
"sentimental fiction." Regardless of his portrait
of himself as a realist, twenty years later *Vanity
Fair* would publish Collins's caricature and crown
him simply as "The Novelist Who Invented Sensation."[2] In that famous portrait, Wilkie Collins
is depicted as a small man with tiny hands and
feet wearing a dark coat and striped trousers,

hunched anxiously on the edge of his seat, his expression obscured by his enormous whiskers and clouded spectacles. Just as his physical features are distorted in this illustration, so too has his literary legacy been misrepresented for over one hundred years. Whereas the distortion and exaggeration of the subject's features are the hallmark of caricature, ultimately a gently parodic gesture bestowed only on the already famous, the last century's undervaluation of Collins's artistic achievements could be said to have distorted seriously and therefore obscured his contributions to English letters. The *Vanity Fair* portrait is certainly symptomatic of the ways in which Collins's varied career is subsumed by his role as the "inventor" of the sensation novel. Like his own Magdalen Vanstone, the expressionless figure in the cartoon has "no name"—he has been effaced, literally and figuratively, by his creation[3]—and is identified only by the caption "The Novelist Who Invented Sensation."

Despite its limited visual framing of Collins's iconic status, *Vanity Fair* did believe that by 1872 Collins had achieved something new and different: in the statement that accompanies his portrait, his work is first contrasted with "that union of Love and Fiction which once was called Romance," and then it is remarked that "every romance that is written makes the next more difficult to write, and deluged as England has been in modern times with works of this class, it must have seemed almost impossible twenty years ago, when Mr. Wilkie Collins first took up the pen, to strike out any distinctly new line of treatment of the old subject."[4] Clearly, the labels that surround Collins's "distinctly new line of treatment"—sentimental fiction, sensation fiction, realism, Gothic fiction, Romance (to which we could also add the terms detective fiction and popular fiction)—have contributed to the difficulties readers have had in assessing it, for the ability to judge is usually preceded by the need to categorize, and it has not always been easy to characterize Collins's work as more than a low "popular" art form.

We see the struggle to pigeonhole Collins's fiction beginning in the nineteenth century. Trollope, in his *Autobiography*, reviews his contemporaries and clearly assumes the literary world is wrestling with a set of binaries:

> Among English novels of the present day, and among
> English novelists, a great division is made. There are
> sensational novels and anti-sensational, sensational novel-
> ists and anti-sensational. The novelists who are considered
> to be anti-sensational are generally called realistic. I am

FIG. 0.1. Wilkie Collins, *The Novelist Who Invented Sensation.* Adriano Cecioni, *Vanity Fair,* 3 Feb. 1872.

realistic. My friend Wilkie Collins is generally supposed to be sensational. The readers who prefer the one are supposed to take delight in the elucidation of character. Those who hold by the other are charmed by the construction and gradual development of a plot. All this is

Maria K. Bachman and Don Richard Cox

I think a mistake, which mistake arises from the inability
of the imperfect artist to be at the same time realistic and
sensational. A good novel should be both—and both
in the highest degree. If a novel fail in either, there is
a failure in art.[5]

There is some qualification here to be sure ("generally called," "generally supposed"), but Trollope indicates that he believes the literary
scene has pretty much been divided into "us" and "them." A few
pages later he returns to his "friend" and says: "Of Wilkie Collins it
is impossible for a true critic not to speak with admiration because he
has excelled all his contemporaries in a certain most difficult branch
of his art"; but he continues, "as it is a branch which I have not
myself at all cultivated, it is not unnatural that his work should be
very much lost upon me. . . . The construction is most minute and
most wonderful. But I can never lose the taste of construction."
"Such work," Trollope concludes, "gives me no pleasure."[6] Despite
Trollope's claim that a good novel should combine both realism and
the sensational, "we" (the realists) turn out to be somehow preferable
to "they" (the writers of sensation who create intricate plots).[7]

Collins was not, in his own mind, a writer who placed plot and
sensation above all, as the unfair stereotypes of him suggest. In his
preface to the second edition of *The Woman in White*, Collins
explains what he calls "a literary principle which has guided me since
I first addressed my readers in the character of a novelist":

I have always held the old-fashioned opinion that the
primary object of a work of fiction should be to tell a
story; and I have never believed that the novelist who
properly performed this first condition of his art was in
danger, on that account, of neglecting the delineation of
character—for this plain reason, that the effect produced
by any narrative of events is essentially dependent, not on
the events themselves, but on the human interest which is
directly connected with them. It may be possible in novel-
writing to present characters successfully without telling
a story; but it is not possible to tell a story successfully
without presenting characters: their existence, as recognizable realities, being the sole condition on which the
story can be effectively told. The only narrative which
can hope to lay a strong hold on the attention of readers

is a narrative which interests them about men and women—for the perfectly obvious reason that they are men and women themselves.[8]

This would not seem to be the Wilkie Collins that Trollope had in mind, a Wilkie Collins who placed "construction" and plot above all; this Collins claims to emphasize "character," "human interest," and "recognizable realities." But, as we can see, this Wilkie Collins is not significantly different from the man who wrote the Dedication to *Basil* nearly a decade earlier, the Collins who stated he would not hesitate to violate the conventions of sentimental fiction in order to pursue the light of reality and truth. The Wilkie Collins of 1852, however, also wrote that he thought it was the novelist's privilege to excite "strong and deep emotions," and moreover contended that he had not "thought it either politic or necessary, while adhering to realities, to adhere to common-place, everyday realities only." He admitted that his fiction would focus on the "extraordinary accidents and events which happen to few men" rather than "the ordinary accidents and events which may, and do, happen to us all." "By appealing to genuine sources of interest *within* the reader's own experience," he continued, "I could certainly gain his attention to begin with; but it would be only by appealing to other sources (as genuine in their own way) *beyond* his own experience, that I could hope to fix his interest and excite his suspense, to occupy his deeper feelings, or to stir his nobler thoughts."[9]

And this, in his own words, is the essence of Collins's fiction—character, realism, plot, suspense, excitement—and, as he boasts in the preface to *No Name* (1862), "a resolute adherence throughout, to the truth as it is in Nature."[10] If we look at Collins's one-time mentor Charles Dickens, we see him, to an extent, struggling with some of the same issues of truth, realism, and the fanciful. In his preface to *Bleak House,* which was being serialized at the same time that *Basil* was published, we find Dickens, like Collins, appealing to outside authorities to validate the truth of his fiction. "I mention here that everything set forth in these pages concerning the Court of Chancery is substantially true, and within the truth," Dickens insists. And when it comes to the very controversial issue of spontaneous combustion, Dickens points to several cases (citing specific page numbers for those who remain skeptical and are scholarly inclined), asserting "I shall not abandon the facts." Having, like Collins, defended the "truth" of his novel, he then employs a strategy very similar to Collins's; he concludes his preface by stating simply: "In *Bleak House*, I have purposely dwelt upon the romantic side of familiar things."[11] This statement, which Dickens does not elaborate upon, would seem to resemble Collins's principle of not adhering to "common-place, every-day realities only," but also focusing on "those extraordinary accidents and events" which happen to only a few. Philosophically and practically, both authors seem to be reaching for a new kind of social realism, and perhaps arriving at a similar kind of fiction while taking different routes. Indeed, *The Moonstone* is a novel that is in some ways the inverse of *Bleak House; Bleak House* might be characterized as a social novel that contains a mystery, while *The Moonstone* is basically a mystery novel that contains a social theme. Collins and Dickens are apparently attempting to fulfill Trollope's dictum that a good novel should be both realistic *and* sensational, and both in a high degree.

Historically, critics have found it difficult to categorize and place a label upon such fiction because for Collins the pursuit of the "Actual" necessitated violating traditional stereotypes and categories. In his prefaces to almost every one of his novels, however, Collins provides a consistent and principled blueprint of his aesthetic vision—a commitment to reshape and expand the contours of nineteenth-century literary realism. As he further states in his preface to *No Name* (1862), "My one object in following a new course, is to enlarge the range of my studies in the art of writing fiction, and to vary the form in which I make my appeal to the reader, as attractively as I can" (*No Name*, xxxvi). Though these treatises seldom deterred contemporary reviewers from finding fault with his stories, Collins neither abandoned his quest for his own kind of realism nor compromised his artistic integrity. While one reviewer of *Basil* lambasted Collins for "enrolling" in the "unwholesome literary school" of Maturin and Eugène Sue and reminded him that "the proper office of Art is to elevate and purify in pleasing,"[12] the author himself had very different ideas about "the proper office of Art." Time and again, Collins, who was undeniably disheartened that his work was not fully appreciated or understood by the critics, professed his unwavering moral responsibility to his readers and to his art by favoring truth and reality in his fiction over amusing or sentimental stories. Wilkie Collins's fictional world is, undeniably, a world populated by oddballs, misfits, and grotesques, characters who sometimes engage in startling and even shocking behavior. From those who are merely eccentric—the con artist

Captain Wragge *(No Name)*, the physical fitness fanatic Geoffrey Delamayn *(Man and Wife)*, or the evangelical spinster Drusilla Clack *(The Moonstone)*—to those who exist on the fringes of society—the opium addict Ezra Jennings *(The Moonstone)*, the scheming poisoner Lydia Gwilt *(Armadale)*, or the scalped frontiersman Mat Marksman *(Hide and Seek)*—to those whom we suspect we might never encounter except in our nightmares—the blue man Oscar Dubourg *(Poor Miss Finch)*, the sadistic vivisectionist Nathan Benjulia *(Heart and Science)*, or the demonic half-man Miserrimus Dexter *(The Law and the Lady)*—Collins creates an extraordinary gallery of bizarre figures in his fiction, which is also peopled by more blind, deaf, mute, or lame characters than that of any Victorian writer. These are the marks of Collins's distinctly modern realist project: "Nobody who admits that the business of fiction is to exhibit human life, can deny that scenes of misery and crime must of necessity, while human nature remains what it is, form part of that exhibition" *(Basil*, xvii–xviii). The dark side of human nature was, for Collins, the very essence of his new, realist project—"[L]ook where we may, the dark threads and the light cross each other perpetually in the texture of human life" *(No Name*, xxxvi).

Collins was, however, well aware that his push for "the light of Reality" would offend, and even outrage, some readers. For example, he says in his preface to *Poor Miss Finch:*

> I have tried to present human nature in its inherent inconsistencies and self-contradictions—in its intricate mixture of good and evil, of great and small—as I see it in the world about me. But the faculty of observing character is so rare, the curiously mistaken tendency to look for logical consistency in human motives and human actions is so general, that I may possibly find the execution of this part of my task misunderstood— sometimes even resented—in certain quarters.[13]

Yet, one receives the impression that Collins almost relishes this sparring with his readers, and it is this aggressive attitude about his art, particularly about violating conventions—we need only look at his legendary cohabitation with two mistresses to see he is not averse to flaunting propriety—that has caused many readers, from both the nineteenth and twentieth centuries, to see his fiction as transgressive. Dickens, who of course kept his mistress a secret, was concerned about Collins's tendency to go out of his way to challenge convention.

Worried about an article Collins was preparing for *Household Words*, Dickens alerted his editor W. H. Wills, "I forgot to mention that I particularly wish you to look well to Wilkie's article . . . and not to leave anything in it that may be sweepingly and unnecessarily offensive to the middle class. He always has a tendency to overdo that—and such a subject gives him a fresh temptation. Don't be afraid of the Truth, in the least; but don't be unjust."[14] Apparently, when it came to offending the middle class, Dickens and Collins may have differed about the nature of the "Truth" and "Reality's light." Collins knew that in order to combat those who wished to "restrict the development of modern fiction,"[15] his work would necessarily have to fly in the face of such Grundyites as his own character from *Armadale*, the villainous Dr. Downward, who clung to the notion that "[t]here may be plenty that is painful in real life—but for that very reason, we don't want it in books." "The English novelist who enters my house," Downward continues, "must understand his art as the healthy-minded English reader understands it in our time. He must know that our purer modern tastes, our higher modern morality, limits him to doing exactly two things for us, when he writes a book. All we want of him is—occasionally to make us laugh; and invariably to make us comfortable" (*Armadale*, 769–70).

Naturally, Collins disagreed. He recognized that in order to direct his characters "toward the light of Reality" he would be seeking darker truths, offending middle-class readers with a portrait of a gloomy modern world that would not make Downward or his friends comfortable, and certainly would not make them laugh. In his foreword to *Armadale* (1866), for example, he acknowledged this:

> Readers in particular will, I have some reason to
> suppose, be here and there disturbed—perhaps even
> offended—by finding that *Armadale* oversteps, in more
> than one direction, the narrow limits within which they
> are disposed to restrict the development of modern fiction.
> . . . Nothing that I could say to these persons, here, would
> help me with them, as Time will help me if my work lasts.
> I am not afraid of my design being permanently misunder-
> stood, provided the execution has done it any sort of
> justice. (*Armadale*, 4)

In 1855, French critic Émile Forgues published what is arguably one of the most significant reviews of Collins. In *Revue des Deux Mondes*, Forgues not only praised Collins for his defiant stand against the "hypocrisy, arrogant prejudices and venal propensities . . . of the day,"[16] but also lauded him for his potential to revolutionize fiction as his own countryman, Gustave Flaubert, would do the following year with the publication of *Madame Bovary*. What was clear to both Forgues and Collins was that to be a leading practitioner of the realist school, though, was to be a cultural villain of sorts; as Collins's own Fosco asserts, "I say what other people only think; and when all the rest of the world is in a conspiracy to accept the mask for the true face, mine is the rash hand that tears off the plump pasteboard, and shows the bare bones beneath" (*The Woman in White*, 239). Certainly this attempt to "show the bare bones beneath" is the essence of Collins's realism and precisely what Margaret Oliphant had zeroed in on when she proclaimed Collins's achievement of "a new beginning in fiction."[17]

And so, throughout his career, Collins continued steadfastly to espouse his artistic vision, but it was a vision that bore the burden of critical scorn. In selecting essays for this volume, we have attempted to represent the range of Collins's aesthetic project from various critical perspectives. Specifically, we sought a balance between new method-ological and theoretical approaches to Collins's fiction while also includ-ing essays that examine his most popular as well as his lesser known works. We have arranged these essays in an order that parallels Collins's publishing history. We begin our collection, then, with an essay that con-siders Collins's first novel set in Victorian England.[18] In "Fatal Newness: *Basil*, Art, and the Origins of Sensation Fiction," Tim Dolin and Lucy Dougan examine the relationship between *Basil* and William Holman Hunt's controversial painting *The Awakening Conscience*, contending that a parallel exists between Collins's vision of modern life and litera-ture and the goals of the Pre-Raphaelite Brotherhood in its challenge of the Royal Academy and the status quo. Hunt's painting of an adulter-ous couple, they argue, seems in fact to have been directly inspired by Collins's novel of adultery and revenge. Because *Basil* retreats into a tra-ditional middle-class domesticity with Basil and his sister Clara setting up a household together after his disastrous marriage collapses, it ulti-mately fails in its mission to create a new kind of fiction, they contend, for it concludes by reaffirming a conservative rather than a transgressive viewpoint. Nevertheless, they point out, its shocking portrait of a sexu-ally unconventional marriage does challenge traditional notions of class and social mobility with a new vision of morality, justifying the claim that *Basil* was the first sensation novel.

Dennis Denisoff, in "Framed and Hung: Collins and the Eco-nomic Beauty of the Manly Artist," explores the changing image of the artist in the nineteenth century, a time when attitudes toward aesthetics "reflected the rising power of the middle class."[19] Successful artists disassociated themselves from the more traditional image of the artist as an individual serving an aristocratic (and effete) patron and began to measure their stature in terms of commercial sales. Associated with this change, Denisoff contends, was a corresponding tendency to identify this profession with a need for serious commitment and masculine labor. Collins thus emphasizes the manly virtues of painters through the figures of Walter Hartright and Valentine Blyth, while a character such as Mr. Fairlie, who represents the spoiled aristocracy, is portrayed as refined, weak, effeminate, and artistically insensitive. Miserrimus Dexter, who possesses "excessive beauty," as well as a taste for flamboyant silk clothing, is also a mediocre artist, an example of someone whose "values fail to accommodate the demands that industry, expansionism, and capitalism were placing on contemporary artists."[20] Although Collins, as a middle-class artist himself, was sensitive to the need of other middle-class men "to establish their masculinity by succeeding in artistic careers," the inclusion of "dissidents" such as Dexter was necessary to satisfy the demands of his genre.[21]

Martha Stoddard Holmes explores representations of physical impairment in Collins's work from a disability studies perspective. "'Bolder with Her Lover in the Dark': Collins and Disabled Women's Sexuality" sets Collins's increasingly sexualized representations of disabled women (from Madonna Blyth in *Hide and Seek* to Lucilla Finch in *Poor Miss Finch*) against contemporary medico-scientific and social science discourses. Collins's novels, Holmes argues, are "counterdiscursive to stereotypes of disability"[22] as he transforms his disabled women characters "from objects of pathos into sexual and domestic subjects with full access to the traditional heroine's desserts of courtship, marriage and motherhood."[23]

In her essay "Chemical Seductions: Exoticism, Toxicology, and the Female Poisoner in *Armadale* and *The Legacy of Cain*," Piya Pal-Lapinski explores the ways in which Collins's fiction reconstitutes the alliance between poison and female agency in mid- to late-Victorian medical and ethnological discourses. Specifically, Pal-Lapinski considers *Armadale* and *The Legacy of Cain* as novels that engage with cultural tropes of empire, exoticism, and cosmopolitanism in far more sophisticated and more destabilizing ways, she argues, than Collins's "representative" colonial text, *The Moonstone*. Pal-Lapinski reads Collins's *empoisonneuses* against the background of contemporary and historical poison epidemics in Britain and France, which were linked to acts of domestic and political resistance, along with medical treatises on poison and the development of methods of poison detection. Ultimately, Pal-Lapinski argues that Collins's female poisoners are inscribed with "a dangerous hybridity" that defies "hegemonic domestic and imperial narratives of race, sexuality, and desire."[24]

Richard Collins, in "Marian's Moustache: Bearded Ladies, Hermaphrodites, and Intersexual Collage in *The Woman in White*," focuses on Marian Halcombe's surprising moustache to construct an analysis of "the social codes and contexts of intersexual phenomena" in the mid-nineteenth century. Looking primarily at the "anatomical curiosities" and sexual "anomalies" that appeared in London exhibition rooms, Richard Collins examines sideshow bearded ladies as well as museum statues of hermaphrodites to argue that in *The Woman in White* Wilkie Collins creates an "intersexual collage" that allows him "to evoke the uncanny in the reader's response."[25] Noting that the author "is careful to place each principal character along a continuum between masculine and feminine poles," Richard Collins contends that the Victorians' interest in sexual anomalies reflected "a flagging trust in the infallibility of Nature." In contrast to Laura Fairlie's extreme femininity, Marian's ambiguous sexuality allows Walter Hartright to experience the dual nature of woman and define his own sexual identity in the process. The ménage à trois that emerges at the end of the novel installs Marian as "surrogate wife and mother," but rather than a threatening hermaphroditism she now projects "a reassuring angelic androgyny" as she and Walter share the governance of the household. The hermaphroditic Marian proves to be the novel's "missing link," Collins assures us.[26]

In "The Crystal Palace, Imperialism, and the 'Struggle for Existence': Victorian Evolutionary Discourse in Collins's *The Woman in White*," Gabrielle Ceraldi examines Collins's novel in relation to contemporary evolutionary debates. Ceraldi foregrounds her argument by pointing out that Walter Hartright's narrative in *The Woman in White* takes place during the Great Exhibition of 1851, yet the optimism and assurance traditionally symbolized by the Crystal Palace are strikingly absent from Collins's novel. In fact, Hartright reminds readers that in 1851 "[f]oreigners, in unusually large numbers, had arrived . . . in England" (*The Woman in White*, 578), tapping into a growing fear that England's cultural supremacy could give way to inevitable processes of devolution and decay. Specifically, Ceraldi argues that *The Woman in White*, serialized immediately following the publication of Darwin's *The Origin of Species* (1859), responds to the collision between the development hypothesis and Darwinian natural selection. Collins, according to Ceraldi, uses foreign characters such as Professor Pesca and Count Fosco to highlight the tenuous relationship between Great Britain and the racialized world that lies beyond her shores.

A. D. Hutter stands conventional readings of *The Woman in White* on their heads as he argues for the survival of the malevolent Count Fosco, last seen in the novel presumably lying dead in the Paris Morgue. Emphasizing that the serial novel invites participation from its readers in a way that the nonserialized novel never can, Hutter examines predominant themes in Dickens and Collins, as well as the nature of Count Fosco himself and the clues Collins places in the text, in order to conclude that Fosco actually fakes his own death to deceive the Brotherhood and live on in anonymity. Engaging the reader in a playful, almost postmodern fashion, Collins invites speculation, creation, and re-creation, Hutter asserts, shaping a form of literature that lies somewhere between fiction and theater. "The particular aesthetic of such works," Hutter argues, "obliges the writer always to be conscious of the reader's extra-textual imagination."[27]

Timothy Carens, like others who have studied *The Moonstone,* finds the novel rife with racial themes. In "Outlandish English Subjects in *The Moonstone,*" however, Carens finds that Collins locates "outlandish" or "foreign" impulses within the English character itself; according to Carens, "regulatory forces which supposedly prevail within the civilized self . . . fail to exert their hold" as "English characters are overmastered by their own 'dark' and irrational obsessions, inordinate desires, unruly aggressions, and self-abasing idolatries."[28] Collins anticipates Freud's insights on the uncanny, Carens contends, with his narrative "that uncovers the forgotten strangeness which inhabits the familiar."[29] Although Victorian culture establishes certain prescribed "lines of demarcation" between itself and the culture of the Orient, the diamond allows English passions to erupt, thereby exposing "the artificiality of the racial oppositions which sustain the imperial project." The "uncanny logic" of the narrative "repeatedly subverts prevailing assumptions about differences between familiar English selves and outlandish Indian others," Carens asserts, revealing that dark desires are truly not restricted to the "otherness" of this "volatile" colony.[30]

Lillian Nayder, in "'Blue Like Me': Collins, *Poor Miss Finch,* and the Construction of Racial Identity," turns to a text from the 1960s,

John Howard Griffith's *Black Like Me,* to establish a parallel with Collins's *Poor Miss Finch,* in which a character also undergoes a treatment that will alter the color of his skin. Oscar Dubourg, who takes silver nitrate as a remedy for epilepsy, becomes transformed into a blue man, although his fiancée, who is blind, is unaware of the transformation. Collins constructs a narrative about racial prejudice, Nayder contends, using Lucilla Finch's irrational aversion to dark-skinned people to underscore his theme of racism and blindness. Lucilla temporarily regains her sight, and, though initially horrified by her fiancé's appearance, comes to choose him over his identical (but nonblue) twin. Although the Indian Mutiny made interracial relations a subject of controversy, Collins ultimately sidesteps the issue of miscegenation and thus qualifies some of the more subversive elements of his fiction, Nayder contends, reinforcing the status quo and concluding his novel by allowing a marriage to take place between a white woman and a man who is, and technically is not, racially different.

In "Plain Faces, Weird Cases: Domesticating the Law in Collins's *The Law and the Lady* and the Trial of Madeleine Smith," Karin Jacobson argues that female sexuality is not easily translated into recognizable legal discourse. Specifically, Jacobson shows how the Madeleine Smith domestic poisoning trial, in which the female defendant was neither convicted nor judged innocent, elucidates the position of Collins's Valeria (*The Law and the Lady*) in relation to the law. Jacobson explains how, in the course of both investigations, the law becomes entwined with the sensational narratives (each woman's letters) it seeks to make "plain" and, in doing so, reveals an uncanny view of the Victorian woman as sexual creature: "[U]ncovering the truth of a woman's story . . . Madeleine Smith's trial begins to embody the gap that has traditionally constituted women's sexuality. [Similarly,] Sara Macallan's missing letter to Eustace, the mystery around which *The Law and the Lady* turns, creates a parallel link between women's writing and sexuality."[31] Thus, both women's textual productions, Jacobson argues, are evidence of "a desire that has never been written," effectively blurring the boundaries between legal and emotional discourse, between the law and the "ladies," and between the domestic and the uncanny.[32]

In "Collins, Race, and Slavery," Audrey Fisch considers the ideological work of race in Collins's fiction and plays. Fisch points out that unlike many of his peers, Collins creates black or mixed-race figures who are *not* alien Others, safely removed from Victorian society or violently intruding into that world. Rather, Collins incorporates mixed-race characters into Victorian society to "detox-ify a contaminated past of English slavery and colonialism" and to imagine how mixed-race people serve to restore Victorian values and social normalcy.[33] Fisch claims that in *Miss or Mrs?* (1871), Collins reaffirms England's decision to abolish colonial slavery, and Fisch explains how, in *Black and White* (1869), Collins offers his audience the "peaceful assimilation of mixed race characters into white society over and against the more dangerous and threatening specter of black alienation and/or rebellion."[34] However, in *The Guilty River* (1886) and *Armadale* (1866), Fisch finds that Collins is "less sanguine" about assimilation as the mixed-race characters in these works, Gerard Roylake and Ozias Midwinter, respectively, must "sacrifice themselves to restore a degraded white society to its rightful position."[35]

In "Yesterday's Sensations: Modes of Publication and Narrative Form in Collins's Late Novels," Graham Law sees the fault lines of Collins's later works as symptomatic of the forms and modes of pub-lication that were available to Victorian writers in the 1870s and 1880s, and of his "uncomfortable" relationship with popular pub-lishers and a mass readership. Specifically, Law argues that Collins's attempts to engage with new narrative forms in *Jezebel's Daughter,* *The Evil Genius,* and *The Guilty River* were stymied by what he iden-tifies as key narrative "moments": the decline of sensationalism in the newspaper serial, the challenge of naturalism to the triple-decker, and the emergence of the best-selling single-volume thriller.

Finally, in an afterword, "Masterpiece Theatre and Ezra Jennings's Hair: Some Reflections on Where We've Been and Where We're Going in Collins Studies," Tamar Heller recalls how she dis-covered Wilkie Collins, and, focusing on the "hybridity" she finds central to contemporary studies of his fiction, speculates on the direc-tions future Collins scholarship might take.

As these introductory remarks and the essays that follow demon-strate, this collection purposefully works to expand Collins's legacy beyond *The Woman in White* and *The Moonstone* and moves well beyond simply viewing Collins's works as "sensation novels," or "detec-tive novels," or even simply "popular fiction," all labels and genres that carry with them a certain pejorative connotation. All of these terms, in the opinion of literary historians even today, suggest lowbrow popular entertainment, which is not worthy of serious critical attention, no mat-ter how well written it may be. The salient features of Wilkie Collins's novels—a striving for psychological realism, the use of multiple narrators, the shifting shape of the plot as it is filtered through different perspectives—these elements that were seen as aesthetically and thematically offensive in Collins's lifetime—have come to be seen as the very bedrock of modernist fiction. Clearly Wilkie Collins, in his determined pursuit of Reality's dark light, has much to teach us in the twenty-first century about the intricacies of life in the nineteenth.

Maria K. Bachman
Don Richard Cox

Notes

1. The *OED* first attributes the term to Henry L. Mansel ("Sensation Novels," *Quarterly Review* 113 [Apr. 1863]: 481–514), but it had appeared in print earlier. For a short history of the term and the genre, see Richard Altick, "The Novel Experience," in *Deadly Encounters: Two Victorian Sensations* (Philadelphia: Univ. of Pennsylvania Press, 1986), 145–58.

2. His "Men of the Day" portrait appeared 3 Feb. 1872.

3. Another illustration from the same year is F. W. Waddy's pen-and-ink cartoon of a bearded and bespectacled Collins pasting up a poster for his recent dramatization. Here again the figure has "no name"; the perfunctory caption which says "He wrote 'The Woman in White'" (*Once a Week*, 24 Feb. 1872) seems to ensconce Collins's reputation even more firmly. Collins apparently never commented publicly on either of these illustrations: as a professional intent on marketing himself and his "product," he certainly might have appreciated and even been flattered by the publicity, but as an artist who was very serious about his work, he might have scorned the inherent limitations of "popular" typecasting.

4. "Men of the Day. No. 39," *Vanity Fair,* 3 Feb. 1872.

5. Anthony Trollope, *An Autobiography,* ed. David Skilton (London: Trollope Society, 1999), 140. Hereafter cited as *Autobiography.*

6. *Autobiography,* 159–60.

7. Although he did not make a public rebuttal to Trollope's judgment, Collins was evidently no more interested in Trollope's fiction than Trollope was in his. At the time of Trollope's death he remarked in a letter: "Call his standard as a workman what you will, he was always equal to it. Never in any marked degree either above or below his own level. In that respect alone, a remarkable writer, surely? If he had lived five years longer, he would have written fifteen more thoroughly readable

works of fiction" (Collins to William Winter, London, 14 Jan. 1883, in *The Letters of Wilkie Collins,* ed. William Baker and William C. Clarke, 2 vols. [New York: St. Martin's Press, 1999], 2:454.)

Although Collins regarded Trollope as a friend and called the author's death "a serious loss," the praise here seems muted—Trollope was "always equal" to his own standards; his fiction was not extraordinary, but always "thoroughly readable." The dichotomy is clearly here: character vs. plot, realism vs. sensation fiction; and, in the case of Trollope in particular, the division was epitomized by his reworking one of Collins's masterpieces, *The Moonstone,* and producing *The Eustace Diamonds,* his own (and to him presumably better) version of a detective story involving stolen diamonds.

8. Wilkie Collins, *The Woman in White,* ed. John Sutherland (Oxford: Oxford Univ. Press, 1999), 4. Hereafter cited in the text as *The Woman in White.*

9. Wilkie Collins, *Basil,* ed. Dorothy Goldman (Oxford: Oxford Univ. Press, 1990), xxxvii. Hereafter cited in the text as *Basil.* Collins further asserted that the narrative, "guided . . . . by my own experiences, and by the experiences incidentally related to me by others . . . would touch on something real and true, in its progress." According to Catherine Peters, the "fact in real life" Collins alludes to in his dedication may have been a now unknown romantic attachment in his own youth. She also identifies the secret marriage of two of Collins's friends, Ned and Henrietta Ward, as well as the liaison of William Holman Hunt and his model Annie Miller as possible "facts" that could have provided the basis for this novel (*The King of Inventors: A Life of Wilkie Collins* [Princeton: Princeton Univ. Press, 1991], 116–17). Annie Miller was also involved with D. G. Rossetti and, among other things, was Hunt's model for his famous painting, *The Awakening Conscience.* See also in this volume Tim Dolin and Lucy Dougan, "Fatal Newness: *Basil, Art, and the Origins of Sensation Fiction.*" The specific source that inspired Collins's story, however, is probably not as important as his insistence that there indeed was one. It was a strategy he was to employ frequently in prefaces as his career unfolded, persistently asserting that his stories—which sometimes seemed fantastic to reviewers—were in fact grounded in truth and reality.

10. Wilkie Collins, *No Name,* ed. Virginia Blain (Oxford: Oxford Univ. Press, 1986), xxxvi. Hereafter cited in the text as *No Name.*

11. Charles Dickens, *Bleak House,* ed. George Ford and Sylvère Monod (New York: W. W. Norton and Co., 1977), 3–4.

12. [D. O. Maddyn], Review of *Basil* by Wilkie Collins, *The Athenaeum,* no. 1310 (4 Dec. 1852): 1323. Quoted in Norman Page, *Wilkie Collins: The Critical Heritage* (London and Boston: Routledge and Kegan Paul, 1974), 47–48.

13. Wilkie Collins, *Poor Miss Finch,* ed. Catherine Peters (Oxford: Oxford Univ. Press, 1995), xxxiii.

14. Dickens to W. H. Wills, Newcastle, 24 Sept. 1858, in *The Letters of Charles Dickens,* ed. Graham Storey and Kathleen Tillotson, vol. 8 (Oxford: Clarendon Press, 1995), 669. The article in question was "Highly Proper!" *Household Words* 18, no. 445 (2 Oct. 1858): 361–63.

15. Wilkie Collins, *Armadale,* ed. Catherine Peters (Oxford: Oxford Univ. Press, 1989), 4. Hereafter cited in the text as *Armadale.*

16. Quoted in Peters, 157.

17. [Margaret Oliphant], "Sensation Novels," *Blackwood's Magazine* 91 (May 1862): 565–74. Oliphant explained that "[a] writer who boldly takes in hand the common mechanism of life, and by means of persons who might all be living in society for anything we can tell to the contrary, thrills us into wonder, terror, and breathless interest, with positive shocks of surprise and excitement, has accomplished a far greater success than he who effects the same result through supernatural agencies, or by means of the fantastic creations of lawless genius for violent horrors of crime" (quoted in Page, 112).

18. Collins's first published novel was *Antonina,* a historical novel set in ancient Rome. His first novel, *Ioláni,* a romance set in Tahiti, was rejected by publishers and did not find its way into print until 1999.

19. Denisoff, this volume.

20. Ibid.

21. Ibid.

22. Holmes, this volume.

23. Ibid.

24. Pal-Lapinski, this volume.

25. Collins, this volume.

26. Ibid.

27. Hutter, this volume.

28. Carens, this volume.

29. Ibid.

30. Ibid.

31. Jacobson, this volume.

32. Ibid.

33. Fisch, this volume.

34. Ibid.

35. Ibid.

References

Altick, Richard. *Deadly Encounters: Two Victorian Sensations.* Philadelphia: Univ. of Pennsylvania Press, 1986.

Collins, Wilkie. *Armadale.* Ed. Catherine Peters. Oxford: Oxford Univ. Press, 1989.

———. *Basil.* Ed. Dorothy Goldman. Oxford: Oxford Univ. Press, 1990.

———. *The Letters of Wilkie Collins.* Ed. William Baker and William M. Clarke. 2 vols. New York: St. Martin's Press, 1999.

———. *No Name.* Ed. Virginia Blain. Oxford: Oxford Univ. Press, 1986.

———. *Poor Miss Finch.* Ed. Catherine Peters. Oxford: Oxford Univ. Press, 1995.

———. *The Woman in White.* Ed. John Sutherland. Oxford: Oxford Univ. Press, 1999.

Dickens, Charles. *Bleak House.* Ed. George Ford and Sylvère Monod. New York: W. W. Norton and Co., 1977.

———. *The Letters of Charles Dickens.* Ed. Graham Storey and Kathleen Tillotson. Vol. 8. Oxford: Clarendon Press, 1995.

Mansel, Henry L. "Sensation Novels." *Quarterly Review* 113 (Apr. 1863): 481–514.

Page, Norman. *Wilkie Collins: The Critical Heritage.* London and Boston: Routledge and Kegan Paul, 1974.

Peters, Catherine. *The King of Inventors: A Life of Wilkie Collins.* Princeton: Princeton Univ. Press, 1991.

Trollope, Anthony. *An Autobiography.* Ed. David Skilton. London: Trollope Society, 1999.

Fatal Newness

Basil, Art, and the Origins of Sensation Fiction

Tim Dolin and Lucy Dougan

ILLIAM HOLMAN HUNT'S *THE AWAKENING CONSCIENCE* (FIG. 1.1) WAS ONE OF THE FIRST VICTORIAN "MODERN-LIFE" PICTURES and one of the most controversial of them.[1] It confounded and offended spectators at the Royal Academy annual exhibition, where it was first shown in 1854. This was not because modern life was deemed too ugly or vulgar for Academic high art, however. In fact, many of those same spectators, members of a rapidly expanding middle-class art public, marveled at William Powell Frith's inaugural modern-life subject, a vast, benign panorama of themselves at play, *Life at the Sea-side (Ramsgate Sands),* hanging nearby. Rather, it was because, in the words of one reviewer, *The Awakening Conscience* drew on "a very dark and repulsive side of modern domestic life," "literally" representing "the momentary remorse of a kept mistress, whose thoughts of lost virtue, guilt, father, mother, and home have been roused by a chance strain of music."[2] Most art historians agree that a significant source for Hunt's depiction of the darkness and repulsiveness of modern life (and, by extension, for the distinctive tradition of what might be called "moral modern-life art" that developed directly out of this painting),[3] was Wilkie Collins's novel *Basil: A Story of Modern Life* (1852),[4] though there is no direct evidence for this. Hunt himself does not mention *Basil* in his copious memoirs, for example,[5] and there are some significant points of difference between the narratives in the two works.[6] Yet certain correspondences remain so compelling that one is led to conclude that *Basil* must indeed have been in Hunt's mind as his painting developed. These correspondences, first noted by Alastair Ian Grieve in 1976, have since been taken up by others.[7] Kate Flint, for example, argues: "Whilst direct collusion is unprovable, we can, importantly, say that painter and novelist shared a common mode of looking at both furniture and gesture, regarding both as social and moral indicators."[8] In *The Awakening Conscience*—a strikingly unpicturesque and uncompromising image— Hunt tried to make his viewers experience middle-class material prosperity as revulsion, inviting comparison with the scene in *Basil* in which Collins's eponymous hero, hypersensitive to the glaring newness of the furniture and objects in the house of the middle-class arriviste, Sherwin, describes them in minute detail:

> Everything was oppressively new. The brilliantly-
> varnished door cracked with a report like a pistol when
> it was opened; the paper on the walls, with its gaudy
> pattern of birds, trellis-work, and flowers, in gold, red,
> and green on a white ground, looked hardly dry yet; the
> showy window-curtains of white and sky-blue, and the
> still showier carpet of red and yellow, seemed as if they
> had come out of the shop yesterday; the round rosewood
> table was in a painfully high state of polish; the morocco-
> bound picture books that lay on it, looked as if they had
> never been moved or opened since they had been bought;
> not one leaf even of the music on the piano was dogs-
> eared or worn. Never was a richly-furnished room
> more thoroughly comfortless than this—the eye
> ached at looking round it. (*Basil*, 1:198–99)

Many of the elements in this description are repeated, almost verbatim as it were, in *The Awakening Conscience*—the varnished and polished woods, the gaudy wallpaper of birds and flowers, the curtains, the bright colors of the carpet, the unopened books on the round rosewood table, and the new music scores. Moreover, the same oppressiveness of the new that Collins describes is conveyed in the picture through Hunt's painterly hypersensitivity: his technique of unmixed colors applied to a wet white ground in order to achieve high saturation, uniform intensity, and sharp detail. This technique allowed him to integrate metonymic signs (the furniture and ornaments, which stand in synecdochically for the vulgarity of an entire class) with arcane and intricately worked-out patterns of symbolism (evident in the wallpaper design, the cat and bird, the sheet music, and so on) and a complicated grammar of gesture and expression.[9] The result is a clutter of equally weighted signifying systems that confounds the expectation (then prevailing in Academic painting) of clear hierarchies of meaning. In this way, Hunt can represent what is for him the distinctive quality of modern life: new things, somehow inherently corrupt in their newness, are the visible signs of the modern; but they are also in some sense unreadable signs, and this is an essential part of their modernity. The hallmark of Hunt's earlier Pre-Raphaelitism, absolute truthfulness to nature, is displaced in *The Awakening Conscience* into an image of the spiritual emptiness and hermeneutic overfullness of modern life. Paradoxically, in the first Pre-Raphaelite painting openly to valorize the modern subject in the ultra-conservative venue of the Royal Academy, the brand new is treated with the deepest suspicion. It is little wonder that the painting was viewed with bewilderment and distaste.

Something of this same paradox underlies *Basil*. In the Letter of Dedication prefacing the 1852 first edition, Collins claims that he is attempting a new kind of serious fiction, yet the novel that follows evinces an undeniable disgust for the new petty-bourgeois suburban classes that are the very source of its self-proclaimed avant-gardism.[10] Like *The Awakening Conscience*, *Basil* is overloaded with narrative and expressive modes that its first readers found difficult to hierarchize, and that acted against ready comprehension.[11] Because it united elements of the contemporary middle-class domestic novel, the Gothic thriller, the early Victorian crime novel, the Romantic confession, and the "Condition of England" novel, *Basil* stood in need of detailed explanation and justification.[12] That Collins devoted seventeen pages to this task in the dedication suggests just how concerned he was that its meanings might be misconstrued; that its pointed mix of melodramatic events, elaborate plots, and taboo subjects, set against a background of respectable middle-class life and couched in a tense, graphic, hyperfactual realism, might misrepresent its author's aesthetic and

FIG. 1.1. William Holman Hunt, *The Awakening Conscience,* 1854. © Tate, London 2002.

political intentions; and that its ostensible antibourgeois shock tactics might appear at odds with its claim to be a morally serious work of art. At bottom, though (again, like *The Awakening Conscience*), *Basil* is anything but antibourgeois. It professes, in its plot and in the character of its narrator-hero, an undeniable yearning for older things, the things of an orthodox, established social order. For contemporary readers of the novel, however, the virtues associated with those things—gentlemanliness, domesticity, family, and womanliness—were not the virtues of ancient blood, in spite of Basil's own class background, but the virtues aspired to by the emergent mid-Victorian middle classes: the virtues of "home."[13] Collins's direct association of those values with upper-class nostalgia indicates a profound political conservatism at odds with the novel's ostensibly radical social and aesthetic aspirations.

To understand this contradiction, it is necessary to situate *Basil* and its politics as precisely as possible within the contexts that produced them. In what follows, therefore, we argue that Collins's novel and Hunt's painting share certain aesthetic aims—broadly, to develop an original form for the representation of contemporary experience—which are responses to common social concerns, but to quite different cultural politics. Only by examining the two works together, in the light of those common concerns and different politics, can we reestablish a provenance for the novel in the aesthetics and politics of modern life, a provenance that has since been obscured by the dominant aesthetics and politics of sensationalism. This essay therefore examines Collins's close personal relationship with the artists, both Pre-Raphaelite and Academic, involved in the moment of modern life, and shows how his fictional treatment of class and social crisis coincides with certain preoccupations and anxieties in Pre-Raphaelite modern-life art, preoccupations and anxieties openly polemicized in John Ruskin's defenses of the movement (and particularly of *The Awakening Conscience*). Our object in this is to show, in the words of Marcia Pointon, "how diverse texts relate": how "the specific historical experience, formed as part of the processes of political, cultural and sexual power, intersects with other (earlier) texts (verbal or visual), also themselves ideologically formed"; and how "ideology is constructed across fields rather than within them."[14] It is also our object to show how these texts and their historical experiences differ. *Basil* is a product of a particular moment in literary culture and Collins's struggle as an ambitious young writer without a stable income or reputation to establish himself in the metropolitan literary marketplace; *The Awakening Conscience* is a product of what has been called the Pre-Raphaelites' struggle "to free themselves of the accumulated artifices and conventions of academic picture-making."[15] Yet when Collins adapts aspects of the latter to his own struggle, we suggest, he initiates a new kind of fiction.

The influence of *Basil* on the evolution of the modern-life problem picture—on Millais as well as Hunt,[16] and on such seminal Academic paintings as Augustus Egg's *Past and Present* (1858)—has tended to overshadow the fact that Collins's novel was also in great part a *product* of the nascent movement toward modern life in the visual arts from the late 1840s onward.[17] Collins's specific use of the words *modern life* in his subtitle, eighteen months before it gained wide currency as the name for this new art, is not coincidental. When he had written to Richard Bentley in November 1849 negotiating terms for *Antonina,* his first published novel (about the fifth-century siege of Rome by the Goths),[18] he had pleaded its worth by claiming to appeal to "other sympathies" than "the modern taste for present times and the horrible," which had "been somewhat surfeited of late."[19] He abandoned the historical mode for a "story of modern life" in his very next novel, however, perhaps because *Antonina* was only modestly successful, or perhaps because in the two intervening years the historical novel had lost ground to the domestic novel, and the Great Exhibition had lent what Martin Meisel calls a "glamour to contemporaneity."[20] Restless for a formula for popular and critical success—between *Antonina* and *Basil* he tried his hand at genres as diverse as the travel book and the Christmas book[21]—Collins quickly decided that he should appeal (as he put it in the dedication) "to the readiest sympathies and the largest number of readers, by writing a story of our own times" (*Basil,* 1:viii). But what would set such a story apart from the surfeit of novels of "present times and the horrible"? To answer this, we must consider Collins's exposure to the new ideas about the representation of modern life circulating in progressive artistic circles around 1850.

Collins was uniquely situated to absorb these ideas because of his close friendships with the Pre-Raphaelites and with members of a small group of Royal Academy painters known as "The Clique"—including E. M. Ward, Augustus Egg, Richard Dadd, and William Frith—who were also beginning to experiment with modern-life subjects at this time.[22] Collins himself had been born into an artistic family. His father was William Collins, the eminent Academician, who had named his son after himself and his friend, the famous genre painter Sir David Wilkie; but his expectations for William Wilkie Collins were not fulfilled. "I do not follow my father's profession," he wrote to the American novelist R. H. Dana in 1849, but added, "I live very much in the society of artists."[23] Over the coming years he would exploit that familiarity with what he called "the varieties of artist-life, and the eccentricities of artist-character" in his journalism and fiction.[24] His younger brother Charles, a close friend of Millais, did follow the profession, however, and took up Pre-Raphaelite subjects after 1850 (though he was never a member of the Pre-Raphaelite Brotherhood).[25] Collins, too, had been a friend of Millais and Hunt since the mid-1840s and closely followed the formation of the Brotherhood in 1848 and the controversies surrounding their first Academy exhibitions in 1850 and 1851. During the period when he was energetically establishing his career as a writer, Collins also "professed a desire" (according to Hunt) to write an article on Pre-Raphaelite methods, "leaving the question of the value of results entirely apart, that the public might understand our earnestness in the direct pursuit of nature, which, if not establishing the excellence of our productions, would at least be convincing proof that our untiring ambition was not to copy any mediaevalists, as it was so generally said we did, but to be persistent rather in the pursuit of new truth."[26]

Hunt supposed that this "intention was never acted upon,"[27] but in fact Collins did write about the Pre-Raphaelites at that time in an unsigned *Bentley's Miscellany* review of the Royal Academy exhibition of 1851.[28] This review reveals a marked ambivalence toward Pre-Raphaelitism, however, and confirms if anything the strength of Collins's loyalty to his own Academic background. In it he summarizes Pre-Raphaelitism as "an almost painful minuteness of finish and detail; a disregard of the ordinary rules of composition and colour; and an evident intention of not appealing to any popular predilections on the subject of grace or beauty."[29] After considering paintings by Hunt, Millais, and his brother, he opines that "they appear to be wanting in one great desideratum of all art—judgment in selection" and have sacrificed truth to their refusal to concede anything "to public taste," concluding:

> we admire sincerely their earnestness of purpose, their
> originality of thought, their close and reverent study of
> nature. But we cannot, at the same time, fail to perceive
> that they are as yet only emerging from the darkness to
> the true light; that they are at the critical turning point
> of their career; and that, on the course they are now to
> take; on their renunciation of certain false principles
> in their present practice, depends our chance of gladly
> welcoming them, one day, as masters of their art—
> as worthy successors of the greatest among their
> predecessors in the English school.[30]

William Collins had been one of those predecessors, and his son's first book, *Memoirs of the Life of William Collins, Esq., R.A.*,[31] had also been something of a history of the "English School" in the nineteenth century. This school was, of course, the chief target of the Pre-Raphaelite revolt, so Collins's reservations are perhaps completely understandable. Just as significant here, though, is the fact that Collins takes up the language of Ruskin's defense of these same paintings, published a few weeks earlier in a letter to *The Times,* in which he too had argued that "these young artists [were] . . . at a most critical period of their career—at a turning point, from which they may either sink into nothingness or rise to a very real greatness."[32] Over the following three years, between 1852 and 1854, this turning point proved decisive, as the Brotherhood began to disintegrate. Millais, fulfilling Collins's hope, achieved popular success by adapting the less contentious Pre-Raphaelite technical innovations (intense coloration, for example) to more conventional anecdotal subjects and treatments. At the same time, Hunt and Rossetti, influenced by Ford Madox Brown, began planning contemporary subjects, to demonstrate that they were not antimodern, not, in the words of Meisel, "archaizing and reactionary," as they were accused of being,[33] but, according to Hunt, "persistent . . . in the pursuit of new truth."[34]

For Frith and his followers, inspired by the buoyant, good-humored crowds in London for the Great Exhibition, modern life was essentially comic.[35] It was epitomized by images of the social classes intermingling happily in airy public spaces: railway stations, parks, post offices, banks, race courses, and omnibuses.[36] For the Pre-Raphaelites, however, the "new truth" of modern life was epitomized by such "stern facts"[37] as emigration and work, and such unpalatable facts as sexual transgression and the loss of respectability.[38] The Pre-Raphaelites were interested in painting problem pictures and were generally far less confident than Frith about the new class formations becoming visible at the midcentury, perceiving in those formations a heavy sense of social instability and threat. In addition, they viewed modern-life art as fundamentally an oppositional art, and they had been thinking and talking about it in these terms since at least 1850. Collins would have been familiar with these discussions, which extended into the Pre-Raphaelite journal *The Germ,* where the sculptor John Tupper argued in 1850: "If, as every poet, every painter, every sculptor will acknowledge, his best and most original ideas are derived from his own time: if his great lessonings to piety, truth, charity, love, honour, honesty, gallantry, generosity, courage, are derived from the same source; why transfer them to distant periods, and make them *'not things of to-day'*?"[39] This commitment to "things of to-day" was a logical progression for the Brotherhood. Having already modernized and radicalized other categories of Academic genre painting—literary subjects, religious genre, sentimental pictures of children and humanized animals, and classic rural genre[40]—the move into contemporary subjects must be seen, in part, as an extension of their critique of the anecdotal tradition of the English School.

As Tupper makes clear, modern life also presented unique opportunities for art's "great lessonings": its essentially moral function. Lynda Nead has shown that midcentury debates over the future of the English School were debates about English moral life that focused on femininity: the virtuous, domestic woman, and the prostitute; the latter, according to Nead, was "an accommodating category" that "could define any woman who deviated from the feminine ideal and lived outside middle-class codes of morality."[41] It is not surprising, then, that so many of the Pre-Raphaelites' inaugural present-day subject-pictures should feature prostitutes (or women deviating from the feminine ideal): not only *The Awakening Conscience* but Rossetti's only modern-life work, the unfinished *Found* (1854–55); the striking series of drawings Millais did in the early 1850s on related themes; and Brown's powerful and mysterious *Take Your Son, Sir!* (begun as early as 1851 and also unfinished).[42] The prostitute was already established in religious and social discourse, fiction, and poetry as the Magdalen figure or "outcast" (an adulteress or a seduced and abandoned woman).[43] The archetypal narratives associated with this figure represent a reactionary sexual ideology to us now, an ideology that, according to Nead, operated for the "wider formation of class identity, nation and empire" through "the regulation of moral behaviour."[44] Thus, we tend to view paintings such as *The Awakening Conscience* as symptomatic and instrumental images, which helped to form bourgeois morality by defining "sexual deviance in terms of its difference to the domestic norm of middle-class marriage and home."[45] But as a Pre-Raphaelite picture exhibited at the Royal Academy in the early 1850s, this image of the fallen woman—painted, in the words of *The Athenaeum* reviewer, "literally" as a fallen woman,[46] and not disguised as a mythological, historical, or literary figure—was also calculated to scandalize bourgeois morality; particularly as Holman Hunt intended *The Awakening Conscience* to be a religious picture, a material counterpart to the (equally scandalous) realistic, humanist image of Christ in *The Light of the World,* also showing at that summer exhibition.

The *Athenaeum* critic, directed by the scriptural message (literally) framing the image,[47] recognized that it was painted in an "earnest religious spirit" but could not reconcile that with its repugnant, modern, secular subject.[48]

This prompted Ruskin to write to *The Times* on 25 May 1854, claiming that "assuredly" *The Awakening Conscience* "is not understood": "People gaze at it in a blank wonder, and leave it hopelessly."[49] In Hunt's absence (against all advice he had left for Syria), Ruskin launched in this letter his own impassioned interpretation of the symbolic function of the various emblems and objects in the picture. He had already attacked the pretensions of the parvenu middle classes elsewhere (in his pamphlet *Pre-Raphaelitism* [1851], for example), and in this letter he rebukes those who set out to buy respectability. Everything in the room—including, by implication, the kept woman—displays its price tag, with appalling consequences for the woman. Ruskin's rhetoric of fallenness gathers such force and momentum that his description soon leaps ahead of Hunt's optimistic, redemptive image into the doomed future awaiting her, when "the very hem of the poor girl's dress . . . may be soiled with dust and rain, her outcast feet falling on the street." Significantly, his reading echoes a similar passage in *Basil* in its condemnation of the "common, modern, vulgar" objects in the room so sharply contrasted with "old thoughts of home": "That furniture so carefully painted, even to the last vein of the rosewood—is there nothing to be learnt from that terrible lustre of it, from its fatal newness; nothing there that has the old thoughts of home upon it, or that is ever to become a part of home? Those embossed books, vain and useless—they also new—marked with no happy wearing of beloved leaves."[50] In Ruskin's view, sexual sinfulness had terrible consequences for women, because they could never be reconciled to their lost virtue, and potentially terrible consequences for society as a whole.[51] That he should associate the fallen woman so strongly with the "fatal newness" of the furniture is not surprising. As Nead points out, the "terrible lustre" of unused things is a sign of the absence of "the rich moral associations of the bourgeois domestic ideal."[52] That this same newness should be associated not only with prostitution but also with the values of the rising small-scale commercial classes, tainted with trade, is also important. Hunt's setting, after all, is a debauched aristocrat's *maison damnée;* Collins's is a linen-draper's house. *The Awakening Conscience* is not, however, a condemnation of upper-class profligacy, but of a society in which material advancement has usurped spiritual aspiration and in which affluence—middle-class affluence—leads only to indulgence and moral depravity. Hunt's tacit alignment of the prostitute and the vulgar petty bourgeois, and Collins's explicit alignment of them in *Basil*, suggests that at the midcentury, as the new prosperity raised paltry shopkeepers into the middle ranks of the middle classes, prostitution was not the only social fear being negotiated in cultural texts.

Collins's daring treatment of sexual transgression in *Basil* was not, therefore, scandalous entirely on its own account but on account of its representation of the sexual fascination and moral repugnance of a new social menace, arrived as if from nowhere (significantly, Collins uses Jewish stereotypes to describe Sherwin),[53] which supplants the familiar object of middle-class social fear from the 1840s: Chartism and lower-class revolt. To underline this connection, Collins borrows in *Basil* from the conventions of the fiction of sensational crime, at that time still predominantly produced in penny numbers by slum publishers for a semi-literate lower-class readership and strongly associated during the forties with radical and republican propaganda.[54] His most notable borrowing is from the sensationally popular *Mysteries of London* (1845–55), written by G. W. M. Reynolds, gentleman turned arch-republican and physical-force Chartist. There was considerable risk in this for an aspiring middle-class writer at the beginning of his career, determined to make a living out of literature. Collins therefore works diligently to subordinate the tense and seductive events of the plot to a stable moral discourse, present both in "little, simple, quiet, womanly Clara" (*Basil*, 3:90), who keeps Basil's conscience awake, and in the scrupulous self-examination that characterizes his own first-person narration; and he is careful to avoid any hint of insurrectionary sentiment. (Nevertheless the *Athenaeum* reviewer was reminded of the "unwholesome" literary school of Maturin and Eugène Sue.)[55] Collins's own politics at this time—he may be described as a liberal intent on living down the Toryism of his father and wary of the radicalism of some of his friends[56]—matter less in this regard, perhaps, than the fact that he was learning to negotiate the complex cultural politics of the literary profession. Letters from the late 1840s and early 1850s show him much preoccupied with money: his own constant shortage of it and, more tellingly, the immense sums that he believed could be earned out of writing.[57] Determined to be a popular novelist and a serious novelist, Collins became "both obsessed by reader approval and rebellious against it," as Sue Lonoff's study has shown.[58] The dedication to *Basil* reflects this ambivalence. It oscillates between progressive and conservative positions, challenging and mollifying its readers by turns, and culminates in a lofty declaration of his enterprise—the union of "Actual" and "Ideal" in a prose "poetry of every-day truth" (*Basil*, 1:xi)—which is at once ambitious in its intentions and reassuringly theoretical in its language.

That language is the language of aesthetics, the language of the Academy and *Modern Painters* alike, and its application in this context suggests that Collins may be trying to explain his own project by referring to recent controversies in the visual arts. Thus, the union of "actual" and "ideal" suggests something vaguely dissident—the Pre-Raphaelites' controversial juxtapositions of literary and religious imagery and symbolism with vulgar or questionable subject matter, and their laborious painterly treatment of a subject intrinsically unworthy of such a treatment—and something safely orthodox, equally at home in the discourses of Sir Joshua Reynolds or the speeches of Sir Charles Eastlake.[59] Similarly, Collins assures his readers that he possesses what Hunt calls "earnestness in the direct pursuit of nature,"[60] by pledging that he is not one of those who "play at writing . . . who coolly select as an amusement 'to kill time,' an occupation which can only be pursued, even creditably, by the patient, uncompromising, reverent devotion of every moral and intellectual faculty, more or less, which a human being has to give" (*Basil*, 1:xv–xvi). This strategy of imparting moral seriousness to his work by investing the *act* of writing itself with moral seriousness recalls Ruskin's defense of Pre-Raphaelitism (1851), which argued that "the mere labour bestowed on these works, and their fidelity to a certain order of truth (labour and fidelity which are altogether indisputable) ought at once to have placed them above the level of mere contempt."[61] This strategy leads Collins to a heavy-handed use of the language of "vocation" and "duty" in the dedication (*Basil*, 1:xv, xix), but his aim is clear: *Basil* shows "the patient, uncompromising, reverent devotion of every moral and intellectual faculty," which could scarcely permit him to "shrink from all honest and serious reference . . . to subjects" thought of in private and talked of in public "everywhere" (*Basil*, 1:xvi, xix–xx). It is the solemn responsibility of any serious "literary man," he declares, to record the ugliness and uneventfulness of modern everyday life. The fantastic coincidences of romance—the "extraordinary accidents and events which happen to few"—are part of that life and are therefore legitimate materials for fiction (*Basil*, 1:xiii).

Basil's first reviewers were not very convinced by these explanations. The "taste of the age" has decreed that the novel's "proper office is to elevate and purify," one of them wrote,[62] and this novel, for all its "artistic merit," falls far short of this sacred office.[63] More pointedly, D. O. Maddyn, in an almost identical phrase, recognized Collins and recognized the allusions to the visual arts in the dedication: "Mr. Collins, as the son of an eminent painter, should know that the proper office of Art is to elevate and purify in pleasing. Without the element of pleasurable emotion, colour and design in painting, like eloquence and fancy in literature, will fail to gain our sympathies. 'Basil' is a tale of criminality, almost revolting from its domestic horrors."[64] In other words, aesthetic abstractions do not redeem *Basil* from its gross offenses against aesthetic propriety—its failure to invoke what Maddyn calls "pleasurable emotion"—by which is meant its offenses against moral order: elevation and purification.[65] Just as early reviews of Pre-Raphaelite paintings sometimes alleged "pictorial blasphemy,"[66] so the *Basil* notices focused on Collins's claim to be writing a moral book. The *Westminster Review,* describing the dedication as a "letter of excessive length and no small pretension," accused *Basil* of offering "nothing which can 'take men from the low passions and miserable troubles of life into a higher region.'"[67] Reproaching Collins for corrupting the "high and holy mission" of the novelist, the review concluded:

> It matters not much whether the artist hold the pencil
> or the pen, the same great rules apply to both. He may
> simply copy nature as he sees it, and then the spectator
> has a pleasure proportioned to the beauty of the scene
> copied. He may give a noble spirit-stirring scene, and he
> will raise high thoughts and great aspirations in those
> who contemplate it. He may take a higher moral ground,
> and move to compassion by showing undeserved suffer-
> ing, or, like Hogarth, read a lesson to the idle and the
> dissipated. He may also paint scenes of cruelty and
> sensuality so gross that his picture will be turned to
> the wall by those who do not choose to have their
> imagination defiled.[68]

The passing reference to Hogarth is telling, however, for it may be argued that *Basil* in fact owes a great deal to Hogarth's coruscating, and often horrific, satires of middle-class society, as does a picture such as *The Awakening Conscience.* (Hunt in fact called Hogarth "the stalwart founder of modern British art.")[69] *Basil* intersects most clearly with the concerns of Pre-Raphaelite modern-life art in an underlying narrative of social relations that both share with Hogarth's *Marriage à la Mode* (1743–45). A devastating morality picture tracing the corrupt union of bourgeois and landed interests in Georgian London, *Marriage à la Mode* is a series of six tableaux depicting the moral progress of a corrupt earl's son and a vulgar merchant's daughter, married solely for the sake of consolidating the social power of their respective families. When Collins was writing *Basil,* these issues were still at the forefront of political and imaginative discourse. For the mid-Victorians, the coalition of the landed classes (who endowed middle-class aspirations to power with the potent symbolism of historical and social continuity in landed property) and the upper middle classes (who infused a moribund and corrupt aristocracy and gentry with capital, commercial energy, and a new moral seriousness) was most potently symbolized in two related figures: the gentleman and the womanly woman. The Victorian idea of the gentleman as someone who transcends the mere obligations of rank and breeding involved complex appropriations of national symbols, most obviously the medieval knight. Popularized in such key texts as Charlotte Yonge's *The Heir of Redclyffe* (1853) and Thackeray's *The Newcomes* (1853–55), the man of breeding and refinement in modern dress helped to endow modern-life literature and art with the high social and moral purpose it needed. The womanly woman, likewise, was figured in this context as the prime agent of social reconciliation, representing in her selflessness and duty a strong image of cultivation and breeding and embodying in her capacity for moral influence nonviolent alternatives to political coercion and rebellion.

The gentleman and the womanly woman were embodiments of a unified and ordered society, who, according to Lynda Nead, together signified "moral purity, private and public virtue, and ultimately national stability."[70] Ruskin's defense of Pre-Raphaelitism in 1851, and later his influential public endorsement of a redemptive moral modern-life art, both urge that art should be the reflection of that society, what he calls in his "Lectures on Art" *"the exponent of its social and political virtues."*[71] The opening section of the Pre-Raphaelite pamphlet is accordingly an attack on the cultural acquisitiveness of the vulgar new-monied classes: "now that a man may make money, and rise in the world, and associate himself, unreproached, with people once far above him, not only is the natural discontentedness of humanity developed to an unheard-of extent, whatever a man's position, but it becomes a veritable shame to him to remain in the state he was born in, and everybody thinks it is his *duty* to try to be a 'gentleman.'"[72] Ruskin's solution to this problem was to encourage a few "benevolent men, undeniably in the class of 'gentleman,'" to "enter into some of our commonest trades, and make them honourable; showing that it was possible for a man to retain his dignity, and remain, in the best sense, a gentleman, though part of his time was everyday occupied in manual labour, or even serving customers over a counter."[73]

Collins takes up this challenge in *Basil*, where, by an accident of fate, his protagonist finds himself in the position of one of those benevolent men, a representative of the new generation of landed gentlemen with a chance to forge an enlightened alliance with the merchant classes; willing, as his father never could be, to serve customers over a counter. Beneath the moderate radicalism of Ruskin's argument there are echoes of Disraeli's nostalgic neofeudal Young Englandism, which may also be heard in *Basil*, effectively a rewriting of Disraeli's *Sybil* (1845). In that novel, Egremont, dressed as middle-class Mr. Franklin, forms a love triangle with Sybil and the moral-force Chartist Stephen Morley and is attacked by Morley under cover of heavy fog. In *Basil*, the hero likewise ventures, ostensibly out of a writer's curiosity, into the streets of the city and suburbs of London and becomes entangled with "the lower orders": but here they are the merchant middle classes. The ensuing triangle of Basil, Margaret, and Mannion therefore represents a more complex set of social relationships than that encompassed by Disraeli's enlightened aristocrat, revolutionary radical, and woman of the future. As a member of a gentry family traced back to Battle Abbey, Basil's power rests with land and with the purity of his English lineage. Like Egremont, however, he is a younger brother and therefore freed from the necessity of maintaining this old social order unchanged. In any case, Collins makes it quite clear in *Basil* that the old order, unreformed, is as corrupt and deficient, in its own way, as the vulgar new order, represented by the equally inassimilable Sherwin. The representative figure for this old order is Basil's father, whose unimpeachable moral standards are themselves the source of his corruption. He has no gouty foot, like one of Hogarth's depraved gentry, but a fateful defect of pride marked in the red spot that appears on his otherwise unruffled face when disobeyed. In defiance of the inassimilable older generation, Basil, a kind of latter-day version of Scott's Ivanhoe, is drawn to the future and loyal to the past. Standing in for a new generation of Englishmen, he is an ideal figure for Ruskin's plan.

Basil's boyish knightly adventure, with its tests of virtue and courtly love, occurs in a strange wasteland, a desert of "half-finished streets and half-inhabited neighbourhoods" (*Basil*, 2:142), which are "desolately silent" after the "mighty vitality of the great city" (*Basil*,

1:125, 165). Collins dwells on this revulsion of unfinished places, connecting it to the unfinished (that is, unconsummated) marriage of Basil and Margaret and to the evil that is allowed to flourish unchecked in the vulnerable spaces where social formations are incomplete and social relationships unresolved: "that worst, deceitful repose, under which the elements of convulsion gather, and lurk unseen" (*Basil*, 2:5). In a long episode early in the novel, Basil describes an encounter on the omnibus (shortly before Margaret gets on) with a veterinarian, whose face and hands are deeply scarred from mad dogs' bites. This grotesque character fascinates and horrifies his captive audience with a matter-of-fact cautionary tale about the imperative of cutting out infection before it destroys you. This bald parable of social infections left untended was clearly either too distasteful or too problematic for Collins and his readers, and he removed it from the 1862 revised edition.

With her "voluptuous, southern-looking beauty" (*Basil*, 1:296), Margaret Sherwin is the dark maiden of Basil's quest, a version of the morally empty lower middle-class woman as femme fatale, the siren of his Romantic (and Rossettian) dream of the woman from the fair hills and the woman from the dark wood (*Basil*, 1:154–59).[74] This vivid, hallucinatory scene sharply accentuates the novel's informing romance typologies of the fair and the dark and uses pictorial conventions to elevate Basil's psychological conflict into the realm of literary or mythological archetypes. But it also allows Collins to penetrate, under cover of those archetypes, "the secret recesses" of sexual desire where the blood burns and the breath fails (*Basil*, 2:158–59), and the hero gives himself up "heart, and soul, and body, to the woman from the dark woods" (*Basil*, 1:159). Moreover, actuality and ideality are so effectively juxtaposed here because, although the reader suspects Margaret's lack of refinement, Basil is impervious to it; and because Collins is careful to shield her personality from the reader until "certain peculiarities" (*Basil*, 2:74) in her character accidentally come to Basil's attention: up to that point she has only been given one sentence of dialogue (*Basil*, 1:135). In this way she is preserved, for a time at least, as pure myth: a falsehood, an icon of respectability produced entirely by money and destined to be traded for the social elevation of her family. In reality, it is Clara, Basil's sister, who truly represents the middle-class ideal of respectable femininity; the actual middle-class woman, on the other hand, only vulgarly apes those virtues. Basil's blindness to Margaret's limitations is vitally important, however, if the novel is to be credible in putting forward the intermarriage of aristocratic blood and middle-class wealth as a possibility. On the other hand, it is critical that Basil and

Margaret remain man and wife in law only, for this is not a relationship that can ever be seriously countenanced; that legitimate "marriage," ironically enough, belongs to Basil and Clara, who will set up house together happily at the end of the novel. This is perhaps where *Basil* comes closest to Dickens. In *Dombey and Son* (1846–48), Dickens had begun to analyze the illicit passions and criminal impulses lurking beneath the surface of middle-class respectability. *Dombey*'s world is one of sexual hypocrisy and cruelty, cynical manipulations of the marriage market, and the looming figure of the middle-class Magdalen.[75] This analysis is continued in *David Copperfield*, where sexual passion— figured in the central image of the "undisciplined heart"—is socially disruptive and threatening.

The marriage of the brotherly and sisterly David and Agnes at the end of *David Copperfield* is intended to resolve those disruptions and defuse those threats, and the denouement of *Basil* performs a similar function, replacing the married couple with a literal brother and sister. Unlike David, however, Basil has endured an ordeal that stealthily erodes the certainties of his own class identity and sends him, in the wake of the novel's traumatic climax in Cornwall, back to the security of his own family. This ordeal occurs with painful slowness, through the gradual and palpable tightening of tension as the months of his "probationary" marriage pass and the heightening erotic interest shifts from Margaret to the mysterious figure of Sherwin's confidential clerk, Mannion. The unconsummated sexual act, displaced into amorous co-reading in the early days of Basil's ordeal, undergoes a further displacement into a fascination with reading Mannion's face. Basil soon becomes obsessed with Mannion and his past when the unreadable face gives him no clue to that past and no clue to Mannion's real class identity. Mannion is, as it were, an entirely new class subject, a ready-made version of the new man, with "all the quietness and self-possession of a thorough gentleman" (*Basil*, 2:28). An arresting composite of Gothic and Romantic types, he is associated with Radcliffean imagery (ice and storm, veil, labyrinth, and void), with *Frankenstein*,[76] and in other important ways with De Quincey's opium eater (he is "an epicure in tea" and "a prodigal . . . in books" [*Basil*, 2:51]).[77] He also points the way to later figures in this mode—*Edwin Drood*'s John Jasper, Dracula, and Holmes and Moriarty. His traumatic past (which Collins encourages us to sympathize with) puts him dangerously outside the class system. He is not a clerk or a shopkeeper or a gentleman, but a monstrous compound of these, and his exile leaves him without need of affection, friendship, or love (he seduces Margaret simply for pleasure and domination before he fixes on revenge against Basil), without need of money or belongings—and without ambition.

Mannion also plainly owes something to Dickens.[78] His scheme to ruin Basil by seducing Margaret closely resembles the elopement in *Dombey and Son* of Carker, Dombey's corrupt confidential clerk and "manager," with Edith Dombey, an elopement also planned to ruin Dombey and bring down the firm. That novel's scathing critique of the commodification of women in the upper middle-class marriage market is also interwoven with a subplot showing the consequences of Carker's vice in the abandoned woman, Alice Marwood, a doubling that Dickens pursues in *David Copperfield,* where Emily, lost in London, is paralleled in the character of the fallen woman, Martha.[79] Just as important for *Basil,* though, are the monstrous doublings of Dickens's benign heroes in these novels: Dombey and Carker, but more especially David and Uriah Heep. In Mannion's sexual magnetism Collins combines elements of the well-educated "fast man," a kind of incognito Steerforth, with elements of the resentful, acquisitive, undermining clerks of *Dombey* and *David Copperfield.* There are also echoes of Redlaw, the embittered protagonist of Dickens's Christmas book *The Haunted Man,* in Mannion. Redlaw is haunted by a ghostly double spawned out of his own painful memories of past injustices, who offers him the gift (actually, curse) of forgetfulness. As with Mannion, the obliteration of bad memories leaves Redlaw incapable of sympathy and human feeling.

At the same time, Mannion can be read as a monster who has been created by schemes such as Ruskin's for an honorable middle class, a gentleman behind the counter, happy with his new lot but secretly nurturing revolt and anarchy. His decidedly (if preemptively) vampirish characteristics—he is cultivated and cool, formal and businesslike, and his real face shows itself only for a second in a lurid flash of lightning—point to a figure capable of undermining an entire civilization. Not surprisingly, then, he is described at one point as "The Great Mystery of London" (*Basil,* 3:141), a clear allusion to G. W. M. Reynolds, who, like Mannion, was a fallen scion of the landed classes seduced by French republicanism and (according to his enemies) monomaniacally driven by his hatred of aristocratic privileges to support full-scale Chartist rebellion against the two enemies of the common people: Sherwin's class and Basil's class. Mannion conceals his abomination of Sherwin and Basil behind a facade of civilized conduct, but the clues to his French allegiances are clear, in his austere post-Revolutionary demeanor (his plain dress and frugal habits) and his impassive neoclassical face: the face of a scholar as well as a cipher, with its bland respectability and blank servitude. All these hints of foreignness make Mannion a power-fully polysemous figure: for conflicting forms of social threat; for Basil's own guilt; and for the menace of modernity. This polysemy is evident in his very name, which carries the contradictory meanings of modern life (of an allegorical "everyman" figure, as well as an odd mixture of "min-ion" and "mammon"), meanings that are too contradictory, in fact, to be resolved other than by his death. Disconnected, uprooted, déclassé, Mannion is a modern man of a later century and has no place in mid-Victorian Britain. When his face is destroyed, his identity is reduced to a single letter mysteriously monogrammed on the handkerchief found on him. "M"—it could stand for Mannion, or Margaret, or middle class, or modern.

Yet Mannion's power is not disabled by any act of Basil's, but by the arrival on the scene of another character with a French connection, Basil's brother Ralph, a scapegrace and a "super-exquisite foreign dandy" who "revolutionized the dinner-table" and scandalized his father whenever he returned home (*Basil,* 1:63, 62). With his buffoon-ish ways and superficial ideas, Ralph ought to be a rather silly charac-ter, but, surprisingly, his appearance breaks a spell in which both Basil and the reader have for pages been held, claustrophobic and paranoid. Suddenly the air is cleared, the diabolical Mannion seems more like a schoolyard bully, and we feel that we, too, have let things get some-what out of proportion. The effect is bracing and emphasizes the vital power of English common sense over all other solutions. Ultimately, of course, Ralph will bring this breezy good sense into a family freed at last from the deadening rule of the father; and through the discipline instilled by his bohemian feminist mistress (a kind of Brompton George Sand), he will be "aroused by his new duties to a sense of his new posi-tion" (*Basil,* 3:295).

Nor is Basil himself able to resolve any of these social contra-dictions: the causes of his horror lie too deep. Rather, that role falls to Clara, his sister. In the struggle between competing forms of influence—Margaret's siren influence over Basil, and Mannion's demonic influence over Margaret—the benevolent influence of the womanly woman prevails over all. Constantly on the verge of losing her self-possession—next to Mannion's composure, a sure sign of deep feeling—Clara is the voice of Basil's conscience. In this, she is able to reach her brother through an ideal of the past that she embodies—a past of homeliness and duty, and the fond associations of childhood. Despite the restitution of this ideal past, however, the novel reaches an impasse: the household that the brother and sister set up is an ideal family and an ideal of middle-class domesticity, but it is wholly at odds with those political narratives that are resolved by the unification of hostile interests in marriage and the issue of an heir to the new generation. By returning to the house of the mother, Basil and Clara escape the regime of the father, with his fanatical genealogical record-keeping, and avoid the corruption and madness attendant upon sexuality and class assimilation. Basil is indeed the baby-husband Margaret predicted, playing at setting up house in a country estate with his sister-wife, outside the perils of history: "Yes! to look away from— but, towards what object? The Future? That way, I see but dimly even yet. It is on the Present that my thoughts are fixed, in the contentment which desires no change" (*Basil*, 3:294). The necessity for a novel about marriage to conclude with a newly constituted family is displaced into the picturesque narrative of the Cornish miner's family who restore the traumatized Basil to Clara. Through this device, the dangers of class hybridity and unreadability are subsumed into noblesse oblige and the highly readable domestic tableau of the rural "good folk." In this sense, *Basil* retreats from modern life to the kind of genre scene only too reminiscent of the work of Collins's father: there is a kind of rustic civility implied in the restoration of social power relations between an enlightened and benevolent landed class (theirs is "not a repose which owns no duty" [*Basil*, 3:296]) and an enlightened working class.[80]

Basil fails, therefore, in what it sets out to do: to make a new kind of fiction out of an act of reconciliation operating on aesthetic, narrative, and social levels, a reconciliation of the actual and the ideal, the past and present, the bourgeois and landed. In the end, it cannot offer a plausible domestic solution to a narrative in which the domestic ideal is threatened by class mobility. But in the process Collins does lay the groundwork for a radical new kind of fiction, one in which "the secret theatre of home" (*Basil*, 1:236) is the medium of the modern: where external signs of social identity such as gesture, expression, environment, dress, and language are no longer trustworthy; and where transgressive identities—the Sherwins, Mannion, Basil himself— disrupt social order and threaten to corrupt bloodlines. Just as the protagonists in *The Awakening Conscience* were compulsively misidentified—the figures were regarded as brother and sister as often as upper-class seducer and lower-class prostitute, and in either case were insistently associated with the vulgarity of the rising lower middle class—these transgressive identities point to a profound anxiety about the preservation of the values of refinement and cultivation, and the protection of fundamental moral values, in the face of the "fatal newness" of these social formations and social relationships. In such a room—in such a society—who can tell aristocrats from shopkeepers, or shopkeepers from clerks? Who can tell sisters from wives, or wives from adulteresses, or adulteresses from prostitutes? It is significant, then, that the central marker for the anxiety these texts evince concerning class identity is the face. Both the novel and the painting focus on the face of the ambiguous class subject as "a mystery for your eyes" (*Basil*, 2:28) and both turn on the disfigurement and erasure of facial expression. Mannion's expression, "impenetrable" and "wholly inexpressive" (*Basil*, 2:28), conceals a "hideously livid hue," a "spectral look of ghastliness . . . glaring and grinning" (*Basil*, 2:73), that must be obliterated or made visibly, permanently monstrous. In 1856, too, Hunt's patron Thomas Fairbairn asked him to repaint the face of the woman in *The Awakening Conscience* because he could no longer bear to live with it: with "the lips half open, indistinct in their purple quivering; the teeth set hard; the eyes filled with the fearful light of futurity."[81]

When Francis Turner Palgrave came to write about this image of a tormented woman a few years later in 1865, the vocabulary of modern life had been displaced by a new vocabulary. Hunt's picture, he wrote, "touched the limits of sensationalism," adding: "Yet we give the name sensational, not to the *Heart of Mid Lothian* [sic] or to *Othello*, but to the dramas of the Victoria or Miss Braddon's novels."[82] By then, moral modern-life art was a tame affair, thoroughly reintegrated into the genre tradition and the Academy. It is significant, then, that *The Awakening Conscience,* a picture that even now confronts and puzzles its viewers, should seem to Palgrave less like the sentimental, humdrum modern-life subjects of the 1860s than the popular novel of domestic crime, mystery, and horror. To attribute this to the influence of *Basil,* however—now commonly cast as the first sensation novel, predating the earliest use of that term by almost a decade[83]—is misleading. *Basil* undoubtedly anticipates sensation fiction. It has what G. H. Lewes identified as the "breathless rapidity of movement" inherent to sensation fiction and introduces many of the devices Collins would later exploit (the "factual" newspaper report, the double).[84] Moreover, as Ann Cvetkovich observes of sensationalism, *Basil* "makes events emotionally vivid by representing in tangible and specific terms social and historical structures that would otherwise remain abstract."[85] But in the early 1850s Collins was not experimenting in isolation with a narrative mode that would await its proper definition for years to come. Indeed *Basil*'s original subtitle, "A Story of Modern Life," suggests an obscured genealogy for sensationalism: a genealogy obscured, in part, by Collins himself when he removed that subtitle in his extensive revisions of the novel in 1862 at the height of the sensation craze. From this standpoint, Hunt was therefore not simply drawing upon the protosensationalism of *Basil* in his anatomy of the "fatal newness" of the new, or Ruskin drawing upon the language of *Basil* in his "sensationalist" defense of *The Awakening Conscience*. On the contrary, all these texts belong to the moment of modern life, which can be legitimately claimed as an important, and overlooked, point of departure for the sensation novel.

Notes

1. Modern-life pictures, according to Martin Meisel, were pictures of the contemporary middle-class scene by painters that were "drawn to identify themselves, through their art, with the energy and concerns of the present age" (*Realizations: Narrative, Pictorial, and Theatrical Arts in Nineteenth-Century England* [Princeton: Princeton Univ. Press, 1983], 375). Furthermore, according to Meisel, "The first painting from the Pre-Raphaelites or their sympathizers likely to be identified as an 'illustration of modern life' and making an impact through its social immediacy was Holman Hunt's *Awakening Conscience*" (375 n. 4).

2. "Royal Academy," *The Athenaeum*, no. 1384 (6 May 1854): 561. Hereafter cited as "Royal Academy."

3. According to Malcolm Warner, Hunt's painting was "the prototype of the many serious, often moralizing scenes from modern life painted by the Pre-Raphaelites and their followers" (*The Victorians: British Painting, 1837–1901* [Washington, D.C.: National Gallery of Art, 1996], 93). Significant Academy pictures in the mode of *The Awakening Conscience* include Augustus Egg's *Past and Present* (1858), William Lindsay Windus's *Too Late* (1858), and Robert Braithwaite Martineau's *The Last Day in the Old Home* (1861). On the history of modern-life subject painting see Caroline H. Arscott, "Modern Life Subjects in British Painting, 1840–60" (Ph.D. diss., Univ. of Leeds, 1987); on Pre-Raphaelitism and modern life, see Tim Barringer, *The Pre-Raphaelites: Reading the Image* (London: Wiedenfeld and Nicolson, 1998), 85–108.

4. The entry on *The Awakening Conscience* in the catalog accompanying the influential 1984 Tate Gallery exhibition, *The Pre-Raphaelites,* for example, notes: "Prostitution was a pressing metropolitan problem, and 'the fallen woman' was the inspiration for contemporary novels such as Wilkie Collins's *Basil* and Mrs Gaskell's *Ruth*, both of which probably influenced [*The Awakening Conscience*]" (Judith Bronkhurst, "William Holman Hunt," in *The Pre-Raphaelites*, ed. Leslie Parris [London: Tate Gallery, 1984], 121). Kate Flint, likewise, finds it "particularly tempting"

to draw a parallel between Hunt's painting and *Basil*. According to Flint, "Hunt saw his friend Collins regularly during his painting of this picture, and there is a strong resemblance between the interior of Woodbine Villa [the 'maison de convenance' in St. John's Wood rented by Hunt and used as the setting for the picture] and North Villa, Holyoake Square, just north of Regent's Park, where Basil's inamorata, daughter of the owner of a large linen draper's shop, lived" ("Reading *The Awakening Conscience* Rightly," in *Pre-Raphaelites Re-Viewed*, ed. Marcia Pointon [Manchester: Manchester Univ. Press, 1989], 51). It has even been suggested, by Collins's most recent biographer, that Hunt's long and apparently unconsummated relationship with his model for *The Awakening Conscience*, Annie Miller, is the "fact in real life" (*Basil: A Story of Modern Life*, 3 vols. [London: Richard Bentley, 1852], 1:x; hereafter cited in the text as *Basil*) on which Basil's relationship with Margaret is based (Catherine Peters, *The King of Inventors: A Life of Wilkie Collins* [Princeton: Princeton Univ. Press, 1991], 116–17). Because the novel was later heavily revised, the first edition, the version actually read by Hunt and his peers, is quoted from in this essay.

5. William Holman Hunt, *Pre-Raphaelitism and the Pre-Raphaelite Brotherhood*, 2 vols. (London: Macmillan, 1905).

6. For example, according to Frederic George Stevens, the male figure in *The Awakening Conscience* is "handsome, as the tiger is,—false, pitiless, and cruel" (*William Holman Hunt and His Works: A Memoir of the Artist's Life, with Description of His Pictures* [London: James Nisbet, 1860], 16), whereas Collins's aristocratic hero is sympathetic and mostly passive; moreover, Margaret Sherwin's conscience awakens only belatedly, on her deathbed.

7. Grieve notes that "a similar use of detail to heighten the pathos of a modern-life subject can also be found in contemporary novels such as *Basil* . . . or *Ruth*. . . . It seems likely that Hunt noticed this and that the subjects of novels such as these gave him the courage to paint *The Awakening Conscience*" (*The Art of Dante Gabriel Rossetti* [Norwich: Real World Publications, 1976], 35).

8. Flint, 52.

9. As summarized by Bronkhurst: "the cat is a straightforward type of the seducer, but the bird it has been tormenting has escaped. The web in which the girl is entrapped is symbolised by the convolvulus in the vase on the piano and the tangled embroidery threads on the carpet. The title of the engraving above the piano . . . ,'Cross Purposes,' is appropriate in the light of the lover being [what Hunt called] 'the unconscious utterer of a divine message'. . . . On the other hand, the sheet music unfurling on the floor is a tribute to Hunt's friend Edward Lear, whose setting of Tennyson's 'Tears, Idle Tears' from *The Princess* was published in October 1853. . . . The message of 'Tears, Idle Tears,' like that of Thomas Moore's 'Oft in the Stilly Night,' which the man has been singing, contrasts past innocence

with present wretchedness. The effect of this on the woman is emphasised by the frame design: marigolds are emblems of sorrow, bells of warning. . . . The wall decoration behind the woman relates back to 'The Hireling Shepherd' [an earlier painting by Hunt] . . . in its warning of the need for vigilance: [according to Hunt,] 'The corn and vine are left unguarded by the slumbering cupid watchers and the fruit is left to be preyed upon by thievish birds'. . . . Chastity is the only weapon by which the human predators can be foiled, and the French clock . . . depicts this virtue binding Cupid" (Bronkhurst, 121).

10. Collins's Letter of Dedication met with strong disapproval from Dickens (see Dickens to Wilkie Collins, London, 20 Dec. 1852, in *The Letters of Charles Dickens*, vol. 6 [1850–52], ed. Graham Storey, Kathleen Tillotson, and Nina Burgis [Oxford: Clarendon Press, 1988], 823–24), as well as from reviewers of *Basil*. One anonymous reviewer called it a letter of "excessive length and no small pretension" ("The Progress of Fiction as an Art," *Westminster Review* 60 [Oct. 1853]: 373; hereafter cited as *Westminster Review*). Another labeled it "crude criticism" ([D. O. Maddyn], Review of *Basil: A Story of Modern Life*, by Wilkie Collins, *The Athenaeum*, no. 1310 [4 Dec. 1852]: 1323; qtd. in Norman Page, *Wilkie Collins: The Critical Heritage* [London and Boston: Routledge and Kegan Paul], 47–48). Significantly, the dedication was cut by almost half in later editions.

11. See the reviews reprinted in Page, 45–53.

12. The integration of elements of domestic and Gothic or sensational crime fiction, present to some extent in the Newgate novel of the 1830s (exemplified by Bulwer's *Eugene Aram* [1832], Dickens's *Oliver Twist* [1837–39], and Ainsworth's *Jack Sheppard* [1839–40]), was pioneered by the Brontës in the late 1840s, when the middle-class domestic novel was coming into vogue.

13. On the centrality of domesticity to Victorian middle-class values, see John Ruskin, "Of Queens' Gardens," in *The Works of John Ruskin, Library Edition*, ed. E. T. Cook and Alexander Wedderburn, 39 vols. (London: George Allen, 1903–12), 18:109–44 (hereafter cited as *The Works of John Ruskin*); Nancy Armstrong, *Desire and Domestic Fiction: A Political History of the Novel* (New York: Oxford Univ. Press, 1987); Mary Poovey, *Uneven Developments: The Ideological Work of Gender in Mid-Victorian England* (Chicago: Univ. of Chicago Press, 1988); and Catherine Hall, "The Sweet Delights of Home," in *A History of Private Life*, ed. Philippe Ariès and Georges Duby, vol. 4, *From the Fires of Revolution to the Great War*, ed. Michelle Perrot (Cambridge and London: Belknap Press, 1990), 47–93.

14. Marcia Pointon, introduction to *Pre-Raphaelites Re-Viewed*, 1.

15. Charles Harrison, Paul Wood, and Jason Gaiger, "*The Times* Critic and John Ruskin (1819–1900) Exchange on the Pre-Raphaelites," in *Art in*

Theory, 1815–1900: An Anthology of Changing Ideas, ed. Charles Harrison, Paul Wood, and Jason Gaiger (Oxford: Blackwell, 1998), 440.

16. Alastair Ian Grieve notes Lindsay Errington's suggestion that *Basil* influenced Millais's modern-life sketches of the early 1850s, in her unpublished dissertation ("Social and Religious Themes in English Art" [Ph.D. diss., London Univ., 1973], 26).

17. It is worth noting that *Basil* was published on 16 November 1852, and the first sketch for *The Awakening Conscience* is dated January 1853.

18. Collins's first novel, *Ioláni; or Tahiti As It Was. A Romance,* remained unpublished in his lifetime. *Antonina,* based on Gibbon's *The Decline and Fall of the Roman Empire* and using Scott and Bulwer-Lytton as its models, was begun in 1846 but was interrupted by Collins's work on his father's *Memoirs* (1848); it was finally published in February 1850.

19. Collins to Richard Bentley, London, 22 Nov. 1849, *The Letters of Wilkie Collins,* ed. William Baker and William M. Clarke (New York: St. Martin's Press, 1999), 1:59. Hereafter cited as *Letters.* It is unclear what Collins is referring to here—the "Condition of England" novel, the "horrible" novels of the Brontës, Elizabeth Gaskell's *Mary Barton* (1848), or perhaps, more distantly, Newgate fiction.

20. Meisel, 375. Sue Lonoff notes that *Antonina* was a *"succes d'estime,"* but "did not sell widely" (*Wilkie Collins and His Victorian Readers: A Study in the Rhetoric of Authorship* [New York: AMS Press, 1982], 68–69). Collins was not alone in abandoning historical fiction at this time, however. Even Bulwer-Lytton, seeing the success of Catherine Gore's shift from historical silver-fork novels to fashionable fictions "of the present day," as well as Dickens's *Dombey and Son* (1846–48) and Thackeray's *Vanity Fair* (1847–48), wrote a domestic novel, *The Caxtons,* in 1849.

21. His travel book, *Rambles Beyond Railways: or, Notes in Cornwall, Taken A-Foot* (London: Bentley, 1851), was used for descriptive background in the climax to *Basil;* his Christmas book was *Mr Wray's Cash-Box* (London: Bentley, 1851).

22. In 1851 Frith was "determined to try [his] hand on modern life, with all its drawbacks of unpicturesque dress." When he was on his summer holiday in Ramsgate that year, he began making sketches of "all sorts and conditions of men and women . . . to be found there" (W. P. Frith, *My Autobiography and Reminiscences,* 2 vols. [London: Richard Bentley, 1887–88], 1:243). On Frith's return, Ward and Egg encouraged him to work those sketches up into the painting that became *Ramsgate Sands.* (On the origin of Frith's modern-life practice, see Meisel, 374–401.) The Pre-Raphaelites were never completely isolated from these Academic painters. With the exception of Rossetti, they had all been trained in the Academy schools themselves, and they remained friends with painters whose work was greatly at odds with theirs. Augustus Egg, for example, organized the commission of *The Awakening Conscience* for Hunt, and

when Hunt left for the Middle East, Egg kept the painting in his studio until the R.A. exhibition. And Millais, initially the most radical and reviled of all the Pre-Raphaelites who exhibited at the R.A. (i.e., not including Rossetti), settled quickly back into an Academy style after the mid-1850s and was ultimately elected president of the R.A.

23. Collins to R. H. Dana, London, 12 Jan. 1849, *Letters*, 1:53. Collins only briefly contemplated a career as an artist. He did have a picture chosen for the Royal Academy exhibition of 1849, but by then he had been studying law at Lincoln's Inn since 1846, "only painting" he tells Dana, "in leisure moments, in humble amateur-fashion, for my own amusement."

24. Wilkie Collins, "Preface to the First Edition," in *Hide and Seek*, ed. Catherine Peters (Oxford: Oxford Univ. Press, 1993), 432. This novel deals explicitly with the Academic art world. When Collins began submitting his first articles to *Bentley's Miscellany* in the early 1850s, many of them concerned the visual arts. See, for example, "A Pictorial Tour of St. George Bosherville," *Bentley's Miscellany* 29, no. 173 (May 1851): 493–508.

25. Charles Collins exhibited *Convent Thoughts* in 1851.

26. Hunt, 1:304.

27. Ibid.

28. Peters, 102–3.

29. "The Exhibition of the Royal Academy," *Bentley's Miscellany* 29, no. 174 (June 1851): 623. Hereafter cited as "Exhibition."

30. "Exhibition," 624–25.

31. Wilkie Collins, *Memoirs of the Life of William Collins, Esq., R.A.* (London: Longmans, 1848). William Collins died in February 1847.

32. John Ruskin to *The Times*, 13 May 1851, 8. Hereafter cited as Ruskin, 13 May 1851.

33. Meisel, 375.

34. Hunt, 1:304.

35. Frith was hailed as the modern Hogarth, although his social panoramas of the 1850s have more in common with David Wilkie and English genre (later series such as *The Road to Ruin* are more explicitly Hogarthian). His version of modern life is also indebted to the topical satire and caricature of middle-class life found in the *Punch* illustrations of John Leech during the late 1840s and early 1850s. Under the editorship of Mark Lemon, and with Thackeray's fierce criticism of Royal Academy complacency and the empty-headedness of contemporary British art, *Punch*'s "gentlemanly party" openly championed its own modern-life aesthetic during this crucial formative period. In April 1853, for example, the magazine deplored "an almost entire want of the Ideas commonly necessary" for the "decent maintenance in the practice" of contemporary art

and suggested that painters institute a new category of genre painting ("Art and Ideas," *Punch* 24 [Apr. 1853]: 171).

36. Frith's paintings inspired such images as William Egley's *Omnibus Life in London* (1859) and George Elgar Hicks's *Dividend Day at the Bank of England* (1859).

37. Ruskin, 13 May 1851, 8.

38. See Brown's *The Last of England* (begun 1851), and *Work* (1852–65), as well as Egg's *Past and Present* (1858).

39. [John Tupper], "The Subject in Art, No. II," *The Germ* 3 (Mar. 1850): 121.

40. For Pre-Raphaelite revisions of literary subjects, see Millais's *Isabella* (1848–49) and Hunt's *Valentine Rescuing Sylvia* (1851); of religious genre, see Rossetti's *Girlhood of Mary Virgin* (1848–49) and Millais's *Christ in the House of His Parents* (1849–50); sentimental animal pictures, Hunt's *Our English Coasts* (1852); sentimental child pictures, Millais's *The Woodman's Daughter* (1850–51); and rural genre, Hunt's *The Hireling Shepherd* (1851–52).

41. Lynda Nead, "The Magdalen in Modern Times: The Mythology of the Fallen Woman in Pre-Raphaelite Painting," *Oxford Art Journal* 7, no. 1 (1984): 30. Hereafter cited as Nead, "Magdalen."

42. *Found* remained unfinished, apparently because Hunt completed *The Awakening Conscience* first. It is significant that there was a kind of race to be the first to paint a modern-life subject at this time. (Frith makes no reference whatever to Pre-Raphaelite experiments in the mode in his memoirs, for example, claiming himself as its sole originator; nor do the Pre-Raphaelites refer to him.) See Ruskin's letter to Rossetti, 5 June 1854: "You feel as if it were not worth while now to bring out your modern subjects, as Hunt has done his first" (*The Works of John Ruskin*, 36: 167). Although *The Awakening Conscience* was the first Pre-Raphaelite modern-life subject to be exhibited, Hunt was clearly influenced by Ford Madox Brown's groundbreaking unexhibited modern-life pictures, especially *Work* and *The Last of England*, both begun in 1852.

43. On the fallen woman in mid-Victorian literature and art, see Nina Auerbach, "The Rise of the Fallen Woman," *Nineteenth-Century Fiction* 35 (1980): 29–52; and Lynda Nead, *Myths of Sexuality: Representations of Women in Victorian Britain* (Oxford: Basil Blackwell, 1988), 77 and passim. Hereafter cited as Nead, *Myths of Sexuality.*

44. Nead, *Myths of Sexuality,* 91.

45. Nead, "Magdalen," 36.

46. "Royal Academy," 561.

47. "As he that taketh away a garment in cold weather, so is he that singeth songs to an heavy heart" (Prov. 25:20). Hunt's stated aim in the painting

was "to show how the still small voice speaks to a human soul in the turmoil of life" (Hunt, 1:347).

48. "Royal Academy," 561.

49. John Ruskin to *The Times,* 25 May 1854, 7. Hereafter cited as Ruskin, 25 May 1854. *The Art-Journal,* for example, found: "Without a title, the purport of this work could not be guessed at; with a title the subject may be recognised by courtesy; yet what light soever the title may throw upon the picture, it is entirely extinguished by the scriptural quotations" ("The Royal Academy: The Exhibition, 1854," *The Art-Journal* 16 [1 June 1854]: 165).

50. Ruskin, 25 May 1854, 7.

51. On prostitution as "the great social evil," and the efforts to contain it imaginatively in the figure of the guilt-ridden, passive fallen woman, see Nead, "Magdalen," 31–37.

52. Nead, "Magdalen," 36.

53. Note, for example, Sherwin's black eyes that are "incessantly in motion," his "sallow" complexion, and the "cringing bow" he gives Basil (*Basil,* 1:201–2).

54. See Richard Altick, *The English Common Reader: A Social History of the Mass Reading Public, 1800–1900* (Chicago: Univ. of Chicago Press, 1963), 286–93.

55. Page, 48.

56. Collins was a contributor to the radical *Leader* under the editorship of his friend Edward Pigott. Letters to Pigott reveal that Collins was uneasy with many aspects of the *Leader*'s radicalism, however, particularly the tendency of some of its political commentators to mix up "the name of Jesus Christ with the current politics of the day" (Collins to Edward Pigott, London, 20 Feb. 1852, *Letters,* 84). Collins was happy to contribute to other departments of the *Leader,* but not to be associated with "heterodoxical opinions." "I don't," he asserts, "desire to be 'one of you'" (Collins to Edward Pigott, London, 16 Feb. 1852, *Letters,* 82).

57. In two separate letters Collins marvels at the sums his fellow authors were making—the "four thousand guineas" that Dickens earned from the Christmas book, *The Battle of Life* (Collins soon tried his own hand at the format, publishing *Mr Wray's Cash-Box* for Christmas 1851), and the "£20,000!" Macaulay earned from sales of two volumes of his *History of England* (Collins to R. H. Dana, London, 12 Jan. 1849 and 17 June 1850, *Letters,* 54, 62). Money was also part of the attraction of Paris for Collins: "The start [*sic*] of a new man in Literature or Art is a matter of intense moment to every individual in this city. . . . Money is to [be] obtained, too, as well as admiration. The average amount yearly of the remuneration to the Dramatists . . . is from £70,000 to £80,000!" (Collins to Mrs. Harriet Collins, Paris, 16 Sept. 1845, *Letters,* 30).

58. Lonoff, 89.

59. See Sir Joshua Reynolds, *Discourses on Art,* ed. Robert R. Wark (New Haven: Yale Univ. Press, 1975), and Charles Lock Eastlake, *Contributions to the Literature of the Fine Arts* (London: John Murray, 1848).

60. Hunt, 1:304.

61. Ruskin, 13 May 1851, 8.

62. "A Trio of Novels," *Dublin University Magazine* 41 (Jan. 1853): 77–79. Hereafter cited as "Trio."

63. According to the anonymous reviewer, "unless the writer keep this object [to elevate and purify] constantly before him, he can never hope to win a lasting popularity" ("Trio," 77).

64. Page, 48.

65. Page, 48. These objections look forward to the standard criticism of Collins's sensation fiction, that it was, in the words of Ann Cvetkovich, like other sensation fiction, "aesthetically inferior, and by implication morally questionable" (*Mixed Feelings: Feminism, Mass Culture, and Victorian Sensationalism* [New Brunswick: Rutgers Univ. Press, 1992], 17).

66. Frank Stone, qtd. in J. B. Bullen, *The Pre-Raphaelite Body: Fear and Desire in Painting, Poetry, and Criticism* (Oxford: Clarendon Press, 1998), 17.

67. *Westminster Review,* 373. The review calls the central incident "absolutely disgusting" and labels the details of the story, "kept so perseveringly before the eyes of the reader," as "hateful" and "revolting."

68. *Westminster Review,* 373.

69. Qtd. in Barringer, 89. Hogarth introduced the technique of investing everything in the picture, down to the most trivial details, with meaning as a way of incorporating what E. D. H. Johnson calls "the artist's own ironic commentary on the scene" (*Paintings of the British Social Scene from Hogarth to Sickert* [London: Weidenfeld and Nicolson, 1986], 35).

70. Nead, "Magdalen," 36.

71. John Ruskin, "Lectures on Art," in *The Works of John Ruskin,* 20:39.

72. John Ruskin, "Pre-Raphaelitism," in *The Works of John Ruskin,* 12:342.

73. Ibid., 343.

74. There are elements of this in the dream scenes of Keats's "The Eve of St Agnes" and "La Belle Dame Sans Merci," both favorites with the Pre-Raphaelites.

75. While writing *Dombey and Son,* Dickens worked closely with Angela Burdett Coutts in the establishment of Urania Cottage, a home for fallen women.

76. See Tamar Heller, *Dead Secrets: Wilkie Collins and the Female Gothic* (New Haven: Yale Univ. Press, 1992), 74–81. Heller argues that Collins's adaptation of the female Gothic in *Basil,* and especially his use of Mary

Shelley's *Frankenstein,* reflect his deep personal anxiety as an aspiring professional in its concern with "the male artist's attempts to differentiate himself from women writers" (Heller, 88).

77. There are many other echoes of De Quincey's *Confessions* in *Basil,* most notably the episode of Basil's delirium, with its "world whose daylight was all radiant flame," its "City of Palaces," and its vision of Margaret and Mannion as "two monsters stretching forth their gnarled yellow talons to grasp at us"(*Basil,* 2:176, 178). Collins, himself an opium addict, draws most extensively on De Quincey in *The Moonstone* (1868).

78. Collins and Dickens met on 12 Mar. 1851. *Basil* was begun early in 1852 but interrupted by tours of the provinces with Dickens's amateur theatrical troupe (performing Bulwer-Lytton's *Not So Bad As We Seem*) throughout the year. It was finished on 15 Sept. 1852 while Collins was staying with Dickens (himself finishing *Bleak House*).

79. The Carker-Edith plot is also echoed in the composition of *The Awakening Conscience,* which uncannily recalls one of Hablot Browne's *Dombey* drawings, "Mr. Carker in his Hour of Triumph." *David Copperfield* was also explicitly acknowledged by Hunt as a key source for *The Awakening Conscience.*

80. William Collins's painting *Rustic Civility* (1837) depicts a peasant boy tugging his forelock to the passing squire.

81. Ruskin, 25 May 1854, 7. In an article on "The Drama" published in *Blackwood's* in 1856, E. S. Dallas lamented the growing similarities between pictorial art and the theater. After characterizing the new drama as Pre-Raphaelite and realist, he catalogs the "very faults we find in the theatre" that have become assimilated into the pictorial arts: "Eternal mannerism, staginess, mimicry, trickery, grimacing, catchwords, red lights and blue lights" ("The Drama," *Blackwood's* 79 [Feb. 1856]: 220).

82. Francis Turner Palgrave, *Essays on Art* (London: George Routledge, 1865), 196–97.

83. Peters, 118.

84. G. H. Lewes, "Farewell Causerie," *Fortnightly Review* 6 (1 Dec. 1866): 894.

85. Cvetkovich, 23.

References

Altick, Richard. *The English Common Reader: A Social History of the Mass Reading Public, 1800–1900.* Chicago: Chicago Univ. Press, 1963.

Armstrong, Nancy. *Desire and Domestic Fiction: A Political History of the Novel.* New York: Oxford Univ. Press, 1987.

Arscott, Caroline H. "Modern Life Subjects in British Painting." Ph.D. diss., Univ. of Leeds, 1987.

"Art and Ideas." *Punch* 24 (Apr. 1853): 171–72.

Auerbach, Nina. "The Rise of the Fallen Woman." *Nineteenth-Century Fiction* 35 (1980): 29–52.

Barringer, Tim. *The Pre-Raphaelites: Reading the Image*. London: Wiedenfeld and Nicholson, 1998.

Bronkhurst, Judith. "William Holman Hunt." In *The Pre-Raphaelites*, ed. Leslie Parris, 120–21. London: Tate Gallery, 1984.

Bullen, J. B. *The Pre-Raphaelite Body: Fear and Desire in Painting, Poetry, and Criticism*. Oxford: Clarendon Press, 1998.

Collins, Wilkie. *Basil: A Story of Modern Life*. 3 vols. London: Richard Bentley, 1852.

———. "The Exhibition of the Royal Academy." *Bentley's Miscellany* 29, no. 174 (June 1851): 617–27.

———. *Hide and Seek*. Ed. Catherine Peters. Oxford: Oxford Univ. Press, 1993.

———. *The Letters of Wilkie Collins*. Ed. William Baker and William C. Clarke. 2 vols. New York: St. Martin's Press, 1999.

———. *Memoirs of the Life of William Collins, Esq., R.A.* London: Longmans, 1848.

———. "A Pictorial Tour of St. George Bosherville." *Bentley's Miscellany* 29, no. 173 (May 1851): 493–508.

Cvetkovich, Ann. *Mixed Feelings: Feminism, Mass Culture, and Victorian Sensationalism*. New Brunswick: Rutgers Univ. Press, 1992.

Dallas, E. S. "The Drama." *Blackwood's* 79 (Feb. 1856): 209–31.

Eastlake, Charles Lock. *Contributions to the Literature of the Fine Arts*. London: John Murray, 1848.

Frith, W. P. *My Autobiography and Reminiscences*. 2 vols. London: Richard Bentley, 1887–88.

Grieve, Alastair Ian. *The Art of Dante Gabriel Rossetti*. Norwich: Real World Publications, 1976.

———. "Social and Religious Themes in English Art." Ph.D. diss., London Univ., 1973.

Hall, Catherine. "The Sweet Delights of Home." In *From the Fires of Revolution to the Great War*, ed. Michelle Perrot, 47–93. Vol. 4 of *A History of Private Life*, ed. Philippe Ariès and Georges Duby. Cambridge and London: Belknap Press, 1990.

Harrison, Charles, Paul Wood, and Jason Gaiger. "*The Times* Critic and John Ruskin (1819–1900) Exchange on the Pre-Raphaelites." In *Art in Theory*,

1815–1900: An Anthology of Changing Ideas, ed. Charles Harrison, Paul Wood, and Jason Geiger, 440–49. Oxford: Blackwell, 1998.

Heller, Tamar. *Dead Secrets: Wilkie Collins and the Female Gothic.* New Haven: Yale Univ. Press, 1982.

Hunt, William Holman. *Pre-Raphaelitism and the Pre-Raphaelite Brotherhood.* 2 vols. London: Macmillan, 1905.

Johnson, E. D. H. *Paintings of the British Social Scene from Hogarth to Sickert.* London: Weidenfeld and Nicolson, 1986.

Lewes, G. H. "Farewell Causerie." *Fortnightly Review* 6 (1 Dec. 1866): 890–96.

Lonoff, Sue. *Wilkie Collins and His Victorian Readers: A Study in the Rhetoric of Authorship.* New York: AMS Press, 1982.

Meisel, Martin. *Realizations: Narrative, Pictorial, and Theatrical Arts in Nineteenth-Century England.* Princeton: Princeton Univ. Press, 1983.

Nead, Lynda. "The Magdalen in Modern Times: The Mythology of the Fallen Woman in Pre-Raphaelite Painting." *Oxford Art Journal* 7, no. 1 (1984): 26–37.

———. *Myths of Sexuality: Representations of Women in Victorian Britain.* Oxford: Basil Blackwell, 1988.

Page, Norman, ed. *Wilkie Collins: The Critical Heritage.* London and Boston: Routledge and Kegan Paul, 1974.

Palgrave, Francis Turner. *Essays on Art.* London: George Routledge, 1865.

Peters, Catherine. *The King of Inventors: A Life of Wilkie Collins.* Princeton: Princeton Univ. Press, 1991.

Pointon, Marcia, ed. *Pre-Raphaelites Re-Viewed.* Manchester: Manchester Univ. Press, 1989.

Poovey, Mary. *Uneven Developments: The Ideological Work of Gender in Mid-Victorian England.* Chicago: Univ. of Chicago Press, 1988.

"The Progress of Fiction as an Art." *Westminster Review* 60 (Oct. 1853): 372–73.

Reynolds, Sir Joshua. *Discourses on Art.* Ed. Robert R. Wark. New Haven: Yale Univ. Press, 1975.

"Royal Academy." *The Athenaeum,* no. 1384 (6 May 1854): 559–63.

"The Royal Academy: The Exhibition, 1854." *The Art-Journal* 16 (1 June 1854): 157–72.

Ruskin, John. Letter to *The Times,* 13 May 1851, 8.

———. Letter to *The Times,* 25 May 1854, 7.

———. *The Works of John Ruskin, Library Edition.* Ed. E. T. Cook and Alexander Wedderburn. London: George Allen, 1903–12.

Stevens, Frederic George. *William Holman Hunt and His Works: A Memoir of the Artist's Life, with Description of His Pictures.* London: James Nisbet, 1860.

Storey, Graham, Kathleen Tillotson, and Nina Burgis, eds. *The Letters of Charles Dickens.* Vol. 6. Oxford: Clarendon Press, 1988.

"A Trio of Novels." *Dublin University Magazine* 41 (Jan. 1853): 77–79.

[Tupper, John.] "The Subject in Art, No. II." *The Germ* 3 (Mar. 1850): 118–25.

Warner, Malcolm. *The Victorians: British Painting, 1837–1901.* Washington, D.C.: National Gallery of Art, 1996.

Framed and Hung
Collins and the Economic Beauty of the Manly Artist

—=◆=—

Dennis Denisoff

ESPITE ITS BREVITY, WILKIE COLLINS'S STORY "A TERRIBLY STRANGE BED" (1852) SUCCESSFULLY ENCAPSULATES THE COMPLEX issues entangled in Victorian efforts to envision the middle-class artist as a manly authority. The narrator of the piece, a portraitist, asks his subject to tell a tale during his sitting. The latter complies by recollecting a time when, as a guest at an inn, he had been mesmerized by the painting of a sinister character "looking intently upward—it might be at some tall gallows at which he was going to be hanged."[1] The joke, of course, is that the character, as the subject of a portrait, will himself be hanged. The more sinister joke is that, like a portrait, the guest's bed at the inn is constructed to contain and control its subjects. The innkeeper, we discover, has converted the piece of furniture into a press that he then uses to suffocate his patrons so that he can rob them. The guest obviously avoided such a fate, having not only lived to tell about his experience, but also remained wealthy enough to have his portrait painted. Or perhaps it would be more accurate to say that he has deferred such a fate, since he escaped only to find himself entrapped by someone even more elusive and controlling—the portraitist to whom Collins gives final authority. "A Terribly Strange Bed" is narrated not by the subject, but by the man painting his likeness. The male commercial artist—and not the wealthy guest, the innkeeper, or for that matter the old soldier or the inn's conspiratorial mistress—is the one who takes control by objectifying the others on canvas and in words.

A number of Victorian writers such as Mary Elizabeth Braddon, Vernon Lee, and Oscar Wilde have written texts that challenge the authority of the status quo by imbuing painting with a sexual dissidence that warns against generic and institutional entrapment.[2] Meanwhile, Collins, in "A Terribly Strange Bed" as well as a number of his novels, comes across as more sympathetic than these other writers to the conservative image of the artist earnestly pursuing a mentally laborious regimen. To further support the persona, he also disputes the cultural and economic productivity of the aristocratic patron while he depicts the man whose physicality is most boldly scripted on the body as exposing an emasculating lack of self-control. And yet, Collins's particular use of sensational literature, in the relegation of traditional signifiers of authority such as wealth and physicality to the margins, ultimately reveals not only his awareness of the actual volatility of the mid-Victorian manly identity, but also the importance of uncommon genders and sexualities to his own career and Victorian culture in general.

Joseph A. Kestner suggests that the gender volatility of the time arises in part through hegemonic efforts to erase or deny the constructed quality of masculinity, which he argues is not a given but includes "the codes of male behaviour in culture, *including* those that construct male dominance in the process of constructing male subjectivity."[3] As Michael Roper and John Tosh emphasize, "men's behaviour—and ultimately their social power—cannot be fathomed merely in terms of externally derived social roles, but requires that we explore how cultural representations become part of subjective identity."[4] Kestner and Paula Gillett have offered excellent historical contextualizations of masculinity in relation to visual art and the artist respectively.[5] Focusing on the male painter in Collins's writing, I will consider the career-based issues behind the sexualized and gendered fashioning of artistic personae during the Victorian era. In the process, I intend to demonstrate the role of verbal and visual rhetoric in efforts to establish a symbiosis between aesthetics and masculinity that would give pro-fessionalized, middle-class men privileged maneuverability within the changing career landscape.

Patronage, Self-Employment, and Masculine Artistry

The shift in British attitudes toward aesthetics and art during the first half of the nineteenth century reflected the rising power of the middle class, which was purchasing artworks in increasing numbers.[6] According to Ruskin, prior to the Victorian era, the fine arts "having been sup-ported by the selfish power of the noblesse, and never having extended their range to the comfort or the relief of the mass of the people[,] . . . have only accelerated the ruin of the States they adorned."[7] Collins, in his novel *A Rogue's Life* (1856), similarly offers an extended derogation of the aristocrats who, rather than thinking for themselves, simply ignored modern artists and blindly venerated the old masters: "It was as much a part of their education to put their faith in these on hearsay evidence, as to put their faith in King, Lords and Commons."[8] The nar-rator happily points out, however, that the situation has finally begun to change:

> Traders and makers of all kinds of commodities
> have effected a revolution in the picture-world. . . .
> The daring innovators started with the new notion of
> buying a picture which they themselves could admire
> and appreciate. . . . From that time good modern pictures
> have risen in the scale. Even as articles of commerce and
> safe investments for money, they have now . . . distanced
> the old pictures in the race. (*A Rogue's Life,* 46–47)

Robert Vaughan noted in *The Age of the Great Cities* (1843) that "successful patronage of the fine arts depends less on the existence of noble families, than upon the existence of prosperous cities."[9] Artistic quality, he proposes, is in fact the result of democracy and an admi-ration for the prosperity of the social state. But as Gillett has demon-strated, although increased middle-class patronage resulted in higher prices, it did not give artists greater freedom so much as it demanded the production of new genres. With minimal church or state patron-age, English painters had to satisfy the bourgeois taste for relatively small pieces evoking domestic life and local scenery.[10]

Collins supported the artist's freedom from aristocratic patrons and, in his own work, is unkind to characters who pride themselves on exclusive aesthetic values. In Collins's *Hide and Seek* (1854), for example, the patriarch Mr. Thorpe sees himself as superior to everybody around him, but not to his portraits of "distinguished" and "very sturdily-constructed" preachers "with bristly hair, fronting the spectator interrogatively and holding thick books in their hands."[11] Thorpe even calls on these visages to participate in his condescension toward other characters in the novel. Indeed, in accord with his rigid lack of emotion, the man signals his own authority by modeling himself on the artworks. It was a familiar view that the purpose of a male's portrait was to celebrate his manly qualities. As Richard Brilliant observes, "the formality and evident seriousness displayed by so many portraits as a significant mode of self-fashioning would seem to be not so much typical of the subjects as individuals as designed to conform to the expectations of society whenever its respectable members appear in public. In this sense, to be portrayed by an artist is to appear in public."[12] In the character of Thorpe, we see the implications of this equation for social interaction; the man chooses to signify his own virtues by constructing his identity in line with the aesthetic conventions of an artistic genre.

Even though Collins's works show less interest in the aesthetics of art than that of personae, he acknowledges early in this novel that, for many Victorians, the two were inseparable. The narrator of *Hide and Seek* articulates a system of aesthetic valuation that ultimately subordinates the quality of the artwork to those of its creator and audience. The visitors to a private exhibition are portrayed as follows:

> Thus, the aristocracy of race was usually impersonated, in his studio, by his one noble patron, the Dowager Countess of Brambledown; the aristocracy of art by two or three Royal Academicians; and the aristocracy of money by eight or ten highly respectable families, who came quite as much to look at the Dowager Countess as to look at the pictures. With these last, the select portion of the company might be said to terminate; and, after them, flowed in promiscuously the obscure majority of the visitors—a heterogeneous congregation of worshippers at the shrine of art, who were some of them of small importance, some of doubtful importance, some of no importance at all. (*Hide and Seek*, 229)

Dennis Denisoff

37

The narrator describes here a form of social segregation inherent, he suggests, to artistic appreciation. Despite Collins's acknowledgment elsewhere that an artist inevitably has monetary concerns, the narrator's delineation of the three aristocracies of race, art, and money emphasizes the view that refined aesthetic appreciation is itself essentially anathema to financial rank. Collins's narrator brushes aside the "obscure majority" with one hand, while the other takes a jab at patronage by having the aristocrats of money be more attracted to the countess than the paintings. Even the members of the Royal Academy are treated rather cursorily, reflecting Collins's sympathy for the growing number of young artists (such as his brother Charles and the Pre-Raphaelite painters with whom he was associated) struggling to establish careers. As Simon Cooke has noted, Collins felt the Pre-Raphaelites should see themselves as "a generation of painters who were casting off their status as craftsmen for a moribund aristocracy and painting their pictures for the up and coming business class."[13] The author was sensitive to their career difficulties and even helped them negotiate commissions not only because he was friends with members of the Pre-Raphaelite Brotherhood such as William Holman Hunt and John Everett Millais, but also because he would have recognized similarities between their chosen profession and his own.

The increased popularity of the visual arts was met by a concomitant increase in the number of men hoping to become professional painters. This also led to the strong possibility that many of them would have to settle for being teachers or for changing careers entirely. The very real economic difficulties experienced by this growing number of men also enhanced the importance of laborious commitment among the criteria by which the artist's social worth was evaluated. In his study *Self-Help* (1859), Samuel Smiles concludes that the major contribution of artists to the morale and character of their society was as exemplars of hard-working, unwavering laborers.[14] And one recalls Ruskin's attack upon Whistler for failing to spend enough time in creating his art, regardless of its intrinsic merits.[15] The image of the artist as an individualist devoted to beauty was being challenged by a persona that painters with overtly commercial concerns hoped to establish as inherently masculine and thus socially superior.[16]

Michel Foucault argues that the Victorian bourgeoisie set up a "technology of power and knowledge" in which sexuality was deployed as a form of self-affirmation, "a defense, a protection, a strengthening, and an exaltation that were eventually extended to others—at the cost of different transformations—as a means of social control and political subjugation."[17] In the realm of the arts, the deployment of sexuality as a standardizing system of categorization resulted in part from a conflict between economic concerns and the view that moral and sentimental qualities were signs of artistic genius. In *Modern Painters,* Ruskin articulates the common Victorian perception that "[p]erfect taste is the faculty of receiving the greatest possible pleasure from those material sources which are attractive to our moral nature in its purity and perfection. He who receives little pleasure from these sources wants taste; he who receives pleasure from any other sources, has false or bad taste."[18] In Dickens's famous article "Old Lamps for New Ones"—which Nuel Pharr Davis describes as "one of the most insulting and blatantly vulgar art criticisms ever printed"[19]—the novelist voices a similar concern that contemporary artists threatened to subordinate the fundamental rule that painting "shall be informed with mind and sentiment" to "a narrow question of trade-juggling with a palette, palette-knife, and paint-box."[20] Dickens argues that the sacrifice of wisdom and sensitivity to economics manifests itself in the works of the perverted and unhealthy Pre-Raphaelites, who depict "the lowest depths of what is mean, odious, repulsive, and revolting."[21] The language attains a sexualized tinge in a critique of a painting by one of Collins's friends, John Everett Millais. In *Christ in the House of His Parents,* Dickens finds Mary so hideous as she kneels between "Two almost naked carpenters" that he feels she would be seen as a "Monster" even in "the vilest cabaret in France."[22] This language is part of a broader cultural process through which certain aesthetic, ethical, and economic views eventually warped into sexualized deformities. Any difficulties that Collins would have had with "Old Lamps for New Ones" would have been exacerbated by the fact that he respected both Dickens and the Pre-Raphaelites.

Dickens's rhetoric accords with the tendency among critics to define what they saw to be good art as masculine and what they saw to be bad art as feminine. In the anonymous piece "Royal Academy: Portraiture" (1849), certain portraitists are congratulated for their "manly character" and "good, honest, sterling style, without affectation."[23] Meanwhile, another artist is criticized because "his taste was not of high caste" and his works "want masculine character in the men, purity in the women, and artlessness in infant life." The painter's demasculinization of male subjects is part and parcel of what this reviewer dubs "the degeneracy of portraiture" that has "spread the evil till it became the epidemic which the walls of our Exhibition rooms now show."[24] For the reviewer, portraiture, throughout its history, has been associated "with the highest names and with the loftiest aim"; it has "hand[ed] down to us the very presence, as it were, of the men who are yet morally with us by their influence on the condition of things amid which we live."[25] These comments reveal an interesting political agenda. Portraits are not being valued here by aesthetic principles, but by their ability to sustain, through a sort of artistic cryogenics, the values of past influential men. The genre is basically admired for how well it has maintained the sociopolitical hierarchy which ensures that it will continue to be valued in the same way. This leaves little room for inspiration, innovation, experimentation, or the participation of women or other people whose success in the field might challenge the hegemonic norms.

The biologized terminology of degeneracy in this review also correlates historically with the mainstreaming of a negative homosexual taxonomy in Britain. Although scientific and legal vocabularies for discussing same-sex male desire were being articulated, a comparably overt aesthetic language was yet to surface. Aestheticism would not acquire a fully formulated example of its homoerotically coded discourse until Walter Pater's *The Renaissance* (1873), and even here the references are necessarily obscure.[26] Likewise, the rhetorical tendency to value most highly that art which signified masculine vitality basically discredited women's participation in the genre because the existence of artistic talent within women would signify deviancy. Even Marion Halcombe, presented as the smartest woman in *The Woman in White* (1860), confidently voices the opinion that "[w]omen can't draw—their minds are too flighty, and their eyes are too inattentive."[27] Similarly, the creative mediocrity of Valentine Blyth, in *Hide and Seek,* is signaled by his inability to paint accurate likenesses of adults, although he is "invariably victorious in the infant department," a genre seen to be one in which women excel (*Hide and Seek,* 54). The review "Royal Academy: Portraiture" reflects the gendered essentialism underlying the disrespect for certain genres when the critic concludes that the best painter of both women and children, but not men, is a female artist—Margaret Geddes Carpenter.

Carpenter happens to have been Wilkie Collins's aunt. In fact, many of Collins's relatives made names for themselves as artists, and his own concerns regarding the demasculinization of the artist is rooted in part in this family history. The novelist was related to the Scottish painter Andrew Geddes through his mother, Harriet Geddes. Two of her sisters became portraitists and one of these, Carpenter, exhibited work at the Royal Academy and made an income from her art.[28] Collins's mother also could have supported herself as a painter, but her husband was against this. The author's paternal grandfather wrote *Memoirs of a Picture* (1805), a biography of the painter George Morland. He also made his living as a picture dealer and cleaner, the latter job involving trips to the gentry to clean private collections. His insecure and often meager income led Wilkie Collins's own father to approach his career as a painter professionally, both by wooing wealthy patrons and by aiming to create broadly popular works. Lillian Nayder points out that William Collins adopted an aesthetic that whitewashed the political instability of his time. His landscapes reinforce an image of national order and coherence, while his paintings of rural life assuage their own dissident potential by implying that lower-class country life is saturated with bucolic bliss.[29] Collins himself notes, in his *Memoirs of the Life of William Collins* (1848), that among his father's paintings of rural life, "No representations of the fierce miseries, or the coarse contentions which form the darker tragedy of humble life, occur. . . . When his pencil was not occupied with light-hearted little cottagers, swinging on an old gate—as in 'Happy as a King'—or shyly hospitable to the wayfarer at the house door—as in 'Rustic Hospitality'—it reverted only to scenes of quiet pathos."[30]

William Collins was a success. He became a member of the Royal Academy and his work was commissioned and purchased by various highly positioned men, including the Prince Regent (later George IV) and Sir Robert Peel.[31] But Diane Macleod notes that—in accord with a general shift in the demographics of British art collectors—William Collins's patrons changed during his career from being primarily titled individuals to being untitled, middle-class buyers.[32] Macleod concludes that William Collins was less motivated to accommodate his patrons than his artistic themes might suggest. However, middle-class patrons were in general becoming the main buyers of art, and their tastes did tend toward the paintings of domestic and local scenery in which he specialized.

Wilkie Collins's own career as a painter led to his exhibition of a landscape painting at the Royal Academy in 1849. But his novel *A Rogue's Life* makes it clear that he was put out by the traditional market system that reduced the artist to an "accomplished parasite" who fawns upon his aristocratic patrons for money (*A Rogue's Life,* 27). According to the narrator of the novel, in the business of portraiture, "Everything is of no consequence, except catching a likeness and flattering your sitter" (22). Echoing these views, Collins's memoirs of his father, as Tamar Heller effectively argues, enact a "desire to construct a masculine artistic identity empowered by the father's example."[33] Codell has also shown that the *Memoirs* mark a transition in Victorian artist biographies toward valuing professionalism and financial stability. Thus, for example, they include records of the pieces that William Collins painted each year, including the location of their exhibition, the people who eventually bought them, and the prices they paid.

With regard to his own career as a writer, Collins claimed that he was free from "the fetters of patronage" because of the growing mass market for both novels and the periodicals in which they were often first serialized (*Memoirs*, 1:6). But while he may not have been dependent on a few wealthy individuals, the success of his career was still dictated by the tastes of the reading public, which he was aware tended to favor sensational scenarios, gothic settings, and characters who were not especially self-restraining and who did not occupy their time with tedious, unacknowledged labor. Involved in various painters' lives, familiar with the sexualized rhetoric around the struggle for control of the standard definition of masculinity, and himself an artist sensitive to his audience's less-than-gentlemanly expectations, Collins was fully enmeshed in the mid-Victorian art world's contest among various personae for the title of the manly.

Idealizing Artists

Victorian men who identified with intellectual careers not characterized by physical labor found themselves struggling to establish a manly identity that would appear staunch and familiar. In his discussion of nineteenth-century French artists, Pierre Bourdieu refers to "a new social personality, that of the great professional artist who combines, in a union as fragile as it is improbable, a sense of transgression and freedom from conformity with the rigor of an extremely strict discipline of living and of work, which presupposes bourgeois ease and celibacy."[34] James Eli Adams, in his study of the Victorian construction of masculinity, also argues that "increasingly, middle-class professionals (including male writers) legitimated their masculinity by identifying it with that of the gentleman," who was rendered "compatible with a masculinity understood as a strenuous psychic regimen, which could be affirmed outside the economic arena, but nonetheless would be embodied as a charismatic self-mastery akin to that of the daring yet disciplined entrepreneur."[35] A man was to appear an intellectually rigorous artist whose gentlemanly qualities fit the positive contemporary image of the capitalist professional.

The term *intellectual*, when applied to the realm of art, was used to distinguish it from the "decorative" arts, the former being seen as having no conventional utilitarian purpose beyond stimulating the mind and moral sentiment. This distinction favored the intellectual and was met with skepticism by William Morris, one of the period's strongest supporters of the decorative arts. Morris argues that there are in fact two types of artists who find security under the umbrella of intellect,

> the first composed of men who would in any age of the
> world have held a high place in their craft; the second
> of men who hold their position of gentleman-artist either
> by the accident of their birth, or by their possessing indus-
> try, business habits, or such-like qualities, out of all pro-
> portion to their artistic gifts. The work which these latter
> produce seems to me of little value to the world, though
> there is a thriving market for it, and their position is
> neither dignified nor wholesome. . . . They are, in fact,
> good decorative workmen spoiled by a system which
> compels them to ambitious individualist effort.[36]

Such doubts about the performance of the intellectual, bourgeois artist exacerbated concerns regarding the artistic community as a site of manly perfection. As a move toward alleviating such uncertainty, Collins's novels turn to rhetoric that pumps up the gentlemanly artist's masculinity.

Walter Hartright, the hero of *The Woman in White,* offers the standard image of the admirable, struggling artist. On first sight, the twenty-eight-year-old teacher of drawing strikes one as "a modest and gentlemanlike young man" (*The Woman in White,* 129). He himself assures us that his deceased father left his dependants secure, having exerted himself in his own career as a drawing master (6–7). But our hero, despite his efforts, continues to find himself unrewarded: "I am an obscure, unnoticed man," he laments, "without patron or friend to help me" (420–21). Ultimately, his hopes shift from a career in the "high" arts to that of getting a permanent commercial position illus-trating for a newspaper, although he still refuses to give up his earlier career aspirations. His character development is rooted in this perse-verance, a virtue that, after many trials, is rewarded not with fame but with financial security and a heteronormative, bourgeois family just like his father's.

The hero of *Hide and Seek,* Valentine Blyth, is similarly portrayed "as an artist, as a gentleman of refined tastes, and as the softest-hearted of male human beings" (*Hide and Seek,* 64). Despite Valentine's gentlemanly sensitivity, he is also defined by strenuous mental labor. For him, "Art wouldn't be the glorious thing it is, if it wasn't all difficulty from beginning to end; if it didn't force out all the fine points in a man's character as soon as he takes to it" (152). The narrator likewise offers the placating bit of wisdom that "[i]t is not all misfortune and disappointment to the man who is mentally unworthy of a great intellectual vocation, so long as he is morally worthy of it; so long as he can pursue it honestly, patiently, and affectionately, for its own dear sake. Let him work, though ever so obscurely, in this spirit towards his labor, and he shall find the labor itself its own exceeding great reward" (33). Coupled with his wife's encouragement, Valentine's perseverance allows him to avoid the "danger of abandoning High Art and Classical Landscape altogether, for cheap portrait-painting, cheap copying, and cheap studies of Still Life" (39). Nevertheless, the character finds it virtually impossible to fulfill his financial goals without being treated as something less than a gentleman:

> No one but himself ever knew what he had sacrificed
> in labouring to gain these things. The heartless people
> whose portraits he had painted, and whose impertinences
> he had patiently submitted to; the mean bargainers who
> had treated him like a tradesman; the dastardly men of
> business who had disgraced their order by taking advan-
> tage of his simplicity—how hardly and cruelly such insect
> natures of this world had often dealt with that noble
> heart! how despicably they had planted their small
> gad-fly stings in the high soul which it was never
> permitted to them to subdue! (39–40)

Affronted by the possibility of being dealt with as one of those "good decorative workmen" to which Morris refers, Valentine is also repulsed by his patrons. In this scene, the hero's business naïveté becomes a virtue abused by those who lack his qualities. While everybody from patrons to tradesmen transmogrify into insects, Valentine alone is marked by an admirable soul and a natural nobility.

Having established their innate gentlemanly virtues, Collins also makes sure to emphasize the manliness of Walter and Valentine. He does so through far-fetched depictions intended to prove that, despite their careers, they can and do partake in physical labor. Of the two, it is the defense offered by the mediocre painter Valentine that is most remarkable. In a rare state of drunkenness that excuses the hero's egotism, he drops his composure in an overt defense of his masculinity specifically *as* an artist:

> When Michael Angelo's nose was broken do you think
> he minded it? Look in his Life, and see if he did—that's
> all! Ha! ha! My painting-room is forty feet long (now this
> is an important proof). While I was painting Columbus
> and the Golden Age, one was at one end—north; and the
> other at the other—south. Very good. I walked backwards
> and forwards between those two pictures incessantly; and
> never sat down all day long. . . . Just feel my legs, Zack.
> Are they hard and muscular, or are they not? (312–13)

This scene makes evident a central conundrum of the persona of the middle-class, masculine artist. In order to reveal the manliness of a hero who is not permitted to brag about or display his physicality, Collins must somehow sanction the man's loss of verbal and physical reserve. He does so by getting him drunk; indeed, the narrator tries to shift blame away from the hero by wondering whether the person who mixed the drinks had given Valentine more liquor than he knew. The end result is that the hero "was not the genuine Valentine Blyth at all,—he was only a tipsy counterfeit of him" (312). And through his fortuitous inebriation, the painter is given a window of opportunity in which to perform overtly the essential masculinity that is otherwise admirably and appropriately restrained.

Collins adopts a different strategy with *The Woman in White*. In this novel, class difference keeps the lowly painter Walter from marrying the woman he loves. Dejected, he decides to go off on an adventure to Central America: "They were last seen entering a wild primeval forest, each man with his rifle on his shoulder and his baggage at his back. Since that time, civilization has lost all trace of them" (*The Woman in White*, 200). After his brush with "[d]eath by disease, death by the Indians, [and] death by drowning," which makes Walter one of the few survivors of the trip, he returns confident that the experience has resulted in his being a stronger and worthier man: "In the stern school of extremity and danger my will had learnt to be strong, my heart to be resolute, my mind to rely on itself. I had gone out to fly from my own future. I came back to face it, as a man should" (414–15). The primitivist retreat strips the hero of the effeminacies of civilization, and his newfound determination and self-reliance erase his image of himself as patron-dependent.

In a further twist that fashions the identity of the humble, industrious artist as superior to all other models of power, Walter, having eventually married his true love, leaves his wife and child in order to fulfill a sketching assignment for the newspaper that now employs him. Upon returning home, he finds a note telling him to go to Limmeridge, the estate of the feeble Mr. Fairlie. There he finds his family, the male child "industriously sucking his coral" as if masculine rigor had already permeated his identity (642). However, the hero seems to have misrecognized his child. "Do you know who this is, Walter?" asks his sister-in-law. "I think I can still answer for knowing my own child," he replies, which leads to her playfully scolding him: "Do you talk in that familiar manner of one of the landed gentry of England? Are you aware, when I present this illustrious baby to your notice, in whose presence you stand? Evidently not! Let me make two eminent personages known to one another: Mr. Walter Hartright—the Heir of Limmeridge" (643). The novel's final flourish, the end result of Walter's "long, happy labor" (643), is the hero and his self-fashioned identity as the masculine, gentlemanly artist usurping the title, authority, and wealth of the decadent upper classes not in spite of, but owing to, his middle-class values and respect for healthy industry.

Monstrous Masculinities

In the characters of Valentine and Walter, Collins offers a glimpse of masculine perfection by coupling aesthetic reverence with mental vigor and restrained physicality. Despite his aggrandizing rhetoric and his association of his heroes with innate artistic sensibilities, however, the author suggests that the heroes are not, on their own, all that convincing in their manliness. Through a portrayal of deviant individuals, Collins differentiates the bourgeois ideal of masculinity both from men who perform physicality at the expense of any intellectual or aesthetic exercise and from the aristocratic individuals whose power is based in old, inactive money.

In *Hide and Seek*, Valentine's drunken display of machismo ends in his asking Zack Thorpe to feel his muscles. A youth who has yet to establish a career path, Zack is expected to attain masculine maturity by emulating someone older like Valentine. In this scene, however, rather than complying with the painter's request for admiration, Zack turns his attention to the other man drinking with them: "I say, Mat, leave off smoking, and tell us something. . . . Bowl away at once with one of your tremendous stories, or Blyth will be bragging again about his ricketty old legs. Talk, man! Tell us your famous story of how you lost your scalp" (*Hide and Seek*, 314). The immature youth turns for his dosage of pure virility to Matthew Grice—a bar-brawling, uneducated loner who had lost his scalp during adventures in the Americas. The man now roams the East End of London, getting beat up because of his skull cap. In contrast to Valentine, Matthew stands for a physical excess that encourages a violently dissident misanthropy and social instability.

For Collins's depiction of the other end of the spectrum, we can turn to *The Woman in White*, in which the evil Baronet Percival Glyde and Count Fosco are identified primarily by their aristocratic lineage and old money. The female victim of the novel actually defines all men of rank and title as untrustworthy (*The Woman in White*, 24). The fact that she has to ask Walter whether he himself is titled emphasizes the difficulty that the artist was having in performing his gentlemanly image and controlling its system of signification. Collins establishes the aristocratic and wealthy men's degeneracy through sexuality and gender ambiguity. Glyde is marked by delicate features explicitly defined as womanly (79), while Count Fosco is portrayed as effeminately vain through his theatrical actions, facial expression, and extreme attention to sartorial detail. Mr. Fairlie, the wealthy man who decides to employ Walter, is described as having "a frail, languidly-fretful, over-refined look—something singularly and unpleasantly delicate in its association with a man, and, at the same time, something which could by no possibility have looked natural and appropriate if it had been transferred to the personal appearance of a woman" (40). When Mr. Fairlie complains that some pictures that he had purchased "smelt of horrid dealers' and brokers' fingers," Walter comments that his own nerves "were not delicate enough to detect the odour of plebeian fingers which had offended Mr. Fairlie's nostrils" (42). Despite the older man's apparent refinement, which attains an unmanly extreme, he lacks true artistic sensitivity, exposing his coarse tastes when he argues that "[w]e don't want genius in this country, unless it is accompanied by respectability" (14). Fairlie's lack of taste reveals his claim to superiority to be unfounded. Meanwhile, although Walter might agree with the wealthy man's concern for respectability, the gentlemanly artist bases his evaluations on "essential" character traits. Ultimately, *The Woman in White* suggests that old money results in impotent, immoral, effeminate men who do not want to work and could not if they had to. Their elitism, the text implies, undermines economic development that requires that society sustain a healthy, civilized exchange of goods and cultural currency across class- and money-based divisions.

Among Collins's negative portrayals of monetary and physical signifiers of masculinity, his most remarkable and most revealing strategy involves a conflation of the two aspects within a single person. From the author's pageant of diverse masculinities, it is the character envisioned by this fusion who is ultimately the most memorable. I refer here to the sensationally gothic individual, Miserrimus Dexter, from the novel *The Law and the Lady* (1873). Max Nordau, in his notorious study *Degeneration* (1892), includes among the characteristics of the degenerate artist immodesty, egotism, impulsiveness, emotionalism, pessimism, and "moral insanity" or a lack of moral sense.[37] Such a person "rejoices in his faculty of imagination, which he contrasts with the insipidity of the Philistine, and devotes himself with predilection to all sorts of unlicensed pursuits permitted by the unshackled vagabondage of his mind; while he cannot endure well-ordered civil occupations, requiring attention and constant heed to reality."[38] Miserrimus offers a textbook example of Nordau's degenerate artist. Although he is extremely masculine, his energy, it turns out, is not coupled with cool, confident restraint. Speeding around his mansion, throwing tantrums, cruelly taunting his devoted female servant, shouting at all who come near him—Miserrimus's force proves to be uncontrollable. His hypervirility becomes grotesque, especially—the narrator claims—in light of the fact that he has no legs.[39] Collins more than once emphasizes the contrast between this lack and Miserrimus's beauty and impressive stature. In an objectifying blazon more often reserved for mid-Victorian heroines, the narrator observes that, "To make this deformity all the more striking and all the more terrible, the victim of it was—as to his face and his body—an unusually handsome and an unusually well-made man. His long silky hair, of a bright and beautiful chestnut colour, fell over shoulders that were the perfection of strength and grace. His face was bright with vivacity and intelligence."[40] At this point, the narrator's intricate portrait takes a distinct turn: "His large, clear blue eyes, and his long, delicate white hands, were like the eyes and hands of a beautiful woman. He would have looked effeminate, but for the manly proportions of his throat and chest: aided in their effect by his flowing beard and long moustache, of a lighter chestnut shade than the colour of his hair" (*The Law and the Lady,* 173). Although Miserrimus's feminine features are defined as enhancing his attractiveness, this excessive beauty is described in a way that signals its potentially dangerous slip into effeminacy. The man of spectacular physicality, rather than standing as an ideal, signals an eccentricity and lack of the cool control found in the intellectual gentlemen.

Encouraging a visualization based in the portraiture conventions applied to women, while indirectly bringing attention to Miserrimus's difficulties with mobility, the narrator concludes that a painter would have reveled in him as a model (214). This objectifying gesture functions as an aestheticization and symbolic disempowerment of the hyper-virile man by the artist. The same strategy occurs in *Hide and Seek* when Valentine is so impressed by Matthew's muscles that he concludes he must capture the man on canvas. Collins suggests that, as an object of admiration, the physical man solicits objectification. It is this invitation to the gaze that allows Collins to join Miserrimus's admirable physique to the persona of the effete aristocrat.

As if to compensate for his handicap, Miserrimus has become more proud of his physical attributes and has developed a strong inclination toward fine clothing. In a foreshadowing of twentieth-century strategic camp, he dons his wardrobe as a sexualized challenge to anybody wishing to abuse him for his differences.[41] In the scene that pays most attention to his clothing, we find him dressed in a jacket of pink quilted silk, while the "coverlid which hid his deformity matched the jacket in pale sea-green satin; and, to complete these strange vagaries of costume, his wrists were actually adorned with massive bracelets of gold" (232). Noticing the effect his clothing has on the novel's heroine, Valeria Woodville, Miserrimus explains that, "Except in this ignoble and material nineteenth century, men have always worn precious stuffs and beautiful colours as well as women" (232). Valeria, who herself challenges sexual convention as one of the first female detectives in literature, remains unconvinced and shows minimal empathy for her partner in gender-bending. Miserrimus's costume—as Collins describes it—connects the man with the normative Victorian woman. The coverlet, which is intended to hide the absence of limbs, is not just any blanket, but a part of his ensemble, a fashion statement signifying a decadent wealth that sanctions his appreciation of self-aestheticization over functionality. Through this makeshift skirt, his handicap is conflated with the assumedly natural passivity of women, which is partly a sartorially imposed immobility.

It should be noted, however, that Miserrimus recognizes that his dress contradicts contemporary standards of gentlemanly performance. His image, he boldly acknowledges, reflects an old-fashioned aesthetic and an aristocratic disrespect for hard-earned money: "A hundred years ago, a gentleman in pink silk was a gentleman properly dressed.

. . . I despise the brutish contempt for beauty and the mean dread of expense which degrade a gentleman's costume to black cloth" (232). Despite Miserrimus's meticulous defense of his attire as a sign of aristocratic confidence, Collins quickly undermines the claim by having the man bring out his knitting basket and begin work on a strip of embroidery. Miserrimus offers another passing defense about the way in which needlework allows him to compose his mind, but the reader is encouraged, through Valeria, not to buy it. A manly man, we are led to conclude, would remain composed without the need of such assistance.

Situating the matrix of concerns in relation to the visual arts, Miserrimus's association with aristocracy and decadent wealth is reinforced by his own aesthetic. How he is visualized, in other words, is made to accord with how he visualizes the world. During her visit to his ancient, dilapidated mansion, Valeria comments on his art collection. "I could see that there were pictures on the grim brown walls," she notes, "but the subjects represented were invisible in the obscure and shadowy light" (203–4). After letting Valeria into the home, Miserrimus's dumb, androgynous cousin leaves through a side entrance hidden by one of the pictures, "disappear[ing] through it like a ghost" (204). The cousin's spectral shift into the artwork conjoins Miserrimus's family to the paintings, obscuring both in the dark murkiness of a past era. The predominant rhetoric of visual art at the time gave preference to an assumedly masculine realistic style and equally masculine subjects such as renowned patriarchs and historical scenes. Miserrimus's tastes, not surprisingly, are unrealistic and anti-industrial. His art collection includes portraits of people suffering from various forms of madness, plaster casts of famous, dead murderers, and the "Skin of a French Marquis, tanned in the Revolution of Ninety Three" (247–48). The works that he has painted himself focus on states of high emotion. The piece entitled "Revenge" depicts "an infuriated man . . . in fancy costume" and "a horrid expression of delight" standing astride the dead body of a similarly attired man while blood drips "slowly in a procession of big red drops down the broad blade of his weapon" (229). The alliteration of Collins's description prolongs the sadistic ecstasy of the experience. In a series of paintings on Cruelty, Miserrimus's subjects include a man disemboweling a horse with his spurs, a scientist gloating over his dissection of a live cat, and two pagans torturing saints— one by roasting and another by skinning (229–30). Needless to say, Miserrimus's sadistic subjects did not fit the values and tastes preferred by mainstream art critics. To represent man's abuse of animals through sport and science in fact exposed the unseemly elements of the aggressive economic drive on which Victorian society depended.

In spite of her admitted ignorance on the subject, the heroine of *The Law and the Lady* concludes that Miserrimus is an inadequate painter: "Little as I knew critically of Art, I could see that Miserrimus Dexter knew still less of the rules of drawing, colour, and composition. His pictures were, in the strictest meaning of that expressive word, Daubs. The diseased and riotous delight of the painter in representing Horrors, was . . . the one remarkable quality that I could discover in the series of his works" (229). But Valeria also grudgingly acknowledges that, notwithstanding his degeneracy, Miserrimus does demonstrate "signs of a powerful imagination, and even of a poetical feeling for the supernatural" (230). The compliment, however, is backhanded. Early in the century, art theorists such as Arthur Hallam associated the imagination with a necessary and valuable womanly component in the male artist.[42] This model lost ground as the traits of industriousness and perseverance became more central such that, by century's end, Nordau would be able to proclaim confidently that too much imagination was, simply put, a sign of degeneracy.[43]

Miserrimus would be the first to admit to his outdated values. On an inscription near a display of his works in his own home, he informs any passing viewer that "Persons who look for mere Nature in works of Art . . . are persons to whom Mr Dexter does not address himself with the brush. He relies entirely on his imagination. Nature puts him out" (229). "My house," he informs some real estate speculators who want to buy the property, "is a standing monument of the picturesque and beautiful, amid the mean, dishonest, and grovelling constructions of a mean, dishonest, and grovelling age" (203). One might expect his devotion to the aesthetic and manly values of a past generation to be interpreted by the middle class as an admirable sign of determination and commitment in the wake of change; this would not be the case, however, because his values fail to accommodate the demands that industry, expansionism, and capitalism were placing on contemporary artists. In order to establish credibility for the new generation of painters, Miserrimus's resilience is interpreted as an outdated quality that has atrophied into elitism and numb inaction.

Victorian efforts to establish an image of the laborious, gentlemanly artist as a manly ideal were never fully successful, with diverse masculinities continuing to form, intermingle, and change throughout the era. Participating in this complex cultural process, Collins tried to make visual a persona whose manly restraint paradoxically encouraged invisibility. Life-threatening adventures in the Americas, drunken descriptions of athletic painting—the author's attempts to establish the bourgeois, male artist as vital to the economic health of his society resulted in proofs that he himself implies are unconvincing or even comical. The ambivalence in Collins's depictions reflects in part his own conflicted position as a middle-class artist whose main product was sensation fiction. For him, it was not simply a choice to include unconventional characters against which to juxtapose an ideal; rather, he relied on the presence of uncommon individuals for his financial and popular success. Those dissidents defined his genre. They ensured his popularity and paid his wage. Miserrimus's awesome charisma, physicality, and imagination fulfilled a generic requirement. Just as Valeria displays shock on viewing the character's sadomasochistic art even while she lingers over its details, readers of sensation literature may have seen themselves as respectable and moral, but they also expected authors such as Collins to use their dexterous imaginations to offer titillating characters and scenarios. Family and friends made Collins sensitive to the growing number of men hoping to establish their masculinity by succeeding in artistic careers, but, notwithstanding the similarities between their struggles and his own, the author's literary niche demanded that he supply his audience with imaginative articulations of diverse gender- and sex-based identities. Not surprisingly, *The Law and the Lady*'s final incarceration of Miserrimus as insane is unconvincing in its suggestion that such characters can be easily excised from Victorian society. The turn to institutional authority is ultimately too uninspired to contain the chestnut-haired, wheel-chair-ridden, hypercreative, beautiful painter—a collection of significations so unusual, so sensational, and yet so characteristic of the popular tastes and interests of the time.

Notes

1. Wilkie Collins, "A Terribly Strange Bed," in *Mad Monkton and Other Stories*, ed. Norman Page (Oxford: Oxford Univ. Press, 1994), 12.

2. I am thinking specifically of portraits and portraitists as they are depicted in Mary Elizabeth Braddon's *Lady Audley's Secret*, Vernon Lee's "Oke of Okehurst," and Oscar Wilde's *The Picture of Dorian Gray*. I discuss painting in these works and others in "Lady in Green with Novel: The Gendered Economics of the Visual Arts and Mid-Victorian Women's Writing," in *Victorian Women Writers and the Woman Question*, ed. Nicola Diane Thompson (Cambridge: Cambridge

Univ. Press, 1999), 151–69; "The Forest beyond the Frame: Picturing Women's Desires in Vernon Lee and Virginia Woolf," in *Women and British Aestheticism,* ed. Talia Schaffer and Kathy Alexis Psomiades (Charlottesville: Univ. of Virginia Press, 1999), 251–69; and "Posing a Threat: Queensberry, Wilde, and the Portrayal of Decadence," in *Perennial Decay: On the Aesthetics and Politics of Decadence,* ed. Liz Constable, Dennis Denisoff, and Matthew Potolsky (Philadelphia: Univ. of Pennsylvania Press, 1999), 83–100.

3. Joseph A. Kestner, *Masculinities in Victorian Painting* (Aldershot, Hants, England: Scolar Press, 1995), 5.

4. Michael Roper and John Tosh, "Introduction: Historians and the Politics of Masculinity," in *Manful Assertions: Masculinities in Britain since 1800,* ed. Michael Roper and John Tosh (London: Routledge, 1991), 15.

5. See Kestner and also Paula Gillett, *Worlds of Art: Painters in Victorian Society* (New Brunswick: Rutgers Univ. Press, 1990). For discussions of the cultural masculinization of the artist during this time, see also James Eli Adams, *Dandies and Desert Saints: Styles of Victorian Masculinity* (Ithaca: Cornell Univ. Press, 1995), and Herbert Sussman, *Victorian Masculinities: Manhood and Masculine Poetics in Early Victorian Literature and Art* (Cambridge: Cambridge Univ. Press, 1995).

6. On the growing popularity of visual art during the Victorian era, see Gillett; Dianne Sachko Macleod, *Art and the Victorian Middle Class: Money and the Making of Cultural Identity* (Cambridge: Cambridge Univ. Press, 1996), 1–4, 20; and Adrian Vincent, *A Companion to Victorian and Edwardian Artists* (Newton Abbot, Devon: David and Charles, 1991), 7–20.

7. John Ruskin, *Two Paths: Being Lectures on Art and Its Application to Decoration and Manufacture,* in *The Works of John Ruskin, Library Edition,* ed. E. T. Cook and Alexander Wedderburn, vol. 16 (London: George Allen, 1900), 341–42. Hereafter cited as *The Works of John Ruskin.*

8. Wilkie Collins, *A Rogue's Life: From His Birth to His Marriage* (New York: Dover Publications, 1985), 43–44. Hereafter cited in the text as *A Rogue's Life.*

9. Robert Vaughan, *The Age of Great Cities: or Modern Society Viewed in Its Relation to Intelligence, Morals, and Religion* (Shannon: Irish Univ. Press, 1971), 134.

10. Gillett, 3–5.

11. Wilkie Collins, *Hide and Seek,* ed. Catherine Peters (Oxford: Oxford Univ. Press, 1993), 14. Hereafter cited in the text as *Hide and Seek.*

12. Richard Brilliant, *Portraiture* (London: Reaktion Books, 1991), 11.

13. Simon Cooke, "'Mistaken for a PRB': Wilkie Collins and the Pre-Raphaelites," *The Wilkie Collins Society Newsletter,* n.s. 3, no. 1 (winter 2000): 3. For discussions of the author's close association with the

Pre-Raphaelites, also see Sophia Andres, "Pre-Raphaelite Painting and Jungian Images in Wilkie Collins's *The Woman in White*," *Victorian Newsletter* 88 (fall 1995): 26–31; Ira B. Nadel, "Wilkie Collins and His Illustrators," in *Wilkie Collins to the Forefront: Some Reassessments,* ed. Nelson Smith and R. C. Terry (New York: AMS Press, 1995), 149–64; and Nuel Pharr Davis, *The Life of Wilkie Collins* (Urbana: Univ. of Illinois Press, 1956), 54–55, 103–5.

14. Samuel Smiles, *Self-Help: With Illustrations of Character, Conduct and Perseverance* (London: John Murray, 1958), 350.

15. James Abbot McNeill Whistler's own account of Ruskin's attack on his painting *Nocturne in Black and Gold* and the subsequent trial can be found in *The Gentle Art of Making Enemies* (London: W. Heinemann, 1890). Linda Merrill offers an extensive analysis of the event in *A Pot of Paint: Aesthetics on Trial in Whistler v. Ruskin* (Washington, D.C.: Smithsonian Institution Press, 1992).

16. For a discussion of the construction of Victorian artists as hard-working, persevering laborers, see Julie F. Codell, "The Public Image of the Victorian Artist: Family Biographies," *The Journal of Pre-Raphaelite Studies* 5 (fall 1996): 5–34. Macleod also explores the unsubstantiated assumption among many Victorians that their successful artists started at the bottom and worked their way up to cultural and economic respectability.

17. Michel Foucault, *The History of Sexuality,* vol. 1, *An Introduction,* trans. Robert Hurley (New York: Vintage, 1980), 123.

18. *The Works of John Ruskin,* 3:110.

19. Davis, 93.

20. Charles Dickens, "Old Lamps for New Ones," *Household Words* 1 (15 June 1850): 266.

21. Dickens, 265.

22. Ibid., 265–66.

23. "Royal Academy: Portraiture," in *Victorian Painting: Essays and Reviews,* ed. John Charles Olmsted (New York: Garland, 1983), 2:17. Hereafter cited as "Royal Academy."

24. Ibid., 16.

25. Ibid., 15.

26. The representation of male-male affection in the visual arts did not see any considerable increase at this time either. For a survey of homosexuality and art in nineteenth-century western Europe, see Emmanuel Cooper, *The Sexual Perspective: Homosexuality and Art in the Last 100 Years in the West,* 2d ed. (London: Routledge, 1994).

27. Wilkie Collins, *The Woman in White,* ed. John Sutherland (Oxford: Oxford Univ. Press, 1999), 35. Hereafter cited in the text as *The Woman in White.*

28. Lillian Nayder, *Wilkie Collins* (New York: Twayne Publishers, 1997), 6.

29. Ibid., 1–6.

30. Wilkie Collins, *Memoirs of the Life of William Collins, Esq., R.A.* (London: Longman, Brown, Green and Longmans, 1848), 2:311–12. Hereafter cited in the text as *Memoirs*.

31. Nayder, 1–2.

32. Macleod, 33.

33. Tamar Heller, *Dead Secrets: Wilkie Collins and the Female Gothic* (New Haven: Yale Univ. Press, 1992), 41.

34. Pierre Bourdieu, *The Rules of Art: Genesis and Structure of the Literary Field*, trans. Susan Emanuel (Stanford: Stanford Univ. Press, 1996), 111.

35. Adams, 6–7.

36. William Morris, *Art and Society: Lectures and Essays by William Morris*, ed. Gary Zabel (Boston: George's Hill, 1993), 21.

37. Max Simon Nordau, *Degeneration* (New York and London: D. Appleton and Co., 1912), 18–19.

38. Nordau, 21.

39. Recently, increased attention has been paid to nineteenth-century representations of disability in relation to gender. See, for example, Lennard J. Davis, "Constructing Normalcy: The Bell Curve, the Novel, and the Invention of the Disabled Body in the Nineteenth Century," in *The Disability Studies Reader*, ed. Lennard J. Davis (New York: Routledge, 1997), 9–28; Martha Stoddard Holmes, "'Bolder with Her Lover in the Dark': Collins and Disabled Women's Sexuality," in this volume; and Cindy LaCom, "'It Is More than Lame': Female Disability, Sexuality, and the Maternal in the Nineteenth-Century Novel," in *The Body and Physical Difference: Discourses of Disability*, ed. David T. Mitchell and Sharon L. Snyder (Ann Arbor: Univ. of Michigan Press, 1997), 189–201.

40. Wilkie Collins, *The Law and the Lady*, ed. Jenny Bourne Taylor (Oxford: Oxford Univ. Press, 1999), 173. Hereafter cited in the text as *The Law and the Lady*.

41. On strategic camp, see David Bergman, "Strategic Camp: The Art of Gay Rhetoric," in *Camp Grounds: Style and Homosexuality*, ed. David Bergman (Amherst: Univ. of Massachusetts Press, 1993), 92–109. Moe Meyer offers a discussion of strategic camp that, although limiting in its definition of camp as a specifically queer phenomenon, offers a useful articulation of the performative quality of the strategy ("Introduction: Reclaiming the Discourse of Camp," in *The Politics and Poetics of Camp*, ed. Moe Meyer [London: Routledge, 1994], 1–22).

42. In a review of Tennyson's *Poems, Chiefly Lyrical*, Hallam celebrates poetry of sensation as the best type of poetry because it aims to stimulate the reader's imagination, thus avoiding conventional thought processes.

For Hallam, the imaginative faculties are connected to women, who, he claims, are more attuned to emotion and imaginative play. See Arthur Henry Hallam, "On Some of the Characteristics of Modern Poetry, and on the Lyrical Poems of Alfred Tennyson," *Englishman's Magazine* 1 (Aug. 1821): 616–28. On the relation of women poets and the feminization of poetry, see Dorothy Mermin, *Godiva's Ride: Women of Letters in England, 1830–1880* (Bloomington: Indiana Univ. Press, 1993). Susan P. Casteras explores a parallel development regarding the relation of gender to genius in the visual arts, in "Excluding Women: The Cult of the Male Genius in Victorian Painting" (*Rewriting the Victorians,* ed. Linda M. Shires [London: Routledge, 1992], 116–46).

43. Nordau, 22.

References

Adams, James Eli. *Dandies and Desert Saints: Styles of Victorian Masculinity.* Ithaca: Cornell Univ. Press, 1995.

Andres, Sophia. "Pre-Raphaelite Painting and Jungian Images in Wilkie Collins's *The Woman in White.*" *Victorian Newsletter* 88 (fall 1995): 26–31.

Bergman, David, ed. *Camp Grounds: Style and Homosexuality.* Amherst: Univ. of Massachusetts Press, 1993.

Brilliant, Richard. *Portraiture.* London: Reaktion Books, 1991.

Bourdieu, Pierre. *The Rules of Art: Genesis and Structure of the Literary Field.* Trans. Susan Emanuel. Stanford: Stanford Univ. Press, 1996.

Codell, Julie F. "The Public Image of the Victorian Artist: Family Biographies." *The Journal of Pre-Raphaelite Studies* 5 (fall 1996): 5–34.

Collins, Wilkie. *Hide and Seek.* Ed. Catherine Peters. Oxford: Oxford Univ. Press, 1993.

———. *The Law and the Lady.* Ed. Jenny Bourne Taylor. Oxford: Oxford Univ. Press, 1999.

———. *Mad Monkton and Other Stories.* Ed. Norman Page. Oxford: Oxford Univ. Press, 1994.

———. *Memoirs of the Life of William Collins, Esq., R. A.* 2 vols. London: Longman, Brown, Green and Longmans, 1848.

———. *A Rogue's Life: From His Birth to His Marriage.* New York: Dover Publications, 1985.

———. *The Woman in White.* Ed. John Sutherland. Oxford: Oxford Univ. Press, 1999.

Constable, Liz, Dennis Denisoff, and Matthew Potolsky, eds. *Perennial Decay: On the Aesthetics and Politics of Decadence.* Philadelphia: Univ. of Pennsylvania Press, 1999.

Cooke, Simon. "'Mistaken for a PRB': Wilkie Collins and the Pre-Raphaelites." *The Wilkie Collins Society Newsletter,* n.s. 3, no. 1 (winter 2000): 1–6.

Cooper, Emmanuel. *The Sexual Perspective: Homosexuality and Art in the Last 100 Years in the West.* 2d ed. London: Routledge, 1994.

Davis, Lennard J., ed. *The Disability Studies Reader.* New York: Routledge, 1997.

Davis, Nuel Pharr. *The Life of Wilkie Collins.* Urbana: Univ. of Illinois Press, 1956.

Dickens, Charles. "Old Lamps for New Ones." *Household Words* 1 (15 June 1850): 265–67.

Foucault, Michel. *The History of Sexuality.* Vol. 1, *An Introduction.* Trans. Robert Hurley. New York: Vintage, 1980.

Gillett, Paula. *Worlds of Art: Painters in Victorian Society.* New Brunswick: Rutgers Univ. Press, 1990.

Hallam, Arthur Henry. "On Some of the Characteristics of Modern Poetry, and on the Lyrical Poems of Alfred Tennyson." *Englishman's Magazine* 1 (Aug. 1821): 616–28.

Heller, Tamar. *Dead Secrets: Wilkie Collins and the Female Gothic.* New Haven: Yale Univ. Press, 1992.

Holmes, Martha Stoddard. "'Bolder with Her Lover in the Dark': Collins and Disabled Women's Sexuality," in this volume.

Kestner, Joseph A. *Masculinities in Victorian Painting.* Aldershot, Hants, England: Scolar Press, 1995.

Macleod, Dianne Sachko. *Art and the Victorian Middle Class: Money and the Making of Cultural Identity.* Cambridge: Cambridge Univ. Press, 1996.

Mermin, Dorothy. *Godiva's Ride: Women of Letters in England, 1830–1880.* Bloomington: Indiana Univ. Press, 1993.

Merrill, Linda. *A Pot of Paint: Aesthetics on Trial in Whistler v. Ruskin.* Washington, D.C.: Smithsonian Institution Press, 1992.

Meyer, Moe, ed. *The Politics and Poetics of Camp.* London: Routledge, 1994.

Mitchell, David T., and Sharon L. Snyder, eds. *The Body and Physical Difference: Discourses of Disability.* Ann Arbor: Univ. of Michigan Press, 1997.

Morris, William. *Art and Society: Lectures and Essays by William Morris.* Ed. Gary Zabel. Boston: George's Hill, 1993.

Nayder, Lillian. *Wilkie Collins.* New York: Twayne Publishers, 1997.

Nordau, Max Simon. *Degeneration.* New York and London: D. Appleton and Co., 1912.

Olmsted, Charles, ed. *Victorian Painting: Essays and Reviews.* Vol. 2. New York: Garland, 1983.

Roper, Michael, and John Tosh, eds. *Manful Assertions: Masculinities in Britain since 1800*. London: Routledge, 1991.

Ruskin, John. *The Works of John Ruskin, Library Edition*. Ed. E. T. Cook and Alexander Wedderburn. 39 vols. London: George Allen, 1903–12.

Schaffer, Talia, and Kathy Alexis Psomiades, eds. *Women and British Aestheticism*. Charlottesville: Univ. of Virginia Press, 1999.

Shires, Linda M., ed. *Rewriting the Victorians*. London: Routledge, 1992.

Smiles, Samuel. *Self-Help: With Illustrations of Character, Conduct and Perseverance*. London: John Murray, 1958.

Smith, Nelson, and R. C. Terry, eds. *Wilkie Collins to the Forefront: Some Reassessments*. New York: AMS Press, 1995.

Sussman, Herbert. *Victorian Masculinities: Manhood and Masculine Poetics in Early Victorian Literature and Art*. Cambridge: Cambridge Univ. Press, 1995.

Thompson, Nicola Diane, ed. *Victorian Women Writers and the Woman Question*. Cambridge: Cambridge Univ. Press, 1999.

Vaughan, Robert. *The Age of Great Cities: or Modern Society Viewed in Its Relation to Intelligence, Morals, and Religion*. Shannon: Irish Univ. Press, 1971.

Vincent, Adrian. *A Companion to Victorian and Edwardian Artists*. Newton Abbot, Devon: David and Charles, 1991.

Whistler, James Abbot McNeill. *The Gentle Art of Making Enemies*. London: W. Heinemann, 1890.

"Bolder with Her Lover in the Dark"

Collins and Disabled Women's Sexuality

Martha Stoddard Holmes

TWO MEMORABLE AND DIVERGENT REPRESEN-
TATIONS OF DISABLED FEMININITY ENTERED
EUROPEAN POPULAR CULTURE IN THE 1870S.
In the first, Wilkie Collins's novel *Poor Miss Finch*
(1872), the wealthy, feisty Lucilla Finch gets engaged successively to each of a pair of identical
twins, regains and re-loses her vision, narrowly
escapes marrying the wrong man, marries the
right one, has babies, and lives happily ever after.
In the second, Phillipe D'Ennery and Eugene
Cormon's play *Les Deux Orphelines* (1874), the
melancholy and childlike Louise is abducted from
the care of her sighted sister Henriette, taken in by
scoundrels who beat her and make her sing in the
streets for alms, and after great suffering reunited
with her sister and long-lost mother. Henriette
marries, while Louise goes home with her mother,
who will take her to an oculist.

English translations of *Les Deux Orphelines* were performed on both sides of the Atlantic

well into the twentieth century, and Stanislavski co-directed a performance of the play in Moscow in the forties.[1] It generated seven silent films, the most famous of which was D. W. Griffith's *Orphans of the Storm* (1921), which starred the Gish sisters. Most recently, the play (loosely) informed Jean Rollins's horror film *Les Deux Orphelines Vampires* (1995).[2] Collins's novel, in contrast, met with mixed reviews and was out of print for most of the twentieth century. *Poor Miss Finch*'s core narrative of a blind woman falling in love, marrying, and having children—without first being "cured"—remains a rarity in fiction and film.[3]

Les Deux Orphelines and *Poor Miss Finch* were both written by successful purveyors of nineteenth-century popular culture, and directed at potentially overlapping audiences, given the speed with which *Les Deux Orphelines* became *The Two Orphans*. While an exhaustive comparison of the play and the novel would necessitate a lengthy analysis of formal and contextual differences (and is thus beyond the scope of this essay), the extreme divergence in the fates of Louise and Lucilla (and the works that featured them) nonetheless suggests that certain kinds of stories about disabled women have long-term cultural purchase, and others do not. Apart from any difference in the works' aesthetic value, or external factors such as competition or the cost of paper, a key factor in *Les Deux Orphelines*' success and *Poor Miss Finch*'s relative failure may well have been nineteenth- and twentieth-century cultural orientations toward "different" bodies and beliefs about the appropriate place of disabled women in the realms of sexuality, marriage, and reproduction. Specifically, contemporary critics and readers alike overwhelmingly seemed to prefer a blind girl who suffered and was rescued, rather than a blind girl who might marry and reproduce.

The question of what kind of future, in love or work, awaited a young woman with an exceptional body was a topic of interest to many Victorian popular writers. Charles Dickens, Elizabeth Gaskell, Edward Bulwer-Lytton, Hall Caine, Dinah Craik, and Charlotte Yonge all created courtship/coming-of-age plots involving young women with physical disabilities.[4] Like Louise, most of these disabled characters do not marry, and very few become mothers. Instead, disability tends to place a woman character on the margins of the plot, making her an adult consigned to eternal childhood, a celibate version of the "fallen" woman, or some other form of "odd" and superfluous female. Her chief importance in the plot is to generate emotion and moral development in others by being innocent and saintly, surprisingly cheerful, justifiably melancholy, tragically frustrated from achieving her goals as woman, suicidal or dead—*or simply by being disabled,* without any of these other conditions.[5]

Selected narratives do construct physically disabled or atypically embodied women beyond the melodramatic identity of emotional catalyst, figuring them as characters who, having accepted the concept of their unfitness for marriage, find happiness in meaningful nondomestic work, the pleasure often denied to women characters with normative bodies. And a select few of these characters, having made a place for themselves apart from mainstream culture, are later heaped with the mainstream rewards of marriage, financial stability, and even motherhood. Significantly, however, the physically disabled women who achieve all these things are marked by emotional control and discretion, "passionlessness" rather than pathos; if presumably sexual, they are never sexualized, and they become mothers through adoption, not reproduction.[6]

Most Victorian literature, then, produces the consistent message that disability, almost by definition, removes or diverts a young woman from the normative sexual economy. Whatever social status or significance she gains, these narratives assert, she will not gain it from marriage. Or, if she is one of the lucky ones who marry, she will become a wife under circumstances as particular and even peculiar as disability itself seems to nondisabled culture.

Wilkie Collins, one of the nineteenth century's most charming iconoclasts, discarded these assumptions. The creator of numerous characters with a range of physical, psychological, and social disabilities, Collins radically replotted disabled women's sexual and reproductive "place" in at least three of his novels, transgressing not only the barrier of marriage but also that of childbearing. Even more significantly, while Collins's novels are mined with references to cultural anxieties about disabled women's capacity to produce disabled children, his narratives' most persuasive message is that we should move beyond the question of "should she marry?" in favor of much more interesting issues (and much more sensational plots). As much as Collins subscribes to conventional, sentimentalized views of bodily "affliction," and shares other writers' exoticizing/pathologizing tendency with regard to disabled sexuality, he never pathologizes a disabled woman's entry, through marriage and motherhood, into the definitionally anti-exotic realms of domestic life.

This essay traces the arc of Collins's progressive transformation of disabled women characters from objects of pathos into sexual and domestic subjects with full access to the traditional heroine's desserts of courtship, marriage, and motherhood. After creating a deaf heroine with a sexual subjectivity in *Hide and Seek,* and giving a "deformed" woman in *The Moonstone* a passionately voiced and indelibly written sexuality, Collins produced in Lucilla Finch a disabled heroine who not only speaks, acts, and writes on her own behalf but also, most significantly, moves beyond the pathetic "if only" narrative structure that in Victorian literature and culture typically brackets and/or pathologizes disabled women's "normal" desire to be wives and mothers.

I place both Collins's work, and the cultural taboos it offends, in a richer cultural context, arguing that Lucilla Finch not only challenged the assumption that disabled (particularly blind) women do not marry, but also threatened this cultural formation at a time when it gravely needed shoring up. In the climate of Victorian hereditarian thought, theories of how impairment moved from one person to another were still very much under construction. Impairments ranging from myopia to insanity were regularly read by social and medical science as signs gesturing both backward to parental sin and forward to generations of intensified "defect." For Collins to move disabled women characters progressively closer to sexual reproduction, while concurrently referencing the very clinical contexts in which "dysgenic" births were theorized, was as risky as it was engaging. A disabled woman's presence in a typical heroine's role was a reminder of significant anxieties surrounding impairment itself and the uncertain rules by which it might pass from person to person. With inadequate distinctions between those impairments that could pass from person to person and those which could not, Collins's essentially normalizing gesture of writing a disabled woman into a typical heroine's story was, in its cultural context, more gothic than domestic. Ironically, while Collins himself shifted the sensational value of disability away from these women characters and onto other plot elements, a Victorian culture not yet ready to abandon the concept of disability's radical difference found a blind woman's marriage a sensation plot too real to be entertaining.

Hide and Seek

Hide and Seek is a bildungsroman *á deux,* a mystery novel about parentage developed through the adventures of Madonna Blyth and Zack Thorpe, two attractive young people who are unknowingly half siblings. Zack Thorpe, the vigorous, picaresque hero, finds relief from his Evangelical father and his stultifying bourgeois home when he meets the painter Valentine Blyth and his family, including Blyth's spinally impaired wife, Lavinia, and their lovely adopted daughter, Madonna, who is deaf. The arrival in the plot of Mat Marksman, a rough woodsman returned from the American West—actually Madonna's uncle—begins the unraveling of Madonna's mysterious past (and ultimately the dismantling of her nascent romance with Zack).

For Collins, Madonna Blyth was a direct challenge to existing modes of representing disability. He remarks in an end note to the novel, "I do not know that any attempt has yet been made in English fiction to draw the character of a 'Deaf Mute,' simply and exactly after nature—or, in other words, to exhibit the peculiar effects produced by the loss of the senses of hearing and speaking on the disposition of the person so afflicted. . . . [T]he whole family of dumb people on the stage have the remarkable faculty . . . of always being able to hear what is said to them."[7] As such, Madonna seems part of Collins's realist project that he had begun in *Basil*. According to him: "the more of the Actual I could garner up as a text to speak from, the more certain I might feel of the genuineness and value of the Ideal which was sure to spring out of it."[8]

Rather than a realistic character drawn "simply and exactly after nature," however, Madonna is a subtly but significantly altered version of Victorian stage representations of deafness and other equally conventional figurations of disability. "Dumb people" were not only features of the comic stage but also significant engines of pathos in the melodramatic theater. Thomas Holcroft's *A Tale of Mystery* (1802), the first English play billed as a melodrama, originated for British audiences the recurrent mute character, which Booth describes as "a sympathetic figure with a terrible and mysterious past . . . meant to evoke great pity."[9]

In other Victorian cultural sites, deaf people were grouped among the "afflicted and neglected" classes for whom pity and alms were regularly solicited, comprised of what the *Charity Organisation Reporter* described as "(1) the blind; (2) deaf; (3) dumb; (4) lame children; (5) deformed children; (6) idiotic; (7) imbecile . . . [and] (8) insane."[10] In positioning deaf people as needy objects, social work and educational writing positioned them as powerful emotional catalysts. The "uninstructed Deaf and Dumb," asserts one charitable appeal, are not only "pitiable objects of compassion" but also "must be causes of unceasing sorrow to their afflicted parents and friends."[11]

Collins bases his characterization of Madonna Blyth on these Victorian cultural conventions that marked deafness as a bodily condition with emotional valence. While he identifies her impairment with pathos, however, he also explicates a complex and disturbing *erotics* of pathos, making it clear that objects of pity are also objects of desire. Further, while Madonna at the novel's end has her own desires bracketed by circumstances, in the middle of the narrative she is an erotic agent, not only desiring but also imagining, like any other heroine, that the man she loves will return her passion.

Collins makes similar alterations to the details he imports to *Hide and Seek* from religious writer John Kitto's autobiographical account of his deafening, treatment, and accommodation to the hearing world, *The Lost Senses* (1845). While his use of Kitto may be Collins's most significant attempt to invite "the Actual" into one of his novels,[12] the overall effect is not so much to bring reality into conventional representations of deafness as to inflect those representations with sexuality, or to mark them as already sexually inflected.

On her first appearance in the novel, Madonna is objectified primarily in erotic, not pathetic, terms. The narrative frame that introduces her playfully posits her association with the "consolations" a married man seeks—ironically—in response to his wife's disability. We first learn the history of Valentine Blyth, an energetic artist, lacking in brilliance, who fell in love with Lavinia, a woman with a history of "spinal malady," and married her against his family's wishes. When the illness returned, Lavinia and Valentine "nobly" hid "the shock" of her disability from each other, but she insisted that Valentine "seek consolation, where she knew he must find it sooner or later, by going back to his studio" (*Hide and Seek*, 35, 37).

After apprising the reader of the Blyths' history, the novel shifts to that studio and the fictional present. While "consolation in the studio" is not necessarily a euphemism for extramarital sex, Collins encourages that connection by describing the entrance in the studio of a "mysterious resident" in the Blyth household, "a Young Lady" who is "in no way related" to either Blyth, and who is "deliciously soft, bright, fresh, pure, and delicate." This object of neighbors' "prying glances . . . and lamenting looks" gives the reader pause, as of course Collins intends her to do. The narrative goes on to detail the physical beauties of this mysterious young woman, articulating them in a sexualized rhetoric that describes her "incomparable blue eyes" as the stuff of elopement fantasies and praises her "'sweet lips smiling at her dimpled chin, / Whose wealth of kisses gods might long to win'" (47–50).

Having thoroughly characterized this being as an object of desire, and one whose connection with Valentine Blyth is both mysterious and intimate, the narrator asks, "What can this absolute and remarkable silence mean between two people who look as affectionately on each other as these two look, every time their eyes meet!" and ends the protracted delay with an answering chapter on "Madonna's childhood," in which her relationship to the Blyths is finally clarified (52–53). Established for the reader as a mysterious and sexually desirable woman, Madonna is only in this later, flashback chapter developed as a mysterious and desirable deaf child.

Valentine has "discovered" the beautiful deaf girl in a country circus. Deafened in an equestrian act, she is now exhibited in front of the circus crowd as

THE MYSTERIOUS FOUNDLING!

AGED TEN YEARS!!

TOTALLY DEAF AND DUMB!!! (56)

While Blyth does not murmur "deaf and dumb!" with the rest of the crowd, he is even more stimulated than they are by the sight of her, and provides a small spectacle in himself:

> From the moment of the little girl's first appearance, ample recreation had been unconsciously provided . . . by a tall, stout, and florid stranger, who appeared suddenly to lose his senses the moment he set eyes on the deaf and dumb child . . . . Mad and mysterious words . . . poured from his lips. "Devotional beauty," "Fra Angelico's angels," "Giotto and the cherubs," "Enough to bring the divine Raphael down from heaven to paint her." (60)

Blyth's artistic appreciation is posed against the crowd's hunger for spectacle, establishing him as an appropriate hero for the rescue tale that follows. He and the child immediately form a dyad so intimate that the crowd seems to evaporate:

> She stopped exactly opposite to Valentine; and when she looked up, she looked on him alone.
>
> Was there something in the eager sympathy of his eyes as they met hers, which spoke to the little lonely heart in the sole language that could ever reach it? Did the child, with the quick instinct of the deaf and dumb, read his compassionate disposition, his pity and longing to help her, in his expression at that moment? It might have been so. . . . He saw the small fingers trembling as

they held the cards; he saw the delicate little shoulders
and the poor frail neck and chest bedizened with tawdry
mock jewelry and spangles; he saw the innocent young
face, whose pure beauty no soil of stage paint could
disfigure, with the smile still on the parted lips, but with
a patient forlornness in the sad blue eyes, as if the seeing-
sense that was left, mourned always the hearing and
speaking senses that were gone—he marked all these
things in an instant, and felt that his heart was sinking
as he looked. (61–62)

Overcome with emotion, and, as before, "losing his senses" ("a
dimness stole over his sight"), Blyth kisses the girl's hand and rushes out
of the circus. It is clear, however, that "[i]f ever man was in love with a
child at first sight, he was that man." When Blyth returns for another
performance, the child is so moved by his presence that she is unable
to perform and leaves the ring. He overhears her crying out while the
circus-master beats her, and swears to "take that injured, beautiful,
patient little angel away from this villainous place" (62, 64, 69).

The emotional and linguistic excess that permeates the passages
that expose Blyth's savior-man spirituality, then, includes a very physical connection between this "good man" and the beautiful, tawdrily
dressed girl he smothers with kisses. Collins amplifies and makes bla-
tant the unspoken erotic context in which numerous Victorian cultural
texts position attractive disabled girls, and he constructs Madonna as
a willing—though literally mute—participant in this potentially disturbing encounter.[13]

In the flashbacks, *Hide and Seek* pursues its project of "representing the character of a 'Deaf Mute' as literally as possible according to nature" by referencing the documentary source of John Kitto's
life story. The child's foster mother, Mrs. Peckover, not only tells how
she met and helped Madonna's mother, a starving, unmarried, yet
clearly middle-class woman, but also recounts the "case history" of
the child's deafening and subsequent medical and educational therapy.
The details of the child's deafness, from the accident that precipitates
it to its diagnosis and treatment, are taken almost verbatim from *The
Lost Senses*. Like Kitto, who was injured while working for his stone-
mason father, Madonna becomes deaf by a fall, is subjected to a number of painful and disgusting treatments, and is diagnosed as having
a paralyzed auditory nerve produced by the shock of the impact.
Collins's version of Kitto's account of deafness, however, transforms

clinical detail into sexual suggestion. Kitto's voice after his accident was "so greatly altered as to be not easily understood";[14] in *Hide and Seek*, this voice change becomes a phenomenon rich in resonances of anxiety regarding little girls and how they should sound. The first time the child speaks after her fall, says Mrs. Peckover, her voice "sounded, somehow, hoarse and low, and deep and faint, all at the same time; the strangest, shockingest voice to come from a child, who always used to speak so clearly and prettily before." This voice, which Mrs. Peckover first thinks is a joking attempt to imitate the child-abusing Jubber, alarms her so much she spills the tea she is carrying. After the diagnosis, when Mrs. Peckover is urged by the doctor to "treat her severely" in order to make Madonna keep speaking aloud, it is not only the little girl's obvious misery upon being asked to do this, but also "the shocking husky moaning voice that . . . didn't belong to her," that make Mrs. Peckover give up the attempt (93, 98, 99).[15]

The disturbing effect of Madonna's deafness on those who are close to her seems based in some sense on her new behavior's violation of gender codes: she loses not only her pretty temper, but also her pretty voice. She is no longer docile and sweet, and she sounds as if she is imitating an unsavory adult man. What is "shocking" about the husky moaning voice is not clear, but it is impossible for a twentieth-century reader to ignore its suggestion of sexuality—a potentially alarming idea in connection with a ten-year-old girl, but one that the narrative reiterates.

After the child is transformed by adoption into Madonna Blyth, the novel continues to devote attention to those particularities of her character it attributes to her sensory impairment—what might be called "deafisms" or "deaf character," borrowing again from Kitto and transforming Kitto's (already intensely melodramatic) narrative into a melodrama of the sexualized female body. Collins's descriptions of Madonna's "deaf experience," for example, develop deafness as a state of physical responsiveness that can only be considered "dangerous" in the context of Victorian ideologies that associated physical responsiveness with primitivity and immorality. A passage in which Kitto elaborates (ironically, through a story of disgust) the aesthetic sense deafness produced in him becomes for Collins an occasion to write Madonna into a sensual rapture in the presence of nature: "She would sit for hours, on fresh summer evenings, watching the mere waving of the leaves; her face flushed, her whole nervous organisation trembling with the sensations of deep and perfect happiness which that simple sight imparted to her" (120).

Many of Collins's changes to Kitto, including the shift from a first-person to a third-person narrative, position Madonna as an object of desire (and even an objet d'art, given her "framing" as a living Raphael Madonna).[16] Within this constraint, however, Collins represents Madonna as doing her own share of looking and desiring, all with regard to Zack Thorpe, the sometime drawing student of her father. An accomplished artist herself, Madonna surreptitiously objectifies Zack as she sketches:

> her eyes wandered timidly once or twice to the place
> where Zack was standing, when she thought he was not
> looking at her. . . . He was over six feet in height; and,
> though then little more than nineteen years old, was
> well developed in proportion to his stature. His boxing,
> rowing, and other athletic exercises had done wonders
> towards bringing his naturally vigorous, upright frame to
> the perfection of healthy muscular condition. . . . He trod
> easily and lightly, with a certain youthful suppleness and
> hardy grace in all his actions, which set off his fine bodily
> formation to the best advantage. (126–27)

If the novel and most of the male characters spend a fair amount of energy looking at Madonna's body in clinical/aesthetic/pathetic/erotic ways, Madonna's own delectation of Zack's frame (and flesh, later in the passage) gives her a form of erotic parity with all those other desiring viewers.

Madonna's reactions to Zack's proximity also trace those stereotypic bodily signs of feminine desire—the blush and the heaving bodice—again giving her parity with "normal" women in love: "A bright flush overspread the girl's face. . . . Her tender blue eyes looked up at him, shyly conscious of the pleasure that their expression was betraying; and the neat folds of her pretty grey dress, which had lain so still over her bosom when she was drawing, began to rise and fall gently now, when Zack was holding her hand" (126). Because a young Victorian woman's sexuality places her in a realm in which oral speech is insufficient or culturally inappropriate, Madonna's desire for Zack is indistinguishable from that of a hearing woman. When Mrs. Blyth suggests to Madonna that "you must like [Zack] very much, love," Madonna does not sign her answer—"her treacherous cheeks, neck, and bosom answered for her" (146).[17]

At this point, a mere glimmer of awareness on Zack's part would send the novel gaily on its way to a courtship and its closure, or so it would seem. There are no other romances afoot and no able-bodied heroines to usurp Madonna's place; the happy Blyth family testifies to disabled women's ability to be exemplary wives and mothers. Zack seems agreeable to reciprocate Madonna's attentions, albeit in the context of a pack mentality; as he cheerfully tells Mat Marksman, "We're all in love with her!" (253). The erotic momentum, however, does not last; the novel seems to recoil from its innovative representation of a disabled woman's sexuality, or at least to remove, abruptly, the context for its expression. When the unfolding of the mystery plot reveals that the repressive Zachary Thorpe Senior is the careless cause of the ruin of Madonna's mother, and Zack is Madonna's half brother, the two young people are whisked apart without ever having occasion to confront their situation together, leaving us in breathless retrospect to imagine a second story that might have made an even better sensation novel.

While the romance never materializes, it is important to note that what officially derails it is a horror of incest, not a horror of deafness. In fact, both the unfolding mystery of Madonna's parentage, and the threat of incest, displace deafness itself as a center of sensationalism. For a woman with a disability—such as Madonna or Lavinia—getting married is a relatively normalized situation.

A more suspicious reading, however, might propose that incest is brought in as an emergency measure to permit Collins to escape a real resolution of the situation between Madonna and Zack. Reluctant to back away from his attempts to create an innovative portrait of not only deafness but also disabled women's ability to play traditional feminine roles, he may have been unwilling at this time to go through with an actual marriage between a deaf woman and a hearing man (especially in light of critics' castigation of the daring plot elements of *Basil*, his previous novel). With the unambiguous horror of brother-sister marriage filling the stage, Collins never has to resolve the thorny issue of whether or not Madonna should marry at all.

The Moonstone

While he continued to explore the cultural and sexual place of physically marginalized women in many other works, it was nearly twenty years until Collins wrote another novel whose heroine was physically disabled. In *The Moonstone,* one of his most famous novels, Rosanna Spearman, a physically and socially disabled woman, is the structural hinge to the novel's mystery narrative. She is also the only clear voice of sexual passion permeating a courtship plot from which she is excluded, while Rachel Verinder, the "official," nondisabled heroine, is literally and figuratively silent for most of the novel. Unlike *Hide and Seek*, *The Moonstone* conforms to the "twin" structure that characterizes many Victorian courtship plots, pairing the stigmatized and disenfranchised Rosanna with the socially gilded, physically beautiful Rachel, who garners all the heroine's rewards including marriage to the man Rosanna loves. Rosanna is a far more memorable character than the heroine, precisely because she is such a compelling container for what cannot be expressed in the Victorian courtship plot. And while her death is necessary to maintain the novel's equilibrium, her imprint on the plot persists.[18]

At first glance, this housemaid with a criminal past and a "deformed shoulder" is a minor character whose main interest is her isolation from not only the people she serves but also most of her fellow servants. Her love for Franklin Blake, a young gentleman in love with his cousin (Rachel Verinder), only exacerbates this isolation, making her a convenient suspect for the crime that launches the mystery plot. When Rachel's priceless Indian diamond is stolen, Rosanna's behavior becomes more and more suspicious, until she disappears and is found drowned. A buried suicide letter reveals that Rosanna believed Franklin was the thief, and consequently she disposed of evidence that she believed would convict him—information that is crucial to Blake's discovery of the real culprit and his happy reunion with Rachel (who also believes he stole her diamond but reacts by refusing to speak to anyone).

Rosanna and Rachel—ostensibly worlds apart in terms of class, normative physical beauty, and, above all, life prospects—are closely connected not only by their love for Franklin Blake but also by their respective functions in the mystery plot. The silence of both women has not only the same source—a belief in Franklin's guilt—but also the same effect on the novel, at least initially; it creates the mystery by blocking the information required to find the thief of the Moonstone. The form the two women's silence takes, however, reiterates the significant differences between them. Rachel maintains her silence until late in the book and, as a result, her consciousness is so slimly represented that she is never a fully realized character. Throughout the novel, Rachel is identified primarily by her withholding of information and emotion. Rosanna's silence, in contrast, is transformed into "buried writing," Tamar Heller's phrase for a recurrent trope in Collins that is "affiliated with a thematics of secrecy, transgression, and illegitimacy."[19] In this case, the literal buried writing is a posthumous letter to the novel's hero, Franklin Blake, which Rosanna hides for him near the Shivering Sands, the quicksand in which she dies. While the letter marks Rosanna's despair of ever reaching Blake as a lover, it nonetheless voices her misery. Rosanna's death is hardly silent; her suicide, in fact, signifies her final appeal for recognition that the novel, if not the other characters, affirms as her rightful due.

Rosanna, despite her silence about her suspicions, is characterized only by her tormented, passion for Franklin Blake. Ultimately, her fate is despair and death, while her nondisabled counterpart's fate is happiness, marriage, and the birth of a child; but because her passion is expressed, preserved in her writing and thus in the "documents" that comprise *The Moonstone,* her effect on the novel and her place in the memories of its readers resonates much more strongly than Rachel's. She herself becomes a form of buried writing, endlessly iterating for Franklin Blake (and the readers) the painful subject position she has occupied.

While *The Moonstone* inscribes the disabled woman's conventional cultural identity as a victimized center of melodramatic pathos, she is also structurally positioned in the novel as a culturally marginal woman whose subjectivity will not be denied, although it may require her death to be fully expressed. Unlike *Hide and Seek,* which for the most part imagines Madonna Blyth's feelings from outside, eliding what could be an increasingly fascinating first-person narrative, *The Moonstone* puts Rosanna in a position to speak her own sufferings, and even to posthumously "frame," in more ways than one, the man who has produced them—according to Donna Haraway, "to mark the world that marked [her] as other."[20] In writing to Franklin, Rosanna articulates the ways in which Franklin's stance toward her named and produced her disability: "'You're a plain girl; you have got a crooked shoulder; you're only a housemaid—what do you mean by attempting to speak to Me?' You never uttered a word of that, Mr. Franklin; but you said it all to me, nevertheless!"[21]

Catherine Peters asserts that Collins even reduced the moral value of the hero to maximize, by contrast, Rosanna's claim on our sympathies; she cites Collins's removal of a passage in which Franklin recognizes the injury he has inflicted on Rosanna and is "overcome by remorse." The omission of this passage in the published version, according to Peters, significantly reduces Blake's insight: "his inability to confront the reality of Rosanna's love makes the reader indignant, and is meant to."[22] While Rosanna's passion may make Franklin Blake uncomfortable, then, the novel itself honors it. As the manservant

Betteredge (whose consciousness, more than anyone else's, shapes the novel) says, "It's natural, sir, in *you*. And, God help us all! . . . it's no less natural in *her*" (*The Moonstone*, 315).

While in its broad structures *The Moonstone* reduces the place *Hide and Seek* constructs for a disabled woman character, Rosanna Spearman nonetheless represents an important expansion of Collins's exploration of disabled women's sexual subjectivity. He not only represents Rosanna as a desiring subject but also structures the novel so that she herself articulates her desire and frustration, uttering a memorable critique of normative culture's view of all the marginal human categories she inhabits. Transgressive in body and voice, Rosanna Spearman not only functions as buried writing; she is arguably the novel's buried heroine.

Poor Miss Finch

In *Poor Miss Finch*, Collins imagined a disabled woman character's trajectory all the way to the culminations of marriage and motherhood. Lucilla Finch is actually allowed what even nondisabled Victorian heroines are usually denied: an assertive, abundantly expressed sexuality that does not lead to prostitution, religious conversion, tragic death, or all three. Her desires, richly reciprocated, eventually lead to marriage and family; wealthy at the start, she is even wealthier at the end. All these happy endings are particularly unusual in representations of blindness, a disability generally treated by nondisabled culture as one that radically separates a person from "normal" life. Further, Collins makes a larger space for Lucilla's subjectivity than in either of the previous novels; she is not only the (talkative) main character but also the writer of the diary that conveys part of the narrative. *Poor Miss Finch*'s combination of female sexuality, disability, and clinical detail, however, inspired in several Victorian critics a vigorous irritation with Collins's work, contributing to the long-term marginalization of both novel and author.

In his preface, Collins articulates his belief that *Poor Miss Finch* (like *Hide and Seek*) will correct previous representations with a dose of realism: "More than one charming blind girl, in fiction and in the drama, has preceded 'Poor Miss Finch.' But, so far as I know, blindness in these cases has been always exhibited, more or less exclusively, from the ideal and the sentimental point of view. The attempt here made is to appeal to an interest of another kind, by exhibiting blindness as it really is."[23] While Collins's effort to explore the experience of blindness and regained sight may at times result in touches of realism, *Poor Miss Finch* is far from being a predominantly realist novel. Lucilla Finch, a young woman of independent income who has been blind since early childhood, pursues and falls in love with Oscar Dubourg, a rich young stranger who moves to the rural town where Lucilla lives with her father, stepmother (Lucilla's mother died when she was a baby), and ever-increasing brood of step-siblings.

Oscar and Lucilla's marriage plans are curtailed, however, when Oscar develops epilepsy after a head injury. Unwilling to wait to see if he will "grow out of" the condition, Oscar presses the doctors for a quicker and more certain remedy and is prescribed silver nitrate, which has a darkening and "bluing" effect on his skin. The fact that Lucilla has an inexplicable but violent prejudice against dark colors—in clothing, and especially in persons—convinces Oscar to hide his transformation until after they are married. To this end, when his identical twin brother comes to town, Oscar attributes his own condition to Nugent in order to smooth over any comments Lucilla may hear about "the blue man." The plan backfires when Nugent—who has fallen in love with Lucilla—brings in a German oculist who cures Lucilla's blindness. Her first vision is of Nugent, whom she assumes is Oscar; the sight of her fiancé, on the other hand, makes her beg to have her bandages replaced. Oscar leaves town and becomes a military nurse. Nugent, still pretending to be Oscar, brings Lucilla to the very verge of the altar before Oscar returns with full knowledge of the deception. Lucilla has lost her eyesight again (largely through the stress of not feeling attracted to the man she is about to marry and not knowing why) but refuses a second operation. The brothers reconcile and Oscar and Lucilla marry and have two children. Nugent goes on an Arctic expedition and freezes to death. The novel is narrated by Madame Pratolungo, a Frenchwoman and radical Republican who is Lucilla's hired companion.

Like *Hide and Seek*, *Poor Miss Finch* positions itself as counterdiscursive to stereotypes of disability but achieves its counterdiscursive effects within a text that alternates between iconoclasm and endorsement of stereotypes. Collins's remark in his dedication that "it is even possible for bodily affliction itself to take its place among the ingredients of happiness" (*Poor Miss Finch*, xxxiv), for example, prepares us to read a stereotypical, morally uplifting story of a woman who has developed a positive attitude toward her disability. The character of Madame Pratolungo is the novel's proxy for this point of view; she approaches her new employment thinking, "Young—lonely—blind. . . . I felt I should love her" (*Poor Miss Finch*, 4). The person known by the local villagers as "Poor Miss Finch" lives in "the ancient portion" of a house formerly a convent, with "one great pleasure to illumine her dark life—music" (13, 4). She first appears as "a solitary figure in a pure white robe" who looks like a Raphael Madonna, except for her "poor, dim, sightless eyes" (13–14). It appears that Lucilla, perhaps even more so than Madonna Blyth, will present disabled femininity solely in terms of sentiment and spirituality.

This pretty tableau of a spiritualized, dependent blind woman is interrupted posthaste, however, as Lucilla recoils from her new companion, convinced she is wearing something dark. The "innocent, afflicted creature," not just the pristine object of seeing eyes, is an objectifier of others, and in much less agreeable terms than Madonna Blyth's admiration of Zack Thorpe's body. Further, the "poor" that is habitually appended to "blind woman" in both fictional and nonfictional Victorian texts, serving as a code word for extreme physical, emotional, and economic dependency, is almost immediately disrupted. On a trip to the village, Madame Pratolungo's attempt to guide Lucilla evokes peals of laughter, as Lucilla, who walks freely through the rural town, is the fitter guide. Lucilla has a legacy on which her father, feeding the increasing family his uxoriousness has produced, depends. Finally, while Lucilla does turn to Madame Pratolungo for emotional support, she habitually takes the lead in interpersonal and emotional affairs (that is, until she is sighted). Her only moments of assuming the role of victim (a stock function of blind characters, including Louise of *Les Deux Orphelines*) come after she has regained her sight.

Lucilla's assertive sexuality is one of her most striking features. By her second meeting with Oscar, her behavior toward him is "so bold" that it terrifies Pratolungo: "Instead of her blindness making her nervous in the presence of a man unknown to her, it appeared to have exactly the contrary effect. It made her fearless" (37). Later, Lucilla explains that she distinguishes Oscar and Nugent only by "something in me [that] answers to one of them and not to the other. . . . When Oscar takes [my hand], a delicious tingle runs from his hand into mine, and steals all over me" (147–48). These expressions of active desire (and their reciprocation) disrupt both the convention of the passively desirable, nondesiring blind woman and the convention of the blind woman whose desires have no place in conventional heterosexual relations. In Madame Pratolungo's analysis, "the most modest girl in existence is bolder with her lover in the dark than in the light," and Lucilla is always in the dark (59).

The specifics of Lucilla's emotions and behavior develop Collins's obvious project of exploring and disrupting cultural conventions of seeing, nonseeing, and desire. While she is blind, Lucilla's sexuality (like her prejudice) has a distinctly specular aspect to it, albeit imagined specularity. Lucilla is obsessed with making Oscar a mental object, visualizing him in all his material specifics. In addition, when Pratolungo questions Lucilla's choice of lover, Lucilla responds by ordering her companion to "Look!" as she directs her fiancé to sit by her, put his arm around her waist, tell her he loves her—"Out loud!"—and kiss her. When Oscar is too embarrassed to comply, Lucilla kisses *him*. While Pratolungo comments that Lucilla, "strong in her blind insensibility to all shafts of ridicule shot from the eye, cared nothing for the presence of a third person," in fact, Lucilla seems to make aggressive use of that third person to witness and react to her sexual commitment to Oscar (175–76).

Her sexualized showing, and forcing Pratolungo to look, offer a meaningful reversal of the usual scenario in which the blind woman is the unknowing object of aggressive looking. Lucilla, shockingly, not only desires but also displays herself as a desiring subject. Her exhibitionism shifts the power relations in the stereotypical scene of looking and desire, especially with reference to blind women.[24]

A similar reversal occurs in terms of literary conventions about blindness, cures, and sexuality. Regained sight is usually the only circumstance in which blind nineteenth-century women characters become sexual and marry; William Paulson observes that in nineteenth-century French popular theater, "the 'awakening' to sight offer[s] a particularly propitious moment for emotional or erotic revelations."[25] According to Paulson, cataract surgery in the French dramas functioned as "a literal ocular equivalent of defloration."[26] In direct contrast, the surgery Herr Grosse performs on Lucilla is not cast as a sexual initiation but as a threat to her existing romance. Similarly, the novel associates Lucilla's regained sight *not* with increased sexuality but rather with the loss of "the delicious tingle," so much so that she shuts her eyes to try to "renew [her] blindness" and regain the excitement. When this fails, she wonders if "the loss of my sense of feeling [is] the price that I have paid for the recovery of my sense of sight" (329). Herr Grosse confirms this, saying that "all those thrill-tingles that she once had when he touched her, belong to [another] time. . . . [I]t is a sort of swop-bargain between Nature and this poor girl. . . . I give you your eyes—I take away your fine touch" (404).

The fact that Lucilla is mistaken about the identity of the man she embraces seems incidental; the effective message of the novel is that blindness is a state of sexual desire that sight removes, rather than the reverse. This is emphasized by the fact that she is blind again when her desire returns:

> For one awful moment, when she first felt the familiar
> touch, the blood left her cheeks. Her blind eyes dilated
> fearfully. She stood petrified. Then, with a long, low cry—
> a cry of breathless rapture—she flung her arms passion-
> ately round his neck. The life flowed back into her face;
> her lovely smile just trembled on her parted lips; her
> breath came faint and quick and fluttering. In soft
> tones of ecstasy, with her lips on his cheek, she
> murmured the delicious words:
> "Oh, Oscar! I know you once more!" (416–17)

At this point, Collins's earlier remarks in the dedication about "bodily affliction" as one of "the ingredients of happiness" take on an entirely new meaning. Lucilla, after she is told of the fraud, still says that it is her blindness, not the return of the real Oscar, that "has given me back my old delightful sensation" (417–18).

Lucilla Finch, like Madonna Blyth before her, is initially framed by the image of a Raphael Madonna. Like so much else in *Poor Miss Finch,* this reference acquires substantial irony by the story's close. While many readers would probably have preferred that a blind hero-ine never become a mother in any way, even through immaculate con-ception, the novel ends with Lucilla married and a biological mother.

Like Madonna, Lucilla stands alone as the heroine. She not only expresses her desire, but also expresses it directly to her love object, who can neither help "seeing" her nor falling in love with her. Were she a sighted heroine, this behavior would surely end in ruin. Lucilla, however, receives all the traditional heroine's desserts. Like Rosanna Spearman, Lucilla authors a part of her own story, producing not so much a central plot hinge as a fuller subjectivity; if Rosanna's buried writing is about secrecy and transgression, Lucilla's journal is about untold stories and unacknowledged subjectivities. The novel gives Lucilla a fuller subjectivity by including her first-person account of her experience of sight, lost sexuality, and—perhaps most significantly— a new, accepting positionality toward dark-skinned people that pre-pares her for her reunion with Oscar. Even if the diary is mediated (and interrupted) by Madame Pratolungo's narration, the fact of its inclusion inscribes Lucilla as subject more than object, giving her an ontological fullness.

Finally, while *Poor Miss Finch* is indeed a sensational novel, with a dizzying series of crises and complications, Lucilla's marriage and motherhood are completely normalized. The novel never broaches the question of whether or not a blind woman should marry (though it does posit that question in reference to Oscar once he has developed epilepsy). While Collins makes Lucilla's immodest behavior a point of commentary, exoticizing her sexuality as he did Madonna's in *Hide and Seek*, Lucilla's ability to fall in love and be loved back is taken for granted; exoticized, perhaps, but not problematized. For Collins, in striking contrast to his contemporaries, the significant question is only *whom* Lucilla will marry, whether she will find the right man in time.

Blindness and blueness notwithstanding, the most sensational aspect of this novel may be how conventional a heroine Lucilla Finch finally is. In fact, it is their conventionality, *not* their sexualization, that is most notable about both Collins's disabled heroines, who are ultimately contained within stories more domestic than sensational. In the case of Madonna, the plot resolution is relatively constricting. Once she is taken from the nomadic, public life of the circus, she is in a situation in which she never leaves the house alone. Her one venture up the stairs to Zack's bedroom (significantly, when he is too ill to know she is there) literally precipitates the discovery that they are blood relatives, effectively putting a halt to any further wandering. The failed romance notwithstanding, Madonna's domestication is drawn as an overwhelmingly positive change from her earlier life. At the same time, one wonders what has happened to the child who was "mad to be carried up in the air on horseback" (*Hide and Seek*, 91). It is tempting to see Madonna's literal fall as a repetition of her mother's figurative one, a moral reproof that must bring about reformation, or if that is impossible, end in death. Madonna's deafening and her subsequent adoption can be seen as the beginnings of her reformation into a middle-class daughter, associated with a home instead of a circus, and her reclamation from Zack's sickroom as a move that protects her from incest and ruination.[27]

Lucilla Finch's transformation—from a single, financially independent woman (who wanders into town alone and meets strange men) into a married mother—can also be read as a regressive rather than an innovative move. Elizabeth Helsinger, Robin Sheets, and William Veeder comment that while Collins's nondisabled heroines are "often aggressive . . . they never seek the feminist goals of a professional career or a parliamentary seat. The goal of his aggressive women is in fact the goal of true woman—marriage with a decent man."[28] His disabled heroines are no different.

Both the content and the significance of "normalization," however, are hardly identical for disabled and nondisabled women, fictional or otherwise. It is difficult to assess the degree of cultural resistance with which a disabled woman, who was not only a worker, a wife, and a biological mother, but also strong minded and sexual, might meet in the nineteenth century or in our own. In either time frame, Lucilla Finch is a radical character precisely because she is normalized, asserting that a woman with a disability can have a life trajectory that is as "regular" as her body is variant.[29]

Cultural Contexts: Disability and Dangerous Generation

Collins's explorations of disability, marriage, and reproduction occurred within a climate of scientific uncertainty that affixed itself with particular fervor to women's bodies, especially physically impaired ones. In "The Cry of the Unborn," Evelyn Hunt observed the following:

> We look around and see the sickly girl uniting herself with an equally sickly man. We *know* that in the families there are fatal tendencies to horrible disease. We see cousins marrying, we know how fatal this will prove to their helpless offspring. . . . And even worse. Heredity. We may call it a catch word, cant, what we will. It exists, nevertheless, and the time has come when it can no longer be ignored. In the smiling, innocent baby may be the fatal taint that will wreck it, body and soul, in spite of all education and environment can do.[30]

For twentieth-first-century readers, adrift in their own time of scientific and ethical turbulence, Victorian concepts of how impairment might move from one person to another offer the pleasure of a scientific muddle distant enough—or so it seems—to laugh at. For many Victorian people, disease and heredity each presented a theoretical challenge in which insufficient knowledge was filled in by fear, anxiety, or circular logic.

The idea that disease could cause some disabilities was immeasurably complicated by conflicting theories about how people became diseased in the first place. Erwin Ackerknecht points out that while the "idea that epidemic diseases were transmitted by contagion, and caused by micro-organisms . . . was not exactly new in the middle of the nineteenth century," resistance to the idea was strong for the first half of the century.[31] An anticontagionist or miasmist would argue that contact with cold air, harsh light, "this evil influence" of impure air, overcrowding, or some other environmental factor caused disease, particularly in individuals with a "scrofulous" or otherwise weak constitution.[32] A contagionist would argue that the cause was contact with infectious material, but might also concede that the environmental factors provided an essential "predisposing cause," a necessary catalyst for the infection to take hold.

And while the individual constitution presented an essential building block in the development of illness and impairment, the "strumous," "scrofulous," or otherwise "defective" constitutions are themselves vague and capacious categories which blend the social, the behavioral, and the physical, and are theorized as both hereditary and caused by environmental influences like overcrowding and unwholesome air. In this context, any physical impairment had the potential to be perceived as transmissible by contact, by miasmatic air, by a combination of contact, environment, and individual constitution, or perhaps simply through the reproductive practices of the lowest (and highest) strata of society. Accordingly, how a condition was constructed rhetorically was perhaps even more significant than it is in our own time.[33] Victorian medical writing on blindness, for example, considers it so often in the context of disease (and often venereal disease) that blindness becomes an emblem for disease and dangerous sexuality, regardless of its many other possible causes.

Hereditary transmission of impairment was also theorized in remarkably fluid rhetorics. The theory of maternal impressions or frights, which posited physical characteristics as something that could be "caught" through the eyes and transmitted to an unborn child, may stretch our credibility far beyond its limits, but it was a commonplace belief among educated people at least through the 1850s. As the following letter to the *Lancet* from a "surgeon-aurist" demonstrates, ideas about hereditary transmission could encompass both direct "impressions" to the fetus via injury to the mother and mental impressions created by things the mother saw:

> The circumstance of a child being deaf on the same side as
> her mother, in consequence of the fall of the mother whilst
> in a state of pregnancy, is not extraordinary, when it is
> considered how many marks and peculiarities children

frequently derive from the mother. At Dover, some years ago, a lady was frightened by a ferrit whilst in a state of pregnancy; the child, when born, had eyes precisely like that animal; every child after had the same kind of eyes, and they all became blind, or nearly so, about the age of puberty.[34]

Impressions are still frequently referenced in medical journals of the 1860s and 1870s as a debatable but not completely dismissible theory.

The belief in maternal impressions represents a logical extreme within Victorian concepts of heredity. Not only the general public but also, according to Charles Rosenberg, most physicians, "assumed that heredity was a dynamic process beginning with conception and extending through weaning."[35] Not only physical traits such as hair color and height but also diseases such as syphilis and addictions such as alcoholism were considered truly hereditary in the nineteenth century; an ill parent would produce a "vitiated sperm or ovum" and finally offspring with "defective" constitutions, if not the parent's particular illness.[36] Both acquired weaknesses and the particular state of the parents' bodies and minds at the moment of conception were believed to influence the formation of the unborn child.

If the parents were weak or "defective," according to followers of degeneration theory, each successive generation of ill parents would be weaker still, with infertility the only factor that would eventually stem the progression of defects. As the physician and protopsychiatrist Henry Maudsley described it, "Certain unfavourable conditions of life tend unquestionably to produce degeneracy of the individual; the morbid predisposition so generated is then transmitted to the next generation, and, if the unfavourable conditions continue, is aggravated in it; and thus is formed a morbid variety of the human kind, which is incapable of being a link in the line of progress of humanity."[37]

As a Victorian cultural sign, then, disability pointed not only backward, to parental transgression and defect, but even more urgently forward, to future generations. Victorian medical and social science reshaped the biblical category of "unclean" into the social-scientific category of the dysgenic or degenerative. The belief that "Beauty, Health, and Intellect Result from Certain Unions, and Deformity, Disease, and Insanity from Others," as Alexander Walker's influential *Intermarriage* (1844) so memorably capsulized it, retained its urgency throughout the century and beyond. An article that appeared in the *London Lancet* asserts the following:

The old should not marry with the young, nor the strong with the weak and debilitated. People with marked hereditary taints should pause ere they run the risk of transmitting their endowments to a long line of suffering successors. The strong and the healthy should beware that it be no act of drunken or insensate folly which records the honour of paternity they have gained. At the moment of conception does the mysterious virtue of the creative force transmit not only an impression of the physical being of the parents, but likewise the moral physiognomy . . . that lies beneath its surface. The impoverished life, the tainted blood, the mental and moral flaws, become the dowry of the descendants.

Included in this dowry are "scrofula, epilepsy, insanity, albinoism, deaf-mutism, idiocy, and defective vision," which are read as "the various impairments of the offspring arising from the influence of too frequent admixture of the same blood."[38]

This fabric of uncertainty and anxiety about bodily conditions and their potential to circulate, in which affliction is reconfigured from a show of Providence and Divine Judgment to one of medical and social pathology, suggests the utility of representing women with disabilities as prepubescent children or as models of womanly self-discipline, especially in light of the powerful and dangerous primacy of the mother's body in Victorian theories of impairment and its genesis. The same medico-socio-scientific context explains the excitement of positing disabled women as desiring women, and the necessity of thwarting that desire before it results in reproduction.

As potential signs of both disease and sexuality, disabled women characters functioned not only in parallel ways to "fallen" women in Victorian literature and culture—as containers for the most dangerous qualities associated with all women—but even as stand-ins for fallen women. As Mary Spongberg argues in *Feminizing Venereal Disease,* in the early nineteenth century all women were conceptualized as diseased, if in varying degrees, as a result of medical research into the transmission of venereal disease and doctors' belief that women were the more significant source, so that "the male body came to represent the standard for health, the female body came to be seen as an aberration from the norm."[39] As the century progressed, however, medical science (and anthropology) created a "gulf between the upright woman and the fallen woman" in which "the prostitute's body continued to be seen as the representative sexualised female body, but it increasingly was also seen as a site of abnormal indulgence."[40] As doctors theorized visible physical anomalies by which one could recognize the prostitute and distinguish her from the upright woman, the prostitute's body came to stand in for disease itself, and to function as a cultural "*cordon sanitaire* that differentiated good women from bad."[41] The signs of the diseased woman, further, included blindness, deafness, paralysis, "deformity and disfigurement," and other forms of physical disability.[42]

Victorian cultural anxieties about both disease and sexual fallenness, I would argue, lurked at various depths beneath courtship plots with disabled women in them. Collins's novels brought these fears to the surface, used them to give tension and interest to the plot, and then dismissed them as nonproblems. If other writers effected various narrative prophylaxes for fears about disabled women—stopping such characters from marrying by drawing them desireless or making their desires unreciprocated—Collins, by *Poor Miss Finch,* stimulated such fears and left them playfully circulating. The clinical details he used in his quest to portray Madonna Blyth "from nature" are in *Poor Miss Finch* both entertaining plot devices and reminders of some of the serious concerns of Victorian medicine.

For example, Oscar's epilepsy is treated with silver nitrate, the same substance to prevent what was referred to as "babies' sore eyes," the congenital blindness caused by the mother's venereal infections and a substantial contributor to infant blindness in the nineteenth century. By pathologizing Oscar rather than Lucilla, Collins plays further with the overall focus on women's bodies as sites of danger and disease; Oscar's disability is treated as a serious barrier to marriage, while Lucilla's is not. The question of Oscar's disability status and its shift from epilepsy to blueness offers one more fascinating, potentially disturbing layer in the novel.

Elsewhere, while Lucilla's congenital cataracts are not only a rare condition but also not the red flag to venereal disease that other kinds of infant blindness might be, the fact that her mother is dead, like so many other mothers of disabled women in fiction, nonetheless evokes suspicions of familiar infirmity. The subplot of Mrs. Finch's awesome fertility and its consequences further develops this atmosphere of (irreverent, it must be said) reference to hereditary weakness, as well as to the miasmist discourse of disease, with its emphasis on air, moisture, and dirt. Mrs. Finch is a "*damp woman* . . . [n]ever completely dressed, never completely dry; always with a baby in one hand and a novel in the other," and the Finch household is a swarm of children, fourteen in all, in "dirty frocks," including one of "deficient intellect" (*Poor Miss Finch,* 10–12). Reverend Finch is a "miserably lean" man with "wizen little legs" and a "contemptible little body," whose face is "deeply pitted with the small-pox" and whose "small whitish-gray eyes had a restless, inquisitive, hungry look in them, indescribably irritating and uncomfortable to see" (67–69).

The oculist's association with both the "clinical" and the "melodramatic" aspects of the novel is similarly hard to pin down to any unitary position. For all the "Actual" that accrues to Herr Grosse— so much so that readers asked Collins for his real name so that they could consult him about their eyes—the medical framework in which he places blindness is essentially thrown out the window by the conclusion; Lucilla says, "Thank God, I am blind" (644), and refuses any further interventions.

Within all these allusions to the transmission of impairment, however, Lucilla's own body is not problematized or pathologized, even if her psyche sometimes is through her obsession with dark colors. The novel is similarly disinterested in the status of Lucilla's children's eyes or any other aspect of their embodiment; they represent the normal, not the sensational—the domestic scene that is Lucilla's place.

Literary "Defects"

Victorian critics seem to squirm on the page in response to *Poor Miss Finch.* One anonymous critic in *The Saturday Review* characterized *Poor Miss Finch* as "a surgical and medical novel" and offered a candid and interesting critique of its failure based on its use of realism:

> Now we are willing to admit that passions sufficiently
> intense, and situations sufficiently sublime, may be born
> of pain and physical afflictions. We know that Poor Miss
> Finch's special burden of blindness has lent itself before
> to the noblest purposes of poetry and romance. But then
> those authors who have turned it to their professional
> purposes have idealized it gracefully, resting lightly even
> on the sightless eyeballs, dealing with the thoughts and
> following the mournful fancies of a mind driven to prey
> upon itself. . . . [W]e have little doubt that Mr. Wilkie
> Collins has made his blind girl more faithful to nature in
> thought, act, and speech than Lord Lytton's Nydia. What

then? Fidelity is, after all, not the foundation of all fiction
. . . we prefer the work of art that suggests to us bright
impressions and graceful fancies.[43]

Another writer simply asked, irritably, "[W]hat is the aim of this
story? That the blind should marry the dark-blue? There is then an
excellent opening for some novelist, distracted for a plot, to write
about the love of the color-blind for the jaundiced."[44]

Perhaps the most fascinating strain of criticism of the novel (and
other Collins novels about disability) engages a thesis of defect encom-
passing not only the writer's aesthetic health but also his physical condition, turning to the physical bodies of the author and reader and the
textual body of the fiction to create a framework in which to place and
thus explain Collins's disabled characters and their "insufficiencies"
(and often, by implication, the significance of any disabled characters).
Notably, John Ruskin attacked Collins's portrayal of physical disabilities in *Poor Miss Finch* as the nadir of the "whole cretinous school" of
"lower fictitious literature" he dubbed the "literature of the Prison-
house" or "Fiction mécroyante," in his "Fiction Fair and Foul" (1880),
a tirade against fiction full of descriptions of illness and violent death,
created by urban, diseased minds and bodies to cater commercially to
other urban, diseased minds and bodies deprived of the healthy stimu-
lation of natural beauty and thus addicted to low fiction.[45] For Ruskin,
physically diseased, "deformed," and (ignobly) dead bodies are symptomatic of equally diseased and deformed genres like sensation fiction
and, ultimately, a morally *and physically* diseased writer catering to
morally and physically diseased readers. "Fiction Fair and Foul" provoc-
atively locates writers, characters, and readers within one web of physical, mental, and moral disease (arguably a schema authorized by the
fluidity of Victorian theories of disease and heredity).

Ruskin reads *Poor Miss Finch* as a prime example of these "anatomical preparations . . . for the general market"[46] in part by *mis*-
reading the novel's ending, in which "evil twin" Nigel Dubourg is
found dead in the Arctic, frozen even as he sat at a table writing the
ship's log. As the novel imagines the point of death, "the hand that
held the pen had dropped into the writer's lap. The left hand still lay
on the table" (*Poor Miss Finch*, 426). Ruskin takes this to mean that
the icy hands have actually "dropped off" Nigel's wrists and fallen on
the table and suggests that a brain malady—Wilkie's—is the source of
this scene: "The reader who cares to seek it may easily find medical
evidence of the physical effects of certain states of brain disease in

producing [such] images of truncated and Hermes-like deformity, complicated with grossness."[47]

Most twentieth-century critics reiterate Ruskin's conviction that variant bodies in fiction come from disorder or variance in the bodies of authors. Robert Ashley, for example, comments that "Where Collins got the idea for a deaf-mute heroine is conjectural," then closes the door on conjecture by stating that Collins "had the chronic invalid's morbid fascination for mental and physical deformities."[48] While Sue Lonoff's readings of Collins's disabled characters are exceptionally astute and well developed, she answers the question of why he created them with a similarly limited emphasis on Collins's own body, saying simply that his "interest in such topics is certainly rooted in his personal history"; Catherine Peters also posits Collins's own body as the "trigger" for his "fascination with physical disabilities and their effect on the psyche."[49] The criticism's cumulative implication is that there can be no "normal" reason to produce fiction about characters with nonnormative bodies, especially narratives that place those characters in normative realms such as courtship, marriage, and parenthood.

All these critical responses indicate a vague discomfort with "different" bodies and in particular with stories that place those different bodies in sexual and reproductive situations rather than making them the stuff of "bright impressions and graceful fancies."[50] What the larger picture I have sketched here should suggest, however, is that this discomfort has a history; it is not self-evident, but was at different pressure points in the history of social relationships and scientific knowledge reinvested with energy and strenuously refortified *as* something self-evident.

What was—and is—distressing about the merging of disability and sexuality bears much more exploration. We still have few stories in which people with disabilities have sexual and reproductive relationships, especially with nondisabled people, suggesting that whatever was disturbing about *Poor Miss Finch* may still be disturbing today.

Notes

1. For a discussion of Stanislavski's work with the play, see Elizabeth Reynolds Hapgood, "Two Orphans in Moscow," *Theatre Arts* (Oct. 1950): 31–35.
2. See Martin Norden's excellent discussion of *Les Deux Orphelines'* film history, which includes all but the Rollins film, in *The Cinema of Isolation: A History of Physical Disability in the Movies* (New Brunswick: Rutgers Univ.

Press, 1994), 36–37, 86, 134. The book integrates a disability studies perspective into a rich, thorough, and readable history of narrative cinema.

3. While twentieth-century literature and film have occasionally figured blind women as sexual objects or as wives, they have almost always concurrently constructed them in the middle of macabre novels such as Susan Sontag's *Death Kit* and crime thrillers *Wait Until Dark, Jennifer 8,* and *Blink,* overdetermining blindness (and, by implication, disability itself) as that which sets one apart from the worlds of "normal" human activities and relationships. From a desexualizing and pathologizing force, disability is readily reframed as an exoticizing force. For further discussion, see Deborah Kent, "In Search of a Heroine: Images of Women with Disabilities in Fiction and Drama," in *Women with Disabilities: Essays in Psychology, Culture, and Politics,* ed. Michelle Fine and Adrienne Asch (Philadelphia: Temple Univ. Press, 1988), 90–110, and Georgina Kleege, *Sight Unseen* (New Haven and London: Yale Univ. Press, 1999).

4. Consider, for example, Dickens's *The Old Curiosity Shop* (The Marchioness), *Our Mutual Friend* (Jenny Wren), *The Cricket on the Hearth* (Bertha Plummer), "Doctor Marigold" (Sophy Marigold), and "Mugby Junction" (Phoebe); Gaskell's "The Well at Pen-Morfa" (Nest Gwynn); Bulwer-Lytton's *The Last Days of Pompeii* (Nydia); Hall Caine's *The Scapegoat* (Naomi); Dinah Craik's *Olive* (Olive Rothesay); and Charlotte Yonge's *The Pillars of the House* (Geraldine Underwood) and *The Clever Woman of the Family* (Ermine Williams).

5. The problematic Victorian binary (both for Victorians and for scholars who assume its validity) between "good" and "bad" women is no less slippery in regard to disabled women. Constructed as ineligible mothers and wives, they do not fit the normative category of good women; constructed as ineligible to be sexual objects/subjects, they do not fit as fallen women either. As such, they approximate the status of the "odd" woman best of all, a category that in itself points out how binaries ineffectively operate on a rational level (an insufficiency that only increases the longing with which binaries are regularly suffused, so desperate are we to have a simple way to organize human diversity and complex human relationships). Cindy LaCom's excellent discussion of the dividing of disabled women into sexless/sexually deviant references some significant exceptions; see "'It Is More than Lame': Female Disability, Sexuality, and the Maternal in the Nineteenth-Century Novel," in *The Body and Physical Difference: Discourses of Disability,* ed. David T. Mitchell and Sharon L. Snyder (Ann Arbor: Univ. of Michigan Press, 1997), 189–201. For a discussion of plots that formalize the attempt to binarize women by pairing a nondisabled woman with a disabled one, see my "The Twin Structure: Disabled Women in Courtship Plots," in *Disability Studies: Enabling the Humanities,* ed. Sharon L. Snyder, Brenda Jo Brueggemann, and Rosemarie Garland-Thomson (New York: MLA, 2002), 222–33. For a discussion of Victorian ideologies of femininity and

critique of twentieth-century scholarship on such binaries, see Elizabeth Langland, *Nobody's Angels: Middle-Class Women and Domestic Ideology in Victorian Culture* (Ithaca: Cornell Univ. Press, 1995). For a discussion of the function of disability in nineteenth-century melodrama, see Peter Brooks, *The Melodramatic Imagination: Balzac, Henry James, Melodrama, and the Mode of Excess* (New Haven: Yale Univ. Press, 1976) and Michael R. Booth, *English Melodrama* (London: Herbert Jenkins, 1965).

6. See especially Craik, and Yonge's *The Clever Woman of the Family* (1865). For a discussion of the power of social performances of "passionlessness" in the nineteenth century, see Nancy Cott, "Passionlessness: An Interpretation of Victorian Sexual Ideology, 1790–1850," in *Women and Health in America,* ed. Judith Walzer Leavitt (Madison: Univ. of Wisconsin Press, 1984), 57–69. The discreet emotional behavior of these disabled heroines parallels that of many nondisabled heroines in Victorian fiction, falling in at the bottom of the range of how emotionally expressive a heroine can be—especially toward men—without turning into a fallen or at least tragically unsuccessful woman. An example at the bottom of the range would be Agnes Wickfield; one at the top would be Jane Eyre. Examples of expressive women who come to tragic ends include Maggie Tulliver, Lucy Audley, and Lydia Gwilt. It should be noted that disabled women characters, because of their plot function as pathos-generators, can exhibit more emotionality than nondisabled ones, but that emotionality produces significant plot disequilibrium when it is directed at men, as in *The Cricket on the Hearth* and *The Last Days of Pompeii.* For further discussion, see chapter 2 of my *Fictions of Affliction: Physical Disability in Victorian Culture* (Ann Arbor: Univ. of Michigan Press, forthcoming).

7. Wilkie Collins, *Hide and Seek,* ed. Catherine Peters (Oxford: Oxford Univ. Press, 1993), 431. Hereafter cited in the text as *Hide and Seek.*

8. Wilkie Collins, *Basil,* ed. Dorothy Goldman (Oxford: Oxford Univ. Press, 1990), xxxv–xxxvi.

9. Booth, 70–71.

10. *Charity Organisation Reporter* (5 Jan. 1876): 1.

11. *An Historical Sketch of the Asylum for Indigent Deaf and Dumb Children, Surrey* (London: Edward Brewster, 1841), iv, xv.

12. See John Kitto, *The Lost Senses* (New York: Robert Carter and Brothers, 1852), 10–19.

13. My essay's purpose is to articulate the ways in which Collins expands the representational place of women with disabilities, not to evaluate the ethics or "positive/negative" social value of his narratives. Any righteously indignant twentieth-century reader, however, is well advised to read James Kincaid's *Child-Loving: The Erotic Child and Victorian Culture* (New York: Routledge, 1992). The discourse of the desirability

(if not necessarily sexualization) of disabled children and the charitable transaction did not originate with this novel and is arguably still an implicit thread in twentieth-century cultural representations of disability.

14. Kitto, 20.

15. The multiple contexts in which this scene is resonant include debates over sign language versus oralism, which would culminate in the 1880s with a resolution against Sign and Victorian gender ideologies. See Elisabeth G. Gitter, "Deaf-Mutes and Heroines in the Victorian Era," *Victorian Literature and Culture* 20 (1992): 179–96, for an excellent discussion of *Hide and Seek* with reference to these issues. See Lillian Nayder, *Wilkie Collins* (New York: Twayne Publishers, 1997), 42–52, for a fascinating discussion of Collins's use of Madonna's deafness and Lavinia's spinal infirmity to critique and challenge (through their transgressive elements) repressive ideals of femininity. Nayder's idea that Collins simultaneously normalizes deafness and pathologizes normative feminine lives is particularly interesting. See Douglas C. Baynton, *Forbidden Signs: American Culture and the Campaign against Sign Language* (Chicago: Univ. of Chicago Press, 1996) for a more developed history of oralism.

16. For art used as a framing device in nineteenth-century literature, and the dangers to heroines who step outside the frame, see Helena Michie, *The Flesh Made Word: Female Figures and Women's Bodies* (New York and Oxford: Oxford Univ. Press, 1987), 79–123.

17. For a discussion of the blush, see Mary Ann O'Farrell, *Telling Complexions: The Nineteenth-Century English Novel and the Blush* (Durham: Duke Univ. Press, 1997).

18. Disabled characters "twin" and threaten to upstage both the hero and heroine of *The Moonstone*. Ezra Jennings, the chronically ill, opium-addicted physician's assistant with a troubled past, is drawn with much more interest and subtlety than Franklin Blake. Like Rosanna, he is central to the forward motion of the plot, amply represented in the text by his first-person writings and acquires a longevity in the imagination that the "major" characters never do, despite the fact that he is sacrificed to their happiness. *The Moonstone*'s use of the twin structure is essentially subversive. I am indebted to Heather Haugen, a student in my "Special Topics: Detective Fiction" course at the University of Colorado in 1992, for her observations about these characters.

19. *Dead Secrets: Wilkie Collins and the Female Gothic* (New Haven: Yale Univ. Press, 1992), 2.

20. Donna Haraway, "A Manifesto for Cyborgs," *Socialist Review* 80 (1986): 65–107. Another disabled woman, Rosanna's friend Limping Lucy, continues her role of conduit of passion and anger after Rosanna's death. Heller reads both characters as figures for womanly rebellion (48). They also form a dyad of differently embodied women whose intimacy acquires

an air of "dangerous" passion, a sinister version of the sacralized bond between Madonna and Lavinia Blyth.

21. Wilkie Collins, *The Moonstone,* ed. John Sutherland (Oxford: Oxford Univ. Press, 1999), 324. Hereafter cited in the text as *The Moonstone.*

22. Catherine Peters, *The King of Inventors: A Life of Wilkie Collins* (Princeton: Princeton Univ. Press, 1991), 310.

23. Wilkie Collins, *Poor Miss Finch,* ed. Catherine Peters (Oxford: Oxford Univ. Press, 1995), xxxiii. Hereafter cited in the text as *Poor Miss Finch.*

24. For useful discussions of sexuality, vision, and blindness with reference to film, see Norden; Linda Williams, "When the Woman Looks," in *Re-vision: Essays in Feminist Film Criticism,* ed. Mary Ann Doane, Pat Mellencamp, and Linda Williams (Frederick, Md.: University Publications of America and the American Film Institute, 1984), 83–99; and Mary Ann Doane, "The Clinical Eye: Medical Discourses in the 'Woman's Film' of the 1940s," in *The Female Body in Western Culture,* ed. Susan Rubin Suleiman (Cambridge: Harvard Univ. Press, 1985), 152–74.

25. William R. Paulson, *Enlightenment, Romanticism, and the Blind in France* (Princeton: Princeton Univ. Press, 1987), 73.

26. Paulson, 82.

27. Kari Weil discusses a relevant erotic context of equestrienne perform-ances in her "Purebreds and Amazons: Saying Things with Horses in Late-Nineteenth-Century France," *Differences* 11 (1999): 1–37.

28. See Elizabeth Helsinger, Robin L. Sheets, and William Veeder, *The Woman Question: Society and Literature in Britain and America 1837–1883* (New York: Garland Publishing, 1983), 3:169–70.

29. For a discussion of disabled women's complex relationship to stereotyp-ical feminine roles, see Adrienne Asch and Michelle Fine, "Introduction: Beyond Pedestals," in Fine and Asch, 1–37. The degree to which Oscar's disability/ies somehow qualifies the extent to which Lucilla's marriage is normalized is worth pursuing. Is this marriage simply a parallel to the (odd) match between Jenny Wren and Sloppy at the close of *Our Mutual Friend,* or between two deaf people in "Doctor Marigold"? The treat-ment of Lucilla's marriage, however, seems normalized, as opposed to the preciousness of the other bonds.

30. Evelyn Hunt, "The Cry of the Unborn," qtd. in Mary Spongberg, *Femin-izing Venereal Disease: The Body of the Prostitute in Nineteenth-Century Medical Discourse* (London: Macmillan, 1997), 161.

31. Erwin H. Ackerknecht, *A Short History of Medicine* (New York: Ronald Press Co., 1955), 162.

32. "Diseases of the Eye Produced by Impure Air," *Lancet* (25 Mar. 1848): 343.

33. See Christopher Hamlin, "Predisposing Causes and Public Health in Early Nineteenth-Century Medical Thought," *Social History of Medicine* 5 (Apr.

1992): 43–70, for an excellent discussion of the complex rhetorics and social dynamics of contagionist-anticontagionist debates. See Erwin H. Ackerknecht, "Anticontagionism Between 1821 and 1867," *Bulletin of the History of Medicine* 22 (1948): 569–93, for the germinal essay on this subject. See Elizabeth Lomax, "Hereditary or Acquired Disease? Early Nineteenth Century Debates on the Cause of Infantile Scrofula and Tuberculosis," *Journal of the History of Medicine* 32 (1977): 356–74, for an excellent discussion of the mysterious scrofula. See Spongberg for an extensive and excellent discussion of Victorian theories of disease and heredity with reference to venereal disease.

34. W. Wright, "On the Causes and Treatment of Deafness, No. II," *Lancet* (9 July 1831): 464.

35. Charles Rosenberg, "The Bitter Fruit: Heredity, Disease, and Social Thought in Nineteenth-Century America," *Perspectives in American History* 8 (1974): 191.

36. Elizabeth Lomax, "Infantile Syphilis as an Example of Nineteenth Century Belief in the Inheritance of Acquired Characteristics," *Journal of the History of Medicine* 34 (1979): 24.

37. Henry Maudsley, "Galstonian Lecture II on the Relations between Body and Mind, and between Mental and Other Disorders of the Nervous System," *Lancet* (30 Apr. 1870): 609–10.

38. "Intermarriage and Its Results," *London Lancet* 1 (1864): 69. According to E. J. Lidbetter, time would enact no significant erosion of the fears associated with "defective" persons reproducing: "not only does like produce like, as we should expect, but . . . there is some subtle and unexplained attraction of like for like in marriage and parenthood among the various forms of defectives. . . . Feeble-minded inter-marry with the feeble-minded; tubercular stocks inter-marry; whilst the mildly incompetent people in a wider, more general way show the same tendency, but show also bad patches where they inter-marry with the more definitely defective." See E. J. Lidbetter, "The Social Problem Group: As Illustrated by a Series of East London Pedigrees," *Eugenics Review* 24 (1932): 7–13.

39. Spongberg, 5.

40. Ibid., 6.

41. Ibid., 14.

42. Ibid., 169.

43. Review of *Poor Miss Finch,* by Wilkie Collins, *The Saturday Review* 33 (2 Mar. 1872): 282–83. Hereafter cited as *The Saturday Review.*

44. Review of *Poor Miss Finch,* by Wilkie Collins, *The Nation* 14 (7 Mar. 1872): 158–59.

45. John Ruskin, "Fiction Fair and Foul–I," in *The Works of John Ruskin, Library Edition,* ed. E. T. Cooke and Alexander Wedderburn (London: George Allen, 1908), 34:276–79.

46. Ibid., 277.

47. Ibid., 278–79.

48. Robert P. Ashley, *Wilkie Collins* (London: Barker, 1952), 37.

49. See Sue Lonoff, *Wilkie Collins and His Victorian Readers: A Study in the Rhetoric of Authorship* (New York: AMS Press, 1982), 158–59; and Peters, 142.

50. *The Saturday Review*, 282–83.

References

Ackerknecht, Erwin H. "Anticontagionism Between 1821 and 1867." *Bulletin of the History of Medicine* 22 (1948): 569–93.

———. *A Short History of Medicine.* New York: Ronald Press Co., 1955.

Ashley, Robert P. *Wilkie Collins.* London: Barker, 1952.

Baynton, Douglas C. *Forbidden Signs: American Culture and the Campaign against Sign Language.* Chicago: Univ. of Chicago Press, 1996.

Booth, Michael R. *English Melodrama.* London: Herbert Jenkins, 1965.

Brooks, Peter. *The Melodramatic Imagination: Balzac, Henry James, Melodrama, and the Mode of Excess.* New Haven: Yale Univ. Press, 1976.

Browne, Susan, Debra Connors, and Nanci Stern, eds. *With the Power of Each Breath: A Disabled Women's Anthology.* San Francisco: Cleis Press, 1985.

Charity Organisation Reporter, 5 Jan. 1876, 1.

Collins, Wilkie. *Basil.* Ed. Dorothy Goldman. Oxford: Oxford Univ. Press, 1990.

———. *Hide and Seek.* Ed. Catherine Peters. Oxford: Oxford Univ. Press, 1993.

———. *The Moonstone.* Ed. John Sutherland. Oxford: Oxford Univ. Press, 1999.

———. *Poor Miss Finch.* Ed. Catherine Peters. Oxford: Oxford Univ. Press, 1995.

Cott, Nancy. "Passionlessness: An Interpretation of Victorian Sexual Ideology, 1790–1850." In *Women and Health in America*, ed. Judith Walzer Leavitt, 57–69. Madison: Univ. of Wisconsin Press, 1984.

"Diseases of the Eye Produced by Impure Air." *Lancet,* 25 Mar. 1848, 343.

Doane, Mary Ann. "The Clinical Eye: Medical Discourses in the 'Woman's Film' of the 1940s." In *The Female Body in Western Culture*, ed. Susan Rubin Suleiman, 152–74. Cambridge: Harvard Univ. Press, 1985.

Fine, Michelle, and Adrienne Asch, eds. *Women with Disabilities: Essays in Psychology, Culture, and Politics.* Philadelphia: Temple Univ. Press, 1988.

Gitter, Elisabeth G. "Deaf-Mutes and Heroines in the Victorian Era." *Victorian Literature and Culture* 20 (1992): 179–96.

Hamlin, Christopher. "Predisposing Causes and Public Health in Early Nineteenth-Century Medical Thought." *Social History of Medicine* 4 (Apr. 1992): 43–70.

Hapgood, Elizabeth Reynolds. "Two Orphans in Moscow." *Theater Arts* (Oct. 1950): 31–35.

Haraway, Donna. "A Manifesto for Cyborgs." *Socialist Review* 80 (1986): 65–107.

Heller, Tamar. *Dead Secrets: Wilkie Collins and the Female Gothic*. New Haven: Yale Univ. Press, 1992.

Helsinger, Elizabeth, Robin L. Sheets, and William Veeder. *The Woman Question: Society and Literature in Britain and America 1837–1883*. 3 vols. New York: Garland Publishing, 1983.

An Historical Sketch of the Asylum for Indigent Deaf and Dumb Children, Surrey. London: Edward Brewster, 1841.

Holmes, Martha Stoddard. *Fictions of Affliction: Physical Disability in Victorian Culture*. Ann Arbor: Univ. of Michigan Press, forthcoming.

———. "The Twin Structure: A Disability Studies Approach to Canonic Victorian Literature." In *Disability Studies: Enabling the Humanities*, ed. Sharon L. Snyder, Brenda Jo Brueggemann, and Rosemarie Garland-Thomson (New York: MLA, 2002), 222–33

"Intermarriage and Its Results." *London Lancet* 1 (1864): 69.

Kincaid, James. *Child-Loving: The Erotic Child and Victorian Culture*. New York: Routledge, 1992.

Kitto, John. *The Lost Senses*. 1845. New York: Robert Carter and Brothers, 1852.

Kleege, Georgina. *Sight Unseen*. New Haven and London: Yale Univ. Press, 1999.

LaCom, Cindy. "'It is More than Lame': Female Disability, Sexuality, and the Maternal in the Nineteenth-Century Novel." In *The Body and Physical Difference: Discourses of Disability*, ed. David T. Mitchell and Sharon L. Snyder, 189–201. Ann Arbor: Univ. of Michigan Press, 1997.

Langland, Elizabeth. *Nobody's Angels: Middle-Class Women and Domestic Ideology in Victorian Culture*. Ithaca: Cornell Univ. Press, 1995.

Lidbetter, E. J. "The Social Problem Group: As Illustrated by a Series of East London Pedigrees." *Eugenics Review* 24 (1932): 7–13.

Lomax, Elizabeth. "Hereditary or Acquired Disease? Early Nineteenth Century Debates on the Cause of Infantile Scrofula and Tuberculosis." *Journal of the History of Medicine* 32 (1977): 356–74.

———. "Infantile Syphilis as an Example of Nineteenth Century Belief in the Inheritance of Acquired Characteristics." *Journal of the History of Medicine* 34 (1979): 356–74.

Lonoff, Sue. *Wilkie Collins and His Victorian Readers: A Study in the Rhetoric of Authorship*. New York: AMS Press, 1982.

Maudsley, Henry. "Galstonian Lecture II on the Relations Between Body and Mind, and Between Mental and other Disorders of the Nervous System." *Lancet*, 30 Apr. 1870, 609–10.

Michie, Helena. *The Flesh Made Word: Female Figures and Women's Bodies*. New York and Oxford: Oxford Univ. Press, 1987.

Nayder, Lillian. *Wilkie Collins*. New York: Twayne Publishers, 1997.

Norden, Martin. *The Cinema of Isolation: A History of Physical Disability in the Movies*. New Brunswick: Rutgers Univ. Press, 1994.

O'Farrell, Mary Ann. *Telling Complexions: The Nineteenth-Century English Novel and the Blush*. Durham: Duke Univ. Press, 1997.

Paulson, William R. *Enlightenment, Romanticism, and the Blind in France*. Princeton: Princeton Univ. Press, 1987.

Peters, Catherine. *The King of Inventors: A Life of Wilkie Collins*. Princeton: Princeton Univ. Press, 1991.

Review of *Poor Miss Finch*, by Wilkie Collins. *The Nation* 14 (7 Mar. 1872): 159.

Review of *Poor Miss Finch*, by Wilkie Collins. *The Saturday Review* 33 (2 Mar. 1872): 282–83.

Rosenberg, Charles. "The Bitter Fruit: Heredity, Disease, and Social Thought in Nineteenth-Century America." *Perspectives in American History* 8 (1974): 189–235.

Ruskin, John. *The Works of John Ruskin, Library Edition*. Ed. E. T. Cooke and Alexander Wedderburn. London: George Allen, 1903–12.

Spongberg, Mary. *Feminizing Venereal Disease: The Body of the Prostitute in Nineteenth-Century Medical Discourse*. London: Macmillan, 1997.

Weil, Kari. "Purebreds and Amazons: Saying Things with Horses in Late-Nineteenth-Century France." *Differences* 11 (1999): 1–37.

Williams, Linda. "When the Woman Looks." In *Re-vision: Essays in Feminist Film Criticism*, ed. Mary Anne Doane, Pat Mellencamp, and Linda Williams, 83–99. Frederick, MD: Univ. Publications of America and the American Film Institute, 1984.

Wright, W. "On the Causes and Treatment of Deafness, No. II." *Lancet*, 9 July 1831, 464–66.

Chemical Seductions

Exoticism, Toxicology, and the Female Poisoner in *Armadale* and *The Legacy of Cain*

Piya Pal-Lapinski

[T]he Orientals are not content, like Mithridates, to make a shield of poison, but also use it as a dagger. In their hands, this science becomes not only a defensive weapon but often an offensive one. The one serves to protect them against physical suffering, the other against their enemies. With opium, belladonna, strychnine, bois de couleuvre or cherry-laurel, they put to sleep those who would rouse them. There is not one of those Egyptian, Turkish or Greek women whom you call here wise women . . . who does not know enough of chemistry to astound a doctor. . . . This is how the secret dramas of the Orient are woven and unwoven.

—Alexandre Dumas
The Count of Monte Cristo, 1844

"Armadale" . . . gives us for its heroine a woman fouler than the refuse of the streets, who has lived to the ripe age of thirty five, and through the horrors of forgery, murder, theft, bigamy, gaol and attempted suicide, without any trace being left on her beauty.

—Review of *Armadale* in *The Spectator,* 1866

I N NINETEENTH-CENTURY BRITAIN AND FRANCE, TOXICOLOGY (THE STUDY OF POISONS) WAS BOTH AN EMERGING DISCOURSE in the field of forensic medicine as well as a seductive strategy for women seeking some element of control over their own lives. Throughout the century, both male and female poisoners baffled forensic toxicologists as they struggled to perfect techniques of poison detection and identification. In fact, Victorian England exploded with one "sensational" poison trial after another—the most famous being those of Madeleine Smith (1857), Dr. William Palmer (1856), Dr. George Lamson (1882), Dr. Thomas Smethurst (1859), and Florence Maybrick (1889)—while in France, the case of Marie Lafarge (1840) revealed the instability and precariousness of forensic toxicology as a criminological procedure.[1]

The indeterminacy of poison, its ability to transform itself, continually evaded and frustrated scientific categories. Readily available, it was used for medicinal, cosmetic, and even aphrodisiacal purposes. Its presence in the fabric of everyday life made it simultaneously insidious, attractive, and dangerous. Poison, in fact, became a social obsession and an art; as a cultural trope, it signified various kinds of border crossings—especially racial "otherness." With its deviousness, "femininity," and tropical contagions, the Orient—or even locations that made up the "near exotic," such as Italy—was the ultimate source of the most beguiling and deadly poisons. In Alexandre Dumas's novel *The Count of Monte Cristo* (1844), the Orientalized hero, Edmond Dantes, discusses the subtleties of the art of toxicology with a female serial poisoner, Madame de Villefort. According to Dantes, the most successful and artistic cases of poisoning are to be found outside France, in "Aleppo or Cairo, or even no further than Naples or Rome," where one can see "people walking along the street, upright, fresh-faced and ruddy with health, of whom the devil, were he to touch you with his cloak, could tell you: 'This man has been poisoned for three weeks and he will be completely dead in a month.'"[2] Poison and poisoners were repeatedly figured in terms of the exotic—Cleopatra was one of the most compelling prototypes of the female poisoner in the nineteenth century, particularly in the French Orientalist tradition. Works such as Alexandre Cabanel's painting *Cleopatra Testing Poisons on Condemned Men* (1887) and Théophile Gautier's novella *Une Nuit de Cleopatre* (1838) constructed the Egyptian queen's sexual and political power through her use of exotic poisons. The myth of the poison damsel (a woman fed on poison and used as a sexual weapon) was available to Orientalist scholars; ethnological texts imagined that racial mixing resulted in "poisoned" or contaminated blood.

The threat of miscegenation, as the gap between "home" and the colonies narrowed, provided a potent metaphor for the infusion of "poison" in the blood. Yet because of the fluid nature of poison, its propensity to invade, dissolve, and be absorbed without a trace, this "otherness" was never absolute. Poison inscribed the bodies of both poisoner and victim with a dangerous sense of hybridity; representations of the body of the female poisoner (in fictional, historical, and medico-legal discourses) mapped out a complex exoticism by which the very architecture of ethnological categories was called into question. I use the term *hybridity* here and throughout this essay in the context of Homi Bhabha's formulation: for Bhabha, hybridity "intervenes in the exercise of authority not merely to indicate the impossibility of its identity but to represent the unpredictability of its presence."[3] Bhabha further defines hybridity as "a process of splitting as the condition of subjection: a discrimination between the mother culture and its bastards, the self and its doubles, where the trace of what is disavowed is not repressed but repeated as something *different*—a mutation, a hybrid. It is such a partial and double force that is more than the mimetic but less than the symbolic, that disturbs the visibility of the colonial presence and makes the recognition of its authority problematic."[4]

Poison was, of course, one of the central preoccupations of Victorian sensation fiction. The lesser-known novels of Wilkie Collins in particular reflect a fascination with poison and with women who resort to poison to carry out their transgressive agendas. In Collins's work, the imperatives of criminology and imperialism/exoticism are seamlessly interwoven and foregrounded through the hybrid bodies of his female protagonists. Here I explore the ways in which Collins's sensational fiction reconstitutes (or reclaims) the links between poison and female agency in mid- to late-Victorian medical and ethnological discourses by looking at two novels: *Armadale* (1866) and *The Legacy of Cain* (1888). Although several of Collins's novels link women and poison, such as *Jezebel's Daughter* (1880) and *The Law and the Lady* (1874), I focus on *Armadale* and *The Legacy of Cain* because of their preoccupation with the ways in which the female poisoner's hybrid body insinuates itself within and challenges discourses of exoticism, empire, and ethnology.

In the colonies, tropical medicine battled what Charlotte Brontë called the "poisoned exhalations of the East,"[5] while at home, outbreaks of "domestic poisonings" in which women poisoned their husbands and lovers periodically occurred. Arsenic, which was used for women's cosmetics, also lurked on the surface of the female body. The notorious Madeleine Smith used the arsenic she regularly purchased for her complexion to murder her unsuspecting lover. Such cases opened up equivocal spaces that enabled Collins to position female acts of poisoning within a politics of transgression and resistance. *Armadale* introduces us to the seductive and resourceful Lydia Gwilt, who, driven by her desire for property and revenge, stages an elaborate poison-plot, while *The Legacy of Cain* uses its dual female protagonists (one of whom, unknown to the reader, is the daughter of a murderess) to investigate issues of heredity and eugenics. In order to fully grasp the implications of Collins's intervention in Victorian cultural narratives of poison, it is necessary to briefly analyze those toxicological discourses with which Collins would have been familiar, both through reading and other encounters.[6]

Victorian Toxicology and the Nature of Poison

The midcentury's leading toxicologist, Dr. Alfred Swaine Taylor, attempted to define the nature, action, and absorption of poisons in his authoritative work, *Poisons in Relation to Medical Jurisprudence and Medicine* (1848). Professor of medical jurisprudence at Guy's Hospital, London, until 1877, Taylor was called in repeatedly as a forensic expert in many criminal trials, including the high-profile poisoning case of William Palmer. Copies of Taylor were in Collins's library, so Collins probably had access to Taylor's work while he was writing *Armadale* and used it to construct the spectacular poison gas episode at the end of the novel in which Lydia Gwilt attempts to poison Allan Armadale with carbonic acid.[7] Taylor begins his text by commenting on the difficulty of arriving at a precise definition of the term *poison* and of distinguishing poisonous from nonpoisonous substances. He warns medical witnesses to avoid the "common" definition:

> A poison is commonly defined to be a substance which, when administered in small quantity, is capable of acting deleteriously on the body. It is obvious that this definition is too restricted for the purposes of medical jurisprudence. It would, if admitted, exclude a very large class of substances, the poisonous properties of which cannot be disputed; as, for example, the salts of lead, copper, tin, zinc and antimony, which are only poisonous when administered in very large doses. . . . Each substance must be regarded as a poison, differing from the other only in its degree of activity and perhaps in its mode of operation.[8]

Taylor goes on to cite cases of death by ingestion of common substances such as salt, sulfate of magnesia (Epsom salts), or even cold water "swallowed in a large quantity, and in an excited state of the system."[9] He repeatedly testifies to the elusive nature of the action of poisons on the body; arsenic, for instance, is particularly confusing in this respect. The signs of inflammation of the stomach from arsenic poisoning might be misleading. Taylor does "not find that the degree of inflammation is in proportion to the quantity of the poison taken; sometimes it is extensive under a small dose, and at others scarcely apparent under a large dose." According to Taylor, although arsenic sometimes does not produce any *local* action (a change in the part of the body with which the poison comes into contact), it operates stealthily by *remote* action ("that power which most poisons possess of affecting an organ remote from the part to which they are applied"). This is also the case with poisons such as "large doses of hydrocyanic acid or strychnia," which "kill with great rapidity, without producing any perceptible local changes."[10] Another subversive effect of poison on the body is absorption into the bloodstream: Taylor concludes that "most if not all poisons can, sooner or later, enter into, and circulate with the blood."[11] Yet, the effect or "operation" of the poison after absorption by the system mystified toxicologists:

Admitting that every poison entered into the blood, and could be chemically detected in this fluid, it would yet remain to be explained *how* it operated when there, to destroy life. At present there is no satisfactory theory to account for the fatal effect. . . . [I]t may be expected that in the progress of microscopical research, the precise effect produced by poisons on the blood will hereafter become a subject of demonstration; but, at present, the *modus operandi* is a perfect mystery. We trace the poison to the circulation, and we observe that death is the result; but neither the chemist nor the microscopist can throw the least light upon the changes produced by the poison in the blood or in the organs necessary to life.[12]

The action of poison therefore remained invisible, covert, and resistant to easy classification.

Arsenic, for instance, turned up everywhere. Since traces of arsenic were found in the bodies of those who had died of natural causes, the foremost toxicologist in France, Matthew Orfila, became concerned that if the earth contained arsenic as well, graveyard seepage would make the testing of exhumed bodies for arsenic poisoning extremely problematic. The landmark French trial of Marie Lafarge in 1840 provided a forum for highlighting the opacity at the heart of these forensic controversies.[13] Marie was accused of systematically and ruthlessly poisoning her husband, Charles Lafarge, by lacing his food with arsenic. The complex ramifications of the case and its relations to class and sexuality emerge in her own memoir, which was published and translated into English in 1841.[14] Matthew Orfila was called in to prove the presence of arsenic in the body of Lafarge. By using the new apparatus developed by the English chemist James Marsh, Orfila demonstrated the existence of an arsenic deposit. However, Orfila also claimed that the sensitivity of the apparatus could produce conflicting results. In other cases in England, the Marsh test was not always reliable in detecting arsenic in suspicious circumstances. The new Reinsch test for arsenic, introduced in 1841, proved to be equally contradictory.[15] Testifying at the trial of Thomas Smethurst (who allegedly poisoned his wife by arsenic in 1859), Taylor admitted that his tests (by the Reinsch method) might have been contaminated.[16] Smethurst was convicted but ultimately pardoned owing to lack of conclusive evidence. Despite scientific advances in the detection of chemical substances, poison continued to veil itself from the clinical gaze, allowing the poisoner powers of infiltration, invasion, and inscription. According to Taylor and Orfila, the power of poison was (hidden) in the amount absorbed, and not in that which was clearly visible in the digestive organs: "It has been truly remarked by Orfila, in regard to arsenic, and it equally applies to all poisons, that that portion which is found in the stomach *is not that which has caused death;* but the *surplus* of the quantity which has produced fatal effects by its absorption into the system."[17]

Poison and Exoticism

In 1837–38, there were 527 deaths by poisoning in England and Wales, with opium and arsenic topping the list. In 1863–67 (the period during which Collins wrote and published *Armadale*), there were more than 2,000 deaths from poison, with opium and its various derivatives accounting for 482.[18] According to Taylor, "there is no form of poisoning so frequent as that by opium and its various preparations."[19] Opium was a pervasive and subtle "poison" masquerading as medicine and recreation—an indisputable part of the fabric of daily life in Victorian England, widely available before the Pharmacy Act of 1868, despite the fact that Robert Christison's pioneering treatise on toxicology in 1829 had classified opium and its derivatives as a "narcotic poison."[20] In 1837–38, opium and its derivatives headed the statistics on poison deaths in the *Lancet* and the *Medical Gazette.*[21] Increasing doses of laudanum (an opium derivative) caused children to become "pale and wan, with a peculiar sharpness of feature," and eventually to "waste away." Habitual opium use or "chronic poisoning by opium" could cause "numbness of the limbs, coldness of the feet, inability to walk far without aching pains . . . and a general sense of lassitude,"[22] and sometimes even death. Yet of all poisons, the status of opium was the most ambivalent, the most hybrid; its seductive uses combined pleasure, languor, and death.

Moreover, opium also signified a kind of racial or cultural "poisoning." Opium smoking was invariably associated—visually and architecturally—with the exoticized interior of the seraglio. French Orientalist paintings that English audiences may have been familiar with, such as Lecomte Du Nouÿ's *L'Esclave Blanche* (*The White Slave,* 1888) and Jean-Léon Gérôme's portraits of the Turkish bath, depicted *hybridized,* white female bodies luxuriating in an atmosphere saturated with the languor induced by opium.[23] Although these bodies were always distinguished from those of black slaves (male or female), their positioning within the harem marked them as racially hybrid. The gradually enveloping languor (a key feature of the visual representations of odalisques, or harem women) was central to the opium experience. Aptly, Taylor noted that the initial symptoms of large doses of opium or its tincture included "giddiness, drowsiness and stupor."[24]

Collins gradually became addicted to laudanum while taking it for his agonizing attacks of gout.[25] In a letter to Charles Kent, he described the effect of laudanum as having a "two fold action on the brain and nervous system—a stimulating and sedative action."[26] Years earlier he had written to Elizabeth Benzon: "My doctor is trying to break me of the habit of drinking laudanum. I am stabbed every night at ten with a sharp-pointed syringe which injects morphia under my skin—and gets me a night's rest without any of the drawbacks of taking opium internally."[27]

Ingesting "poisons" such as arsenic and opium and, in the process, building up a systemic tolerance was evocative not only of the East but also of places on the border between the Orient and the Occident, such as Eastern Europe (parts of which were under the Ottoman regime until the late nineteenth century). In a later edition of *Poisons* published in 1875, Taylor referred to the legendary practice of arsenic-eating in that region: "It is stated that in certain parts of Styria and Hungary, there are human beings who have so accustomed themselves to the use of arsenic, as to be able to take this substance not only without the usual symptoms of poisoning, but with actual benefit to health. This subject would hardly require serious notice . . . but that it has already formed part of the medical evidence in some criminal trials for poisoning."[28] Despite Taylor's assertion that "[t]here is no reason to believe that arsenic-eating is practiced in this country,"[29] there were at least two celebrated poison trials in which the slow, voluntary ingestion of arsenic was cited as evidence for the defense. Madeleine Smith, tried for poisoning her lover Emile L'Angelier in 1857, claimed that she had applied arsenic to her "face, neck, and arms, diluted with water"—to beautify her complexion. Significantly, she mentioned that she "had been advised to the use of arsenic" by "the daughter of an actress." Similarly, when Florence Maybrick was accused of murdering her husband in 1889, the defense attempted to provide evidence of James Maybrick's "arsenic habit." The testimony of the druggist at the Maybrick trial suggested that "arsenic-laced tonics" were popular with gentlemen for their supposed ability to improve sexual performance.[30]

Victorian historiography often associated a desire for political power and an unnatural sexual appetite with female poisoners. Gaetano Donizetti's popular opera *Lucrezia Borgia* (based on Victor Hugo's play *Lucrèce Borgia*), was performed in London between 1839 and 1888. As an opera fan, Collins was familiar with it.[31] Initially, the opera attempts to "normalize" Lucrezia by focusing on her relationship with her son, Gennaro, although their exchanges are charged with erotic overtones. In the final act of the opera, Lucrezia poisons her enemies (including her son) at a sumptuous banquet. The German historian Ferdinand Gregorovius announced his intention to "rehabilitate the honor of the unfortunate woman" and "to clear up the Lucretia legend" in the introduction to his book *Lucrezia Borgia, According to Original Documents and Correspondence of Her Day* (1874).[32] Accusing Hugo and Donizetti of having transformed Lucrezia into "the type of all feminine depravity," Gregorovius set out to present her as "amiable, gentle, thoughtless, and unfortunate"—a victim, lacking agency.[33] Yet, for Victorian women writers, the myth of Lucrezia the poisoner was essentially a transgressive one. George Eliot drew on this myth in her portrayal of her enigmatic, cryptic female poisoner Bertha in *The Lifted Veil* (1859). In Eliot's text, the feminized hero is mesmerized by Lucrezia Borgia's portrait: "This morning I had been looking at Giorgione's picture of the cruel eyed woman, said to be a likeness of Lucrezia Borgia. I had stood alone before it, fascinated by the terrible reality of that cunning, relentless face, till I felt a strange poisoned sensation, as if I had long been inhaling a fatal odour, and was just beginning to be conscious of its effects."[34]

The other two legendary women poisoners who dominated the landscape of Victorian historiography were the Marquise of Brinvilliers, convicted of poisoning in the France of Louis XIV, and Cleopatra. Marie Brinvilliers's glamorous, nefarious poisonings and her eventual torture and forced public confession at the scaffold became a historical fetish, generating biographies, novels, and visual representations, both in the seventeenth century and after. Witnessing her execution, the sympathetic Madame de Sévigné sensed the "infectiousness" of her crimes, which pervaded the very air of Paris: "Well, it's all over and done with, Brinvilliers is in the air. Her poor little body was thrown after the execution into a very big fire and the ashes to the winds, so that we shall breathe her, and through the communication of the subtle spirits we shall develop some poisoning urge which will astonish us all."[35]

Among the most shocking features of the case was her strategy of masquerading as a "nurse"—she would visit hospitals in order to test out her poisons on the sick. Her erotic appetite and her desire for economic independence and power were emphasized in a mid-Victorian novel by Albert Smith, entitled *The Marchioness of Brinvilliers* (1846). The Brinvilliers case was also noted as having set off a "poison epidemic" or the "Affair of the Poisons" in seventeenth-century France, in which various women, such as Catherine Deshayes (otherwise known as "La Voisin"), regularly resorted to poison and witchcraft. Several of these women, perceived as a threat to the state, were imprisoned and/or executed. The king's mistress, Athenais De Montespan, who "surrounded herself with a brilliant luxury" and was noted for her extravagance, was also involved, as was the dramatist Jean Racine.[36]

Exoticism, luxury, political authority, erotic power, and poison—all these converged in the body of Cleopatra. The French artist Cabanel, in his painting *Cleopatra Testing Poisons on Condemned Men* (1887), imagined the Egyptian queen as a languorous odalisque who nevertheless is in supreme control (fig. 4.1). Clinical and detached, Cleopatra uses men for her toxicological experiments. Her languor serves as a mask; her apparent passivity is a veil that conceals deliberation, force, and strength. The irreducible surface of her body becomes an enigma that destabilizes the observer's gaze, blocking attempts to decipher it. The painting can be seen as an extension of Théophile Gautier's *Une Nuit de Cleopatre* (1838), which casts the queen as imaginatively staging her own spectacles of excess, but never being consumed by them herself. She offers herself to the slave Meiamoun, who must pay for his erotic encounter by submitting to death by poison. As in the Lucrezia Borgia narrative, he is poisoned during a voluptuous banquet, the feverish Orientalism of which is visualized in hyperbolic detail by Gautier. However, this moment (in which the queen's body becomes ambivalently encoded as the perfect receptacle of imperial desire/erotic male fantasy and the signifier of absolute female power over the male body) also looks forward to her suicide, a powerful anti-imperialistic gesture that preserves her political and personal sovereignty. In response to the question "What signifies this corpse upon the pavement?" Cleopatra replies, "only a poison I was testing with the idea of using it upon myself should Augustus take me prisoner."[37] If we position the figure of the Victorian female poisoner in Collins's fiction against the background of these cultural narratives of exoticism, we can begin to understand the power and sense of agency created by her alliance with poison.

FIG. 4.1. A. Cabanel, *Cleopatra Testing Poisons on Condemned Prisoners*, 1887. Koninklijk Museum voor Schone Kunsten–Antwerpen (Belgie).

Race and the Female Poisoner in *Armadale*

When *Armadale* (1866) burst upon the Victorian literary scene, the novel was both topical and exciting. Collins had been "obsessed" with the novel for some time, as he mentioned in a letter: "the characters themselves were all marshaled in their places, before a line of 'Armadale' was written. And I knew the end two years ago in Rome, when I was recovering from a long illness."[38] The Victorian "sensations" and excessive pleasures and terrors of *Armadale* offer insight into an inextricable tangle of race, sexuality, power, and criminality that dominated the cultural life of the British Empire both at home and in the colonies. While *Armadale*'s heightened awareness of the complexity of the exotic subject allows for a more subtle engagement with issues of race than *The Moonstone,* its multilayered approach to these concerns must necessarily problematize any straightforward postcolonial reading of the text. At the core of the narrative is the seductive, resourceful, and tortured female poisoner, Lydia Gwilt—one of Collins's most transgressive figures and a character who horrified many contemporary critics.[39]

The novel also has as its focus the figure of the biracial, feminized male hysteric, Ozias Midwinter, whose relationship with the Anglo-Saxon, propertied Allan Armadale is mediated through Lydia. (This is further complicated by the fact that both men bear the name "Armadale"—a symptom of Collins's strange doubling of dark and light throughout the novel.) Lydia's sexual and intellectual desire for Midwinter coexists with her hatred of Allan Armadale. Her repeated attempts to poison him are assaults not only on his property (which Lydia hopes to claim through a complicated masquerade and a play on names), but also on his "Englishness"—a national identity that aggressively homogenizes dissident elements. I read Lydia's body as a racially hybrid one, which, through its use of poison and its existence on the margins of Victorian society, is driven to a radical dislocation of imperial and domestic authority. Exoticism and poison in *Armadale,* far from working to bolster ethnological stereotypes, become an integral part of Lydia's hybridity. This hybridity leads her to effect strategies through which she can stage her resistance.[40]

Armadale begins in the German spa town of Wildbad, with the deathbed confession of Ozias Midwinter's father, Allan Armadale (né Matthew Wrentmore), a West Indian proprietor. In this confession, the dying Armadale/Wrentmore reveals a fiendishly complicated history that threatens to haunt his son and future generations of Armadales.

By a twist of fate, Wrentmore had become possessor of the name and colonial estates of the disinherited Allan Armadale. In retaliation, Fergus Ingleby, the "real Armadale," had destroyed the prospects of a marriage between Wrentmore and Miss Blanchard, daughter of another West Indian colonial. While Wrentmore languished from an illness caused by "negro-poison," Ingleby/Armadale had assumed his identity, gained the affections of Miss Blanchard, and, assisted by the "wicked dexterity" of her "precocious" maid (Lydia Gwilt), had married her (*Armadale*, 31, 34). Thus, in one fell swoop, Armadale had deprived Wrentmore of the ideal colonial wife as well as an addition to his colonial property. Mad with rage, Wrentmore had murdered Armadale while investigating a shipwreck. Haunted forever by his criminal act, Wrentmore passes on his legacy of guilt to his biracial son, Ozias Midwinter (also named Allan Armadale, as Collins's enigmatic doubling continues). Meanwhile, the murdered Armadale's widow has given birth to a son whom she has also named "Allan Armadale."

From the beginning, the text represents the precariousness of mixed racial identities as well as the seductive "contagion" of those identities. Midwinter is nervous and dark and succumbs frequently to both languor and hysteria—in short, he is the perfect *male* odalisque. He inherits his exotic qualities from his Creole mother, the "other" Mrs. Armadale, whose marginalized presence hovers over Wrentmore's confession of loss and murder. Shut out from her husband's narrative, yet inescapably implicated in the burden of "contamination" that has been handed down from father to son, Mrs. Armadale represents that which Wrentmore has fallen into through his failure to make a suitable colonial marriage with the "fair" Miss Blanchard. Yet her exoticism is inscribed on her body in complex ways. Both her sexuality and her gaze are unsettling precisely *because* of their rejection of ethnological categories. She is described as "a woman of the mixed blood of the European and African race, with the northern delicacy in the shape of her face, and the southern richness in its colour—a woman in the prime of her beauty, who moved with an inbred grace, who looked with an inbred fascination, whose large languid black eyes rested on him" (*Armadale*, 21). *Armadale* continues to be haunted by the ghost of the biracial woman. Her "contagion" is passed on to her feminized son, Midwinter, with his "tawny complexion, his large bright brown eyes," his "dusky hands," and "foreign look" (*Armadale*, 60). A homeless wanderer, he suddenly invades the "stable" existences of the propertied Norfolk Armadales, making their Anglo-Saxon flesh "creep." As he recovers from "brain-fever," his "savage" otherness is immediately apparent to the rector, Mr. Brock: "his tawny, haggard cheeks . . . his tangled black beard; his long, supple, sinewy fingers, wasted by suffering, till they looked like claws. . . a nervous restlessness in his organization which appeared to pervade every fibre in his lean, lithe body. The rector's healthy Anglo-Saxon flesh crept responsively at every casual movement of the . . . supple brown fingers, and every passing distortion of the . . . haggard yellow face" (64). Fascinated by his exoticism, Allan Armadale befriends Midwinter, his namesake and alien double, precisely because he "wasn't like all the other fellows in the neighborhood." In contrast to Midwinter's darkness, Allan is blond, muscular, "noisy, rosy, light-haired, good-tempered" (66, 284), with all the attributes of the man of property and "perfect" English squire. In his relationship with Allan, Midwinter finds himself increasingly caught up in this process of domestication, which seeks to homogenize and manage the plurality of his nomadic identity, distancing him from his mixed heritage and his mother's "negro blood." It is this pattern of assimilation, initiated by the homosocial bonding between Allan and Midwinter, which is interrupted and utterly dislocated by the seductive Lydia Gwilt. Lydia eventually appears in Norfolk as a governess employed by Allan's tenants, the Milroys.

Lydia herself is repeatedly exoticized, but in ways which heighten her sense of agency and relate directly to her pursuit of power. Her connections with poison reinforce and intensify her carefully constructed strategies that aim to control her own and others' narratives. What makes her remarkable among Collins's heroines is not so much the successive masquerades and manipulations of her body (Magdalen Vanstone in *No Name* and Valeria Macallan in *The Law and the Lady* also use disguise to further their own ends), but rather a strange awareness of the seductiveness of hybridity that surfaces through her actions (the most important being her attempts to poison Allan Armadale) and erotic choices (such as Midwinter and the Cuban, Manuel). Both realize that they present threats to Allan Armadale's "Englishness"— but while Lydia revels in and exploits her exoticism, Midwinter suffers the perpetual burden of his mixed racial heritage.

Lydia's affinities with exoticism appear in her dress—on several occasions she is described as being dressed in "a thick black veil, . . . a black silk dress, and a red Paisley shawl" (105). Her use of the veil defies successive attempts to connect her with her past, frustrating Mr. Brock's attempts to identify her in order to protect Allan Armadale. For Lydia, the veil signifies the freedom to conceal and manipulate her identity, to block the detective's gaze. Female observers in the British

Orientalist tradition had noticed in their observations of Eastern women and the harem that the veil could be equivocal; a simultaneous marker of captivity and freedom.[41] The veil provided an inner space, a vantage point from which the "obliterated" female body, observing without being observed, might rethink the link between visibility and power.

Significantly, Lydia's frequent lapses into odalisquelike languor are tied to her love of music and laudanum. Both bring her "delicious oblivion." In moments of crisis, she soothes herself alternately with her "darling drops" of opium and Beethoven's "Moonlight Sonata." She admits to being a laudanum addict: "Who was the man who invented laudanum? I thank him from the bottom of my heart. . . . I have had six delicious hours of oblivion" (426–27).

Such bodily engagements with laudanum intensify Lydia's connections with the exotic Orient. Travelers and Orientalist historians emphasized the tenacious hold opium had on Oriental bodies. Colonial historian James Tod, in his well-known work on Northern India, *Annals and Antiquities of Rajasthan* (1829), gave several examples of this: from the use of poisoned shirts or robes as strategic weapons by the warrior classes of India to their eventual degeneration owing to excessive opium use. Others claimed that Indian children were given opium at an early age for its soothing properties, and female infanticide was effected by smearing the mother's nipple with "a fatal dose of opium."[42] Another facet of the Oriental poison myth, existing in a fascinating and unique relation to the female body—was the "poison-damsel," located in the shadowy contact zone between history and fantasy.

Orientalist scholarship invariably located poison-women within narratives of political violence and intrigue. Fed on poison from childhood, these women built up a tolerance and thus became immune to poison themselves. Used as weapons of war, they were apparently able to poison their victims through sexual intercourse or simply by mixing their bodily secretions, such as perspiration or saliva, together with that of their victim. Although her own agency was limited, the poison-woman was able to penetrate and dissolve the permeable boundaries of the male body while remaining impenetrable herself.[43] Therefore, the image of the female body in control of poison might be interpreted as undermining what Elizabeth Grosz, in her study *Volatile Bodies,* has called the "solidity" of male seminal fluids. Grosz theorizes that seminal fluid may be understood "primarily as what it makes, what it achieves, a causal agent and thus a thing, a solid: its fluidity, its potential seepage, the element in it that is uncontrollable, its spread, its formlessness, is perpetually displaced in discourse onto its properties, its capacity to fertilize, to father, to produce an object."[44] This "solidity" according to Grosz, is the result of a disavowal, a "refusal to acknowledge the effects of flows that move through various parts of the body," which make it more vulnerable, female, and hybrid.[45] Through the exchange of poisonous body fluids, the exotic poison-woman, whom the Orientalist scholar H. H. Wilson called the "messenger of certain death,"[46] compels the male body to acknowledge its own fluidity.

In complete control of her own sexuality, Lydia manages to construct it as simultaneously excessive, fraught, and restrained. In a telling scene with Midwinter, her aggressive yet subtle sexual power mocks the Victorian cult of domesticity by concealing itself under the "veil" of the fetishized domestic ritual of tea-drinking.[47] The original *Cornhill Magazine* illustration of this scene (fig. 4.2) communicates this tension effectively through its depiction of Lydia's hauntingly cold and detached facial expression. In the illustration, her hair (signifying her energy and sexuality throughout the novel) is also tightly braided and "domesticated." Midwinter senses the tremendous tension between Lydia's unnameable, restless desires and the "dainty neatness" (*Armadale*, 383) of the space within which she is forced to contain herself while she plays the role of the respectable woman. Indeed, Lydia's dangerousness consists partly in her ability to assume respectability and discard it at will:

> Her hands moved about among the tea things with a
> smooth, noiseless activity. Her magnificent hair flashed
> crimson . . . as she turned her head hither and thither,
> searching, with an easy grace, for the things she wanted
> in the tray. Exercise had heightened the brilliancy of her
> complexion, and had quickened the rapid alternations of
> expression in her eyes—the delicious languor that stole
> over them when she was listening or thinking, the bright
> intelligence that flashed from them softly when she spoke.
> . . . Perfectly modest in her manner, possessed to perfection
> of the graceful restraints and refinements of a lady, she had
> all the allurements that feast the eye . . . a subtle suggestive-
> ness in her silence, and a sexual sorcery in her smile. (383)

In terms of both race and class, Lydia's origins are blurred. James Bashwood, the detective employed to trace her history, discovers the impenetrability of certain areas of her past: "She may be the daughter

Fig. 4.2. *The Moth and the Candle*, from *Armadale*. George W. Thomas, *Armadale* in *Cornhill Magazine*, Oct. 1865.

of a Duke, or the daughter of a costermonger. . . . Fancy anything you like—there's nothing to stop you" (520–21). As a child with "a beautiful complexion and wonderful hair," she is adopted by a quack doctor and his wife, the Oldershaws, who exploit her hair as an advertisement for their perfumery business. Entering the Blanchard family as a maid and "Miss Blanchard's new plaything," she uses the ensuing events involving the confusion between Wrentmore and Ingleby to consolidate her position and blackmail the family into providing her with a Continental education. After being involved in a sexual scandal, Lydia opts for a convent (another haremlike space), where one of the priests fears she is "possessed by the devil." Leaving the convent, she supports herself by "playing the pianoforte at a low concert room in Brussels," adamantly resisting all male sexual advances. Ultimately falling in with a Russian Baroness, a card sharp whose "name is unpronounceable by English lips," she wanders all over Europe with her new companion. On the Baroness's eventual exposure and imprisonment, Lydia marries one of her admirers, an Englishman named Waldron (522–24). Her nomadism and rootlessness, as well as her constant association with the "foreign," are symptomatic of her rejection of a stable national or sexual identity. Every attempt to convert her body into property, to fix or contain it, is met with resistance.

Nineteen years after the publication of *Armadale*, the Italian ethnocriminologist Cesare Lombroso published *The Female Offender* (1895), the culmination of his research into the psychology and physiology of female criminals. Professor of forensic medicine at the University of Turin, Lombroso laid the cornerstones of criminal anthropology/anthropometry when he published *The Criminal Man* (1876). His views continued to be influential well into the first half of the twentieth century. Lombroso's measurements of the skulls and brains of a wide range of women from different ethnic backgrounds (mainly Italian) who were convicted of crimes as diverse as murder, theft, infanticide, complicity in rape, and poisoning led him to formulate the concept of the inherent "atavism" of the female criminal; an atavism that was an inevitable symptom of racial degeneration. For instance, he concluded that "[f]emale poisoners, thieves, and assassins are most remarkable for cranial asymmetry and strabismus; while the female assassin has most often a virile and Mongolian type of face."[48] Lombroso also cataloged the attributes of women in whom the degenerative process had taken hold more firmly than in men.[49] While other women (whom Lombroso called "occasional criminals") may have been "led into crime either by the suggestion of a third person or by irresistible temptation," the women in whom "the complete type" of degeneration appears seem to have criminal propensities that "are more intense and more perverse than those of their male prototypes."[50] Among other qualities, these women display cruelty, "want of maternal affection," vengeance, "intense . . . erotic tendencies," greed, religiosity, contradictions, sentimentalism, and intelligence.[51] Discussing several well-known female poisoners in the course of his work, such as Marie Brinvilliers and Marie Lafarge, Lombroso praised their superior cranial capacities, acute minds, and ability to write "extremely well."[52] At the same time, he observed that "naturally poisoners are not wanting amongst hysterical criminals."[53] (Interestingly, Lydia Gwilt's and Helena Gracedieu's diaries, in *Armadale* and *The Legacy of Cain*, respectively, provide evidence of their ability to construct their own narratives, manipulate events, and reimagine their bodies.)

"Virility" was another marker of the "reversion" to the "primitive type." Looking at portraits of "Red Indian and Negro beauties," Lombroso and Ferrero argue that it is difficult to "recognize [them as] women, so huge are their jaws and cheek-bones, so hard and coarse their features."[54] *The Female Offender* brings together images of the poisoner, the hysteric and the exotic woman in order to subject their bodies to the relentless discipline of criminal anthropology. Yet their bodies are never fully contained by the text; female criminals are more unclassifiable, more *hybrid* than male ones, ambiguously positioned along the spectrum of civilization and savagery. They occasionally display "Darwinian traits" of beauty and feminine softness; they use makeup to disguise their atavistic features. Everywhere, the body of the exoticized female criminal eludes Lombroso. *Armadale* both anticipates and challenges Lombroso's discourse through its focus on Lydia Gwilt's complex negotiation with hybridity.

Lydia first uses poison as a weapon against domestic violence. Obsessed by jealousy and his fear of her sexuality, her husband, Waldron, asserts his claims to absolute ownership of her body by imprisoning her in an isolated mansion in Yorkshire. His physical abuse of her is precipitated by her clandestine sexual liaison with a Cuban officer, Captain Manuel. When Waldron strikes Lydia with his whip, she feigns submission before turning to poison as a way out of her intolerable marital situation:

> From that moment, the lady submitted as she had never sub-
> mitted before. For a fortnight afterwards, he did what he
> liked; and she never thwarted him—he said what he liked;
> and she never uttered a word of protest. Some men might
> have suspected this sudden reformation of hiding something
> dangerous under the surface. . . . All that is known is, that
> before the mark of the whip was off his wife's face, he fell
> ill, and that in two days afterwards, he was a dead man. . . .
> The evidence of the doctors and the evidence of the servants
> pointed irresistibly in one and the same direction; and Mrs.
> Waldron was committed for trial, on the charge of murder-
> ing her husband by poison. (*Armadale,* 527)

Like other famous "best-selling" female poisoners of the period, among them Marie Lafarge, Madeleine Smith, and Florence Maybrick, Lydia manages to escape the death penalty owing to the contradictions in the forensic evidence at her trial. Her affair with the exoticized Manuel is thought to have provided her with access to the poison "unless she con-trived, guarded and watched as she was, to get the poison for herself, the poison must have come to her in one of the captain's letters" (529). Written by the ethnic "other," Manuel, the letter containing poison is itself a hybridized document as it mimics Englishness "perfectly." For Lydia, both the letter and the poison, superimposed on each other, open the way to freedom and renewed control over her own body.

Exotic men such as Manuel and Midwinter, therefore, are crucial to the driving force of Lydia's desire. Her sexual desire for them is underscored by a deep sympathy for their "otherness," an otherness that she continually senses in herself. Unlike Midwinter, Manuel is comfortable with his ethnic identity. He reappears in Lydia's life, during a performance of Bellini's *Norma* in Naples, after her marriage to Midwinter and just before her second attempt to poison Allan Armadale. The opera is significant here, as the plot involves political rebellion; in occupied Gaul, the Druid priestess Norma resists colonization by the Romans, even as she is simultaneously caught up in a sexual relationship with the colonizer. (Manuel is costumed as one of the Druids.) Located in an intermediate space between colonizer and colonized, Norma's dilemmas mirror those of Lydia Gwilt. Furthermore, like Norma, whose suicide by fire symbolizes both resistance and capitulation, Lydia is destined to die by voluntarily suffocating herself with poisonous carbonic acid. By the end of the nineteenth century, *Norma* was translated into sixteen languages and had gone on to be performed in thirty-five different countries.[55] In *Armadale*, Lydia's visit to the opera at a critical narrative juncture reinforces the problematic link between exoticism, power, and resistance. Catherine Clément speculates that although the exotic heroines of nineteenth-century European opera often succumb to violence (at times self-inflicted), nevertheless their revolutionary insurgence confounds psychiatric and ethnological discourses:

> These furies, these goddesses, these women with
> fearsome arms and inspired eyes, these Turandots and
> Normas collected the witch's inheritance in the nineteenth
> century. Behind the metal sheaths covering their grotesque
> nails—and the Far East always mirrors the colonial image
> of our Torture gardens and our napalm in Vietnam—these
> women are thinly disguised resistants to the enemy. Look
> at these foreign women . . . these recalcitrant women,
> bent on their own destruction, determined to leave their
> lives behind. Turandot resists the Mongol rapist, Norma
> resists Rome . . . Carmen the Gypsy resists all men.
> These woman are all exotic. . . . Resistant women,
> burned women: that was the fate of the Sorceress,
> and it is Norma's.[56]

Cixous and Clément's theoretical paradigm of the Sorceress can be applied to the female poisoner as well. Iconographically, the poisoner and the sorceress were often interchangeable. In his famous work on medieval witchcraft hysteria, *La Sorcière* (1862), the French sociologist and historian Jules Michelet referred to the use of the healing properties of poisons by "sorceresses" or female medical practitioners: "All the plants which were confounded together under the name of *Witches' herbs* were supposed ministers of death. Found in a woman's hands, they would have led to her being adjudged a poisoner or fabricator of accursed spells."[57] Cixous and Clément analyze the radical *La Sorcière* (*Satanism and Witchcraft*) and other texts, including those by Freud, and argue that the sorceress and hysteric exist along the same continuum, and use their spectacular and pathological bodily symptoms to "revolt and shake up the public, the group, the men, the others to whom they are exhibited": "The sorceress heals, against the Church's canon; she performs abortions, favors non-conjugal love, converts the unlivable space of a stifling Christianity. The hysteric unties familiar bonds, introduces disorder into the well-regulated unfolding of everyday life."[58] Situated at the margins, these figures create spaces for themselves in which they encounter "a relationship with the other that is not yet stable but metastable—uneasy, such that one can pass without fixed identity from body to body: from woman into beast, from woman into woman."[59] By exhibiting what Michelet calls their "pathological symptoms," they rupture the terms of the discourse which marks them as pathological.[60]

Equipped with her knowledge of toxicology, Lydia becomes obsessed with murdering Allan Armadale. Superficially, her motive appears to be the possession of Armadale's Thorpe-Ambrose property—by going through a marriage ceremony with Midwinter (whose name is also Armadale), and manipulating events cleverly, she will be able to pose as "Mrs. Armadale" and inherit the property on Allan's death. Beneath the surface, however, Lydia's desperate attempts to poison Allan signify an attack on everything he stands for—the hierarchies of class and imperial identity that refuse to acknowledge their own ideological fissures.

For Lydia, Allan's response to *Norma* in Naples betrays an "Englishness" that is confident in its own hegemony: "Armadale said—with an Englishman's exasperating pride in his own stupidity, wherever a matter of Art is concerned—that he couldn't make head or tail of the performance" (*Armadale*, 557). She also wishes to prevent his marriage to Neelie Milroy, "his darling Neelie" (552)—a nauseating

FIG. 4.3. *The End of the Elopement*, from *Armadale*. George W. Thomas, *Armadale* in *Cornhill Magazine*, Feb. 1866.

version of the Victorian child-woman. Lydia's frantic desire to separate Midwinter from Allan, to "decolonize" the former—is based on a recognition of Englishness itself as fraught, unstable, and incoherent. Another *Cornhill Magazine* illustration shows Lydia mediating between the "fair" and "dark" Armadales (fig. 4.3); from the beginning, in Wrentmore's confession it was she who had initiated the confusion between them. In the illustration, her dress is literally split, in terms of light and shadow, complicating the very notion of "whiteness." Since both Allan and Midwinter desire Lydia sexually, her body becomes the embattled site upon which their racial and cultural anxieties are played out. Adept at the art of poisoning, she herself becomes the "poison" that once absorbed, induces vulnerability and dissolution.

Lydia is also allied with two other figures who constantly move back and forth between center and periphery in Victorian society. The first is Mother Oldershaw of the "Ladies' Toilette Repository"—Lydia's foster mother, correspondent, and business partner, based on the notorious beauty expert, Sarah Rachel Leverson. The sensational trials of Madame Rachel for fraud, which took place in London during the period that Collins was writing *Armadale,* stirred up Victorian England's deepest fears about ambitious and resourceful female tricksters.[61] An "exotic" outsider herself, the Jewish Madame Rachel had opened a cosmetics shop on Bond Street in the mid-1860s that converted the Victorian fascination with exoticism into a wildly successful business enterprise. Here she promised to use her Eastern cosmetics, "preparations made up of the purest, rarest, and most fragrant productions of the East," such as "the Magnetic Dew of Sahara," "Jordan Water," "Favourite of the Harem's Pearl White," "the Royal Arabian Toilet of Beauty as arranged by Madame Rachel for the Sultana of Turkey," "Arab Bloom Powder," and the "Arabian baths" to "remove all personal defects, put a bloom on old visages . . . and thus manufacture antiquated belles into charming juveniles."[62] By trading on "colonial desires," Madame Rachel was able to invade the bastions of the wealthy bourgeoisie, even getting herself a box at the opera. At her second trial in 1868, she was convicted for massive fraud and accused of prostitution. For Victorians, the most horrifying aspect of the trial was the fact that female criminals such as Madame Rachel—women who could construct and control their own master-narratives—might exist at the heart of respectable society. The newspapers compared Madame Rachel to women authors of sensation fiction such as Mary Elizabeth Braddon: "For here is sensation and plot quite as thrilling as *Lady Audley's Secret,* with situations and morals nearly as offensive as those which the purveyors, foreign and domestic, of fornicating literature commonly venture upon. . . . Mrs Levison, we are asked to believe, could invent this plot, and is master of this language; and yet Mrs. Levison cannot write, and probably can hardly read."[63] Cosmetics and poison, were of course, aligned in Victorian discourses on the female body. "Arsenic Complexion Wafers" were in use till the beginning of the twentieth century, and beauty guides claimed that cosmetics for the skin contained "the most deadly poisons in the whole catalogue for chemical products," such as corrosive sublimate, prussic acid, and arsenic.[64] The idea of sculpting an artificial body with the use of poisonous cosmetics could also dissolve the boundaries between one's body and that of the racial other. As one American doctor commented, the use of lip salve was necessitated by "lives of dissipation" that "impoverish[ed]" and "decolorize[d]" the blood. Frequent use "thickens" the lips giving a "peculiar tint to the mouth," likening it to the "shriveled, purplish one of a sick negress." The *Cornhill Magazine* cautioned its female readers against the dangerous effects of rouge and pearl powder, pointing out that pearl powder was mainly used by "foreign actresses" and that Englishwomen should not attempt to "pass" by altering "obstinately brown" complexions by such means.[65] The alliance between Lydia and Mother Oldershaw (Rachel) heightens the poison-maquillage connection in *Armadale;* both women are involved with "poisons" that threaten to corrode and destroy stable cultural identities.

Lydia's other associate is the abortionist and quack psychiatrist, Dr. Downward, who helps her to initiate her plan to murder Allan Armadale with poison gas in his newly designed "sanatorium." The madhouse becomes the final space in which Lydia passionately tries to "reclaim" Midwinter and force him to confront his own "otherness" or hybridity, an acknowledgment that would also find expression through his renewed desire for her. By now, her antipathy toward Allan Armadale and the kind of normalization he represents has reached fever pitch, as she reveals in her Italian diary:

> If some women bring such men as this into the
> world, ought other women to allow them to live? It is
> a matter of opinion. *I* think not.
>
> What maddens me, is to see, as I do see plainly,
> that Midwinter finds in Armadale's company, and in
> Armadale's new yacht, a refuge from *me*. (553)

On a tour of the sanatorium, Dr. Downward explains the architectural features of certain rooms, which contain hidden "fumigation apparatuses," so that asthmatic nervous patients can be "noiselessly" provided with oxygen (640). For Lydia, this is the Panopticon perfected, where she can flood the room with poisonous carbonic acid and observe Allan Armadale without herself being seen. The ingeniously constructed madhouse gas chamber allows her to envision regaining control of the gaze and compelling Armadale to experience profound alienation. Downward explains the action of the poison, contained in a "purple flask":

> Quantities of little bubbles will rise at every pouring;
> collect the gas in those bubbles; and convey it into a
> closed chamber—and let Samson himself be in that
> closed chamber, our Stout Friend will kill him in
> half-an-hour! Will kill him slowly, without his seeing
> anything, without his smelling anything, without his
> feeling anything but sleepiness. Will kill him, and tell
> the whole College of Surgeons nothing, if they examine
> him after death, but that he died of apoplexy or conges-
> tion of the lungs! What do you think of *that*, my dear
> lady . . . ? (642)

Yet Lydia ultimately turns her elaborate poisoning device on her own body. When Midwinter, suspicious of her actions, changes places with Allan, Lydia drags him out and then enters the poison chamber to die. Her suicide, far from being the sacrificial act that enthralled Dickens and Forster,[66] is a frantic, tragic gesture of defiance—she evades a criminal trial, her body resisting reappropriation and reinscription by the legal system. If we read hybridity and poison as interchangeable, then Lydia's final exhibition of agency is to allow the poison (carbonic acid) to envelop her body completely. The exposure to the gas creates a spectacle whereby the poison pervades and inscribes the body. Like Cleopatra, she stages the spectacle of her own death. To succumb to poison is to embrace her own nomadism; her exoticism and estrange-ment from herself is what Bhabha calls a "tragic and intimate act of violence" that is rooted in "a kind of self-love that is also the love of the 'other,'"[67] or rather the "other-in-herself." The embrace of poi-son is also an escape from a body continuously subject to the pres-sures of normalization and surveillance. Choosing Allan over Lydia, Midwinter resists this embrace to the very end. Lydia's final gesture marks what Bhabha designates as an "unhomely moment"—a moment that "relates the traumatic ambivalences of a personal, psychic history to the wider disjunctions of political existence."[68] As Collins himself remarked in the letter to Harriet Collins (cited above): "My own idea is that I have never written such a good end to a book . . . at any rate I never was so excited myself, while finishing a story. . . . Miss Gwilt's death quite upset me."[69]

The Legacy of Cain and
Hereditary Poison

In his last completed novel, *The Legacy of Cain* (1888), Collins uses the figure of the female poisoner to intervene in contemporary discussions of heredity and degeneration. Lombroso had already laid out the fundamental concepts of his theory of criminal atavism in *The Criminal Man*. The other major post-Darwinian investigator of issues relating to heredity was the British ethnologist Sir Francis Galton, who, like Lombroso, helped to revolutionize criminology by pioneering the development of fingerprinting techniques. Regarded as the founder of the eugenics movement, Galton published *Hereditary Genius: An Inquiry into Its Laws and Consequences* (1869).[70] In his introduction, Galton clearly set forth his agenda, emphasizing the importance of "natural inheritance" and advocating the necessity of selective breeding:

> I propose to show in this book that a man's natural
> abilities are derived by inheritance, under exactly the
> same limitations as are the form and physical features
> of the whole organic world. Consequently, as it is easy,
> notwithstanding these limitations, to obtain by careful
> selection a permanent breed of dogs or horses gifted with
> peculiar powers of running, or of doing anything else, so
> it would be quite practicable to produce a highly-gifted
> race of men by judicious marriages during several
> consecutive generations.[71]

However, as Robert J. C. Young has demonstrated in his study, *Colonial Desire: Hybridity in Theory, Culture and Race,* in Victorian ethnological discourses, the tortured question of "civilization" was inextricably tied to that of degeneration. Young points out that for ethnologists like Galton, Paul Broca, Darwin, and even the overtly racist Comte de Gobineau, "hybridity" or racial intermixture was an essential component in the survival of "civilized" races. Unions with "proximate" species would be fertile, and were somehow necessary if the white races were to continue to develop, whereas those with "distant species" would produce "a corruption of the originals, degenerate and degraded."[72] The very notion of degeneracy, argues Young, threatens to implode the category of whiteness:

> [T]he naming of human mixture as "degeneracy"
> both asserts the norm and subverts it, undoing its
> terms of distinction, and opening up the prospect

of the evanescence of "race" as such. Here, therefore, at the heart of racial theory, in its most sinister, offensive move, hybridity also maps out its most anxious, vulnerable site: a fulcrum at its edge and centre where its dialectics of injustice, hatred and oppression can find themselves effaced and expunged.[73]

The Legacy of Cain investigates the discursive fragility of degeneration theory through the intertwining bodies of its two heroines, Helena and Eunice. Like Lydia Gwilt, they narrate their own version of events through their diaries. Eunice is the daughter of a murderess, convicted and hanged for her crime. Although the text does not explicitly name the crime, it hints at poisoning, since the evidence at the trial reveals "deliberate and merciless premeditation."[74] Her daughter is adopted by a minister, Mr. Gracedieu (the name a peculiar echo of the wrecked ship in *Armadale*), who brings her up with his own daughter without allowing either of them to know their real ages, so that Eunice's heritage, with its "poisonous" maternal taint, may be suppressed, if not erased. The doctor at the prison, a Galtonian, predicts a disaster: "When I think of the growth of that poisonous hereditary taint, which may come with time—when I think of passions let loose and temptations lying in ambush—I see the smooth surface of the Minister's domestic life with dangers lurking under it which make me shake in my shoes. . . . I should come down to breakfast with suspicions in my cup of tea, if I discovered that my adopted daughter had poured it out" (*The Legacy of Cain*, 34). Collins deliberately confuses the bodies of the two sisters, so that it becomes impossible to classify them or trace either one to the murderess. Eunice has odalisquelike qualities: she is dark and indolent, with a pale complexion. Helena is fairer, with gray eyes and light brown hair. However, Helena finds Eunice's languor contagious: "I noticed the old easy indolent movements again . . . which I can never contemplate without feeling a stupefying influence that has helped me to many a delicious night's sleep" (66).

Both women acknowledge and are ready to act on their sexual desires, focusing on the same man, the weak and vacillating Philip Dunboyne, who cannot decide between the sisters. Collins reverses the gaze so that Philip's sexual attractions are repeatedly the subject of female erotic fantasies in the novel; as Eunice comments, "His hair curls naturally. In colour, it is something between my hair and Helena's. He wears his beard. How manly! It curls naturally, like his hair; it smells deliciously of some perfume which is new to me" (82). Helena consumes Eunice's articulation of her desire while reading the latter's diary: "If I had not seen the familiar handwriting, nothing would have induced me to believe that a girl brought up in a pious household . . . could have written that shameless record of passions unknown to young ladies in respectable English life" (150). For Philip, the object of their desires, the two sisters' bodies are constantly impinging on one another as he moves back and forth between them.

While Eunice has a near-pyschotic episode in which her mother's spirit exhorts her to murder Helena, it is Helena who, in the end, resorts to poison. When Philip lies ill in their house, Helena gradually poisons him. She confesses in her diary that she is motivated by his sexual rejection of her: "I had made my poor offering of love to a man who secretly loathed me. I wonder that I survived my sense of my own degradation" (410). As Eunice wrestles with her "hereditary taint," Helena embraces poison to gain absolute power over the male body. Like the Italian opera and French novels to which she had been denied access by the harsh regime of her fanatically religious father, poison is seductive and "foreign." It also provides a way for Helena to articulate her "furious, overpowering, deadly rage" (409).

In her diary, Helena records her experience of reading about "a strange case of intended poisoning" in which a married woman seeks revenge for some "unendurable wrong . . . at the hands of her husband's mother" (388–89). When caught in the act, this young woman "of strong passions" had cleverly disguised her guilt by implicating her maid. The contemplation of poison as a way out eventually leads to a legal separation, freeing the wife from her oppressive marriage. Helena comments on the impact of the poisoner's "extraordinary courage and resolution": "A remarkable story, which has made such an impression on me that I have written it in my Journal" (390). She returns to it repeatedly as she contemplates the art of toxicology and its place in her own life: "I went back to my bedroom, and opened my Diary, and read the story again. . . . Would it be running too great a risk to show the story to the doctor, and try to get a little valuable information in that way? It would be useless. He would make some feeble joke; he would say, girls and poisons are not fit company for each other" (421).

Through her reading of this poisoning case, Helena recognizes the female poisoner as a transgressive woman struggling to recover agency in a world which consistently encourages her to discipline her desires. As she begins to live this narrative, she is tempted to flaunt her knowledge of it as a signature of her rebellion and agency. The governor notes that Helena's "insolence" and "audacity" springs from a self constructed through "a secret course of reading" (272). (Her father, the

Reverend Gracedieu, is a harsh and repressive parent who forbids his daughters to read novels and newspapers.) Yet, Helena's engagement with poison is more complex than this. By taking on Eunice's poisoned maternal "inheritance," she exoticizes herself and triggers the collapse of classification systems based on theories of inherited criminality. Helena is convicted, goes to prison, and escapes to the United States, where, as "the Reverend Miss Gracedieu," she carries on her masquerades by becoming the "distinguished leader of a new community" (480). Like Madeleine Smith, who wrote passionate love letters to her lover Emile before poisoning him, Helena will not allow her sexuality to be silenced or denied.

In *The Legacy of Cain,* the male body is vulnerable to infiltration by various types of poison. The prison governor speculates that Eunice's upbringing in the minister's household, together with "the better qualities in her father's nature" (299) will counteract her mother's poisonous blood. Yet the minister himself "degenerates" into imbecility and madness, his collapse supposedly brought on by fanaticism and overwork. Consumed by sexual jealousy, he savagely attacks the picture of his "virtuous" dead wife (who had rejected the murderess's daughter and attempted to prevent her entry into the household). The threat of degeneration seems to be contained *within* the Gracedieu family as Collins shifts the source of poison from the maternal body to that of the father. As their father degenerates, Eunice and Helena both experience varying degrees of freedom and agency. Meanwhile, Philip Dunboyne, initially seduced by Eunice's "poisonous" exoticism, is literally poisoned by Helena.

Collins's *empoisonneuses* use poison to inscribe bodies (their own and that of others) with a dangerous hybridity that dismantles the formulation of fixed national and imperial identities. The crime of poisoning opens up for them "the point of departure" through which, muses Hélène Cixous, "we suddenly become the stranger, the foreigner in ourselves. We separate ourselves from ourselves."[75] They consistently resist attempts to classify or contain their bodies through the lens of Victorian ethnocriminology. In Collins's fiction, the links between poison and exoticism open up a space for the articulation of anxieties about "Englishness" and explore the ways in which these ideological fissures are negotiated and exploited by powerful women. Seduced by poison's exotic "otherness," Collins's female poisoners are ultimately able to defy hegemonic domestic and imperial narratives of race, sexuality, and desire.

Notes

1. For general accounts of these trials, see Mary Hartman, *Victorian Murderesses, A True History of Thirteen Respectable French and English Women Accused of Unspeakable Crimes* (New York: Schocken Books, 1977); Donald Thomas, *The Victorian Underworld* (New York: New York Univ. Press, 1998); and Thomas Boyle, *Black Swine in the Sewers of Hampstead: Beneath the Surface of Victorian Sensationalism* (New York: Viking, 1989).

2. Alexandre Dumas, *The Count of Monte Cristo* (London: Penguin, 1996), 506–7.

3. Homi K. Bhabha, *The Location of Culture* (London: Routledge, 1994), 114.

4. Ibid., 111.

5. Charlotte Brontë, *Shirley* (Harmondsworth: Penguin, 1996), 399.

6. In the appendix to *Armadale,* Collins claimed: "Wherever the story touches on questions so connected with Law, Medicine, or Chemistry, it has been submitted, before publication, to the experience of professional men. The kindness of a friend supplied me with a plan of the Doctor's Apparatus—and I saw the chemical ingredients at work, before I ventured on describing the action of them in the closing scenes of this book" (Wilkie Collins, *Armadale,* ed. John Sutherland [London: Penguin, 1995], 678–79. Hereafter cited in the text as *Armadale*).

7. See William Baker, *Wilkie Collins's Library: A Reconstruction* (Westport, Conn.: Greenwood Press, 2002), 155.

8. Alfred Swaine Taylor, *Poisons in Relation to Medical Jurisprudence and Medicine* (Philadelphia: Lea & Blanchard, 1848), 13. Hereafter cited as Taylor (1848). For an excellent survey of the development of toxicology in Victorian England, see Thomas Forbes, *Surgeons at the Bailey: English Forensic Medicine to 1878* (New Haven: Yale Univ. Press, 1985).

9. Taylor (1848), 18.

10. Ibid., 26–27.

11. Ibid., 32.

12. Ibid., 36.

13. Orfila's role in the Lafarge case is discussed in detail in Jürgen Thorwald, *The Century of the Detective,* trans. Richard and Clara Winston (New York: Harcourt Brace, 1965), 267–92.

14. Marie Lafarge, *The Memoirs of Madame Lafarge; Written by Herself* (Philadelphia: Carey & Hart, 1841). After finding herself trapped in a provincial marriage with the petty bourgeois Lafarge, the semi-aristocratic Parisienne apparently became desperate after she found he was embroiled in debt and refused to release her from the contract. In her memoir,

Marie described her extreme anxiety as she warded off attempted rapes by her husband. In December 1839, she sent him a poisoned cake while he was in Paris. After he developed cholera-related symptoms and returned home, she continued to hover over his sickbed, lacing his food liberally with arsenic.

15. The Marsh test involved a delicate and complex procedure whereby fluid containing arsenic was mixed with zinc and acid, producing arsine gas that, once ignited, left a metallic deposit of arsenic on a porcelain bowl. However, the chemicals themselves had to be tested for traces of arsenic in order to ensure accurate results. Traces of graveyard earth, tested with the Marsh apparatus also produced arsenic, intensifying the possibility of contamination. In 1842, the German chemist Hugo Reinsch devised another method—that of mixing the arsenic solution with hydrochloric acid and boiling it to produce a coating on a copper mesh. For a detailed description of these two tests in their historical context, see Thorwald, 277–81, 340–41.

16. Forbes, 138–39.

17. Taylor (1848), 117.

18. For statistics on poisoning, see Forbes, 128–29, and Taylor (1848), 178–79.

19. Taylor (1848), 466.

20. The Pharmacy Act of 1868 included "opium and all preparations of opium or of poppies" in the list of poisons, restricted its sale to professional pharmacists, and also initiated labeling restrictions. However, because of the variety of opium preparations, there were several loopholes, such as the exclusion of opium-based medicines. For a detailed discussion of the complexities of the act, see Virginia Berridge and Griffith Edwards, eds., *Opium and the People: Opiate Use in Nineteenth Century England* (London: Allen Lane; New York: St. Martin's Press, 1981), 113–22. As Griffith and Edwards point out, "the way the 1868 Act operated in practice was rather different from legislative intentions" (122). For Christison's classification, see Robert Christison, *A Treatise on Poisons* (New York: AMS Press, 1973), 510–30.

21. *Lancet* 1 (1839): 597–99; for the *Medical Gazette* statistics, see Alfred Swaine Taylor, *Poisons in Relation to Medical Jurisprudence and Medicine* (Philadelphia: Lea & Blanchard, 1875), 176. Hereafter cited as Taylor (1875).

22. Taylor (1875), 474–75.

23. According to Alison Smith, "The impact of French salon painting on the formation of the English nude was such that by the 1870's audiences had become accustomed to viewing the works of Gérôme and Cabanel at important venues in both London and the provinces" (*The Victorian Nude: Sexuality, Morality and Art* [Manchester: Manchester Univ. Press, 1996], 168).

24. Taylor (1875), 468. According to John Sweetman, the development of "Arab" smoking rooms in private houses—such as the billiard room at Newhouse Park in Hertfordshire in the later part of the century—drew on the connection between opium and the East. Such interiors themselves were often "hybrid," such as the breathtaking Arab Hall at the home of the artist Frederick Leighton, built in 1877–79, composed of motifs from Sicily, Persia, Syria, and Turkey (*The Oriental Obsession: Islamic Inspiration in British and American Art and Architecture, 1500–1920* [Cambridge and New York: Cambridge Univ. Press, 1988], 196). The association of hybridity and opium use turns up in Collins's *The Moonstone* (1868), in which the racially ambiguous Ezra Jennings is not only an opium addict himself but also reveals the crucial role played by opium in the narrative of the Indian diamond.

25. Tamar Heller points out the resemblance between Collins and Ezra Jennings, arguing that "Jennings becomes the novel's most important mirror of its author. Collins and his creation have obvious similarities: both are opium addicts who live on the margins of respectability" ("Blank Spaces: Ideological Tensions and the Detective Work of *The Moonstone*," in *Wilkie Collins,* ed. Lyn Pykett [New York: St. Martin's Press, 1998], 262).

26. Collins to Charles Kent, London, 8 Aug. 1884, *The Letters of Wilkie Collins,* ed. William Baker and William M. Clarke (New York: St. Martin's Press, 1999), 2:472. Hereafter cited as *Letters.*

27. Collins to Elizabeth Benzon, London, 26 Feb. 1869, *Letters,* 2:319.

28. Taylor (1875), 68.

29. Ibid.

30. See Madeleine Smith's statement in Alexander Forbes Irvine, *Report of the Trial of Madeleine Smith* (Edinburgh: T. & T. Clark, 1857), 73. For analyses of the Maybrick trial, see Hartman, 247, and George Robb, "The English Dreyfus Case: Florence Maybrick and the Sexual Double-Standard," in *Disorder in the Court: Trials and Sexual Conflict at the Turn of the Century,* ed. George Robb and Nancy Erber (New York: New York Univ. Press, 1999), 57–77.

31. In *The Woman in White,* Walter Hartright spots Count Fosco at the opera house during a performance of this work.

32. Ferdinand Gregorovius, *Lucrezia Borgia, According to Original Documents and Correspondence of Her Day* (New York: D. Appleton and Co., 1903), xvii–xxiii.

33. Gregorovius, 361. For a brief account of Donizetti's opera, see Charles Osborne, *The Bel Canto Operas of Rossini, Donizetti, and Bellini* (Portland: Amadeus Press, 1994), 224–27.

34. George Eliot, *The Lifted Veil* (Oxford: Oxford Univ. Press, 1999), 18–19.

35. Madame de Sévigné, *Selected Letters,* trans. Leonard Tancock (Harmondsworth: Penguin, 1982), 196.

36. For the cases of Marie Brinvilliers and La Voisin, see Frances Mossiker, *The Affair of the Poisons: Louis XIV, Madame de Montespan, and One of History's Great Unsolved Mysteries* (New York: Alfred A. Knopf, 1969), Frantz Funck-Brentano, *Princes and Poisoners: Studies of the Court of Louis XIV* (London: Duckworth, 1901), and Albert Smith, *The Marchioness of Brinvilliers* (London: Bentley, 1846).

37. Théophile Gautier, *One of Cleopatra's Nights* (New York: Brentano's, 1927), 77.

38. Collins to Reverend Dr. Deems, Turnbridge Wells, 5 Oct. 1865, *Letters*, 2:259.

39. For Victorian critics' reactions to Lydia Gwilt, see Catherine Peters, *The King of Inventors: A Life of Wilkie Collins* (Princeton: Princeton Univ. Press, 1993), 272–80.

40. Poison is an important motif in several of Collins's lesser-known novels. Some of these have been somewhat neglected by critics and have only recently been rediscovered. See Wilkie Collins, *Jezebel's Daughter* (New York: Collier, 1900), in which the would-be chemist Madame Fontaine experiments with the poisons of the Borgias, and *The Law and the Lady*, ed. Jenny Bourne Taylor (Oxford: Oxford Univ. Press, 1994), based on the Madeleine Smith poisoning case.

41. For a range of European women travelers' responses to the veil, see Billie Melman, *Women's Orients* (Ann Arbor: Univ. of Michigan Press, 1992).

42. James Tod, *Annals and Antiquities of Rajasthan, or the Central and Western Rajpoot States of India* (London: Routledge and Kegan Paul, 1972), 35. For a discussion of Oriental poison myths, see N. M. Penzer, *Poison Damsels and Other Essays in Folklore and Anthropology* (London: privately printed for Chas. J. Sawyer Ltd., 1952), 3–71.

43. In both Sanskrit and Arabic sources, imperialists such as Alexander or the Indian king, Chandragupta Maurya, are saved from poison-women by the advice of their ministers. Several of these sources were translated into different European languages. The ninth-century Sanskrit play *The Signet Ring of Rakshasha*, by the dramatist Visakadatta, in which the poison-woman is frequently mentioned, but is never actually seen onstage, was translated into English by the Orientalist scholar H. H. Wilson at the beginning of the nineteenth century.

44. Elizabeth Grosz, *Volatile Bodies: Toward a Corporeal Feminism* (Bloomington: Indiana Univ. Press, 1994), 199.

45. Ibid., 200.

46. Qtd. in Penzer, 15.

47. The ritual of presiding over tea is presented as erotic fetish in another popular Victorian sensation novel involving a murderess. See Mary Elizabeth Braddon, *Lady Audley's Secret* (New York: Oxford Univ. Press, 1987), 222. Braddon describes her heroine, the "fair demon" Lucy

Audley, seated amidst "floating mists from the boiling liquid" that envelop her in "a cloud of scented vapour."

48. Cesare Lombroso and William Ferrero, *The Female Offender* (London: T. Fisher Unwin, 1895), 86.

49. Ibid., 147–91.

50. Ibid., 147.

51. Ibid., 152, 159.

52. Ibid., 171.

53. Ibid., 235.

54. Ibid., 112–13.

55. Osborne, 338.

56. Catherine Clément, *Opera, or the Undoing of Women* (Minneapolis: Univ. of Minnesota Press, 1999), 103.

57. For the sorceress, see "The Guilty One," in Hélène Cixous and Catherine Clément, *The Newly Born Woman,* trans. Betsy Wing (Minneapolis: Univ. of Minnesota Press, 1986), 1–39.

58. Ibid., 5.

59. Ibid., 19.

60. Jules Michelet, *Satanism and Witchcraft* (New York: Citadel Press, 1939), 83.

61. *The Extraordinary Life and Trial of Madame Rachel* (London: Diprose and Bateman, 1868).

62. Ibid., v–vii.

63. Ibid., 122.

64. Richard Corson, *Fashions in Makeup* (London: Peter Owen, 1981), 376.

65. Qtd. in Corson, 344–50.

66. For their reactions to Lydia's death, see Collins to Mrs. Harriet Collins, London, 4 June 1886, *Letters,* 2:275–76.

67. Bhabha, 17.

68. Ibid., 10–11.

69. *Letters,* 2:275.

70. Although I have not been able to find evidence that Collins was familiar with this work, it is very likely that he would have known it because of his interest in issues of heredity and degeneration, not only in *The Legacy of Cain* but also in previous novels such as *The Law and the Lady,* where the links between madness, degeneration, and genius are explored through the character of Misserimus Dexter. Galton was *not* among the books in Collins's library, however. See Francis Galton, *Hereditary Genius* (New York: St. Martin's Press, 1972).

71. Galton, 45.

72. Robert J. C. Young, *Colonial Desire: Hybridity in Theory, Culture and Race* (London: Routledge, 1995), 18. The theoretical framework of my essay is much indebted to Young's reading of Victorian ethnological theories and the problem of hybridity, particularly his groundbreaking analysis of the "conflicted" category of whiteness.

73. Ibid., 19.

74. Wilkie Collins, *The Legacy of Cain* (New York: Collier, 1900), 7. Hereafter cited in the text as *The Legacy of Cain.*

75. Hélène Cixous, "Bathsheba," in *Stigmata: Escaping Texts* (London: Routledge, 1998), 8.

References

Baker, William. *Wilkie Collins's Library: A Reconstruction.* Westport, Conn.: Greenwood Press, 2002.

Berridge, Virginia, and Griffith Edwards, eds. *Opium and the People: Opium Use in Nineteenth Century England.* London: Allen Lane; New York: St. Martin's Press, 1981.

Bhabha, Homi K. *The Location of Culture.* London: Routledge, 1994.

Boyle, Thomas. *Black Swine in the Sewers of Hampstead: Beneath the Surface of Victorian Sensationalism.* New York: New York Univ. Press, 1998.

Braddon, Mary Elizabeth. *Lady Audley's Secret.* Ed. David Skilton. New York: Oxford Univ. Press, 1987.

Brontë, Charlotte. *Shirley.* Harmondsworth: Penguin, 1996.

Christison, Robert. *A Treatise on Poisons.* New York: AMS Press, 1973.

Cixous, Hélène. *Stigmata: Escaping Texts.* London: Routledge, 1998.

Cixous, Hélène, and Catherine Clément. *The Newly Born Woman.* Trans. Betsy Wing. Minneapolis: Univ. of Minnesota Press, 1986.

Clemént, Catherine. *Opera, or the Undoing of Women.* Minneapolis: Univ. of Minnesota Press, 1999.

Collins, Wilkie. *Armadale.* Ed. John Sutherland. London: Penguin, 1995.

———. *Jezebel's Daughter.* New York: Collier, 1900.

———. *The Law and the Lady.* Ed. Jenny Bourne Taylor. Oxford: Oxford Univ. Press, 1994.

———. *The Legacy of Cain.* New York: Collier, 1900.

———. *The Letters of Wilkie Collins.* 2 vols. Ed. William Baker and William M. Clarke. New York: St. Martin's Press, 1999.

Corson, Richard. *Fashions in Makeup.* London: Peter Owen, 1981.

de Sévigné, Madame. *Selected Letters.* London: Penguin, 1982.

Dumas, Alexandre. *The Count of Monte Cristo*. London: Penguin, 1996.

Eliot, George. *The Lifted Veil*. Oxford: Oxford Univ. Press, 1999.

The Extraordinary Life and Trial of Madame Rachel. London: Diprose and Bateman, 1868.

Forbes, Thomas. *Surgeons at the Bailey: English Forensic Medicine to 1878*. New Haven: Yale Univ. Press, 1985.

Funck-Brentano, Frantz. *Princes and Poisoners: Studies of the Court of Louis XIV*. London: Duckworth, 1901.

Galton, Francis. *Hereditary Genius*. New York: St. Martin's Press, 1972.

Gautier, Théophile. *One of Cleopatra's Nights*. New York: Brentano's, 1927.

Gregorovius, Ferdinand. *Lucrezia Borgia, According to Original Documents and Correspondence of Her Day*. New York: D. Appleton and Co., 1903.

Grosz, Elizabeth. *Volatile Bodies: Toward a Corporeal Feminism*. Bloomington: Indiana Univ. Press, 1994.

Hartman, Mary. *Victorian Murderesses, A True History of Thirteen Respectable French and English Women Accused of Unspeakable Crimes*. New York: Schocken Books, 1977.

Heller, Tamar. "Blank Spaces: Ideological Tensions and the Detective Work of *The Moonstone*." In *Wilkie Collins*, ed. Lyn Pykett, 244–70. New York: St. Martin's Press, 1998.

Irvine, Alexander Forbes. *Report of the Trial of Madeleine Smith*. Edinburgh: T. & T. Clark, 1857.

Lafarge, Marie. *The Memoirs of Madame Lafarge; Written by Herself*. Philadelphia: Carey & Hart, 1841.

Lombroso, Caesar, and William Ferrero. *The Female Offender*. London: T. Fisher Unwin, 1895.

Melman, Billie. *Women's Orients*. Ann Arbor: Univ. of Michigan Press, 1992.

Michelet, Jules. *Satanism and Witchcraft*. New York: Citadel Press, 1939.

Mossiker, Frances. *The Affair of Poisons: Louis XIV, Madame de Montespan, and One of History's Great Unsolved Mysteries*. New York: Alfred A. Knopf, 1969.

Osborne, Charles. *The Bel Canto Operas of Rossini, Donizetti, and Bellini*. Portland: Amadeus Press, 1994.

Penzer, N. M. *Poison Damsels and Other Essays in Folklore and Anthropology*. London: privately printed for Chas. J. Sawyer Ltd., 1952.

Peters, Catherine. *The King of Inventors: A Life of Wilkie Collins*. Princeton: Princeton Univ. Press, 1993.

Robb, George. "The English Dreyfus Case: Florence Maybrick and the Sexual Double-Standard. In *Disorder in the Court: Trials and Sexual Conflict at the Turn of the Century*, ed. George Robb and Nancy Erber, 55–77. New York: New York Univ. Press, 1999.

Smith, Albert. *The Marchioness of Brinvilliers*. London: Bentley, 1846.

Smith, Alison. *The Victorian Nude: Sexuality, Morality and Art*. Manchester: Manchester Univ. Press, 1996.

Sweetman, John. *The Oriental Obsession: Islamic Inspiration in British and American Art and Architecture, 1500–1920*. Cambridge and New York: Cambridge Univ. Press, 1988.

Taylor, Alfred Swaine. *Poisons in Relation to Medical Jurisprudence and Medicine*. 1875. Philadelphia: Lea & Blanchard, 1848.

Thomas, Donald. *The Victorian Underworld*. New York: New York Univ. Press, 1998.

Thorwald, Jürgen. *The Century of the Detective*. Trans. Richard and Clara Winston. New York: Harcourt Brace, 1965.

Tod, James. *Annals and Antiquities of Rajasthan or the Central and Western Rajpoot States of India*. 1829. London: Routledge and Kegan Paul, 1972.

Young, Robert J. C. *Colonial Desire: Hybridity in Theory, Culture and Race*. London: Routledge, 1995.

Marian's Moustache
Bearded Ladies, Hermaphrodites, and Intersexual Collage in *The Woman in White*

Richard Collins

The mention of Hermaphrodite conjures up a reclining figure in some museum at Florence, London or Rome, stretched out on its side, its forehead resting on a cushion, whom visitors approach from behind. They must walk round it to discover its secret.
—Marie Delcourt, *Hermaphrodite,* 1956

When all the archetypes burst out shamelessly, we plumb Homeric profundity. Two clichés make us laugh but a hundred clichés move us because we sense dimly that the clichés are talking among themselves, celebrating a reunion.
—Umberto Eco
"*Casablanca*: Cult Movies and
Intertextual Collage," 1979

Cult Movies, Cult Novels, and Intersexual Collage

THE POPULARITY OF *THE WOMAN IN WHITE* HAS ALWAYS BEEN AN ISSUE IN CRITICISM OF THE NOVEL, WHETHER TO IGNORE IT BECAUSE such a popular work could not be serious or to examine it all the more closely for how it resonates in the culture, upholding or questioning received values. That Collins's novel has never been out of print also suggests another resonance beyond specific cultural contingencies, tapping into deeper archetypal desires and fears. The novel also spawned a whole industry of what we would now call merchandise franchising (though Collins received no royalties on this merchandise), disseminating the "Woman in White" trademark into expressions of material culture—including posters, clothing, and umbrellas—far beyond the limits of the book's covers, its stage and film versions, or even its influence on imitators. According to John Sutherland, "It is a tribute to the procreativity of [Collins's] novel that Allen J. Hubin's massive *Crime Fiction: A Comprehensive Bibliography* (New York, 1994), lists no fewer than nine *Woman in Black*s, four *Woman in Red*s, two *Woman in Grey*s, a *Woman in Mauve,* and a *Woman in Purple Pajamas.*"[1] The novel took on the status of what we would now call a cult.

At the center of the novel's cult status is Marian Halcombe, whose bodily and moral beauty is crowned by the contradiction of a repulsive head, signified by her moustache. Yet readers were able early on to look beyond Collins's defacement of his heroine to see her moustache for what it was: a defect that made her all the more appealing, just as the moustache painted by Marcel Duchamp on the lip of the Mona Lisa was an encouragement to take women and art off their pedestals.[2] Edward Fitzgerald, for example, responded to her powerful appearance and personality by proposing to name his boat the *Marian Halcombe* after "the brave Girl in the Story"[3] while other men responded by proposing marriage. Marian's appeal has extended well beyond her extraordinary popularity in the nineteenth century, and her androgynous appearance has inspired novelists of our own time to create female characters who point up what Marjorie Garber has called our own "category crisis" of postmodern gender identity.[4]

Recent critics have turned to Wilkie Collins as a precursor of this crisis.[5] As many of these commentators have pointed out, the period surrounding the publication of *The Woman in White* (1859–60) provides a rich cultural period for the intersex topos. Darwin's theories of natural selection were notorious even before the appearance of *The Origin of Species* (1859) and were informed in large part by his eight-year investigation into the status of hermaphroditic barnacles in the 1840s.[6] This notoriety provided fertile ground for the public displays of anatomical curiosities in the London exhibition rooms during the 1850s, an atmosphere exploited by P. T. Barnum and other promoters of sensational exhibits of racial and sexual "nondescripts."[7] As Michel Foucault has pointed out, "The years from around 1860 to 1870 were precisely one of those periods when investigations of sexual identity were carried out with the most intensity, in an attempt not only to establish the true sex of hermaphrodites but also to identify, classify, and characterize the different types of perversions. In short, these investigations dealt with the problem of sexual anomalies in the individual and the race."[8] The focus on gender confusions culminated in the decades after 1870, so that today, according to Elaine Showalter, "gender criticism has found its ideal text-milieu in the fin de siècle, a period described by historians and writers as both a crisis in masculinity and an age of sexual anarchy."[9]

Yet, while many critics have noted the importance of gender in *The Woman in White,* none has yet brought to the discussion the social codes and contexts of sexual teratology, the popular sideshow exhibitions of sexual freaks such as bearded ladies, or the transgressive semiotics of the hermaphrodite, whether seen in the sideshow or in the extensive literature on the double-sexed figure as myth and art in the nineteenth century. This essay examines the social codes and contexts of intersexual phenomena, as found in the intertextual presence of figures from high art and popular entertainment in Collins's novel, to discuss how Hartright comes to view the spectrum of gender, including his own sexual identity.

Umberto Eco's analysis of *Casablanca* provides a useful way of thinking about the enduring popularity of *The Woman in White* as an intertextual cultural and cult artifact and about Marian Halcombe as an intersexual figure.[10] Eco suggests, for example, that a cult movie provides "a hodgepodge of sensational scenes" presented as an "unhinged text" rather than a unified narrative, which would also describe both Collins as a sensation novelist and the multiple first-person narrative of *The Woman in White.* Further, Eco defines the cult object as "a palimpsest for future students" and "a paramount laboratory for semiotic research into textual strategies."[11] Although *The Woman in White* could be read, as Eco reads *Casablanca,* more thoroughly in terms of how it reunites narrative clichés, I want here simply to examine two of what Eco calls "'magic' intertextual frames" or "intertextual archetypes": the Bearded Lady and the Hermaphrodite.[12] Eco's definition of this term is useful because it does away with psychoanalytic or mythic connotations to emphasize a recurring narrative situation, "cited or in some way recycled by innumerable other texts and provoking in the addressee a sort of intense emotion accompanied by the vague feeling of déjà vu, that everybody yearns to see again."[13] One need not, in other words, consider the intertextual archetype as universal but only as "a topos or standard situation that manages to be particularly appealing to a given cultural area or historical period."[14] While *The Woman in White* may owe its emotive effect, its early cult status, and its enduring popularity to its evocative "intertextual collage," it can be shown that the specific clichés, magic frames, or intertextual archetypes that Collins draws upon in his portrayal of characters are largely androgynous or hermaphroditic figures in high art and popular entertainments. The result is an "intersexual" collage that allows Collins to evoke the uncanny in the reader's response as Walter Hartright undertakes his investigations into identity.

Hartright's investigations are inspired by two originating "shock" events, in each of which he meets a woman, and each of which has a dreamlike quality. The first is his meeting with Anne Catherick, the mysterious woman in white, who touches him on the public road. This scene has been analyzed by D. A. Miller as a "primal scene" that the novel "obsessively repeats and remembers" as a "trauma" that needs to be worked through because her touch constitutes a "female contagion," feminizing Walter and the (male) reader by an initiation into the nervous world of sensation. Later sightings of the woman in white will bring up similar questions of "gender slippage"[15]—"Was it a man, or a woman?"—to which Marian's answer is: "It seems useless to inquire. I cannot even decide whether the figure was a man's or a woman's. I can only say that I think it was a woman's."[16] The erotic charge of the first traumatic scene is repeated in the second "shock" when Walter meets the androgynous Marian. When he first sees her from behind, his description is put in terms of an aesthetic appreciation of the beauty of her figure, but culminates in a horror of the sublime when she turns around and he sees her moustache:

> My first glance round me, as the man opened the door,
> disclosed a well-furnished breakfast-table, standing in the
> middle of a long room, with many windows in it. I looked
> from the table to the window farthest from me, and saw a
> lady standing at it, with her back turned towards me. The
> instant my eyes rested on her, I was struck by the rare
> beauty of her form, and by the unaffected grace of her
> attitude. Her figure was tall, yet not too tall; comely and
> well-developed, yet not fat; her head set on her shoulders
> with an easy, pliant firmness; her waist, perfection in the

eyes of a man, for it occupied its natural place, it filled out its natural circle, it was visibly and delightfully unde- formed by stays. She had not heard my entrance into the room; and I allowed myself the luxury of admiring her for a few moments, before I moved one of the chairs near me, as the least embarrassing means of attracting her attention. She turned towards me immediately. The easy elegance of every movement of her limbs and body as soon as she began to advance from the far end of the room, set me in a flutter of expectation to see her face clearly. She left the window—and I said to myself, The lady is dark. She moved forward a few steps—and I said to myself, The lady is young. She approached nearer— and I said to myself (with a sense of surprise which words fail me to express), The lady is ugly! (*The Woman in White*, 31)

The undeniable erotic charge of this scene is heightened rather than lessened by the repulsion that replaces the initial attraction. Fascinated, Walter is almost unable to put his uncanny experience into words. In the paragraph that follows "The lady is ugly!" Walter tries to account for his complex reaction (erotic desire, aesthetic horror) by anatomizing or dissecting Marian's freakish appearance in terms of her contradictory sexual characteristics, notably her woman's body and her man's face. Moreover, Andrea Stulman Dennett notes, "It was deeply arousing to Victorians to touch a strange woman in a legiti- mate, respectable setting."[17] While Dennett's remark about Victorians' arousal by public touching refers to their behavior at freak shows,[18] Walter touches Marian in the respectable setting of Limmeridge House. When she offers her "rather large, but beautifully formed" hand, though, the effect is just as titillating. Unlike Anne Catherick's touch on the road in a setting that is neither legitimate nor respectable, Marian's touch is reassuring, as it is later when she takes both his hands in hers with "the strong, steady grasp of a man" as she pledges herself to him as a "friend" and "sister," putting to rest any hopes or fears he may have had about the transgressive erotic possibilities of their relationship (32, 125).

Walter's meeting of the two women gives birth to the investiga- tion that is the central action of the novel. The woman in white impreg- nates him with her touch, while Marian makes him see himself as pregnant with the mystery that will result in the long difficult "labour" of writing the book, which allows Walter not only to identify the woman in white but to cure himself of her "contagion" by exorcising the woman within. The woman in white is also the woman in Walter. The process of unveiling the mystery of Walter's own place in the world of Victorian gender is accomplished only with the help of Marian, who provides Walter with a mirror in which he is able to see the masculine and feminine in his own character. Faced with an "anomaly" of gender in Marian, Walter sees a reflection of his own uncertain, or as yet unrealized, gender identity. Walter must leave his sexuality—("all the sympathies natural to my age")—"in my employer's outer hall, as coolly as [he] left [his] umbrella there," while Marian carries a "horrid, heavy, man's umbrella" (64, 214). And when Hartright goes to Central America, where he comes into his own manhood at last, it is with the help of Marian, who takes vicarious pleasure in imagining an adventure of the sort normally reserved for men.

The use of intertextual collage, or assemblage, is not simply a literary technique, it is the embodiment and metaphor for a way of seeing the world as a complex weave of signs more or less indecipherable. In *The Woman in White*, the collage of textual records that Hartright and Marian assemble displays a multiplicity of first-person points of view, subjective, fragmentary, and contradictory. Like the bearded lady or hermaphrodite, these texts require a medico-legal investigation to reveal their true character. But what such investigations always reveal is the social construction of gender that the investigator brings to the object. Walter and Marian undertake an epistemological investigation into the identity of the woman in white, but in the mirror of Laura's blank, they end by revealing themselves. While the woman in white is the ostensible object of his and Marian's investigation, it is their own (gender) identity that is the underlying motivation for their researches. Laura, as the shared focus of their love, becomes the blank sheet that receives their inscriptions. Marian's moustache, as the focal sign for all the other "anomalies and contradictions" of the novel, is the best emblem for the epistemological puzzle that Hartright is driven to solve.

Like Dickens, Collins knew that the popular entertainment provided by sideshows could tap deep social and psychological fears. In *The Woman in White* Collins taps the primordial fears of sexual identity and sexual desire by invoking a number of "shock" spectacles current in London at the time he was writing the novel, such as the exhibition of the celebrated bearded ladies Madame Clofullia and Julia Pastrana in the 1850s. These spectacles, however, had precedents

in more traditional representations of hermaphrodites in myth, literature, and art, with which Collins, growing up the son of an artist in
Florence and Paris, would have been familiar. By combining these
intersexual sources from high and low culture in the attractive figure
of Marian Halcombe, Collins created an intertextual collage that
questioned and subverted Victorian notions of gender.

Bearded Ladies in the Exhibition Rooms of the Actual

Marian's moustache is the key to the shock Hartright feels in his first
meeting with Marian, and the key to Collins's observation of ambiguous gender because Victorians considered facial hair to be the male's
"distinguishing characteristic" *(Irish Quarterly)*, or the "distinctive
appendage" *(London Methodist Quarterly Review).*[19] *The Habits of
Good Society: A Handbook of Etiquette for Ladies and Gentlemen*
(1859) even went so far as to say that in addition to being "gossips
and mischief-makers," barbers were eunuch-makers: "Who, in fact,
can respect a man whose sole office is to deprive his sex of their distinctive feature?"[20] These attitudes in the years leading up to the publication of *The Woman in White* convey the shock that facial hair on
a woman might elicit.

Personally, Collins was sensitive to the issue of facial hair
because of his inability to grow whiskers as "glorious" as those of his
friend Dickens. In 1853, while on tour in Italy with Dickens and the
artist Augustus Egg, Wilkie entered into a wager with them to see who
could grow the greatest whiskers. Dickens took pleasure in taunting
his younger friends for their inability to keep up with him in this, as
in every endeavor; his condescending tone is evident in his comment
that Collins and Egg "compliment each other on that appendage."
Dickens describes the three of them at the opera, "Collins with incip-
ient moustache" and Egg with "a straggly mean little black beard."[21]
Collins's moustache was no competition for that of Dickens, who
bragged of his own "glorious, glorious" whiskers: "They are charming, charming. Without them Life would be a blank."[22] Davis notes
that Collins saw moustaches as "daringly un-English" and thought his
public would see his as "a hairy certificate of lunacy."[23]

Dickens was something of a connoisseur of popular entertainments of all kinds, including the freak show, and it would have been
odd indeed if some of his enthusiasm had not rubbed off on his

companion. The freak show was a time-honored British institution. Bartholomew Fair included exhibitions of human anomalies and curiosities every September since the twelfth century until it was suppressed by proclamation in July 1840, when the tradition did not cease but only moved to more upscale venues called exhibition rooms. Dickens and Collins are likely to have visited these together, even though, according to Philip Collins, "various organizations, mainly religious in inspiration and membership, were urging the authorities to act against 'vicious' pleasures."[24] Dickens would use the topic of curiosities in Mr. Venus's shop in *Our Mutual Friend* (1865), but he had already explored the subject in his most sustained novel on the grotesque in nature, *The Old Curiosity Shop* (1840), which opens with a meeting on the road at night between the narrator and Little Nell, a meeting that bears a striking resemblance to Walter Hartright's meeting with Anne Catherick. There are also similarities between Little Nell and the childish Laura Fairlie. Like Nell, whom, according to Paul Schlicke, "Dickens conceived from the outset in juxtaposition to the 'crowd of uncongenial and ancient things,'"[25] Laura is the foil to everything that is threateningly dark and ugly (Marian), brutal (Glyde), or evil (Fosco). As Sue Lonoff notes, "Dickens's relish for all forms of physical distortion, his love of the grotesque, his interest in insanity, can only have struck a responsive chord in a protégé with Collins's proclivities," but while Dickens "thrilled" his Victorian audience, Collins "elicited condemnation."[26] There is good reason for this, since Dickens's caricatures rarely transgress the most closely held prejudices of his audience, while Collins's characters rarely fail to challenge the stereotypical Victorian assumptions about gender.

The *anomaly*, like the *curiosity*, was a good Victorian word for a freak of nature. Other terms were the *What Is It?* and the *nondescript,* deriving from the exhibitions of human freaks that were such a popular form of entertainment in the decade preceding *The Woman in White*. These terms had a scientific air about them, so when P. T. Barnum and other entrepreneurs introduced the freak show stars of bearded ladies and "half-and-half" hermaphrodites to Victorian audiences, they could justify their curiosity as scientific discovery, even as they experienced the frisson of erotic horror, the better to deny that they were in some way related to the teratological example before them.[27]

Among the more striking of the sideshow exhibitions were those of the celebrated bearded ladies Madame Clofullia and Julia Pastrana, who reached the height of their notoriety in London in the 1850s. Two years before P. T. Barnum unveiled Madame Clofullia (née Josephine

Boisdechene) at his American Museum in New York, this Bearded Lady of Geneva had caused a stir in London, where she was examined by a physician to prove that she was not a man in drag.[28] A comparison of the description of Madame Clofullia in the much-publicized physician's report of 1851 with that of Marian in Walter Hartright's narrative provides examples of two different kinds of descriptive discourse: the medico-legal of the physician and the pseudo-legal erotic and aesthetic description of the artist Hartright.[29] While one intends to solve a riddle by forming a judgment, the other poses a riddle by describing an impression. The structures of the two descriptions are suitably reversed, with the doctor listing masculine then feminine characteristics, while Hartright details first his attraction to Marian's femininity and then his repulsion from her masculinity. Both discourses, however, show men struggling with their attraction and repulsion (that is, their fascination) for a hermaphroditic woman.

First, the paragraph that follows Walter's realization, "The woman was ugly!"—which will be followed by the physician's report:

> Never was the old conventional maxim, that Nature
> cannot err, more flatly contradicted—never was the fair
> promise of a lovely figure more strangely and startlingly
> belied by the face and head that crowned it. The lady's
> complexion was almost swarthy, and the dark down on
> her upper lip was almost a moustache. She had a large,
> firm, masculine mouth and jaw; *prominent, piercing,*
> *resolute brown eyes*; and *thick, coal-black hair, growing*
> *unusually low down on her forehead.* Her expression—
> bright, frank, and intelligent—appeared, while she was
> silent, to be altogether wanting in those feminine attrac-
> tions of gentleness and pliability, without which the beauty
> of the handsomest woman alive is beauty incomplete. To
> see such a face as this *set on shoulders that a sculptor*
> *would have longed to model*—to be charmed by *the mod-*
> *est graces of action* through which the symmetrical limbs
> betrayed their beauty when they moved, and then to be
> almost repelled by *the masculine form and masculine*
> *look of the features* in which the perfectly shaped figure
> ended—was to feel a sensation oddly akin to the helpless
> discomfort familiar to us all in sleep, when we recognize
> yet cannot reconcile the *anomalies and contradictions* of
> a dream. (*The Woman in White*, 32; emphases added)

Here, then, is the report of W. D. Chowne, M.D., of Charing Cross Hospital, dated September 22, 1851:

> I have this day seen, professionally, Josephine Boisdechene, and, in relation to the legal question referred to me, hereby certify, that although she has *beard and whiskers, large, profuse, and strictly masculine,* on those parts of the face (*the upper lip excepted*) occupied by the beard and whiskers in men, and, although on her limbs *and back,* she has even more hair than is usually found on men, she is *without malformation.* Her breasts are large and fair, and strictly characteristic of the female.[30] (emphases added)

Several comparative details will strike the reader familiar with Collins's description of Marian Halcombe. The first is that the doctor, after viewing Josephine's back, decides that she is "without malformation," while Marian is "delightfully undeformed" by stays and corsets. The second is that while Josephine's hair is found everywhere but on her upper lip, that is the only place it appears on Marian.

Even more famous than Madame Clofullia was Julia Pastrana, who was exhibited as "The Ugliest Woman in the World" in Regent Street in 1857. Pastrana died in childbirth at age twenty-eight in 1860, the year of *The Woman in White* (see fig. 5.1). After her death, Pastrana was put on display (with her dead child) in a glass case in London as "The Embalmed Female Nondescript," capitalizing on the term that, coined for a species heretofore undescribed, was related in the popular imagination with Darwin's missing link. In *Curiosities of Natural History* (1900), Francis T. Buckland describes Pastrana in much the same fashion that Chowne describes Madame Clofullia, carefully moving from masculine to feminine features.

> [H]er eyes were deep black, and somewhat *prominent,* and their lids had long, thick eyelashes; her features were simply hideous on account of the *profusion of hair growing on her forehead,* and her black beard; *but her figure was exceedingly good and graceful,* and her tiny foot and well-turned ankle, *bien chaussé,* perfection itself. She had a sweet voice, great taste in music and dancing, and could speak three languages. She was very charitable, and gave largely to local institutions from her earnings. I believe that her true history was that she was simply a *deformed* Mexican Indian woman.[31] (emphases added)

FIG. 5.1. Julia Pastrana. Date unknown.

Marian's "modest graces of action" are reflected in the dancer Pastrana's "good and graceful figure"; Marian's "clear, ringing, pleasant voice" is echoed in the singer Pastrana's "sweet voice." Indeed, Collins's description of the "highly-bred" Marian could almost stand in for that of Julia Pastrana with her "great taste" in the arts and her linguistic skills.

Marian's portrait suggests that Collins was familiar with the bearded ladies of the exhibition rooms, if not with the medico-legal literature on them as well. Some differences in detail seem to argue for rather than against this connection. For example, Josephine Boisdechene had a beard and not a moustache, but Collins must have realized that he could not get away with a *bearded* lady in the drawing room of Victorian fiction. Also, it was conceded that Boisdechene was not ugly but was a handsome woman; still, her marriage to a young landscape painter who was tutoring her in watercolors bears an intriguing resemblance to Marian's relationship with Walter. As for Julia Pastrana, "The Ugliest Woman in the World" came from the region of Central America, while the "ugly" Marian sends Walter to work as an illustrator on an archaeological expedition to the same region.[32]

Collins sums up the uncanny experience of first viewing Marian as the inability to "reconcile the anomalies and contradictions of a dream," but his readers would have experienced similar sensations viewing the anomalies and curiosities of freaks in the exhibition rooms. According to Richard Altick, "Intently examined, the history of the Victorians' involvement with human freaks is a fair index to certain aspects of their psyche. But the macabre return of Julia Pastrana, the bearded Mexican lady who sang in a sweet voice and spoke three languages, perhaps suggests more than do most such tales."[33] The timing and popularity of these exhibitions on the eve of Darwin's *Origin of Species* and in the midst of imperial expansion suggest that Victorian doubt was even deeper than a creeping agnosticism and had penetrated every level of Western man's epistemological identity categories, from his ontological status as the crown of creation, to his ethnic status as the most powerful being on earth, to his psychological status of gender identity.

Like Marian, bearded ladies and hermaphrodites called into question "the old conventional maxim, that Nature cannot err." But Collins's phrase "anomalies and contradictions" suggests a more dialogical relationship between dream and reality than the "anomalies and curiosities" used in medical treatises on teratology.[34] Doctors and judges attempted to answer the question so often asked about hermaphrodites and bearded women—"what sex is it?"—but even they, for all their analytical and dissective skills, were sometimes in doubt about whether such anomalies could be reconciled as either male or female, or constituted some *tertium quid,* a third, intersex between man and woman. In the realm of the sexually monstrous, science and imaginative literature seemed equally at loss for words.[35]

Similar attempts at a dissective analysis of the physical signs of gender occur whenever Hartright meets another male character. Of the neurasthenic Frederick Fairlie, he notes that his feet were "effeminately small" and shod in "womanish" slippers (*The Woman in White*, 39–40).[36] "Upon the whole, he had a frail, languidly-fretful, over-refined look—something singularly and unpleasantly delicate in its association with a man, and, at the same time, something which could by no possibility have looked natural and appropriate if it had been transferred to the personal appearance of a woman" (42–43). Hartright's analysis, which suggests the viewing of a "What Is It?" discovers only that Fairlie is neither this nor that, a confusion of gender that is far less acceptable in a man than a woman. In *In Memoriam* Tennyson praised the androgynous ideal of perfect balance, "manhood fused with female grace,"[37] but his tolerance for mixed gender identities stopped at the "effeminate" man or "mannish" woman.[38] In "On One Who Affected an Effeminate Manner," a quatrain published in 1889, Tennyson wrote:

> While man and woman still are incomplete,
> I prize that soul where man and woman meet,
> Which types all Nature's male and female plan,
> But, friend, man-woman is not woman-man.[39]

The balance of visible gender characteristics, in other words, should fall on the person's "real" or appropriate sex; "Men should be androgynous and women gynandrous," Tennyson wrote in a late notebook, "but men should not be gynandrous nor women androgynous."[40] Like Tennyson, Hartright can look beyond Marian's apparent androgyny to see that she is actually gynandrous, but he cannot abide Fairlie's gynandry: "My morning's experience of Miss Halcombe had predisposed me to be pleased with everybody in the house; but my sympathies shut themselves up resolutely at the first sight of Mr. Fairlie" (*The Woman in White*, 40).[41] That Hartright makes his judgment at the "first sight" of Fairlie suggests that his analysis is based entirely on visible signs of gender without taking into account the man's annoying personality.

Similar first-sight descriptions of Percival Glyde and Count Fosco cast them too in ambiguous sexual roles. Walter focuses on Fairlie's feet; Anne Catherick also describes Glyde synecdochically: "his nose straight and handsome and delicate enough to have done for a woman's. His hands the same" (79).[42] Capable of a deceitful charm, Glyde is normally brusque and brutal, except in the presence of Count Fosco, whose approval he looks for, Marian notices, "more than once in the course of the evening" (231). Fosco himself is "noiseless in a room as any of us women" and "nervously sensitive as the weakest of us," starting at "chance noises as inveterately as Laura herself" (222). Among "his effeminate tastes and amusements" are sweets and small pets, and when Fosco sings Figaro's song, he looks "like a fat St Cecilia masquerading in male attire" (225, 230). Yet he also possesses a mesmeric power over Marian, both in his eyes and in his speech: his "most unfathomable gray eyes" force her "to look at him" and cause in her "sensations, when I do look, which I would rather not feel" (221). His talk causes her to reflect: "Women can resist a man's love, a man's fame, a man's personal appearance, and a man's money; but they cannot resist a man's tongue, when he knows how to talk to them" (260).[43] Marian herself confesses she has a woman's tongue, and Hartright remarks that she grows "womanly the moment she [begins] to speak" (32).

In developing his approach to gender in the novel, Collins is careful to place each principal character along a continuum between masculine and feminine poles. Most readers have agreed that the principal interest is not to be found in the purported main characters of Laura and Walter, but in the secondary characters. As one reviewer in *Dublin University Magazine* wrote, "Both hero and heroine are wooden, commonplace, uninteresting in any way apart from the story itself."[44] Collins knew that he had to *have* a hero and heroine, the more commonplace the better, but the wooden Walter and the anemic Laura are poles of standard Victorian notions of gender, controlled subjects created for mass consumption, by whom we measure the more interesting characters of mixed gender who transgress the usual boundaries and subvert Victorian standards. This is why most critics and modern readers have recognized the "couple" of true interest in the novel to be Marian Halcombe and Count Fosco. Fosco's cynical European amorality (which Collins admitted was his own) offsets Walter's British righteousness, while Marian's dark hermaphroditic sublimity provides a subversive aesthetic to undermine the standard of Laura's pale and childish prettiness.

The Victorian period's unusual interest in such "anomalies and contradictions" was an indication of a flagging trust in the infallibility of Nature. It was also a reflection of the crumbling cosmology that placed man at the crown of creation, European man at the crown of the empire, and man as the crowned head of the family. Not everyone liked what they saw in Darwin's mirror. If species progressed through change and adaptation, was there not the possibility of an adaptive throwback, especially if women could adapt to changing conditions for their own survival? Freaks were living proof that Nature could, in Hartright's phrase, "err." Nature might get its signals mixed and toss off various mutations, adaptations, and whimsies, which in effect would prove that Nature sometimes transgresses itself, or at least the Victorian constructions of Nature. In such a mirror, the Victorian's dream of replacing faith with science became a nightmare, and the freak show became an opportunity to say, "there but for the grace of God, go I." Normative physiology, as in the Middle Ages, remained the sign of God's favor.[45]

Nature is mentioned some fifty times in the early pages of the book. Hartright gives an excellent refutation of the Wordsworthian view of nature as an important instinctual component of our moral lives. This is a typical Victorian reaction to Romanticism: even though everyone gave lip service to the sublimity of Nature, no one really trusted its essential morality, which was more likely to be "red in tooth and claw" than nursemaid. One needed a more pragmatic basis for morality in some sort of faith, if not faith in religion then in science or art. Hartright argues:

> We go to Nature for comfort in trouble, and sympathy
> in joy, only in books. Admiration of those beauties of
> the inanimate world, which modern poetry so largely
> and eloquently describes, is not, even in the best of us,
> one of the original instincts of our nature. As children,
> we none of us possess it. No uninstructed man or woman
> possesses it. Those whose lives are most exclusively
> passed amid the ever-changing wonders of sea and land
> are also those who are most universally insensible to every
> aspect of Nature not directly associated with the human
> interest of their calling. Our capacity of appreciating the
> beauties of the earth we live on is, in truth, one of the
> civilised accomplishments which we all learn, as an Art.
> (*The Woman in White*, 53)

This passage is important to an understanding of how Walter observes and learns to appreciate not only the beauties of Nature but also its so-called errors. Hartright gives a comic example of Nature's incompetence in Mrs. Vesey:

> Nature has so much to do in this world, and is engaged in
> generating such a vast variety of co-existent productions,
> that she must surely be now and then too flurried and
> confused to distinguish between the different processes
> that she is carrying on at the same time. Starting from this
> point of view, it will always remain my private persuasion

that Nature was absorbed in making cabbages when
Mrs Vesey was born, and that the good lady suffered
the consequences of a vegetable preoccupation in the
mind of the Mother of us all. (46)

Considering that this reflection comes directly after Hartright's first meetings with Marian and Fairlie, it is difficult not to read this as a comic displacement of a far more disturbing question about how Nature "errs."

As a teacher of art, Hartright understands that one must learn to observe and interpret Nature in its moral sense as an Art. Walter's initial description of Marian shows a painterly eye for detail worthy of a Pre-Raphaelite artist, but he must learn to look at her as a critic might learn to look at a new and startling representation of nature. The more he stares at her, the less she is a woman and the more she becomes his metaphor for her, a statue, a work of art that only then can be compared to the works of Nature. Wisely, Walter learns to see beyond the surface of the natural error of Marian's hermaphroditic ugliness, and to see instead the beauty of her moral accomplishments. The more inclusive one's vision of Art, the more inclusive is one's moral being. Marian's own view of art is pragmatic: some acquaintance with the arts is a necessary social accomplishment, but she has no faith in a woman's ability to have any real knowledge of art, a view of which Laura seems the proof. An inept artist, Laura appreciates Hartright's painting entirely for its sentimental value. In women, then, artlessness appears to be a virtue, while in men, placing too high a value on art is a sign of moral weakness. Isolated from nature and locked up with his drawings, Frederick Fairlie has become a monster of aestheticism. He loses all feeling for anyone but himself, abdicating responsibility for his family and considering children to be mere annoyances except as the legless, lungless angels of Raphael, the props of art, like his servant who, by the same token, is not a human being but "simply a portfolio stand" (44, 159).

Acting as Walter's instructor in moral appearances, Marian compares herself to Laura in the least favorable light: "I am dark and ugly, and she is fair and pretty. Everybody thinks me crabbed and odd (with perfect justice); and everybody thinks her sweet-tempered and charming (with more justice still). In short, she is an angel; and I am—Try some of that marmalade, Mr Hartright, and finish the sentence, in the name of female propriety, for yourself" (34). The pause allows Walter, and the reader, to fill in the blank; by the end of the novel, however, we will all use the same word to describe both Laura and Marian: angel. At this point, though, we have several choices for angel's complement: devil? monster? human? Some early reviewers called this reticence a clever trick of Collins's composition, like the ellipses in *Tristram Shandy*, a gimmick of mystification to get his readers to do the work of writing his books for him.[46] Actually it is precisely what Marian says it is, a concession to "female propriety," since what she is, is the opposite of sexless Laura. Laura's angelic aura stems from her diaphanous sexuality, the androgyny of the child whose gender is as yet undifferentiated; what is *not* angelic about Marian is the material actuality of a highly charged, *doubled* sexuality, the hermaphrodism of the already consummated and taboo fetish.

The relative sensuousness of Laura and Marian is reflected in the activities they pursue, and especially in the arts that Walter associates with them. Laura's talent is for music, the least material art, and is associated with watercolors, the least material of painting media; Marian does not know "one note of music," but at such mathematical and geometric pursuits as "chess, backgammon, écarté, and (with the inevitable female drawbacks) even at billiards as well," she claims to be able to "match" Walter, who associates her with the most material of the arts, sculpture (35). Schopenhauer's aesthetic hierarchy ranked the arts according to their relative freedom from the material, with music at the top and sculpture at the bottom. Since, according to Pater, "All art constantly aspires towards the condition of music,"[47] Walter naturally prefers Laura, who, like all well-bred Victorian women, aspires to the *production* of music. Walter himself, the drawing master, begins by appreciating art and music but ends by appreciating the written word: "Miss Halcombe's graceful figure, half of it in soft light, half in mysterious shadow, bending intently over the letters in her lap" (55). The "letters" in her lap indicate the "masculine" power of her literacy.[48] Walter continues, "We all sat in the places we had chosen—Mrs Vesey still sleeping, Miss Fairlie still playing, Miss Halcombe still reading" (56). These are less "chosen" activities than symbolic performances of Victorian gender roles.

Collins did not see the gender curiosities he found in the exhibition (or drawing) rooms to be confusions but realistic specimens of "the Actual." In his Letter of Dedication to *Basil* (1852), he puts forth his theory of the Actual as a living text to draw from: "My idea was that the more of the Actual I could garner up as a text to speak from, the more certain I might feel the genuineness and value of the Ideal which was sure to spring out of it."[49] This theory shows Collins moving from a painterly or illusionist collage in his earlier literary portraiture (in *The Dead Secret* a maid is described two-dimensionally as having a young face framed in an old woman's gray hair) to a sculptural or actualist collage in which contradictory physical characteristics must be seen in the round (as when Walter says of Marian: "To see such a face as this set on shoulders that a sculptor would have longed to model" [34]). Like the circumspection of multiple narratives, the collage technique seems to have borne fruit for Collins in creating complex characters pieced together from contradictory fragments of personality and anatomy.[50] Collins's metaphor for the Actual was any London omnibus where various classes and temperaments were found "oddly collected together" and "contrasted with each other" in "a perambulatory exhibition-room of the eccentricities of human nature" (*Basil*, 27). Such exhibition rooms were just the place to encounter such eccentricities and varieties of human anatomy as those suggested by Marian Halcombe's moustache.

The Erotic Hermaphrodite: High Art and Popular Entertainment

Collins's theory of seeing characters in the round was conceived not only in omnibus rides and exhibition rooms but also in art galleries. Like the bearded ladies of popular entertainments, the hermaphrodite has a long history in myth, literature, and art, but it became ubiquitous in the nineteenth century, which, as Foucault asserts, "was so powerfully haunted by the theme of the hermaphrodite—somewhat as the eighteenth century had been haunted by the theme of the transvestite."[51] Collins would have been familiar with the hermaphrodite from his youth and later travels, but its fascination for the Pre-Raphaelite poets and painters would have brought its significance up to date.[52] Two works of art in particular seem to have contributed to the portrait of Marian Halcombe: John Everett Millais's painting *Mariana* (1851, fig. 5.2) and Bernini's restoration of the Hellenistic statue *Hermaphrodite endormi* in the Louvre.

The connection between Millais's portrait of Mariana and Collins's portrait of Marian has been overlooked, perhaps because of the facial beauty of Millais's model.[53] Yet Millais was supposedly with Collins when he allegedly met Caroline Graves, the original woman in white, and his *Mariana* was notorious for the frank sensuality of its portrayal of a woman seen at a window from behind in a dress that shows off her

FIG. 5.2. John Everett Millais, *Mariana,* 1851. © Tate, London 2002.

figure, "visibly and delightfully undeformed by stays." That Collins's novel takes place from 1849 to 1851 also locates it as the contemporary of Millais's painting. Millais's frontispiece for Collins's next novel, *No Name* (1862), presents an almost identical setting as his *Mariana* and features the same model (fig. 5.3).

FIG. 5.3. John Everett Millais, frontispiece to *No Name* (London: Sampson Low, 1864).

A further intertextual frame linking Millais's portrait of Mariana with Collins's portrait of Marian is the *Sleeping Hermaphrodite*. One difference between painting and novel is that Mariana is standing while Marian is reclining on a sofa. But the extraordinary resemblance among the figures in the painting, the novel, and the statue can be seen clearly by turning a picture of the statue of the recumbent *Sleeping Herma-phrodite* on end and placing it next to Millais's painting. This very difference is what argues for the subtext of the statue and painting in the novel. Like the figures in the painting and the statue, Marian is first seen from behind, Collins's preferred perspective for viewing women.[54] And like them, she is shown in a state of reverie. Daydreaming about Walter in Central America, she is reclining on a sofa, lulled by "The quiet in the house, and the low *murmuring hum of summer insects* outside the open window. . . . In this state, my fevered mind broke loose from me, while my *weary* body was at rest" (277; emphases added). This passage echoes Tennyson's "Mariana," on which Millais's painting is based, in which Mariana, while waiting for Angelo at the "moated grange," hears the humming of insects ("The blue fly sung in the pane"), and sings her refrain "I am aweary, aweary."[55]

Collins's familiarity with the hermaphrodite in art would go back to his childhood, growing up as the son of an artist in cities where the museums offered several sculptural examples of the *Sleeping Herma-phrodite* in replicas housed in Paris (the Louvre), Florence (the Uffizi), Rome (the Villa Borghese), as well as London (the British Museum).[56] By age thirteen Collins had a variety of sexual experiences, the nature of which may have raised questions of gender. In Italy he fell for "one of the most consummate rascals in Rome—a gambler, a thief, and a *stiletto* wearer, at twelve years of age." This boy was one of his father's models, "a beautiful boy, with features dazzlingly perfect, who had sat to every one for cupids, angels, and whatever else was lovely and refined."[57] The homoerotic subtext of this friendship would have contributed to an informed viewing of the *Sleeping Hermaphrodite* in the Villa Borghese.

Collins may have been reminded of these early experiences during his trip to Paris in 1856 with Dickens to enjoy "*en garçon* . . . the festive diableries of Paris," when Collins is said to have conceived several elements of *The Woman in White*.[58] In addition to popular entertainments such as wrestling matches and shady ballrooms, the friends on holiday also attended the theater and art galleries.[59] At the Louvre they would have seen not only the *Venus de Milo* but also the *Hermaphrodite endormi,* already immortalized by Shelley in *The Witch of Atlas* and Théophile Gautier in his poem "Contralto" (1849).[60] Seeing the *Sleeping Hermaphrodite* while forming the novel in his mind would have provided Collins with the ultimate expression of mixed gender that unifies the portrayal of all the principal characters in *The Woman in White*.[61]

In addition to providing the key to the puzzle of his intersexual collage, the *Sleeping Hermaphrodite* would also have given Collins the sensational experience of viewing this perplexing figure. Three years after the publication of Collins's novel, Swinburne would narrate his own reaction to Bernini's sculpture in his poem "Hermaphroditus," dated "*Au Musée du Louvre, Mars 1863*." Swinburne's homage to the statue is an occasional poem in the best sense of the term, capturing the poet's vivid experience in a narrative of how one looks at statuary, and this statue in particular. The first of four sonnet stanzas begins by asking the figure to "turn round, look back for love," but ends in frustration: "And whosoever hath seen thee, being so fair, / Two things turn all his life and blood to fire; / A strong desire begot on great despair, / A great despair cast out by strong desire." Later, the narrator realizes that for all the figure's sexual tension, "the fruitful feud of hers and his" turns into "the waste wedlock of a sterile kiss." The poem ends in an ironic question: "But Love being blind, how should he know of this?"[62] Both Swinburne's description of Hermaphroditus and Collins's description of Marian begin by looking at the feminine figure from behind, continue by focusing on the ambiguous figure's lips when she/it turns around, and end on her/its sexual unavailability: "so dreadful, so desirable, so dear." Whether Swinburne borrowed from Collins, poet and novelist describe both an object of sexual ambiguity and the narrativity of viewing such an object.

Most critics agree that there is a "spectacular" or "textual" quality about Walter's viewing of Marian.[63] As a drawing master, he views her aesthetically with a critic's eye to composition, the play of light on her body, the ease of her posture, and so on. As a man, he also views her erotically, noting the absence of stays. As Kimberley Reynolds and Nicola Humble point out, "Marian's body is described with a lascivious textual attention, anatomised feature by feature, in marked contrast to the textual and visual evasions employed to describe Laura. Far from the revelation of Marian's ugliness forming a shocking reversal that would deny the previous eroticisation, it is precisely *because* she is ugly—and therefore not textually available as a wife for Walter—that she can be seen as an erotic spectacle."[64] Harvey Peter Sucksmith agrees: "Significantly, it is only Marian's face that is ugly; the discrepancy between her face and her beautiful figure reflects the dissociation between sexual feeling and the sexual instinct." Pointing out "the classic case" of John Ruskin's traumatic wedding-night disgust with Effie Gray, Sucksmith goes further: "Marian is unattractive, yet that other nether-face of sexuality, with other lips and other cheeks, which is secretly displaced upwards in Marian's form, is at once both ugly and attractive; body and face are unconsciously reversed in such a way as to conceal yet betray the true state of things."[65]

Walter's conflicting reaction takes us back to our discussion of the conflict between Nature and Art. While Walter's bodily instinct tells him that Marian is attractive, his socially constructed aesthetic sense tells him that she is not. Leslie Fiedler begins his chapter on "Beauty and the Beast: The Eros of Ugliness": "All Freaks are perceived to one degree or another as erotic. Indeed, abnormality arouses in some 'normal' beholders a temptation to go beyond looking to *knowing* in the full carnal sense the ultimate other."[66] This is especially true of the Bearded Venus, who makes us call "into question—in a troubling but by no means anaphrodisiac way—our belief in the bipolarity of the sexes."[67]

Walter is afraid that his initial physical attraction to Marian is not normal, but he consoles himself by convincing himself that it is Nature who has erred. A great reader of French literature, Collins would have been familiar with similar scenes in Casanova, Hugo, Balzac, and Gautier. In Casanova's *Memoirs* (1826–38) and in Gautier's *Mademoiselle de Maupin* (1834), the narrators are attracted to effeminate boys who turn out to be women in disguise, a Shakespearean paradigm that suggests that Nature does *not* err and that the attraction was simply Nature's way of seeing through the disguise of Art (as artifice). No social taboos are ultimately transgressed. Collins's treatment, however, leaves the question of Walter's physical attraction for Marian open.

Walter's uncanny discomfort with Marian's moustache is possibly a variation on Freud's interpretation of the Medusa as a "genitalized head," which Elaine Showalter explains as "an upward displacement of the sexual organs, so that the mouth stands for the *vagina dentata*."[68] This would seem to be supported by the way Walter in his detailed description moves from Marian's moustache not to her nose (the facial feature most often associated with masculinity—Glyde's effeminate nose gives away his essential weakness) but to her "large, firm, masculine mouth" (*The Woman in White*, 32). Freud saw the fear of our universal bisexuality as the fear of castration, a common fear, exemplified during the Victorian era by Ruskin's (and perhaps Hartright's) fear of frank adult female sexuality. This reading of Walter's reaction to Marian's hermaphrodism suggests that she represents a challenge to his own developing gender identity, an originating anxiety about his sexual maturity that will take the rest of the novel to work out.

If Marian's moustache represents a Medusa archetype of castration anxiety, the hermaphrodite may be seen as the remedy, replacing the penis in a dream of surgical restoration. If so, why does the hermaphrodite cause such disturbing reactions? One answer may be that the hermaphrodite stands for the female's usurpation of the penis, a superaddition to femininity, a doubling of female empowerment. In the Ovidian myth, the nymph Salmacis loses her female identity by being added (wed) to Hermaphroditus; she loses her name but gains a penis, increasing her power but becoming anonymous, while decreasing his power and making him infamous. The vagina dentata, on the other hand, simply subtracts the male's penis without adding anything to the female except the exercise of destructive power itself. The simpler explanation would be that Walter suffers from a simple case of frustrated desire. Walter's fear of finding a penis already attached to the "perfection" of Marian's waist ruins his desire, preempts it, blocking what would otherwise be accessible to him. His desire for Marian's body is frustrated by the sign of her moustache, but whether this invokes a taboo against homosexuality, justified later as an incest taboo in her role as his "sister," or simply a taboo against mating with a highly sexed woman is debatable.

Marian's moustache is less an indication of her masculinity than of her obvious adult female sexuality, the dash of testosterone, without which, as we know today, neither male nor female can be fully sexual. This dash Walter himself lacks, at least early in the novel. With a discomforting reflexivity, Walter identifies with Laura's asexuality: "At one time it seemed like something wanting in *her;* at another, like something wanting in myself" (50–51). In contrast to Laura, in whom "incompleteness" signifies the "sacred weakness" of her role as "angel" and "child," Marian wears her sex, we might say, not on her sleeve but on her lip. What Walter and Laura lack is the resolution and strength of character signified by Marian's moustache. In many of the depictions of the hermaphrodite, such as those in the National Museum in Stockholm and in the Wallace Collection in London, the double-sexed figure is shown in an attitude of displaying its sexual organs, or *anasyrma*. While the Sheela-na-gig of British folklore reveals the sexual organs of a female, the purpose is the same as that of the hermaphrodite; according to Delcourt, "The revealing of the sexual organs had a double purpose, both positive, to stimulate the powers of life, and prophylactic, to ward off evil forces."[69] A similar purpose has been ascribed to certain bearded ladies, notably St. Wilgeforte or Vigiforte, also known as St. Liberata or St. Uncumber, to whom women prayed to be rid of their husbands; she was not born with a beard, but, according to Fiedler, prayed to God "to afflict her in some way that would make her sexually undesirable."[70] Marian's moustache is a kind of *anasyrma*, an unveiling that reveals her sex, turns her hidden sex inside out, making immediately available what the Victorian male would have felt should be earned. Marian's ambiguous effect on Walter is thus both to stimulate his erotic instinct before he meets Laura and simultaneously to ward off his advances on Marian herself.

If Walter is put off by Marian's sexuality and textualizes it, Fosco reads her like a book. In his first meeting with Marian, Walter is careful to undress her stealthily from behind, although he seems less to undress her with his eyes than to be unaware of her clothing, as though she is already naked, only noting the absence of stays. Later too he views Marian's sexuality textually when he notices her "graceful figure, half of it in soft light, half in mysterious shadow, bending intently over the letters in her lap" (55). Fosco, however, undresses Marian immediately with his eyes, seeing through her masculine disguise, "reading" her sex even before he violates her by reading the text of her journal. The darkness and moustache that Walter takes to be signs of her "ugliness," Fosco interprets as attractive, reading her facial hair not as a sign of hidden masculinity (that "pushes through from within," as D. A. Miller puts it),[71] but as the physical sign of her heightened female sexuality. As Victor Hugo says in *The Man Who Laughs*: "Ugliness is insignificant, deformity is grand. Ugliness is a devil's grin behind beauty; deformity is akin to sublimity."[72] Fosco sees only a "sublime creature, . . . this magnificent Marian" (*The Woman in White*, 343).

The opposite of Marian's masculinity (or sexual availability), indicated by her darkness and hairiness, is Laura's extreme femininity or asexuality, signified by unmodulated lightness, fairness, and transparency veiled in the ultra-symbolic white fabrics variously construed as the swaddling clothes of an infant, the hospital gown of an invalid or madwoman, the robes of an angel, or the winding sheet of the dead. This light and shadow imagery has caused Sophia Andres to argue that Anne Catherick (and later Laura) represents Walter's *anima*, "the shadowy figure [who] becomes an integral part of Hartright's quest for psychic integration."[73] While this makes sense, the argument is not complete without considering that the woman in white who leads him on his quest is not the only shadow figure he has to deal with, nor the most important. It is rather the dark and fully present Marian rather than the pale Anne/Laura (their sexuality displaced and diluted through doubling) who presents the greater challenge to his ability. Collins "aroused and allayed the fear of the Other"[74] by integrating it psychically into Walter. While the woman in white presents a puzzle about legal identity, it is the dark lady who presents a far more disturbing puzzle about sexual identity. As Sucksmith points out, the confrontation with *anima* is more complex than a simple working out of light and dark imagery, which is why Collins needed "two heroines in the novel but only one hero, for Collins achieves psychological validity with this trio by representing in Victorian terms what have been called the *anima* and the *shadow*—that is, here, the Victorian male's idealized image of woman together with much of a contradictory nature that is excluded from that ideal. Collins, the man who later lived with two women, depicts a hero who experiences the dual nature of woman."[75]

As in *The Taming of the Shrew*, the social constructions of gender that Laura and Marian represent to Walter are only as superficial as those that differentiate between the supposedly submissive Bianca and the supposedly shrewish Kate, whose divergence from the feminine norm similarly provokes prospective suitors to assume that she is "not fair"—suitors, that is, who are less imaginative and resourceful than Petruccio. As men of the world who know what they want in a woman, Fosco and Petruccio are able to see beneath such superficial constructions. Fosco knows that Marian's moustache, like Kate's discourse, is a decoy, the clever defense of a highly sexed virgin, anti-aesthetic camouflage to ward off unwanted sexual advances. Bianca is all that her name promises only in name and refuses to come when her husband calls, just as Miss Fairlie is fair to eye and ear but has other ways of making herself sexually inaccessible, such as the Victorian female's neurasthenia. Marian cannot help but be flattered when she overhears Fosco chiding Glyde for treating Marian "as if she was no sharper and no bolder than the rest of her sex," such as "that poor flimsy pretty blonde wife" of his (*The Woman in White*, 331). "Where are your eyes?" Fosco asks Glyde. "Can you look at Miss Halcombe, and not see that she has the foresight and the resolution of a man?" (330).

Ironically, it is Marian who is Hartright's primary role model in his discovery of his masculinity. Laura is a mirror image of Walter's immature sexuality, as undifferentiated as a child's, while Marian's hermaphrodism mirrors Walter's as yet unachieved sexual maturity. It is Marian who instructs him to how to deal with his first feeling of love for Laura: "Crush it! . . . Don't shrink under it like a woman. Tear it out; trample it under foot like a man" (71). When he cannot crush it in spite of Marian's "generous faith in [his] manhood," she instructs Hartright to leave Limmeridge House and gets him a post as draughtsman on the Central American expedition that turns out to be his rite of passage into manhood. When Walter returns, he is "a changed man," ready to face his future "as a man should" (415).

Significantly, on his return Walter is also able to read any number of ambiguous new signs. Not only can he read Fosco's scheme, he is also ready to interpret the ambiguities of Marian's appearance and of his relationship with her. While his duties on his journey to Central America would not have included collecting "nondescripts" for London sideshows, Walter would have had to illustrate hieroglyphic Mayan sculptures of figures that were both textually and sexually indecipherable.[76] Hartright's education in textual indecipherability coincides with Collins's interest in sexual indecipherability, just as Hartright's education in sculpture coincides with Collins's development of his theory of the Actual.

Marian is not simply Walter's tutor in masculine etiquette, she is also his role model in his *amour,* teaching him how to win Laura away from her for himself. Playing Cyrano to Walter's Christian, Marian must be convinced that Walter will make Laura happy, but once she is won over she is loyal and self-effacing, no longer worrying that, as she tells Laura earlier, "no man tolerates a rival—not even a woman rival—in his wife's affections" (188). This fear turns out to be unfounded, since Walter will not only tolerate Marian but encourage the bond between Laura and Marian. An example of René Girard's "triangulation of desire," the relationship between the three of them can be seen in terms of Eve Kosofsky Sedgwick's discussion of homosocial bonding in *Between Men,*[77] except that here, instead of an exchange of women that mediates between men, the exchange of Laura is between Marian and Walter. This bonding exchange removes the competition between Marian and Walter so that they can share Laura.

By the final scene, all of Walter's original uncanny discomfort at seeing the hermaphroditic Marian has disappeared. With the three of them settled in a ménage, Walter appears to have the best of both worlds at his disposal: a fair wife heroically rescued and an intelligent and sexually mature woman of ability. The ambiguity of the household's arrangement is emphasized by the fact that Laura is bedridden and by the suggestive visual pun of Marian's lifting up (literally "bearing") Walter's child, to present him with "the Heir of Limmeridge." At this moment Collins invokes several narrative clichés to show that Walter's masculine destiny is perfected. He has slain the dragon, rescued the maiden, and sired a child, but these mythic signs of maturity are not enough to prove his manhood in the Victorian economy. He comes fully into his manhood only when Frederick Fairlie's death conveniently gives him his financial "independence" (a word ironized by his having married money) and his six-month-old heir something to inherit. The death of the effeminate Fairlie signals the death of Walter's own effeminacy, thus fully enfranchising him in the Victorian economy. If Marian's transformation is from ugly hermaphrodite to good angel, Walter's is from a sexless and subservient "domestic animal," who must leave his umbrella in his employer's outer hall, into a man who has mastered the roles of manliness as explorer, hero, knight-errant, advocate, forensic analyst, lover, husband, *and* property owner. According to Ann Cvetkovich, "the sign of his class difference is his desexualization."[78] Now when Marian announces the *heir* of Limmeridge, we may recall Walter's first encounter with her, when a very different sort of "hair" was on her lips. Having overcome his fear of the "hair" of Limmeridge (Marian's moustache) that brought his own sexuality into question in the first place, Walter is able to celebrate his own "heir" (his son) which settles the question of his gender once and for all. To the extent that *The Woman in White* is Walter's bildungsroman, what has been torn down and rebuilt is the construction of his gender, the architect of which is Marian.

At Limmeridge House little has changed except that Walter is in charge instead of Frederick Fairlie, whose position as the resident invalid Laura assumes, while Marian directs the household for her invalid sister, keeping her mediating position between Hartright's ideal Victorian male and Laura's ideal Victorian female. An archetype of what Susan Balée calls the Victorian "surplus woman,"[79] Marian cannot have offspring of her own, but she cares for theirs, the ideal Victorian infant. Walter's transformation from surplus male to property owner could not have taken place without first turning Marian into a surrogate wife and mother, nursemaid, governess, and housekeeper. Even in her role of presiding over the birth and presumably the rearing of Walter and Laura's child, Marian's moustache is not without precedent in antiquity; according to Fiedler, "among the oldest Freak forms of the goddess of love (antedated only by the Fat Aphrodite) are the Bald Venus and the Bearded Venus, who in Cyprus were combined into a single deity believed to preside over childbirth."[80] And as Ajootian notes, "Roman sculptures of Hermaphroditos as a *kourotrophos,* holding a baby or Eros, also attest to a nurturing aspect for this divinity."[81] If not for this safely unsexed role that Marian plays in the household, their threesome might have come under scrutiny, as did Dickens's arrangement with his wife and her sister

Georgina, or Collins's own dual households. Having split himself between two women, each of whom presumably provided him with something that the other could not, Collins knew that one man living with two women under the same roof needed some decoy of respectability, some practical justification for the arrangement to be accepted, a justification that Collins is more careful to provide to his readers than he was to his neighbors.

Now, far from being "almost repelled" by Marian or seeing her as a "rival" for Laura's affection, Walter accepts Marian as "the good angel of our lives" (*The Woman in White*, 643). Marian has been transformed from a disturbing diabolical hermaphrodism (monstrously sterile) to a reassuring angelic androgyny (the Madonna's parthenogenesis or impregnation through the word).[82] Significantly, Walter does not have the last word but gives it to Marian: "So she spoke. In writing those last words, I have written all. The pen falters in my hand; the long, happy labour of many months is over! Marian was the good angel of our lives—let Marian end our Story" (643). All anxieties about power, position, and privilege having been dissolved, Walter puts aside his pen, allowing Marian to have the last (spoken) word. While Marian's writing is as good as any man's, Marian has the tongue of a woman. Walter's final rhetorical strategy of magnanimous self-effacement disguises the fact that he could not have achieved his place as head of the household without subordinating both Laura and Marian, although not as brutally as Glyde would have done.

Quite apart from the subtext of patriarchal hegemony inscribed here, Walter's rhetorical strategy keeps a neat balance between his and Marian's ascendancy, between his de jure power and her de facto power over the household and over Laura. Walter and Marian share governance of the household, with Laura fulfilling the role she has had throughout the story as the dependent child and angel of the house. Instead of the letters of the earlier scene, the baby is now in Marian's lap, suckling a "coral" nipple that, like Marian's breast, yields no milk. Yet Marian is no less the surrogate mother, presenting the "illustrious baby" to his father while Laura sits idly by, a mere spectator. That Marian has both the baby and the last word implies that while Walter fathered the biological child of Laura, it is Marian who fathered the rhetorical fruit of Walter's "labour of many months," the novel itself, whose title embodies the luster, illumination, clarity, or elucidation that Walter—as editor and "illustrator"—has tried to convey in assembling the story. Tired out by his effort, Walter allows Marian to have the "last words" (642–43). But even these words would have evaporated had not Walter preserved them. Still, Walter recognizes that he could not have produced the book on his own. Like Hermes, Marian presides, but over communication; like Aphrodite, over love; but like Hermaphroditus, she presides over childbirth even though she cannot herself reproduce. As the mediator who brings Walter to manhood and his book to completion, Marian is the missing link who is found in the evolution of the text.

Notes

1. John Sutherland, introduction to *The Woman in White* (Oxford: Oxford Univ. Press, 1999), xiii.
2. Duchamp's famous painting is entitled *L.H.O.O.Q.*, a pun on *Elle a chaud au cul,* which translates loosely as "she has a hot behind," as though to remind us that art does not belong behind glass in museums, nor should women be idealized out of their sexual bodies. Collins's defacement of his heroine inscribes a similar message.
3. Edward Fitzgerald to Frederick Tennyson, 29 Jan. 1867. Qtd. in *Wilkie Collins: The Critical Heritage,* ed. Norman Page (London and Boston: Routledge and Kegan Paul, 1974), 124.
4. Marjorie Garber, *Vested Interest: Cross-Dressing and Cultural Anarchy* (New York: Routledge, 1992), 16–17. Shirley Peterson ("Freaking Feminism: *The Life and Loves of a She-Devil* and *Nights at the Circus* as Narrative Freak Shows," in *Freakery: Cultural Spectacles of the Extraordinary Body,* ed. Rosemarie Garland Thomson [New York: New York Univ. Press, 1996], 291–301) locates the origins of Fay Weldon's *The Life and Loves of a She-Devil* (1983) and Angela Carter's *Nights at the Circus* (1984) in circus freak shows, but Carter's novel in particular seems to owe a debt to Marian Halcombe as a predecessor. In *Nights at the Circus,* Sophie Ruth is seen by her suitor Walser in the same way Walter Hartright sees Marian, as a sculpture with a magnificent body and an androgynous head: "Her face, in its Brobdingnagian symmetry, might have been hacked from wood and brightly painted up by those artists who build carnival ladies for fairgrounds or figureheads for sailing ships. It flickered through his mind: Is she a man?" ([New York: Viking, 1985], 35). In explaining the power of the women in Weldon and Carter, Peterson also unwittingly explains the uncanny power of Marian Halcombe: "Like such sideshow attractions as bearded ladies and hermaphrodites, they function as sites of contradiction, challenging notions of stable identity and pointing to cultural dissonance" (Peterson, 294).
5. While there is consensus on Collins's interest in sexual indeterminacy, especially in *The Woman in White,* several interpretive approaches have been applied to the novel's exploration of gender from the psychological

to the postcolonial. Harvey Peter Sucksmith, for example, calls upon the *anima* of Jungian theory (introduction to *The Woman in White*, by Wilkie Collins [New York: Oxford Univ. Press, 1975], xviii). Lillian Nayder argues that "Hartright's manhood . . . is 'engendered' in an imperial out-post" ("Agents of Empire in *The Woman in White*," *Victorian Newsletter* 83 [spring 1993]: 1). D. A. Miller's use of reader-response theory is perhaps the most influential and controversial of recent readings, with its discussion of the novel's exploration of "gender slippage" and its exploita-tion of "female contagion" and "homosexual panic" as part of the sensa-tion novel's affective technique ("*Cage aux folles*: Sensation and Gender in Wilkie Collins's *The Woman in White*," in *Speaking of Gender*, ed. Elaine Showalter [New York and London: Routledge, 1989], 187–215). It is clear that Collins is interested in the cultural construction of gender, especially the dichotomy embodied in what Philip O'Neill calls Marian's "fusion of masculine intellect and female physique" (*Wilkie Collins: Women, Property and Propriety* [London: Macmillan, 1988], 188), but while Miller asserts that Collins served the status quo, Pamela Perkins and Mary Donaghy argue for Collins's "genuine desire to expose the inequities of Victorian gender and social conventions" ("A Man's Resolution: Narra-tive Strategies in Wilkie Collins' *The Woman in White*," *Studies in the Novel* 22 [winter 1990]: 392). Similarly, Susan Balée reads the social agenda of the novel as "a subversion of Victorian stereotypes (the angel in the house, the manly man) in order to promote new icons"; "by its lauda-tory portrayal of an androgynous old maid, Wilkie Collins helped the movement towards broadened opportunities for single women" ("Wilkie Collins and Surplus Women: The Case of Marian Halcombe," *Victorian Literature and Culture* 20 [1992]: 201, 210). Tamar Heller takes the mid-dle path, arguing for Collins's "ideological doubleness" (*Dead Secrets: Wilkie Collins and the Female Gothic* [New Haven: Yale Univ. Press, 1992], 163). My reading of the novel attempts to add to these studies by provid-ing the intertextual echoes of intersexual figures, such as bearded ladies and hermaphrodites from popular culture and art, that lurk in the novel's background and even provide the necessity for the type of medico-legal investigation that Walter and Marian undertake in discovering not only Laura's legal identity but also their own "medical" identity in terms of gender. The extent of Collins's conscious intent in this venture is more or less irrelevant, since, like Umberto Eco's analysis of *Casablanca* as "a sort of textual syllabus, a living example of living textuality," my analysis of *The Woman in White* assumes that "[w]orks are created by works, texts are created by texts, all together they speak to each other independently of the intention of their authors" ("*Casablanca*: Cult Movies and Intertextual Collage," in *Travels in Hyper Reality: Essays*, trans. William Weaver [San Diego: Harcourt Brace Jovanovich, 1986], 199). Collins's ideas, in short, are less important than the ideological *multiplicity* imported into the text by intertextual echoes.

6. Darwin admitted that he owed a great debt to the idea of the hermaphrodite as the prototype of an "original ancestor," and made his most important preparatory discoveries in his development of his theory of the origin of species during his research on a bisexual barnacle, the cirripede hermaphrodite: "my species theory convinced me, that an hermaphrodite species must pass into a bisexual species by insensibly small stages" (qtd. in William Irvine, *Apes, Angels, and Victorians: The Story of Darwin, Huxley, and Evolution* [New York: McGraw Hill, 1955], 84).

7. According to James W. Cook Jr., "significantly, it is at this very moment—as Barnum is searching for the right language to describe his new character—that the term 'nondescript' first appears in the English language as a noun defining 'a person or thing that is not easily described, or is of no particular class or kind'" ("Of Men, Missing Links, and Nondescripts: The Strange Career of P. T. Barnum's 'What Is It?' Exhibition," in Thomson, *Freakery*, 147). Cook goes on to assert that to move from nondescript animals "to nondescript *people*, however, represented a significant conceptual leap, one Barnum appears not to have fully undertaken until the American debut of 'What Is It' in 1860" (147). As Altick (*The Shows of London* [Cambridge and London: Harvard Univ. Press, 1978]), Fiedler (*Freaks: Myths and Images of the Secret Self* [New York: Simon and Schuster, 1978]), and Nigel Rothfels ("Aztecs, Aborigines, and Ape-People: Science and Freaks in Germany, 1850–1900," in Thomson, *Freakery*, 158–72) show, however, exhibitions of racial and intersex human specimens reached the height of their notoriety in London and Germany during the 1850s, so Barnum's "conceptual leap" is somewhat belated.

8. Michel Foucault, introduction to *Herculine Barbin: Being the Recently Discovered Memoirs of a Nineteenth-Century French Hermaphrodite*, trans. Richard McDougall (New York: Pantheon, 1980), xi–xii.

9. Elaine Showalter, "Introduction: The Rise of Gender," in *Speaking of Gender*, ed. Elaine Showalter (New York and London: Routledge, 1989), 9.

10. Coincidentally, *Casablanca* and *The Woman in White* share several elements: mysterious women in white (Ilsa Lund/Anne Catherick), mysterious white cities that stand out in contrast to the darkness that surrounds them (Casablanca/Copán), and male protagonists who are fighting for their masculine identity (Rick Blaine/Walter Hartright). They also share Sidney Greenstreet playing Italians: Ferrari in *Casablanca* (1943) and Fosco in the film of *The Woman in White* (1948). As Eco suggests, this is just the sort of associative web of trivia that perpetuates the allure of cult objects and makes them natural texts for "the best deconstructive readings" (202).

11. Eco, 197.

12. Ibid., 200. In Russian Formalist terms, Eco distinguishes between the "visual stereotypes" and "more complex archetypical situations," which might be applied respectively to the Bearded Lady and the Hermaphrodite.

As in Eco's discussion of *Casablanca*, however, the general term "'magic' intertextual frame," or "intertextual archetype," will suffice for our purposes.

13. Ibid., 200.

14. Ibid., 201.

15. Miller, 150, 191.

16. Wilkie Collins, *The Woman in White*, ed. John Sutherland (Oxford: Oxford Univ. Press, 1998), 267, 270. Hereafter cited in the text as *The Woman in White*.

17. Andrea Stulman Dennett, "The Dime Museum Freak Show Reconfigured as Talk Show," in Thomson, *Freakery*, 323.

18. According to Dennett, "Sex was a powerful component of the performance text of the freak show" because bearded ladies "inspired images of transgressive sex, ambiguous sex, homosexuality, bisexuality, and group sex, challenging the conventional boundaries between male and female, self and other. . . . Sometimes patrons were allowed to touch the limbs of Fat Ladies or pull the whiskers of Bearded Ladies. It was deeply arousing to Victorians to touch a strange woman in a legitimate, respectable setting" (322–23).

19. Qtd. in Richard Corson, *Fashions in Hair: The First Five Thousand Years* (London: Peter Owen, 1980), 408.

20. Qtd. in Corson, 413.

21. Kenneth Robinson, *Wilkie Collins: A Biography* (New York: Macmillan, 1952), 82–83.

22. Qtd. in Corson, 405.

23. Nuel Pharr Davis, *The Life of Wilkie Collins* (Urbana: Univ. of Illinois Press, 1956), 142.

24. Philip Collins, "Dickens and Popular Amusements," *The Dickensian* 61 (1965): 9.

25. Paul Schlicke, *Dickens and Popular Entertainment* (London: Allen & Unwin, 1985), 88.

26. Sue Lonoff, *Wilkie Collins and His Victorian Readers: A Study in the Rhetoric of Authorship* (New York: AMS Press, 1982), 159.

27. That the audience might recognize in the freak a possible ancestor was explicitly reflected in P. T. Barnum's advertising slogan, "What Is It?", that evoked medical and scientific discourse (Cook, 139). The question was not lost on Dickens, whose interest in the grotesque drew him to Barnum's exhibits. Fiedler suggests that it was Dickens (or the Prince of Wales) who applied the name "What Is It?" to Zip, Barnum's "feral man," an American Negro who was billed as the Missing Link, or "Man Monkey" (165).

28. Frederick Drimmer, *Very Special People: The Struggles, Loves and Triumphs of Human Oddities* (New York: Bell Publishing Co., 1985), 118.

Richard Collins

29. Collins would have appreciated the highly publicized court case in which Barnum and Madame Clofullia were put on trial for fraud at the Tombs Court, New York, in July 1853. A Mr. William Charr, as plaintiff, charged that he had been defrauded of his twenty-five cents by a man posing as a bearded lady. The case was dismissed after several depositions by doctors who certified Madame Clofullia's biological sex. Very probably Charr was a shill for Barnum himself who may have instigated the ridiculous litigation as a (successful) publicity stunt (Drimmer, 117–19).

30. Qtd. in Drimmer, 114–15.

31. Francis T. Buckland, *Curiosities of Natural History*, 4th series (London: Macmillan and Co., 1900), 42.

32. Richard Altick notes that "Central America was a favorite putative source of prodigies in these years. The 'nondescript' What Is It? was advertised as having been captured in the mountains of Mexico, and in 1857 the Baboon Lady, Julia Pastrami [*sic*], would be ascribed to the same region" (284 n).

33. Altick, 267.

34. George M. Gould and Walter L. Pyle, *Anomalies and Curiosities of Medicine* (Philadelphia: W. B. Saunders, 1896).

35. For the medico-legal investigations of hermaphrodites, see Alice Domurat Dreger, *Hermaphrodites and the Medical Invention of Sex* (Cambridge: Harvard Univ. Press, 1998), Foucault's introduction to Barbin (vii–xvii), and Aileen Ajootian, who notes the irony of a female doctor who had to prove her own sex in court: "Usually in the context of a court trial, a woman must raise her dress to confirm her true sex. Agnodike, the Athenian 'first female doctor' who practised medicine disguised as a man, revealed her woman's body not only to her female patients but also at the trial where she was accused by jealous male colleagues of seducing the women she cured" ("The Only Happy Couple: Hermaphrodites and Gender," in *Naked Truths: Women, Sexuality, and Gender in Classical Art and Archaeology*, ed. Ann Olga Koloski-Ostrow and Claire L. Lyons [London: Routledge, 1997], 236–37 n).

36. Collins is clearly indulging in autobiographical self-parody here, since his own hands and feet were famously delicate.

37. "In Memoriam," 109.17.

38. For a discussion of the ideal of a "supreme androgynous splendour" as imagined by Winckelmann and others especially in the Romantic period, see Joel Black, "The Aesthetics of Gender: Zeuxis' Maidens and the Hermaphrodite Ideal," in *Fragments: Incompletion and Discontinuity*, ed. Lawrence D. Kritzman (New York: New York Literary Forum, 1981), 205. According to Black, "conceived in its immediate actual, physical totality—as a fragment or compilation of fragments—the ideal is hardly the becoming hermaphrodite admired by Winckelmann, but rather a grotesque, un-becoming monster" (205).

39. *The Poems of Tennyson,* ed. Christopher Ricks (London: Longman, 1969), 1424.

40. Qtd. in Tennyson, 1424.

41. Titled to echo Pope's Dunciad, *The Gynandriad: A Satire of the Day on Women's Rights* (London: John Camden Hotten, 1873) reveals the anonymous author's fear that the women's rights movement would turn women not into the ideal androgyne but the monstrous gynander.

42. The stylistic similarity of Walter's and Anne Catherick's descriptions is one example of what Dickens told Collins, that three of the narrators in the novel had "a DISSECTIVE property in common, which is essentially not theirs but yours" (qtd. in Page, 80).

43. Mrs. Oliphant, reviewing the novel ("Sensation Novels," *Blackwood's Magazine* 91 [May 1862]: 565–74), is even more taken with Fosco than Marian is and never turns against him: "The reader shares in the unwilling liking to which, at his first appearance, he beguiles Marian Halcombe; but the reader, notwithstanding the fullest proof of Fosco's villainy, does not give him up, and take to hating him, as Marian does" (qtd. in Page, 113).

44. *Dublin University Magazine* 57 (Feb. 1861): 200–203. Qtd. in Page, 105.

45. For a discussion of the hermaphrodite in relation to nature in the Middle Ages, see David Williams, *Deformed Discourse: The Function of the Monster in Mediaeval Thought and Literature* (Montreal and Kingston: McGill-Queen's Univ. Press, 1996). According to Williams, "The Middle Ages commonly defined and described the monstrous in terms of the dimensions of the physical body. From Isidore of Seville and others came the idea that monsters were constituted by violation of the body's limits: excrescence of parts, deprivation of parts, and other abnormalities. This physical explanation could, however, be extended to a conceptual explanation that saw all these deformities as transgressions of logical categories" (173). "The negation of the structural order of physical nature is another means of transgressing the affirmative limitations placed upon reality," he continues. "Like the human body, nature's 'body' provides a kind of text of the mind and its rational workings that, through rearrangement and deformation, can be expanded and rewritten to include its own negation. While the body as microcosm provided the key for the interpretation of the Cosmos, Nature as a macrocosm governed the structure of the human body that was its reflection" (177).

46. Collins invites the reader, for example, to collaborate in writing the novel by filling in the blanks of his description of Laura with the reader's own sensations of first love. See *The Woman in White,* 50.

47. Walter Pater, *The Renaissance: Studies in Art and Poetry,* ed. Donald L. Hill (Berkeley: Univ. of California Press, 1980), 106.

48. For a discussion of oral and literate "phallogocentrism," "those cultural or theoretical systems in which there is a conflation of the phallus and the

logos (speech, thought)," see Howard Eilberg-Schwartz, "The Nakedness of a Woman's Voice, the Pleasure in a Man's Mouth: An Oral History of Ancient Judaism," in *Off With Her Head! The Denial of Women's Identity in Myth, Religion and Culture*, ed. Howard Eilberg-Schwartz and Wendy Doniger (Berkeley: Univ. of California Press, 1995), 166, and Mary O'Brien, *The Politics of Reproduction* (Boston: Routledge, Kegan & Paul, 1981). Hartright objectifies Laura and Marian as works of art (watercolors and sculpture respectively); for a related discussion of the "sexually coded nature of image/text relations" in which decorative illustration is typically seen as the female handmaiden to the male text, see Lorraine Janzen Kooistra, *The Artist as Critic: Bitextuality in Fin-de-Siècle Illustrated Books* (Brookfield, Vt.: Scolar Press, 1995), 11.

49. Wilkie Collins, *Basil,* ed. Dorothy Goldman (Oxford: Oxford Univ. Press, 1990), xxxv–xxxvi. Hereafter cited in the text as *Basil.*

50. Another example of Collins's grotesque portraiture in the round would be his sketch of Miserrimus Dexter as "half man, half chair" (Wilkie Collins, *The Law and the Lady,* ed. Jenny Bourne Taylor [Oxford: Oxford Univ. Press, 1992], 206). On Collins's Darwinian comment in the novel, "We were all monkeys before we were men, and molecules before we were monkeys!" (321), Sue Lonoff says that Dexter "cannot be dismissed as a 'monkey' or a 'monster,' any more than he can be dismissed as imitation-Gothic; he escapes easy categorization" (Lonoff, 166). The same can be said of Collins's intended effect in all of his character collages, whether these are composites of furniture or gender.

51. Foucault, xvii.

52. For a discussion of the hermaphrodite in the nineteenth century, see A. J. L. Busst, "The Androgyne in the Nineteenth Century," in *Romantic Mythologies,* ed. Ian Fletcher (London: Routledge & Kegan Paul, 1967), 1–95.

53. Collins stated that Marian was a composite of many women. Catherine Peters suggests that Marian's manly appearance and mannerisms were based on George Eliot *(The King of Inventors* [London: Secker and Warburg, 1991], 217). Peters also mentions Collins's reading of the Robin Hood stories (32), which might indicate that Collins was punning on [Old] Maid Marian. No one, however, has until now suggested a Mariana/Marian connection.

54. According to Davis, "For Wilkie's tenacious conviction that a woman should be judged by her walk, preferably as viewed from the rear, see 'Give Us Room!' *Household Words,* 23 Feb. 1858" (Davis 321 n). In 1887, at age sixty-three, Collins commented on a nude study by the photographer Napoleon Sarony: "I think the back view of a finely formed woman the loveliest view" (William M. Clarke, *The Secret Life of Wilkie Collins* [London: Alison and Busby, 1988], 64). Frederick Walker, the illustrator who designed the poster for the stage version of *The Woman*

in White, also chose to depict his fleeing subject from behind (*The Woman in White,* appendix A, 656).

55. Tennyson, 187–90.

56. Marie Delcourt, *Hermaphrodite: Myths and Rites of the Bisexual Figure in Classical Antiquity,* trans. Jennifer Nicholson (London: Studio Books, 1961), 62.

57. Clarke, 35–36. Davis notes another homoerotic attachment of Collins's at the Maida Hill Academy, where he became a male Sheherazad by talking an older boy to sleep every night in return for protection and pastry: "In this early contact with art for pay, Wilkie perhaps took the first step toward understanding his father" (23), but it was also his first step away from painting, his father's profession, and towards his own as storyteller.

58. Davis, 168. On this trip Collins bought Mejan's *Recueil des Cause Célèbres,* a primary source for the plot of *The Woman in White.*

59. According to Robinson, "Dickens arranged a continuous round of theatres, art galleries, and social occasions of every kind" (96). Davis adds "wrestling matches and shady ballrooms" (184). In his own recollections of this trip to Paris, Collins recalls spending two weeks sick in bed, watching the city from his apartment in the Champs Elysees ("Laid Up in Lodgings: My Paris Lodging," in *My Miscellanies* [New York: Peter Fenelon Collier, 1900], 85–104). At the theater they saw two productions that point to their mutual interest in sexuality and hair. They managed to get tickets to a sold-out stage production of *Paradise Lost,* which, as rumor had it, promised to feature Adam and Eve on stage naked, but the original couple turned out to be modestly dressed. They also saw a farce, *Les Chevaux de ma Femme,* in which a man takes a lock of his wife's hair to a clairvoyant, who tells him that the owner of the hair is debauching herself; the husband discovers, however, that his wife is bald and wears a wig made of the hair of another woman.

60. For the connection between Shelley's, Gautier's, and Swinburne's treatments of the statue of the *Sleeping Hermaphrodite,* see Catherine Maxwell, "Swinburne, Gautier, and the Louvre Hermaphrodite," *Notes and Queries* 238 (Mar. 1983): 49–50.

61. We last see Fosco laid out on a marble slab in the Paris Morgue, near the Louvre, where the *Hermaphrodite endormi* reclines on its marble pillows. Hartright describes the scene in terms that would apply to any freak show: "There was evidently something inside which excited the popular curiosity, and fed the popular appetite for horror." Inside, Fosco's naked corpse is "exposed to the flippant curiosity of a French mob" (*The Woman in White,* 639–40).

62. Algernon Charles Swinburne, *The Poems of Algernon Charles Swinburne* (London: Chatto & Windus, 1905), 1:79–81. See Dorothy Mermin, "'The fruitful feud of hers and his': Sameness, Difference, and Gender in

Victorian Poetry," *Victorian Poetry* 33 (1995): 149–68, for a discussion of the hermaphrodite figure in Swinburne and other Victorian poets, who all "can be read as women" (165).

63. Helena Michie notes that "the unfolding of the mystery simultaneously textualizes [Laura] and makes it imperative that she be interpreted" (*The Flesh Made Word: Female Figures and Women's Bodies* [New York: Oxford Univ. Press, 1987], 122). In a Derridean reading of the novel, Diane Elam makes a similar point: "The doubling of woman by her whiteness in effect creates the indeterminacy of her position, an indeterminacy which leads us to question the situation and representation of identity" ("White Narratology: Gender and Reference in Wilkie Collins's *The Woman in White*," in *Virginal Sexuality and Textuality in Victorian Literature,* ed. Lloyd Davis [Albany: State Univ. of New York Press, 1993], 61). See also M. Kellen Williams, who argues that the novel "seeks to stabilize . . . identities by making the difference upon which they depend not only female, but physiological" ("'Traced and Captured by the Men in the Chaise': Pursuing Sexual Difference in Wilkie Collins's *The Woman in White*," *Journal of Narrative Technique* 28, no. 2 [spring 1998]: 92). All three of these critics focus on Laura rather than Marian, whose doubled sexuality, while dark, is also "undecidable" and thus in even greater need of textual interpretation.

64. Kimberley Reynolds and Nicola Humble, *Victorian Heroines: Representations of Femininity in Nineteenth-Century Literature and Art* (New York: New York Univ. Press, 1993), 54.

65. Sucksmith, xviii. Sucksmith's view of Marian resembles René Magritte's *Le Viol* (The Rape), a surrealist painting of a female torso as a face. See Wendy Doniger for a discussion of Magritte's painting ("'Put a Bag over Her Head': Beheading Mythological Women," in Eilberg-Schwartz, 27). O'Neill sees a similar oral-genital displacement in relation to Margaret in *Basil:* "Concentrating on her lips, Basil decides that maternity would somehow complete her. He wants to make eloquent and productive those other lips and have her bear children" (O'Neill, 189).

66. Fiedler, 137.

67. Ibid., 143. Fiedler mentions the witches in *Macbeth,* as well as references to bearded young women in the diaries of John Evelyn and Samuel Pepys (144–45).

68. Elaine Showalter, *Sexual Anarchy: Gender and Culture at the Fin de Siècle* (New York: Viking, 1990), 145.

69. Delcourt, 163. Ajootian also notes that in Herodotus "Egyptian women traveling by boat on the Nile to a festival for Artemis at Bubastis lifted their dresses and yelled obscenities at local women standing on shore" (224). Similarly, gypsy women in Eastern Europe today, for example in Romania, still reveal their genitals as a form of insult.

70. Fiedler, 145.

71. Miller, 207.

72. Qtd. in Fiedler, 138.

73. Sophia Andres, "Pre-Raphaelite Paintings and Jungian Images in Wilkie Collins's *The Woman in White,*" *Victorian Newsletter* 88 (1995): 28.

74. Andres, 27.

75. Sucksmith, xvi–xvii.

76. The sculpture at Copán, for example, included Janus-like bicephalic monsters. According to Claude-François Baudez, "When the monster has contrasting heads, the front head is living and oriented normally (from an anatomical point of view); the rear head is skeletal and often placed in an abnormal position" (*Maya Sculpture of Copán: The Iconography* [Norman and London: Univ. of Oklahoma Press, 1994], 256). It is often unclear whether the figures in these sculptures—even when not monstrous—depict a woman or a man (103). For a complete discussion of the sources of Hartright's Central American experience in travel literature of the time, and how he uses his experience as an illustrator to interpret his experience on his return to England, see Richard Collins, "The Ruins of Copán in *The Woman in White*: Wilkie Collins and John Stephens's *Incidents of Travel in Central America, Chiapas, and Yucatan,*" *The Wilkie Collins Society Journal,* n.s., 2 (1999): 5–17.

77. See Eve Kosofsky Sedgwick, *Between Men: English Literature and Male Homosocial Desire* (New York: Columbia Univ. Press, 1985).

78. Ann Cvetkovich, "Ghostlier Determinations: The Economy of Sensation and *The Woman in White,*" in *Wilkie Collins,* ed. Lyn Pykett (New York: St. Martin's Press, 1998), 114.

79. See Balée.

80. Fiedler, 143.

81. Ajootian, 228.

82. Rather than posing an erotic threat to either Walter or Laura, Marian is, like the hermaphrodite, sufficient unto herself. Ajootian notes that "According to Horace Walpole, Lady Townsend described his modern bronze copy of an ancient *Sleeping Hermaphrodite* sculpture as the only happy couple she had ever seen" (220).

References

Ajootian, Aileen. "The Only Happy Couple: Hermaphrodites and Gender." In *Naked Truths: Women, Sexuality, and Gender in Classical Art and Archaeology,* ed. Ann Olga Koloski-Ostrow and Claire L. Lyons, 220–42. London and New York: Routledge, 1997.

Altick, Richard D. *The Shows of London*. Cambridge and London: Harvard Univ. Press, 1978.

Andres, Sophia. "Pre-Raphaelite Paintings and Jungian Images in Wilkie Collins's *The Woman in White*." *Victorian Newsletter* 88 (1995): 26–31.

Auerbach, Nina. *Woman and the Demon: The Life of a Victorian Myth*. Cambridge: Harvard Univ. Press, 1982.

Balée, Susan. "Wilkie Collins and Surplus Women: The Case of Marian Halcombe." *Victorian Literature and Culture* 20 (1992): 197–215.

Baudez, Claude-François. *Maya Sculpture of Copán. The Iconography*. Norman and London: Univ. of Oklahoma Press, 1994.

Black, Joel. "The Aesthetics of Gender: Zeuxis' Maidens and the Hermaphroditic Ideal." In *Fragments: Incompletion and Discontinuity*, ed. Lawrence D. Kritzman, 189–209. New York: New York Literary Forum, 1981.

Buckland, Francis T. *Curiosities of Natural History*. 4 vols. London: Macmillan, 1900.

Busst, A. J. L. "The Androgyne in the Nineteenth Century." In *Romantic Mythologies*, ed. Ian Fletcher, 1–95. London: Routledge & Kegan Paul, 1967.

Carter, Angela. *Nights at the Circus*. New York: Viking, 1985.

Clarke, William M. *The Secret Life of Wilkie Collins*. London: Alison & Busby, 1988.

Collins, Philip. "Dickens and Popular Amusements." *The Dickensian* 61 (1965): 7–19.

Collins, Richard. "The Ruins of Copán in *The Woman in White*: Wilkie Collins and John Stephens's *Incidents of Travel in Central America, Chiapas, and Yucatan*." *The Wilkie Collins Society Journal*, n.s., 2 (1999): 5–17.

Collins, Wilkie. *Basil*. Ed. Dorothy Goldman. Oxford: Oxford Univ. Press, 1990.

———. *The Law and the Lady*. Ed. Jenny Bourne Taylor. Oxford: Oxford Univ. Press, 1998.

———. *My Miscellanies*. New York: Peter Fenelon Collier, 1900.

———. *The Woman in White*. Ed. John Sutherland. Oxford: Oxford Univ. Press, 1999.

Corson, Richard. *Fashions in Hair: The First Five Thousand Years*. London: Peter Owen, 1980.

Cvetkovich, Ann. "Ghostlier Determinations: The Economy of Sensation and *The Woman in White*." In *Wilkie Collins*, ed. Lyn Pykett, 109–35. New York: St. Martin's, 1998.

Davis, Nuel Pharr. *The Life of Wilkie Collins*. Urbana: Univ. of Illinois Press, 1956.

Delcourt, Marie. *Hermaphrodite: Myths and Rites of the Bisexual Figure in Classical Antiquity.* Trans. Jennifer Nicholson. London: Studio Books, 1961.

Dreger, Alice Domurat. *Hermaphrodites and the Medical Invention of Sex.* Cambridge: Harvard Univ. Press, 1998.

Drimmer, Frederick. *Very Special People: The Struggles, Loves, and Triumphs of Human Oddities.* New York: Bell Publishing, 1985.

Eco, Umberto. "*Casablanca:* Cult Movies and Intertextual Collage." In *Travels in Hyper Reality: Essays,* trans. William Weaver, 197–211. San Diego: Harcourt Brace Jovanovich, 1986.

Eilberg-Schwartz, Howard, and Wendy Doniger, eds. *Off With Her Head! The Denial of Women's Identity in Myth, Religion, and Culture.* Berkeley: Univ. of California Press, 1995.

Elam, Diane. "White Narratology: Gender and Reference in Wilkie Collins's *The Woman in White.*" In *Virginal Sexuality and Textuality in Victorian Literature,* ed. Lloyd Davis, 49–63. Albany: State Univ. of New York Press, 1993.

Fiedler, Leslie. *Freaks: Myths and Images of the Secret Self.* New York: Simon and Schuster, 1978.

Foucault, Michel. Introduction to *Herculine Barbin: Being the Recently Discovered Memoirs of a Nineteenth-Century French Hermaphrodite,* by Herculine Barbin. Trans. Richard McDougall. New York: Pantheon, 1980.

Garber, Marjorie. *Vested Interests: Cross-Dressing and Cultural Anxiety.* New York: Routledge, 1992.

Gould, George M., and Walter L. Pyle. *Anomalies and Curiosities of Medicine.* Philadelphia: W. B. Saunders, 1896.

The Gynandriad: A Satire of the Day on Women's Rights. London: John Camden Hotten, 1873.

Heller, Tamar. *Dead Secrets: Wilkie Collins and the Female Gothic.* New Haven: Yale Univ. Press, 1992.

Irvine, William. *Apes, Angels and Victorians: The Story of Darwin, Huxley, and Evolution.* New York: McGraw-Hill, 1955.

Kooistra, Lorraine Janzen. *The Artist as Critic: Bitextuality in Fin-de-Siècle Illustrated Books.* Brookfield, Vt.: Scolar Press, 1995.

Lonoff, Sue. *Wilkie Collins and His Victorian Readers: A Study in the Rhetoric of Authorship.* New York: AMS Press, 1982.

Maxwell, Catherine. "Swinburne, Gautier, and the Louvre Hermaphrodite." *Notes and Queries* (Mar. 1993): 49–50.

Mermin, Dorothy. "'The fruitful feud of hers and his': Sameness, Difference, and Gender in Victorian Poetry." *Victorian Poetry* 33 (1995): 149–68.

Michie, Helena. *The Flesh Made Word: Female Figures and Women's Bodies.* New York: Oxford Univ. Press, 1987.

Nayder, Lillian. "Agents of Empire in *The Woman in White.*" *Victorian Newsletter* 83 (spring 1993): 1–7.

O'Brien, Mary. *The Politics of Reproduction.* Boston: Routledge, Kegan & Paul, 1981.

O'Neill, Philip. *Wilkie Collins: Women, Property and Propriety.* London: Macmillan, 1988.

Page, Norman, ed. *Wilkie Collins: The Critical Heritage.* London and Boston: Routledge and Kegan Paul, 1974.

Pater, Walter. *The Renaissance: Studies in Art and Poetry.* Ed. Donald L. Hill. Berkeley: Univ. of California Press, 1980.

Perkins, Pamela, and Mary Donaghy. "A Man's Resolution: Narrative Strategies in Wilkie Collins' *The Woman in White.*" *Studies in the Novel* 22 (winter 1990): 392–402.

Peters, Catherine. *The King of Inventors: A Life of Wilkie Collins.* London: Secker & Warburg, 1991.

Reynolds, Kimberley, and Nicola Humble. *Victorian Heroines: Representations of Femininity in Nineteenth-Century Literature and Art.* New York: New York Univ. Press, 1993.

Robinson, Kenneth. *Wilkie Collins: A Biography.* New York: Macmillan, 1952.

Schlicke, Paul. *Dickens and Popular Entertainment.* London: Allen & Unwin, 1985.

Sedgwick, Eve Kosofsky. *Between Men: English Literature and Male Homosocial Desire.* New York: Columbia Univ. Press, 1985.

Showalter, Elaine, ed. *Speaking of Gender.* New York: Routledge, 1989.

———. *Sexual Anarchy: Gender and Culture at the Fin de Siècle.* New York: Viking, 1990.

Swinburne, Algernon Charles. *The Poems of Algernon Charles Swinburne.* 5 vols. London: Chatto & Windus, 1905.

Sucksmith, Harvey Peter, ed. Introduction to *The Woman in White,* by Wilkie Collins. New York: Oxford Univ. Press, 1973.

Tennyson, Alfred. *The Poems of Tennyson.* Ed. Christopher Ricks. London: Longman, 1969.

Thomson, Rosemarie Garland, ed. *Freakery: Cultural Spectacles of the Extraordinary Body.* New York: New York Univ. Press, 1996.

Williams, David. *Deformed Discourse: The Function of the Monster in Mediaeval Thought and Literature.* Montreal and Kingston: McGill-Queen's Univ. Press, 1996.

Williams, M. Kellen. "'Traced and Captured By the Men in the Chaise': Pursuing Sexual Difference in Wilkie Collins's *The Woman in White.*" *Journal of Narrative Technique* 28, no. 2 (spring 1998): 91–110.

The Crystal Palace, Imperialism, and the "Struggle for Existence"

Victorian Evolutionary Discourse in Collins's *The Woman in White*

Gabrielle Ceraldi

EAR THE END OF WILKIE COLLINS'S *THE WOMAN IN WHITE*, WALTER HARTRIGHT REMINDS READERS, "THE YEAR OF WHICH I am now writing was the year of the famous Crystal Palace Exhibition in Hyde Park. Foreigners, in unusually large numbers, had arrived already, and were still arriving, in England. Men were among us, by thousands, whom the ceaseless distrustfulness of their governments had followed privately, by means of appointed agents, to our shores."[1] With these words, Collins reveals that the entire dastardly plot against Laura Fairlie has resulted indirectly from the Great Exhibition of 1851, which occasioned the visit to England of Mr. and Mrs. Rubelle, accessories to the plot, and the mastermind himself, Count Fosco. For Collins, writing in 1860, the Great Exhibition is associated with fears of invasion by hordes of foreign spies and secret agents. Such anxieties form a pointed contrast to earlier responses to the Great Exhibition of the Works of Industry of All Nations. According to George W. Stocking Jr., the Great Exhibition provoked an outpouring of British patriotism and self-congratulation; the various exhibits seemed to prove Britain's racial, cultural, and industrial superiority to the rest of the world: "the character of the different national exhibits . . . led one along a line of progress from the Tasmanian savage through the 'barbaric' civilizations of the East, northwest across the European continent toward an apex in Great Britain."[2] This "line of progress" echoed current evolutionary theories that posited a teleological development in both the biological and the social realms. As Robin Gilmour points out, "before the 1850s [evolution] was chiefly associated with the work of the French naturalist Jean-Baptiste Lamarck," who believed that "Nature was purposive; its innermost processes encouraged the peaceful evolution of the higher animals from the lower, and rewarded individual success in adaptation with the passing on of desirable qualities to offspring."[3] Lamarck's theories were promulgated in England by scientists and sociologists such as Robert Chambers and Herbert Spencer. Chambers's *Vestiges of the Natural History of Creation* (1844) combined Lamarck's idea of the gradual transformation of species with current theories of paleontology and anthropology in order to posit a "law of development" that Gilmour sees at work in the world of plants and animals, "propelling it on to ever more complex forms of organisation."[4] Though it challenged religious orthodoxy, this teleological understanding of biological development was congenial to Victorian ideals of progress.

Spencer's "The Development Hypothesis" (1852) adapted the idea of biological development to the social sphere; as his famous phrase "survival of the fittest" implies, he believed that progress, both social and biological, favored the morally deserving. Such optimism was widespread at midcentury, when the Crystal Palace, according to Stocking, was making Britain's status as a civilized nation and leading world power "not so much a problem as an assumption."[5] Spencer's theories of social evolution respond to what Stocking describes as a cultural need to explain "why it was that not all men had shared equally in the process [of evolutionary development]—why it was that though the whole world had been invited to attend, the Crystal Palace had been a uniquely British creation."[6] Yet the optimism and assurance symbolized by the Crystal Palace—that "glass cathedral to the Goddess Progress"[7]—are strikingly absent from Collins's fictional treatment of the Exhibition era. In *The Woman in White*, the gleaming walls of the Crystal Palace are replaced by a bleaker symbol of the Industrial Revolution: the ugly, half-finished town of New Welmingham. Here, the "Goddess Progress" has abandoned the snug, picturesque old village and substituted for it a scene of "clean desolation" and "neat ugliness." Walter views the town as an "arid exile of unfinished crescents and squares" surrounded by "dead house-carcases that waited in vain for the vivifying human element to animate them with the breath of life." In this ugly town, England surpasses the world only in its grim barrenness; Walter concludes that "[t]he deserts of Arabia are innocent of our civilised desolation; the ruins of Palestine are incapable of our modern gloom!" (*The Woman in White*, 445). Such images direct a certain skepticism toward the optimistic Spencerian theory that Britain was on a smooth, teleological course toward biological, social, and moral supremacy.[8] Walter's pessimism situates him amid an emerging trend that would replace evolutionary ambitions with fears of devolution. Jenny Bourne Taylor traces such anxieties as far back as 1857, when Andrew Wynter "argued against a growing fear that 'lunacy is on the increase.'. . . Over the next twenty years such fears absorbed and helped to shape a discourse of 'degeneration' that was to establish its hegemony by becoming assimilated across biological, psychological, and social theory."[9] A key moment in this transition was, of course, the publication of Charles Darwin's *The Origin of Species* (1859). Darwin's theory of natural selection implies a random, aimless process involving all the earth's creatures in a desperate struggle for survival. Gilmour observes that "the bleaker implications of natural selection do not seem to have registered with most of [Darwin's] contemporaries," who continued to cling to Victorian ideals of progress, but "the idea of a struggle for existence did strike a chord with contemporaries, who were used to high mortality rates, especially among the young."[10]

Serialized from November 1859 to August 1860, *The Woman in White* responds to the intersection of the development hypothesis and Darwinian theories of natural selection.[11] Through "foreign" characters such as Professor Pesca and Count Fosco, Collins examines the relationship between Great Britain and the racialized world that lies beyond her shores.[12] As his skeptical treatment of the Crystal Palace Exhibition would suggest, Collins attacks complacent Spencerian assumptions of British evolutionary supremacy. In *The Woman in White*, foreign characters are invariably stronger and more virile than their pallid English counterparts. By the end of the novel, however, it has become clear that the real threat facing Britain is not embodied in foreigners such as

Fosco; rather, England is undermined from within by its growing ability to shelter itself from the rigors of evolutionary struggle. Collins's denouement reveals that the cultural superiority that was trumpeted by the Great Exhibition ironically has shielded Britain from the very "struggle for existence" that would guarantee its future development. Anticipating later adventure narratives, Collins can counter this threat only by turning to the imperialist enterprise as a source of cultural rejuvenation.

In the early pages of the novel, Collins satirizes vulgar prejudices against foreigners through the narrow-minded attitudes of Sarah Hartright and Philip Fairlie. Even the solicitor, Mr. Gilmore, who claims to have held "the soundest Conservative principles all my life" (*The Woman in White*, 142), is enlightened enough to disapprove of the late Mr. Fairlie's decision to strike his sister out of his will upon her marriage to Count Fosco; in Mr. Gilmore's opinion, Fosco's credentials are impeccable: "He had a small, but sufficient income of his own; he had lived many years in England; and he held an excellent position in society. These recommendations, however, availed nothing with Mr. Fairlie. In many of his opinions he was an Englishman of the old school; and he hated a foreigner, simply and solely because he was a foreigner" (133).

In Gilmore's mind, such stubborn, unreasoning hatred is a relic of an older age, when the Napoleonic Wars encouraged a harder xenophobia, before political reforms such as the Catholic Emancipation Act (1829) opened up participation in British political life to Irish Catholics and others who would once have been excluded as "foreign." Rejecting the bigotry of the "old school," Gilmore aligns himself with what he evidently regards as a more open-minded liberalism characteristic of the peaceful and enlightened Victorian age. Gilmore's disapproval of Mr. Fairlie duplicates Walter's attitude toward his sister Sarah, whose inability to accept the "puzzling foreign peculiarities" of the comically eccentric Professor Pesca brands her as a dour, humorless spinster. Like Mr. Gilmore, Walter associates such "insular notions of propriety" with days gone by: "I never saw my mother and my sister together in Pesca's society, without finding my mother much the younger woman of the two" (5–6).

In contrast to the ignorant prejudices of Sarah and Mr. Fairlie, Walter adopts and encourages what he would consider a more "enlightened" attitude of amused condescension. If Sarah seems older than her years because of her "insular" notions, Walter, like Mr. Gilmore, distances himself from such old-school prejudices and treats

Pesca with affectionate ridicule. He remarks indulgently on Pesca's "harmless eccentricity" (3), gently poking fun at his friend's ardent Italian nature. Describing Pesca as "happily and fussily unconscious of the irreparable wrong which the crockery had suffered at his hands," Walter encourages the reader to view him as an endearing and comic "little man" (6, 3). Though he derives considerable humor from Pesca's attempts to re-create himself in the mold of a stereotypical English gentleman, Walter makes it clear that his friend is to be pitied, rather than hated, for his constitutional inability to achieve the English identity he so admires. Although Pesca does "his utmost to turn himself into an Englishman," his efforts are doomed to failure (3). His exertions at the fox hunt and on the cricket field make him no more than a comic parody of English customs and manners. Similarly, his attempts to reproduce English idiom form a ludicrous contrast to his exaggerated Italian excitability. Pesca peppers his conversation with exclamations of "Deuce-what-the-deuce!" and "my-soul-bless-my-soul!" culminating in his *coup de grace*: "When your sun shines in Cumberland (English proverb), in the name of Heaven, make your hay" (8, 7, 13).

Through his portrait of Professor Pesca, Collins briefly encourages his readers to adopt the attitude of complacent superiority that characterized responses to the Great Exhibition. The supremacy of all things English is attested to, not only by Pesca's frank admiration but also by his inability to achieve the "Englishness" he strives for. As the novel progresses, however, Collins undermines the very attitude his introductory chapters encourage. Where Pesca is likable but incompetent, his countryman, Count Fosco, is chillingly adept. Pesca's amusing idiomatic peculiarities are conspicuously absent from Fosco's speech. Marian comments that "until I saw Count Fosco, I had never supposed it possible that any foreigner could have spoken English as he speaks it. There are times when it is almost impossible to detect, by his accent, that he is not a countryman of our own; and, as for fluency, there are very few born Englishmen who can talk with as few stoppages and repetitions as the Count" (197). Fosco's linguistic competence not only makes him immune to ridicule, it even allows him to out-English the English.

Fosco's ability to learn "our strong, hard Northern speech" (197) emphasizes, by way of contrast, the limitations of Englishmen who, like Pesca, are incapable of transcending their origins. Frederick Fairlie assures Walter that he has "none of the horrid English barbarity of feeling about the social position of an artist. . . . So much of my early life has been passed abroad, that I have quite cast my insular skin in that respect" (33). As it turns out, however, Mr. Fairlie's skin has stuck to him far more firmly than he suspects; a moment later, when he addresses Walter in the same peremptory tone he uses with his browbeaten servants, he provides "a practical commentary on the liberal social theory which he had just favoured me by illustrating" (34). Similarly, Sir Percival Glyde has pretensions to a cosmopolitan identity; as Tamar Heller observes, "Percival was born on the Continent; the Glydes are thus associated with revolution and like Fosco, the 'Italian,' are linked to the invasion of 'foreign' ideas."[13] But no amount of travel or experience is able to efface Sir Percival's congenital Englishness; as Fosco repeatedly insists, Percival is the epitome of a number of British stereotypes. Fosco is fond of making such exclamations as "My good Percival! how I like your rough English humour!" or "My good Percival! how I enjoy your solid English sense!" (200). As these half-mocking statements reveal, Count Fosco tolerates his friend with an air of amused indulgence—in much the same way Walter tolerates Pesca. Count Fosco "puts the rudest remarks Sir Percival can make on his effeminate tastes and amusements quietly away from him . . . smiling at him with the calmest superiority; patting him on the shoulder; and bearing with him benignantly, as a good-humoured father bears with a wayward son" (200). Even Sir Percival's outbursts of temper are treated with belittling paternal patience: "'Poor, dear Percival!' cried Count Fosco, looking after him gaily; 'he is the victim of English spleen'" (210).

Through Count Fosco, Collins turns the tables on his readers; Fosco views English behavior with fond condescension, taking over the attitude of aloof benevolence that Walter and his readers had adopted toward Pesca. In his comments about English political and social policies, however, Fosco reveals attitudes that are less than affectionate. Pesca's enthusiastic admiration for his adopted country typifies the response many Britons expected from the foreigners who came to the Great Exhibition. The Crystal Palace attracted crowds of visitors from within England, as well as from abroad, and, according to Stocking, "*Punch* felt [these well-behaved British crowds] were a 'magnificent lesson' for the Prussian Princes—'a splendid example of that real freedom . . . and perfect security . . . which are the result of our constitutional monarchy.'"[14] Whatever the "Prussian Princes" might have thought, Collins reveals that at least one Italian Count is unimpressed by what he sees in Great Britain. In a key confrontation, Marian insists on the moral superiority of England to the more primitive governments that are found elsewhere in the world: "The Chinese authorities kill thousands of innocent people, on the most horribly frivolous pretexts," Marian exclaims, adding earnestly, "We, in England, are free from all guilt of that kind—we commit no such dreadful crime—we abhor reckless bloodshed, with all our hearts." Fosco's reply is polite, but contemptuous: "John Bull does abhor the crimes of John Chinaman. He is the quickest old gentleman at finding out the faults that are his neighbours', and the slowest old gentleman at finding out the faults that are his own, who exists on the face of creation" (*The Woman in White*, 212). That stinging remark is backed up by a catalog of social injustices that confirms Fosco's suggestion that English patriotic fervor attests more to British blind egotism than to actual British greatness.

The emptiness of England's patriotic self-image is complemented by the falseness of the Italian identity that had seemed so unshakable in Pesca. For Count Fosco, Italianness is a mask that can be assumed at his will and convenience. For instance, Fosco turns English prejudices against Marian and Laura when he invites Marian to witness the signing of Sir Percival's mysterious document. "We Italians are all wily and suspicious by nature, in the estimation of the good John Bull," Fosco observes. "Set me down, if you please, as being no better than the rest of my race. I am a wily Italian and a suspicious Italian" (218). On this occasion, Fosco evokes English prejudices both to authorize his behavior and to manipulate Marian and Laura. He asks the ladies to indulge what may seem like suspicious behavior on the grounds that he is ruled by his inescapable Italian temperament. Simultaneously, he makes it difficult for Laura to raise scruples that would seem equally trifling and suspicious; as an Englishwoman, she is expected to shun behavior that would be characteristic of a dark, wily Italian.

Most startling of all, perhaps, is the final revelation that even Pesca's Italianness is, like Fosco's, merely a performance. A covert member of the terrorist "Brotherhood," Pesca wears a mask of harmless eccentricity; his "every-day respectability" hides a "secret self which smoulders in him" (535). The condescending laughter Collins elicits in his initial portrayal of Pesca proves to be a snare; from that point on, Collins proceeds to undermine the cultural overconfidence that characterized English responses to the Crystal Palace. As it turns out, Collins's satirical portrait gallery does not indict merely the overt prejudice of Sarah Hartright or Philip Fairlie; it also mocks the self-righteous hypocrisy of Mrs. Michelson, who prides herself on having "cultivated a feeling of humane indulgence for foreigners. They do not possess our blessings and advantages." As she reminds Lady Glyde, it is essential "not to be hasty in our judgments on our inferiors—especially when they come from foreign parts" (332–33). Mrs. Michelson's much-vaunted open-mindedness is both hypocritical, as her sharp-tongued caricature of Mrs. Rubelle reveals, and naive, as it blinds her to the real threat posed by Count Fosco to Laura's health and well-being.

Through his characterization, Collins draws attention to the danger that Britain's cultural egotism will blind her to the strength of her adversaries. The novel sets up a series of pairings that juxtapose weak English characters with strong, powerful foreigners. The first of these pairings contrasts Laura Fairlie to her half-sister, Marian Halcombe. Blonde and blue-eyed, Laura is a perfect English lady: Walter describes her as a "fair, delicate girl, in a pretty light dress . . . with truthful innocent blue eyes" (41). By contrast, Marian is dark and ugly. Where Laura's appearance establishes her social and racial credentials, Marian's suggests a gypsy heritage: "The lady's complexion was almost swarthy, and the dark down on her upper lip was almost a moustache. She had a large, firm, masculine mouth and jaw; prominent, piercing, resolute brown eyes; and thick coal-black hair, growing unusually low down on her forehead" (25). Point for point, Marian's physical description matches that given by George Borrow in his study, *The Zincali: An Account of the Gypsies in Spain* (1841). Borrow describes the English gypsies: "their complexion is dark, but not disagreeably so; their faces are oval, their features regular, their foreheads rather low."[15] Laura and Marian are clearly aware of the resemblance implied by this description; when Laura returns from Italy, she is thrilled to see Marian's "dear, dark, clever gipsy-face" again (191). Furthermore, Marian's psychic dream-vision, in which she foresees Walter's Central American perils, reveals her possession of the legendary gypsy ability to interpret dreams. Such psychic and spiritual strength is typical of Marian; in their first conversation, she indicates to Walter the nature of her relationship to her more passive half-sister: "I won't live without [Laura], and she can't live without me" (27).[16] The entire novel supports this contrast between gypsy-faced Marian's superior strength and resolution and Laura's English helplessness and dependence.

The virtuous friendship of Laura and Marian has its evil counterpart in Sir Percival's friendship with the Italian Count Fosco. Again, the power dynamics suggest the superior energy and cunning of the foreigner. Despite his violent temper and constant peevishness, Sir Percival is more to be despised than dreaded, as Marian realizes: "I had no such fear of Sir Percival as I had of the Count" (282). Her evaluation shows insight; it is indeed Count Fosco who concocts the plan that nearly deprives Laura of both her fortune and her sanity. When

Walter attempts to vindicate Laura, the difference between his adversaries is vast; strengthened by his experiences in Central America, Walter is more than a match for Sir Percival and his English henchmen. Using techniques "against suspected treachery" that he had learned "in the wilds of Central America," Walter eludes Sir Percival's spies as he dodges through London traffic (418). Such strategies are ineffective, however, against Fosco. Walter's veneer of foreignness does not enable him to outwit his truly foreign adversary; as Marian reveals, "You were followed, Walter, on returning here, after your first journey to Hampshire—by the lawyer's men for some distance from the railway, and by the Count himself to the door of the house" (506–7). Because Walter had been especially careful, on that final leg of his journey, to glance back "over the open space behind" him, Fosco's tracking ability borders on the magical: "How he contrived to escape being seen by you, he did not tell me," Marian concludes (418, 507).[17]

To be foreign is to be a formidable foe, and that connection is reaffirmed in the contrast between Walter's pursuit of Sir Percival and his plot against Count Fosco. By his own unaided efforts, Walter unearths Sir Percival's secret and hounds him to his fiery death in the Welmingham church vestry. His victory over Fosco, by contrast, is far less independent. Like Laura and Sir Percival, Walter must rely on a foreign friend in his time of greatest need. The count, who had outmaneuvered Walter with such superb confidence and aplomb, is reduced to a quivering lump of terror at the mere sight of Professor Pesca: "The leaden hue that altered his yellow complexion in a moment, the sudden rigidity of all his features, the furtive scrutiny of his cold grey eyes, the motionless stillness of him from head to foot, told their own tale. A mortal dread had mastered him, body and soul—and his own recognition of Pesca was the cause of it!" (531). As Walter's tone of amazement makes clear, this incident must subtly alter the relationship between the two friends; never again will Walter be able to view his funny little friend with the same dismissive humor. Thus, by the end of the novel, the third friendship between Englishman and foreigner has been brought into conformity with the other two.

This succession of pairings sets up a dichotomy between English and non-English characters that blurs distinctions among the various foreigners. To be Italian, in this novel, is to be a racialized Other who has far more in common with gypsies and Creoles than with pure, white Englishmen. In viewing the Italians as a separate race, Collins echoes Victorian race theories that placed England at the top of a hierarchy of races. For example, Edward Burnett Tylor's *Primitive Culture* (1871) creates a scale of civilizations that positions Europe and America "at one end of the social series and savage tribes at the other, arranging the rest of mankind between these limits according as they correspond more closely to savage or to cultured life."[18] According to Stocking, in Tylor's ladder, "the Australian, Tahitian, Aztec, Chinese, and Italian 'races' stood in precisely that ascending 'order of culture'—although its implied but missing apex might give pause to those south of the Alps."[19] Tylor's refusal to name Britain as the apex of his hierarchy suggests an immense cultural gulf between British civilization and the continuum of savagery that was seen to exist beyond its borders. In a similar vein, George Henry Lewes carefully preserves the wealthy English gentleman from all taint of savagery, even as he admits that "savage" characteristics can be observed "lingering amongst ourselves, either in remote provinces, in uncultivated classes, or in children." Nevertheless, Lewes is willing to collapse the categories of "civilized" and "savage" by demonstrating the resemblance between Africa and Italy: "The fatiguing and universal mendicancy of Africa . . . is little less than what the traveller meets with throughout the Neapolitan dominions. . . . In like manner the delight in bargaining which the Africans display is much the same as that exhibited by the Italians generally."[20]

Collins participates in this dichotomization of England and the rest of the world by associating the Italian Count Fosco with a number of racial groups. In the eyes of Frederick Fairlie, for example, Count Fosco "looked like a walking-West-Indian-epidemic" (*The Woman in White*, 322). The Count's own words, by contrast, associate him with the East; he begins his narrative by identifying himself as the "PERPETUAL ARCH-MASTER OF THE ROSICRUCIAN MASONS OF MESOPOTAMIA" (557). Most pervasive of all, however, is Fosco's relation to the gypsy. During Marian's illness, the attending physician, Mr. Dawson, is horrified by Fosco's attempts to "try his quack remedies (mesmerism included) on my patient" (334–35). Indeed, Marian could already attest to Fosco's mesmeric qualities; even at a first meeting she is struck by "the extraordinary expression and extraordinary power of his eyes" (197). His abilities extend to the animal realm as well; Fosco is able to tame a vicious bloodhound merely by looking him "straight in the eyes" (199).

In the nineteenth century, mesmerism was popularly associated with the gypsy; as Maria M. Tatar explains, the erotic and occult connotations of mesmerism were exploited by "itinerant magnetizers who made the rounds of carnivals and festivals with their trance maidens in order to cash in on the latest fad sweeping the Continent."[21] Such itinerancy links the mesmerist not only to the wandering gypsy but also to Fosco himself, who has accompanied Sir Percival "in London, in Paris, and in Vienna—but never in Italy again; the Count having, oddly enough, not crossed the frontiers of his native country for years past" (201). The connection between gypsies and mesmerism is not based merely on common habits of nomadism, however; in addition, gypsies, like mesmerists, were reputed to have psychic powers. As Antony Harrison points out, Matthew Arnold's "The Scholar-Gipsy," which depicts a student who learns the gypsy art of thought-control, was originally entitled "The Wandering Mesmerist."[22] Count Fosco, of course, is no stranger to such telepathic arts, as Marian is well aware: "He fixed his unfathomable grey eyes on me, with that cold, clear, irresistible glitter in them, which always forces me to look at him, and always makes me uneasy, while I do look. An unutterable suspicion that his mind is prying into mine, overcomes me at these times" (240). In Fosco, Collins brings together images of West Indian disease, Mesopotamian mystery, and gypsy magic.

Such racial ambiguity is even more marked in Mrs. Rubelle, whose racial origins are indeterminate. As Fosco admits, Mrs. Rubelle is one of his spies, employed by an unnamed government. Her surname indicates possible French origins—a hypothesis supported by the fact that before her arrival in England she had spent time in Lyons (384)—but Mrs. Michelson describes her face as having "a dark brown, or Creole complexion" (333). If these details are inconclusive, the waters are muddied still further by Walter's description of the final foreigner in the novel. After pointing out Count Fosco to Professor Pesca at the opera, Walter notices beside him the man who will eventually become the instrument of divine retribution against Fosco. He is described as a "slim, light-haired man . . . with a scar on his left cheek," and though Walter observes that he "was a mild gentlemanlike man, looking like a foreigner," no more specific information is ever given (530–31). At this point in the novel no further information is needed; we know that he is not English, and beyond that, little else matters.

Like Tylor and Lewes, Collins sets up a clear dichotomy between the English upper and middle classes, and the dark, racial-ized world outside. At first glance it might seem, however, that Collins has reversed the hierarchy: his English characters are weak and nervous, while his foreign characters are strong and vigorous. Nor has England any clear moral supremacy: the dark, gypsy-faced Marian is good, while the ultra-English Sir Percival is evil. Despite such details, however, Collins has not completely broken away from current teleological evolutionary theories that depicted England as the most advanced of the world's nations. According to Gilmour, in Victorian evolutionary theory, the savage tribes of the world represent the "childhood" of the human race: "Progressive evolutionism . . . assume[d] that mankind had evolved up a ladder of progress currently resting at white, European, industrial civilisation; those primitive peoples who had failed to take this main route of progress were not just different . . . but [were] "living fossils" who could be studied for the light they threw on the pre-historic past. As they are now, so we were then."[23]

So pervasive were such comparisons that even antievolutionary thinkers were affected by this concept of a chronology of races. William Whewell, according to Stocking, "would not allow [Darwin's] *Origin* on the shelves of Trinity College library."[24] Whewell responded to the Crystal Palace by noting that there "the infancy of nations, their youth, their middle age, and their maturity" were displayed side by side.[25]

Collins employs this concept when he attempts to resolve the problem of how England should evaluate the rest of the world. Throughout the novel, Collins explores and rejects various responses to foreigners, ranging from Philip Fairlie's hatred, to Sarah's fastidious dislike, to Mrs. Michelson's self-righteous tolerance. The dilemma cannot be solved, however, until Professor Pesca himself, in a heartfelt and impassioned speech, instructs Walter on how to view the refugee. As Pesca reveals, "every great city on the continent of Europe" is a hotbed of covert violence (534); concealed behind picturesque avenues are secret societies and furtive brotherhoods dedicated to the revolutionary cause. England alone is exempt from such inner agitation, and, for that very reason, the English must treat their foreign brethren with respect, awe, humility, and genuine tolerance:

> It is not for me to say in what frightful circumstances
> of oppression and suffering this Society took its rise. It is
> not for you to say—you Englishmen, who have conquered
> your freedom so long ago, that you have conveniently
> forgotten what blood you shed, and what extremities
> you proceeded to in the conquering—it is not for *you* to
> say how far the worst of all exasperations may, or may
> not, carry the maddened men of an enslaved nation. The
> iron that has entered into our souls has gone too deep
> for *you* to find it. Leave the refugee alone! Laugh at him,
> distrust him, open your eyes in wonder at that secret self

which smoulders in him . . . but judge us not! In the time of your first Charles you might have done us justice; the long luxury of your own freedom has made you incapable of doing us justice now. (535)

In his notes to the Oxford World's Classics edition of the novel, Harvey Peter Sucksmith reads this passage as an attack on "the smug hypocrisy of many Victorian Englishmen who cannot bear to acknowledge that their freedom, despite the Restoration and Burke, was bought and guaranteed with Eliot's imprisonment, Prynne's ears, the head of Charles I, and the blood of those who died in the Civil Wars"[26] Whether or not such images of historical bloodshed were palatable to the Victorian memory, surely the point here is that the age of violent unrest, in England at least, is securely locked away in the past. Assassinations, revolutions, and random murders are all part of contemporary experience for Continental Europeans, Collins suggests. England, by contrast, has buried such civil unrest three hundred years in the past: "As they are now, so we were then."[27]

By Pesca's own account, Great Britain stands at the pinnacle of evolutionary development, centuries ahead of the rest of Europe, and presumably millennia ahead of the primitive tribes of Africa, Australia, or America. The impetuous violence of Italy links it to Pesca's own adolescent impetuosity: he was first shipped off to England because, in his youthful zeal, he "ran the risk of compromising myself and others" (535). By contrast, Britain has settled into the staid satisfactions of a prosperous middle age. Taken by itself, Pesca's speech thus suggests a full endorsement of the most optimistic manifestations of the development hypothesis. But Collins's depiction of the state of the English race is, for the most part, far less reassuring. Not only are English characters physically and mentally weaker than their foreign counterparts but the bloodline seems to be declining with each successive generation. Instead of developing onward and upward, as Spencer or Chambers might suggest, the Fairlie family appears to be devolving into an abyss of madness.

French psychopathologist B. A. Morel's *Treatise on the Physical, Intellectual and Moral Degeneracy of the Human Race* (1857) provides a model for the devolution of the Fairlie family. According to Morel, "The first generation of a degenerate family might be merely nervous, the second would tend to be neurotic, the third psychotic, while the fourth consisted of idiots and died out."[28] The Fairlies follow this pattern with frightening accuracy. Frederick Fairlie is a hypochondriac and an imaginary invalid; he constantly complains of his tortured nerves, but as Walter observes, "Mr. Fairlie's selfish affectation and Mr. Fairlie's wretched nerves meant one and the same thing" (*The Woman in White*, 33). Mr. Fairlie's sufferings may not be as intense as he pretends, but clearly he is not psychologically healthy either. By contrast, his niece, Anne Catherick, must surely fill Morel's category of "neurotic" rather than "merely nervous." Anne's monomaniacal worship of the late Mrs. Fairlie subjects her to incarceration in an Asylum—a fate that is all too soon inflicted on her half-sister, Mr. Fairlie's other "neurotic" niece, Laura. Although Laura's "madness" is initially fabricated by Fosco, her stay in the asylum permanently enfeebles her delicate constitution; throughout the second half of the novel, Laura is infantilized, as Walter and Marian take her for walks, feed her "delicate strengthening food," and play "children's games at cards" with her (401). Even upon her return to Limmeridge, when her recovery is supposedly complete, she is little more than a body on display for the gawking eyes of the villagers: Laura is "so completely overwhelmed" by her neighbors' cheers of support that Walter is "obliged to take her from them, and carry her to the door" (577).

The apparent degeneration of the Fairlie family combines with the universal weakness of the purely English characters to undermine any sense of confidence British readers might otherwise have gained from reading Pesca's stirring speech. Nevertheless, these details do not simply contradict Pesca's views; rather, the devolution of the English race is a direct result of the evolutionary supremacy that Pesca describes. As the professor reveals, the process of sociocultural evolution has carried England to a time of peace and security; political and revolutionary struggles still rage on the Continent, but in England all is calm. As flattering as such images might seem, they carry a much more disturbing connotation in the context of Darwin's theory of natural selection. According to Darwin, evolutionary change occurs because competition for resources pits the strong against the weak: "as more individuals are produced than can possibly survive, there must in every case be a struggle for existence, either one individual with another of the same species, or with the individuals of distinct species, or with the physical conditions of life."[29] This "struggle for existence" guarantees that "individuals having any advantage, however slight, over others, would have the best chance of surviving and of procreating their kind," while "any variation in the least degree injurious would be rigidly destroyed."[30] By removing England from the theater of revolutionary struggle, Collins suggests that biological stagnation is inevitable.

If Pesca locates the struggle for existence in European political conflict, Walter locates it in the depths of working-class London. After his reunion with Marian and Laura, Walter chooses to make their abode "in a poor and populous neighbourhood—because the harder the struggle for existence among the men and women about us, the less the risk of their having the time or taking the pains to notice chance strangers who came among them" (*The Woman in White*, 397). The hardships faced by the working poor of London ensure that their biological evolution will continue according to the Darwinian model: the strong will survive, and the weak will be ruthlessly weeded out. Needless to say, however, it is not on the basis of its poorest classes that England's cultural supremacy rests: the very struggle for existence that ensures biological evolution also precludes any real cultural progress; Walter's neighbors have no time to write novels or visit the opera.

By contrast, Limmeridge, the seat of high culture in the novel, is a haven for biological and psychological disorders that would not survive a day in the teeming streets of London. For most of the novel Frederick Fairlie is ensconced at Limmeridge among all the trappings of civilization and high culture; in Mr. Fairlie's den, Walter finds "a long bookcase of some rare inlaid wood . . . adorned with statuettes in marble," as well as "two antique cabinets," a "picture of the Virgin and Child, protected by glass, and bearing Raphael's name," and several "little stands in buhl and marquetterie, loaded with figures in Dresden china, with rare vases, ivory ornaments, and toys and curiosities" (31). Mr. Fairlie himself is a frail, richly garmented specimen of England's degenerate upper class:

> His beardless face was thin, worn, and transparently
> pale, but not wrinkled; his nose was high and hooked;
> his eyes were of a dim greyish blue, large, prominent,
> and rather red round the rims of the eyelids; his hair
> was scanty, soft to look at, and of that light sandy colour
> which is the last to disclose its own changes towards grey.
> . . . His feet were effeminately small, and were clad in
> buff-coloured silk stockings, and little womanish
> bronze-leather slippers. Two rings adorned his white
> delicate hands. . . . Upon the whole, he had a frail,
> languidly-fretful, over-refined look. (32)

Through his portrayal of the weak, effeminate, "over-refined" Mr. Fairlie, Collins anticipates what Stocking describes as "the more pessimistic social Darwinism of those who . . . saw in modern society not so much an affirmative model of evolutionary process, but the evidence of a recent disjunction between social and biological evolution."[31] One such pessimist, Stocking contends, was Francis Galton, whose writings on heredity would suggest that "[t]he very operation of natural selection had in fact become problematic. . . . [C]ivilization had diminished the 'rigour' of natural selection, the simple fact of inherited wealth alone preserving 'very many rightful victims.'" For Galton, the problems of inherited wealth were exacerbated by the fact that Britons who still retained a spirit of enterprise and adventure too often "left fewer children or emigrated," leaving England to collapse into barbarism.[32]

The marriage of imperialist adventurer Walter Hartright to the culturally wealthy but biologically degenerate Laura Fairlie is Collins's tenuous solution to the problems posed by natural selection. Initially, Walter seems weak and enervated. After his departure from Limmeridge, he nearly suffers a nervous breakdown: as Mr. Gilmore observes, "His face looked pale and haggard—his manner was hurried and uncertain—and his dress, which I remembered as neat and gentlemanlike when I saw him at Limmeridge, was so slovenly, now, that I should really have been ashamed of the appearance of it on one of my own clerks" (139). Walter can be healed only in the jungles of Central America, where he engages in an epic battle for survival against "the perils of a bad climate, a wild country, and a disturbed population"(164)—forces that would certainly eliminate all but the fittest opponents. Marian's prophetic dream foretells Walter's survival of the threat of foreign pestilence, which is figured as a white "exhalation" from the "hideous stone idols" of "an immense ruined temple." As Marian dreams on, however, these idols come to life and take the form of "dark, dwarfish men" who lurk "murderously among the trees, with bows in their hands, and arrows fitted to the string" (248–49). Walter survives this threat as well, though many of his companions do not. Upon his return, he confirms Marian's visions; he is one of few survivors, but he has come back "a changed man. In the waters of a new life I had tempered my nature afresh. In the stern school of extremity and danger my will had learnt to be strong, my heart to be resolute, my mind to rely on itself" (373).

Peter Thoms identifies Walter's expedition to Central America as the moment of his escape from the plot society has scripted for him: "by journeying to 'the wilds and forests of Central America,'" Thoms suggests, "Hartright rejects the prevailing structure for his life." What Thoms sees as Walter's "quest for the condition of selfhood which exists outside the plans of others,"[33] however, Patrick Brantlinger would see as a point of transition between two plots, both of which are socially determined. In *Rule of Darkness,* Brantlinger discusses the transition in Victorian fiction from domestic realism to intrepid adventure: "The domestic, as in *Middlemarch,* is often associated with issues of democratic reform and with the difficulties involved in personal and political compromise. Against these complexities . . . imperialism offers a swashbuckling politics and a world in which neither epic heroism nor chivalry is dead. Both are to be rediscovered in crusading and conquering abroad."[34] Collins does not narrate Walter's imperialistic adventures; instead, he demonstrates the power of imperialism to counteract the dangers of "peace and prosperity, feminine wiles and domestic tranquillity," both for Walter himself and for England as a whole.[35]

The expedition to Central America enables Walter to act as what Taylor calls the "revitalizer of the stagnant and incipiently morbid Fairlie family."[36] Through Walter and Laura's marriage, Collins remarries the processes of biological and sociocultural evolution. Young Walter Hartright Jr., the heir of Limmeridge, inherits his great-uncle's cultural artifacts, along with his access to music, art, and education. At the same time, he inherits the spirit of struggle acquired by his father in Central America. Though pure English blood flows through his veins, he is hedged round by strong "foreign" godparents: the gypsy Marian and the Italian Pesca. It is fitting, then, that the final image of the novel is of the infant Walter "kicking and crowing" in his Aunt Marian's capable arms (*The Woman in White,* 583). The healthy exuberance of the new heir suggests that imperialist endeavor might well jolt Britain out of the peaceful complacency produced by the unquestioned evolutionary supremacy that the Crystal Palace had demonstrated.[37] Though England might have lapsed into a state of genteel decay, sites of struggle in India, Africa, and Central America beckon beyond her shores. By depicting the dangerous weakness that lies at the heart of English society, Collins lures the imagination to scenes of strife where the nation might win back the youthful energy and virility that time had begun to steal away. In this context, it becomes clear that Collins's critique of Crystal Palace optimism emerges, not from any real disloyalty to British patriotic ideals, but from a fear that England might lose her evolutionary advantage by resting on her laurels. Collins satirizes British self-congratulatory smugness in order to ensure that such complacency never undermines what he depicts as England's real racial and cultural superiority to Europe and the rest of the world.

Notes

I am grateful to the Social Sciences and Humanities Research Council of Canada for funding that allowed me to complete this paper.

1. Wilkie Collins, *The Woman in White*, ed. Harvey Peter Sucksmith (Oxford: Oxford Univ. Press, 1980), 525. Sucksmith's edition reproduces the original serialized version of the novel, which Collins revised for the subsequent book editions. Hereafter cited in the text as *The Woman in White*.

2. George W. Stocking Jr., *Victorian Anthropology* (London: Collier Macmillan, 1987), 5.

3. Robin Gilmour, *The Victorian Period: The Intellectual and Cultural Context of English Literature, 1830–1890* (London: Longman, 1993), 121.

4. Gilmour, 123.

5. Stocking, 45.

6. Ibid.

7. Ibid., 1.

8. Gilmour points out that Spencer's coining of the phrase "survival of the fittest" casts evolutionary debate in implicitly moralistic terms: "only those survive who *deserve* to survive" (133).

9. Jenny Bourne Taylor, *In the Secret Theatre of Home: Wilkie Collins, Sensation Narrative, and Nineteenth-Century Psychology* (London: Routledge, 1988), 67. The term *degeneration* pulls together a constellation of fears about Britain's racial, cultural, and social future. Though pre-Darwinian evolutionary theories focused on the notions of progress and teleological development, the suggestion that humans had evolved from animals inevitably raised the possibility of biological and cultural devolution, sparking fears that Britain's imperial power and dominance might give way to invasion from without or collapse from within. Though fears of "counterimperialism" became most widespread at the end of the century, concerns about the weakening of the social body can be found as early as the 1850s, when confidence in the forces of "progress" was counterbalanced by fears of madness and disease affecting not only individuals but also British culture as a whole. For discussions of degeneration in the late Victorian period, see Stephen Arata, *Fictions of Loss in the Victorian Fin de Siècle* (Cambridge: Cambridge Univ. Press, 1996), and William Greenslade, *Degeneration, Culture, and the Novel, 1880–1940* (Cambridge: Cambridge Univ. Press, 1994). For an examination of degeneration in the mid-Victorian period, see Daniel Pick, *Faces of Degeneration: A European Disorder, c. 1848–1918* (Cambridge: Cambridge Univ. Press, 1989).

10. Gilmour, 133.

11. As Christopher Kent points out, Collins "was surely better read and informed than is often recognized"; as a former contributor to *The Leader,* an avant-garde newspaper, Collins would have been acquainted with the evolutionary theories espoused by fellow contributors, such as G. H. Lewes, Herbert Spencer, and George Eliot ("Probability, Reality and Sensation in the Novels of Wilkie Collins," in *Wilkie Collins to the Forefront: Some Reassessments,* ed. Nelson Smith and R. C. Terry [New York: AMS Press, 1995], 55–56).

12. Criticism of *The Woman in White* has tended to dismiss or ignore issues of race. Stephen Bernstein outlines the parameters of critical response to the novel when he indicates that Collins takes on "the historical narratives of class, gender, and genre" ("Reading Blackwater Park: Gothicism, Narrative, and Ideology in *The Woman in White*," *Studies in the Novel* 25, no. 3 [1993]: 291). Indeed, the novel has provoked many Marxist, feminist, and narratological analyses, but race has emerged as a concern only briefly and in passing. Taylor, for example, alludes to the "foreignness" of Fosco only to demonstrate Collins's avoidance of narrow stereotypes: "There is clearly a close relationship between his sexual power and his 'foreignness' . . . but here he eludes any stable stereotypical framework, partly by his opposition to Pesca, the other Italian" (123).

13. Tamar Heller, *Dead Secrets: Wilkie Collins and the Female Gothic* (New Haven: Yale Univ. Press, 1992), 132.

14. Stocking, 2.

15. George Henry Borrow, *The Zincali: An Account of the Gypsies of Spain* (London: John Murray, 1901), 15.

16. Presumably, Marian's gypsy identity is metaphorical, rather than actual. Nevertheless, there is an intriguing air of mystery in the novel about Marian's paternal origins. Marian admits that her father "was a poor man," but after that Mr. Halcombe disappears from the text, though not without a trace. Although Mr. Gilmore comments that Marian "strongly reminds me" of the late Mrs. Fairlie, who also "had dark eyes and hair," it is evident that Marian's ugliness, at least, comes from the other side of the family, for Walter is confident that Mrs. Catherick is lying when she asserts that Mrs. Fairlie was "a remarkably plain-looking woman" (*The Woman in White,* 27, 113, 495).

17. Unlike Walter's, Marian's own attempts to outwit Count Fosco are often successful; when she asserts that her midnight move to Fulham went "quite unobserved," her words are allowed to stand uncontradicted (*The Woman in White,* 509).

18. Edward Burnett Tylor, *Primitive Culture* (1871; rpt. as *The Origins of Culture* [New York: Harper & Row, 1958]), 26 (page citation is to the reprint edition).

19. Stocking, 162.

20. George Henry Lewes, "Uncivilised Man," *Blackwood's* 89 (Jan. 1861): 39.

21. Maria M. Tatar, *Spellbound: Studies on Mesmerism and Literature* (Princeton: Princeton Univ. Press, 1978), 31.

22. Antony Harrison, "Matthew Arnold's Gipsies: Intertextuality and the New Historicism," *Victorian Poetry* 29 (winter 1984): 376.

23. Gilmour, 59.

24. Stocking, 5–6.

25. Qtd. in Stocking, 5–6.

26. Harvey Peter Sucksmith, explanatory notes to *The Woman in White*, 622.

27. Gilmour, 59. Tylor employs a similar logic when he deduces a primitive culture from history and archeology, concluding that "[t]his hypothetical primitive condition corresponds in a considerable degree to that of modern savage tribes, who, in spite of their difference and distance, have in common certain elements of civilization, which seem remains of an early state of the human race at large." Just as for Tylor the "savage" races represent civilization at an earlier stage of development, so also for Collins does Italy represent an earlier moment in English history (Tylor, 21).

28. Qtd. in Tylor, 68.

29. Charles Darwin, *The Origin of Species,* in *The Darwin Reader,* ed. Mark Ridley (New York: Norton, 1987), 74.

30. Ibid., 85.

31. Stocking, 233.

32. Ibid., 95.

33. Peter Thoms, "Escaping the Plot: The Quest for Selfhood in *The Woman in White*," in Smith and Terry, *Wilkie Collins to the Forefront*, 184.

34. Patrick Brantlinger, *Rule of Darkness: British Literature and Imperialism, 1830–1914* (Ithaca: Cornell Univ. Press, 1988), 36.

35. Brantlinger, 36. Walter is not the only English character who is strengthened and rejuvenated by imperialist enterprise; there is also evidence that better times are ahead for the decaying Blackwater Park when it falls into the hands of its true heir, "an officer in command of an East Indiaman." As Walter observes, this stalwart adventurer "would find his unexpected inheritance sadly encumbered; but the property would recover with time, and if 'the captain' was careful, he might be a rich man yet, before he died" (*The Woman in White*, 503).

36. Taylor, 108.

37. In a rare discussion of English nationalism in the novel, Cannon Schmitt reads *The Woman in White* as a tale of the reconstruction of English national identity. Schmitt argues that by expelling foreign invaders such as Fosco, Hartright is able to supplant a decayed aristocracy; at the end of the novel, Hartright has come to represent a "new Englishness" of "middle-class manliness possessed of the signs of the rural gentry" (*Alien*

Nation: Nineteenth-Century Gothic Fictions and English Nationalism [Philadelphia: Univ. of Pennsylvania Press, 1997], 133). I would add that this "new Englishness" should be understood not only in terms of class and gender, but also in terms of race and evolutionary discourse.

References

Arata, Stephen. *Fictions of Loss in the Victorian Fin de Siècle*. Cambridge: Cambridge Univ. Press, 1996.

Bernstein, Stephen. "Reading Blackwater Park: Gothicism, Narrative, and Ideology in *The Woman in White*." *Studies in the Novel* 25, no. 3 (fall 1993): 291–305.

Borrow, George Henry. *The Zincali: An Account of the Gypsies of Spain*. London: John Murray, 1901.

Brantlinger, Patrick. *Rule of Darkness: British Literature and Imperialism, 1830–1914*. Ithaca: Cornell Univ. Press, 1988.

Chambers, Robert. *Vestiges of the Natural History of Creation*. London: J. Churchill, 1844.

Collins, Wilkie. *The Woman in White*. Ed. Harvey Peter Sucksmith. Oxford: Oxford Univ. Press, 1980.

Darwin, Charles. *The Origin of Species*. In *The Darwin Reader*, ed. Mark Ridley. New York: Norton, 1987.

Gilmour, Robin. *The Victorian Period: The Intellectual and Cultural Context of English Literature, 1830–1890*. London: Longman, 1993.

Greenslade, William. *Degeneration, Culture, and the Novel, 1880–1940*. Cambridge: Cambridge Univ. Press, 1994.

Harrison, Antony. "Matthew Arnold's Gipsies: Intertextuality and the New Historicism." *Victorian Poetry* 29, no. 4 (winter 1991): 365–83.

Heller, Tamar. *Dead Secrets: Wilkie Collins and the Female Gothic*. New Haven: Yale Univ. Press, 1992.

Lewes, George Henry. "Uncivilised Man." *Blackwood's* 89 (Jan. 1861): 27–41.

Pick, Daniel. *Faces of Degeneration: A European Disorder, c. 1848–1918*. Cambridge: Cambridge Univ. Press, 1989.

Schmitt, Cannon. *Alien Nation: Nineteenth-Century Gothic Fictions and English Nationality*. Philadelphia: Univ. of Pennsylvania Press, 1997.

Smith, Nelson, and R. C. Terry, eds. *Wilkie Collins to the Forefront: Some Reassessments*. New York: AMS Press, 1995.

Spencer, Herbert. "The Haythorne Papers. No. II—The Development Hypothesis." *The Leader*, 20 Mar. 1852, 280–81.

Stocking, George W., Jr. *Victorian Anthropology*. London: Collier Macmillan, 1987.

Tatar, Maria M. *Spellbound: Studies on Mesmerism and Literature.* Princeton: Princeton Univ. Press, 1978.

Taylor, Jenny Bourne. *In the Secret Theatre of Home: Wilkie Collins, Sensation Narrative, and Nineteenth-Century Psychology.* London: Routledge, 1988.

Tylor, Edward Burnett. *Primitive Culture.* 1871. Rpt. as *The Origins of Culture.* New York: Harper & Row, 1958.

Fosco Lives!

———◆———

A. D. Hutter

THE *WOMAN IN WHITE*, COLLINS'S FIRST MAJOR LITERARY ACHIEVEMENT AND PERHAPS HIS GREATEST SUSPENSE NOVEL, remains a model of fiction told from limited narrative perspectives. Many of Collins's contemporaries were deeply moved by the novel—Thackeray, for example, ill at the time of its full publication, nevertheless read it straight through the night[1]—while a number of Victorian writers considered it the best work Collins had ever done.[2] It has become, along with *The Moonstone*, the most highly regarded of his mystery novels. Not all Victorian reviewers, however, were so moved; in fact, some adopted a distinctly hostile position. According to Julian Symons, "reviews . . . were for the most part condescending or sharply critical, and Collins was both surprised and annoyed that his story should be so unappreciated."[3]

Victorian reviewers remained obdurate, unable to appreciate what we now recognize as a unique achievement in a particularly demanding form of storytelling. The constantly maintained suspense of exposition, at once advanced and restricted by the perspectives of its many narrators, allows the mysteries of plot to develop naturally into a reflection of intense social and emotional mysteries, the deepest conflicts of the period. Just as imperialism and sexual desire are central to *The Moonstone,* so are sexuality and physical appearance, like the broader issues of class, government, foreign policy, and foreign politics central to a full understanding of *The Woman in White.* Collins understood the profound importance of Italian immigrants and revolutionaries, through friends and family, as he also understood the power of the revolutionary movement that would result in the unification of Italy. The impact of Italian political refugees and the growing fervor of revolution and change are embodied in "The Brotherhood" and particularly in the characters of Pesca and Fosco: their actions profoundly alter the lives of Walter, Laura, and Marian, and their backgrounds are integral to understanding *The Woman in White.*

The mysteries of *The Woman in White,* like those of *The Moonstone,* are firmly rooted in nineteenth-century events. The more we know about the historical fabric of Collins's works, the more immediate and persuasive are the bases for their suspense—the rich and textured detail of description, dialogue, and character. Many of the most interesting characters in these works were drawn from life, so much so that Collins, in two published interviews, would later describe numerous letters written to him by readers complaining of public recognition or humiliation because of his apparently exact description of their physical similarities, homes, or personal quirks and reputations.[4] Finding himself so uncannily and accurately exposed (as Fosco was exposed by Walter), one Parisian in fact insisted on a duel of honor with Collins.

Historical sources for the novel's characters could indeed be found in Europe, and not necessarily among only Collins's personal acquaintances. For example, the novel's famous villain, Count Fosco, apparently owed his charm, as well as his delightful and much sought-after conversation, to Giuseppe Mazzini, one of the nineteenth-century founders of a united Italian kingdom. Other qualities, including his name, were derived from the Italian poet and revolutionary, Ugo Foscolo, who lived in England most of his adult life and died there in 1827.[5] François Eugène Vidocq—criminal, informer, one of the first and most brilliant of criminologists and criminalists, and founder of the French Sûreté—was also a particularly important source for Fosco.[6] Other essential characteristics of this most intriguing villain are to be found in numerous figures known to and observed by Collins. The novelist estimated that more than a hundred people "posed" for Fosco. Collins probably did not include his wry but accurate rendition of many of his admitted radical views and bohemian vices, although he repeatedly acknowledged how much of Fosco derived from his sense of himself. One of his biographers imagines Collins delivering his final installment of *The Woman in White* and simultaneously unburdening himself of the overwhelming reality of his famous villain: "Blinking, he awakened slowly from the world of Count Fosco, who for two years had been the most real person in his life."[7]

Sensation fiction, particularly as Collins developed it, demands first that the author provide constant interest through the intricate movements and suspense of story itself, so that the reader is always absorbed by action. But Collins would inform his sensational plots with a depth of social commentary and social conflict, sharpening our interest as the range of issues used for the novel's action invariably furthers our understanding not simply of characters but of the period's central values. The strongly reciprocal relationship between surface event and cultural or political meaning would increasingly distinguish Collins's fiction until it became virtually a different genre from, for example, the sensation fiction of Charles Reade. In Collins's best writing it is impossible for us to understand the action without understanding its cultural context—the hidden, social conflicts from which the surface action develops.

Our changing understanding of the novel, like our changing views of history and historiography, combined with the evolution of different ways of reading complex texts, insistently demand that we reappraise in particular those writers, such as Collins, whose subtlety of thought and originality of form are carefully concealed whenever they threaten to slow suspense and sensation. Collins's aesthetic continues to make it all too easy to overlook the originality of his thought—and thus his increasing importance in literary history.

I establish here readings of *The Woman in White* and, implicitly, of Collins's major works that make them if not unique then extraordinarily rare in the history of English literature, perhaps in all literatures. In planning out the text in full, Collins may have decided to avoid the more blatantly censorious responses he had experienced in the publication of earlier works such as *Basil*[8] and to create a double ending—primarily or even purely to satisfy himself—while protecting his work from the more savage reviews he had experienced prior to 1860.

For almost all of his contemporary readers, as indeed for most readers up to and including the present, he offers a standard solution of rewarding the good and disposing of his villains. Fosco's apparently violent death, in fact, seems particularly fitting. But a closer inspection of the novel's ending demonstrates that Fosco cannot, in fact, be dead. Rather he manages to escape retribution and in his own characteristic way continues to thrive. In so doing he inevitably reverses the stated moral premises of the novel and thus offers a thoroughgoing repudiation of Victorian pretense. Using a hero whose heart is right but whose perceptions and strength of character grow steadily weaker, Collins manages at once to frame within his editor's heartfelt Victorian morality a parody of that morality.

As editor, Walter himself unwittingly reveals the most powerful support for the mistaken belief that the Count has been murdered: by the inconsistencies of Walter's own narrative; by the limited and brief view he has of Fosco's supposed corpse in the Paris Morgue;[9] and, above all, by noting and then citing from the posthumous publication of Fosco's hagiography. Brought out a year after Fosco's alleged death, the biography is purportedly written by his wife and published under her name. But everything we know about Madame Fosco makes this impossible. When such unlikely authorship is combined with the quotation Walter provides from the ending of Fosco's biography, we see the unmistakable hand of Fosco himself.[10] Walter, indeed all the narrators of the novel, have made it abundantly clear that the former Eleanor Fairlie would be incapable of writing such a work—even after years of married life to the count. Fosco does manage to transform a silly, aging spinster into a quiet and obedient, or quietly terrified, wife. But in every way the evidence of the novel shows us that this posthumous biography—in its content, its voice, its aims, and especially in its style of writing—could have been written by only one person.

Because Collins was not writing a modernist or self-consciously open ending, the proof for my argument must first focus on the text.[11] In addition to close textual analysis there are at least six further ways of corroborating the idea of an alternate ending. And most important, the idea of such an ending opens an entirely new reading of *The Woman in White.*

First, if we examine the sources for significant figures in the text, particularly for Count Fosco, we discover that their lives and personal characteristics, all familiar to Collins, are reflected in an ending that allows Fosco to live. And this, in turn, permits a fuller understanding of what happens at the close. Fosco's miraculous escape from death and his commentary on that death make far more sense than any other version of this novel's last installment—indeed of the novel as a whole. Second, by looking at what we do know of Collins's work in general we are able to define a theme so dominant and so consistent throughout his life it becomes a topos: "the dead alive." Third, that topos should make us more sensitive to a strikingly similar theme of the dead returned to life, of miraculous resurrection, as it first appears in Dickens's *A Tale of Two Cities* and was then developed by both writers over the following eleven years. Dickens's novel of the French Revolution ends in the same number of *All the Year Round* in which *The Woman in White* begins, and the theme of resurrection would remain central to Dickens's last three novels.[12]

Fourth, each writer's work draws from and adds to that of the other. Dickens would publish *Great Expectations* (1860–61) and *Our Mutual Friend* (1864–65), while in 1868 Collins would publish his other great mystery novel, *The Moonstone.* Just as Pip dies and is reborn into Joe's arms as we move toward the concluding section of *Great Expectations,* and just as *Our Mutual Friend* is dominated by recurring passages of death and resurrection, so the very title image of Collins's novel depends upon taking the Indian jewel from its rightful place, like a resurrectionist robbing a grave of its body, before it is finally returned at the close. Dickens's career would end with the half-completed *The Mystery of Edwin Drood* (1870). *Drood* in particular depends throughout on a variety of different views of death and ritual resurrection—from Druids, to being buried alive, to the central question of whether the protagonist himself will be found alive or dead or "returned to life," like Manette in *A Tale of Two Cities,* in what Dickens seems to have been building toward in the second and unwritten half of his final novel. In many ways the absence of direct corroboration from their correspondence allows us to see more clearly how two major writers influenced one another, often unconsciously, and how, during an eleven-year period, each one would work out, in very different ways, versions of the same theme.

Fifth, the aesthetically horrifying but revealing—and often unintentionally amusing—changes Collins introduced into his theatrical adaptation of *The Woman in White* (1870), a decade after publishing his novel, clarify much of what, at first, he deliberately obscured—particularly as it affects our understanding of Fosco.

Finally, understanding how and why readers read and constantly create and re-create fictions of their own, which often extend or vary—or even contradict—the very stories they are reading—is central to the ways in which both Collins and Dickens thought about serial publication and its relationship—*their* relationship—to the readers of their publications. Readers of serial fiction are encouraged to imagine far more than the works describe, to create for themselves alternate aspects of character and plot. They are especially encouraged to anticipate and imagine a variety of endings, for in the closure, or partial closure, or even lack of closure of a single number and certainly of the work as a whole, such stories oblige readers to play with and refictionalize what has already been read. We know that these readers continued to reconsider and reorder details of story, until finally the meanings of specific details and clues, as well as general comments and important choices reflected on for a year or longer, would finally cohere. This, more than anything, returns us to the profound importance of a double or open ending to *The Woman in White*.

The concern of serial novelists to promote and provoke solutions and resolutions beyond anything stated in weekly or monthly numbers is essential to their work: so much of this process determines the increasing involvement and interest of their audience. Everything from critical reception to increased sales depends upon that audience's imagined involvement with a story—one that readers have a great deal of time to think about between monthly or even weekly parts. And it is above all true when, added to a normal publication in serial parts, we find the catalyst of a story, told over time, by a series of subjective narrators each contributing an incomplete account. Collins thrived on readers who identified themselves with characters, good and evil, readers who wrote to him, involving themselves right down to the end of each number—and beyond. In considering the activity of individual readers creating and altering their own imaginary fictions based on published fictions, we better understand the central concepts of *re-creation* in the *recreational* activity of all reading. Such activity is wonderfully illustrated by Collins, as by a few of our most important writers from Melville to Henry James and well into the twentieth century.[13]

The excitement surrounding the appearance of a new number and especially that engendered by the arrival of the final number has grown into one of the great clichés of Victorian fiction: we still see New York harbor on a cold, rainy day, with tens of thousands crying out to know whether Little Nell was dead; we imagine the thousands of readers of *Vanity Fair* searching frantically backward through earlier numbers to find out precisely whom Becky could mean when she tells Sir Pitt Crawley that she is already married. One of the psychological issues I discuss later in this essay is that the very capacity to imagine alternate stories, to read fiction and to engage with it, is itself symptomatic of the health of an individual's imagination; while an inability to do so, an inability to read fiction in the first place, is one of the earliest symptoms of depression.

I am thus writing in the spirit of the original *essai*—a try or attempt to establish the possibility of a new approach to Collins that shall ultimately lead us to a fresh perspective of his work from sources we are only now beginning to discover. My conjectures are meant to extend a unique view of a uniquely popular writer catering to the demands of an unusually demanding audience. Victorians, we know, insisted on rewarding their heroes and punishing their villains. But Collins would simultaneously open this narrow view into an unself-conscious modernism so that he could, at the same moment, satisfy the demands of his audience and the atypical demands of his own far more radical and unusual tastes. Like Dickens, Collins fully under-stood the nature of good reading, which necessarily includes the orig-inal or fundamental meaning of *re-creation* as the OED defines it: "The action of creating again; a new creation."

Collins and Dickens understood that serial publication not only involved but *provoked* readers between numbers. In analyzing Collins's special gift for novels told by multiple narrators, we must keep in mind that we are reading a form somewhere between litera-ture and theater. The particular aesthetic of such works obliges the writer always to be conscious of the reader's extratextual imagination. If fiction in general stimulates one's continued growth and develop-ment, then we might make the strongest case for serial fiction told from multiple perspectives. Fiction should be enjoyable; but good fic-tion necessarily expands its readers' creativity—perhaps most effec-tively when that reader is unaware of anything but the pleasure of the reading experience itself.[14]

The Text

The Woman in White has two villains. Sir Percival Glyde is a despi-cable bully willing to lie, to cheat, and even to murder in order to obtain whatever he wishes. By contrast, Count Fosco consistently repudiates every stereotype of the villain—from his obesity to his intel-ligence and wit, even his love for one of the two heroines of the novel. More than half a century after its original publication, Dorothy Sayers, referring to Collins's second published novel, *Basil*, would speak of "Basil's love-affair and its abominable ending . . . told with a kind of grim actuality which has little relation to anything in contemporary English fiction. It is a story of passion without sentiment, more French than English in its frank facing of sexual facts."[15] Sayers herself seems more Victorian English than French in her rush to judgment over frank sexual descriptions, her evaluation of *Basil* a magisterial dismissal rather than a critical appraisal. "Not until *Armadale*," she adds, "did [Collins] attempt anything of the same kind again, and then only with safeguards. *Basil* alone remains to show that it was in him to become, long in advance of this period, a frank exponent of physical passion." She concludes that *Basil* was indeed "a young man's book, crammed with errors and crudities,"[16] although with enough promise to prevent total disregard of his future work. And she punctuates her dismissal with the most damning of faint praise: according to Sayers, Swinburne offers the best Victorian critique of *Basil*. Swinburne's remarks on the novel are scarcely temperate. He notes how "violent and unlovely and unlikely as it is, this early story had in it something more than promise. . . . The horrible heroine, beast as she is, is a credible and conceivable beast; and her hapless young husband is a rather pathetic if a rather incredible figure. But . . . the book would hardly be remembered for better or for worse if the author had not in his future stories excelled its merits and eschewed its faults."[17]

Following her citation of Swinburne, Sayers subsequently refers to *Basil* as alone revealing two Collinses, one of whom "was arrested in his development."[18] But whether the British critic of Collins's time or of a later but equally puritanical period in English literary criticism had recourse to such outrageous name-calling, what both Sayers and the occasionally conventional Swinburne have noted is indeed not something Collins outgrew or somehow *un*arrested. Rather, he was obliged to learn from his critics. By the time he wrote *The Woman in White* he knew how to provide his audience with what he correctly assumed they would require. He continued, throughout his life, to enjoy an exposition of villainy that he found neither villainous nor odious, which he was capable of separating into ethical evil, the misuses of considerable and even admirable intelligence, and the portrayal of a passion that, in Fosco's reaction to Marian, for example, was intellectual and emotional as well as physical and domineering.

However, Collins carefully avoided anything too shockingly frank or direct in *The Woman in White*. By 1860 he had learned to conceal such enjoyment so thoroughly it would not be remarked on in the same way by future critics. Yet its presence, like his unabashed pleasure in so many of his villains, would remain unmistakably clear until his death.[19] Marian herself sets the tone for the reader, finding Fosco irresistibly charming in spite of what she knows to be his sometimes odious morality. It is indeed difficult for us, like Marian, not to be charmed and delighted with Fosco, not to look forward to his appearances, his inimitable style, his relish for machinations, even his narcissism. Fosco feeds a Rabelaisian appetite for his own cleverness, much as he takes such delight in the immensity of his person. From the outset of her description of Fosco, Marian acknowledges: "I am almost afraid to confess it, even to these secret pages. The man has interested me, has attracted me, has forced me to like him. In two short days, he has made his way straight into my favourable estimation" (*The Woman in White*, 219–20). In spite of his villainy, Fosco has the same attraction for the readers. Marian's initial description of Fosco is an attempt to parse out how and why he has so rapidly overcome her objections to what he stands for and still manages to compel her attraction. Her description is also quite lengthy, so I am able to summarize only its most essential points.

She begins by first describing Madame Fosco *née* Eleanor Fairlie (aged seven-and-thirty)—if only to get her out of the way to focus on Count Fosco himself! Prior to her marriage to Fosco, Eleanor "was always talking pretentious nonsense, and always worrying the unfortunate men with every small exaction which a vain and foolish woman can impose on long-suffering male humanity. As Madame Fosco (aged three-and-forty), she sits for hours together without saying a word, frozen up in the strangest manner in herself" (218). She has ceased to dress inappropriately and "look[s], for the first time in her life since I remember her, like a decent woman." Sitting mute but attentive, she either embroiders or rolls "endless cigarettes for the Count's own particular smoking." She generally does not look at anyone but her husband, and then with a "mute submissive inquiry which we are all familiar with in the eyes of a faithful dog." Her only other emotion seems to be a pent up but fierce, almost tigerish, jealousy of any woman to whom Fosco speaks or shows particular attention. The remarkable change in Eleanor Fairlie results in "a civil, silent, unobtrusive woman, who is never in the way." She may also, concludes Marian, have developed "something dangerous in her nature" which only time will reveal (218–19).

However remarkably Fosco has transformed his wife, a foolish and voluble woman now turned quiet and unobtrusive, it has necessarily been by suppressing her flaws. Not even Fosco may imbue her with qualities she did not possess in the first place, qualities, for example, of intelligence, or of wit and language, qualities he is to find so admirable in Marian. He does not dwell on Marian's physical beauty, but

Marian's internal strength is for Fosco inextricably linked with the beauty of her figure and her skill with language:

> Just Heaven! with what inconceivable rapidity I learnt to adore that woman. At sixty, I worshipped her with the volcanic ardour of eighteen. All the gold of my rich nature was poured hopelessly at her feet. My wife— poor angel!—my wife, who adores me, got nothing but the shillings and the pennies. Such is the World, such Man, such Love. What are we (I ask) but puppets in a show-box? Oh, omnipotent Destiny, pull our strings gently! Dance us mercifully off our miserable little stage!
>
> The preceding lines, rightly understood, express an entire system of philosophy. It is Mine.
>
> I resume. (614–15)

When Marian turns to "the magician who has wrought this wonderful transformation" in his wife, she notes that he looks to be a man who could tame anyone—even Marian herself. Her admission is followed by an embarrassed confession of her attraction to Count Fosco. But why? Taken individually, his features, like too many aspects of his domineering personality, are not prepossessing: "For example, he is immensely fat" (220). Marian not only finds such corpulence unattractive in itself; it is often mistakenly associated with joviality and good nature. She introduces Henry the Eighth and "Mr Murderer and Mrs Murderess Manning" to support her argument. Perhaps then Fosco's attractions are in his face rather than his body. "It may be his face. He is a most remarkable likeness, on a large scale, of the great Napoleon. His features have Napoleon's magnificent regularity—his expression recalls the grandly calm, immovable power of the Great Soldier's face. This striking resemblance certainly impressed me, to begin with" (221). It would have impressed, even more, a British public for whom Napoleon represented everything they most feared. Marian here allies herself with Fosco in her most unconventional and, to her contemporaries, her outspokenly radical views.

Other compelling qualities emerge in Marian's detailed examination of Fosco's behavior and achievements. But more than the initial resemblance to what she calls "the great Napoleon," she is impressed by Fosco's eyes, "the most unfathomable grey eyes I ever saw." At times they have "a cold, clear, beautiful, irresistible glitter in them which forces me to look at him, and yet causes me sensations, when I do look, which I would rather not feel" (221).[20] He listens closely and with deference, rare enough in men but particularly rare in a Victorian man listening to a woman. Above all, his mastery of English impresses Marian: "There are times when it is almost impossible to detect, by his accent, that he is not a countryman of our own, and as for fluency, there are very few born Englishmen who can talk with as few stoppages and repetitions as the Count." For all his apparent obesity he also moves with an unaccountable grace and speed, and "is as noiseless . . . as any of us women" (222).[21] Marian's detailed description will further include Fosco's unusually clear, if "sallow-fair" complexion, at variance with the rest of his coloring and hair, suggesting that he wears a wig. Above all, his complexion is so free of wrinkles and marks, freer indeed than Marian's, it bears no resemblance to that of a man supposed to be sixty. She comments at length on his unusual love for pets, such as the white mice that run about his body, and his accomplishments in science, in particular the fact that "among other wonderful inventions" he has discovered "a means of petrifying the body after death, so as to preserve it, as hard as marble, to the end of time" (223).

This is Collins at his very best. The elaborate, eight-page description of Fosco in no way slows the progress of the story by simply painting the portrait of a complex character. On the contrary, it is first of all a double portrait, telling us as much about Marian as about Fosco, while it contains throughout detailed references to Fosco's ability to seem to be that which he is not. It implies that he may be a skilled hypnotist (mesmerist), and that he is in disguise. His grace, speed, and noiseless movements suggest someone who may be giving the impression of a false obesity; if one wishes to disguise oneself in such ways, the use of padding and, given Fosco's scientific knowledge, something which adds a misleading sense of weight to his features is possible, whereas one could hardly disguise oneself in the opposite way, somehow transforming obesity into the slight and nimble! Almost as a footnote, Marian notes Fosco's knowledge of how to maintain the dead in perpetuity "to the end of time." This final piece of information will be of great importance when we presumably see him, or some substitute for him, in the Paris Morgue. Under the guise of a most intelligent but perplexed heroine describing in detail a man who so quickly fascinates her against her will, Marian amasses details that are all essential to the mystery itself, to the story of Fosco's crimes and, ultimately, to the basis for the novel's double ending.

Much later, and much more superficially, Walter ponders Fosco's changed appearance, so changed that Pesca cannot recognize him.

Hartright's thinking is far less thorough than Marian's. However, Walter's conclusions, such as the idea that Fosco's "immense corpulence might have come with his later years" (593) are separated from Marian's more detailed observations not so much by 350 pages, but by several months for those reading the story in parts. Walter thus helps the reader to *mis*perceive or gloss over what Collins has gone to so much trouble to set before us much earlier in the novel. In this, as in so many ways, Walter is Fosco's greatest, if unwitting, ally in making us believe in Fosco's death.

While Walter describes Sir Percival Glyde in great detail over many pages, the time and concern he devotes to Fosco are more limited. However objective Walter may wish to be in his reporting and in his role as editor of the manuscript as a whole, his interests are, first and foremost, concerned with Laura. He marries Laura after he finishes with Sir Percival but before dealing with Fosco. And by then his actions are always restricted by his love for his new wife—to complete her restoration to her rightful position as Lady Glyde and to reverse the harm done to her by the substitutions of Laura for Anne Catherick and Anne for Laura. The rest, as he says, even the knowledge of, and punishment for, Fosco's crimes, does not concern him:

> The one question to consider was, whether I was justified
> or not in possessing myself of the means of establishing
> Laura's identity, at the cost of allowing the scoundrel who
> had robbed her of it to escape me with impunity. I knew
> that the motive of securing the just recognition of my
> wife in the birthplace from which she had been driven
> out as an imposter, and of publicly erasing the lie that
> still profaned her mother's tombstone, was far purer, in
> its freedom from all taint of evil passion, than the vindic-
> tive motive which had mingled itself with my purpose
> from the first. And yet I cannot honestly say that my
> own moral convictions were strong enough to decide
> the struggle in me, by themselves. (606)

Following his marriage to Laura, Walter loses strength, not just morally but in his clarity of observation, in his ability to be more objective and less biased, in virtually every way—physically and emotionally. He will move from the cant in the passage cited above to a "far purer" motive, and then claim that the still-frightening memory of Percival's horrible death by fire has snatched retribution "from [Walter's own] feeble hands" (606). Surely he is aware that he stands to gain by Laura's restoration to her rightful place, whereas punishing Fosco for his misdeeds is far more altruistic. He wonders if he has the right to decide to allow "in my poor mortal ignorance of the future, that this man [Fosco], too, must escape with impunity because he escaped *me*" (606). This last comment is particularly interesting given that he will not only escape Walter but escape in part *because of* Walter. Walter's increasing concern with Laura and the weakening of his resolve everywhere else contribute, as we shall see, to his blindness, even cowardice, in his final dealings with Fosco.

Walter protects himself unnecessarily, another example of a growing moral weakness and personal fear that corrupts his judgment as it corrupts his integrity: he openly exposes Pesca's identity when there is not only no need to do so, but every reason to avoid such exposure. "You have," Pesca tells Walter, "drawn your own conclusion already. . . . I see it in your face. Tell me nothing; keep me out of the secret of your thoughts. Let me make my one last sacrifice of myself, for your sake—and then have done with this subject, never to return to it again. . . . [I]f the man you pointed out at the Opera knows *me,* he is so altered, or so disguised, that I do not know *him.*" He then begs Walter to leave him for a few moments because the evening's revelations have so frightened him: "He dropped into a chair; and turning away from me, hid his face in his hands. I gently opened the door, so as not to disturb him—and spoke my few parting words in low tones, which he might hear or not, as he pleased" (591–92).

Walter's response appears to be sincere: "'I will keep the memory of tonight in my heart of hearts,' I said. 'You shall never repent the trust you have reposed in me'" (592). But Walter immediately proceeds to use Pesca's revelations to gain ascendancy over Count Fosco. Whatever Pesca knows or does not know, Fosco finds himself in immediate peril:

> I have said that I felt certain of the purpose in the
> Count's mind when he escaped us at the theatre. How
> could I doubt it, when I saw, with my own eyes, that he
> believed himself, in spite of the change in his appearance,
> to have been recognised by Pesca, and to be therefore in
> danger of his life? If I could get speech of him that night,
> if I could show him that I, too, knew of the mortal peril
> in which he stood, what result would follow? Plainly this.
> One of us must be master of the situation—one of us
> must inevitably be at the mercy of the other. (593)

Within less than a page, Walter seems to have forgotten his promise to Pesca that he shall "never repent the trust you have reposed in me." And why? Always for the same reason: "I owed it to myself to consider the chances against me before I confronted them. I owed it to my wife to do all that lay in my power to lessen the risk" (593–94). In spite of his friend's plea not to involve him in the matter unless absolutely necessary, Walter uses Pesca to guarantee that Fosco cannot harm him during or immediately after their interview. This allows Walter to secure what he needs for Laura's restoration but puts Pesca in considerable danger, when something as simple as an envelope without a name, or the name of an intermediary, or a prearranged drop at a different address for Pesca—virtually anything requiring half a moment's thought to save the life of someone so loyal to him—would guarantee the safety of Pesca as well as Walter. And Pesca has literally begged Walter to do all he possibly can to protect him. Yet by the end of his negotiations with Fosco, Walter simply addresses a note to Pesca that Monsieur Rubelle, Fosco's henchman, will deliver. Fosco naturally asks Rubelle to show the letter to him and then closely examines the name and address: "'I thought so!' he said, turning on me with a dark look, and altering again in his manner from that moment" (612).

It is essential to perceive just how much Walter weakens during this final period of the novel, not simply because it explains his mistaken conclusion about the death of Fosco: most important in The Third Epoch is the repeated textual evidence for the protagonist/editor's unreliability, shown so frequently that it makes us believe Walter must be as deceptive to his readers as he is to himself. There is, for example, no question but that, from his very first meeting with Laura, Walter both perceives something wrong with her and is bent here, too, on deceiving himself *and* deceiving us. He tries to make what he wants to believe for himself equally acceptable to the reader. For most Victorians, nothing would seem easier to explain the mental weakness and lack of determination in a woman, especially a beautiful woman, than to see her as an adorable child. Walter does all he is able to do to make such explanations work. Yet Collins is not Walter. It may seem unnecessary for a contemporary critic to make this point, but too many recent critics of this novel continue to confuse the two. And Collins will not let his protagonist avoid what he instead obliges Walter to note, and regularly to acknowledge:

> Mingling with the vivid impression produced by
> the charm of her fair face and head, her sweet expression,
> and her winning simplicity of manner, was another

impression, which, in a shadowy way, suggested to me
the idea of something wanting. At one time it seemed
like something wanting in *her:* at another, like something
wanting in myself, which hindered me from understanding her as I ought. . . . I was most conscious of the
harmony and charm of her face, and yet, at the same
time, most troubled by the sense of an incompleteness
which it was impossible to discover. Something wanting,
something wanting—and where it was, and what it was,
I could not say. (50–51)

Throughout his initial experiences of Laura he regularly delights
in her childlike qualities. Certainly Laura's incarceration in a madhouse, her kidnappings, the brutal treatment she receives from Sir
Percival, her limited strengths to begin with, now render her absolutely
childlike—and often childish. One of many examples is her need to be
of use when she cannot provide for herself, much less provide for
Walter or Marian. Walter pretends that she does bring in an income, as
one might humor a very young child. He claims to sell her drawings
along with his own (489–90).[22] And Walter plays on this feeling, enjoying Laura as so childlike that she finally becomes, at times, an infant.

As Walter prepares for his final confrontation with Count Fosco,
Marian in turn reacts like a good wife, and together they behave like
a couple who share the responsibility of protecting a retarded child.
Marian's intelligence and intuition tell her what Walter is about to do
when he sets off to see Fosco. At first she helps him without raising
questions, but finally she cannot contain herself. She speaks to him "in
a low eager whisper," saying, "You are trying the last chance tonight."
Walter whispers back a yes, "the last chance and the best." And she
begs—one intimate, loving adult to another—to join him: "Not
Alone! Oh, Walter, for God's sake not alone! Let me go with you.
Don't refuse me because I'm only a woman. I must go! I will go! I'll
wait outside in the cab!" (597).

But Walter needs Marian for something much more important. As
we have just seen, he is not alone. He has a trump card in Pesca and he
means to *use* his friend in every sense of that word. Marian's most
important task is to protect the child they both love; he asks her to
watch over Laura and to sleep in her room that night. Only a few
moments before this conversation with Marian, Walter himself looks in
on Laura, sleeping like an angel, ignorant of the dangers that surround
her, and ignorant, too, of all that these two parental figures are doing
for her. Her role is precisely that of a beloved infant, adored by both

Marian and Walter, inspiring them, and protected by them in all those ways parents will protect a child. She is told nothing, suspects nothing, but she inspires Walter by the very childlike nature of her innocence:

> [We had not been married quite a month yet.] If my heart was heavy, if my resolution for a moment faltered again, when I looked at her face [turned faithfully to *my* pillow] in her sleep—when I saw her hand resting open on the coverlid, as if it was waiting unconsciously for mine—surely there was some excuse for me? I only allowed myself a few minutes to kneel down at the bedside, and to look close at her—so close that her breath, as it came and went, fluttered on my face. I only touched her hand and her cheek with my lips at parting. She stirred in her sleep and murmured my name—but without waking. I lingered for an instant at the door to look at her again. "God bless and keep you, my darling!" I whispered—and left her. (596–97; brackets mine)

I have used this passage, unidentified, with students familiar with Victorian fiction and Victorian conventions. When I have simply deleted the first sentence and dropped five other words (as shown above in brackets), my students have universally identified the characters as a parent speaking about a child.

And appropriately so. To use one of these students' favorite terms, there is something increasingly "pathological" about Walter's relationship with Laura. Bad enough at the outset, Walter grows more and more protective, parental, and, were the story one of a parent in actuality, he would only further infantilize Laura by lying to her, protecting her from the world's harsh reality. Walter uses Laura, who starts out with something notably lacking and grows worse, to rationalize his own questionable behavior. In thinking about how much more clever and dangerous Count Fosco is than anyone else, including Sir Percival, Walter argues that he owes it to himself "to consider the chances against me, before I confronted them" (593–94). And he owes it to his wife, in every way, to lessen the risk. But as we have just seen, he does not feel much of an obligation for someone such as Pesca, who helps in spite of the risk, but who begs Walter to remember that "[i]f what I say to you now is ever known by others to have passed my lips . . . I am a dead man" (589). So much for Pesca.

And what about us? When we start to examine Walter's editing we should also begin to wonder just how much Walter's lying for the benefit of others is a screen for manipulation and self-protection in general. Certainly, when we come across the following remarkable, editorial footnote, something we would more likely expect from a narrator in a Borges story, we need to evaluate everything we have been told and *not* told all along by Walter:

> It is only right to mention here, that I repeat Pesca's statement to me, with the careful suppressions and alterations which the serious nature of the subject and my own sense of duty to my friend demand. My first and last concealments from the reader are those which caution renders absolutely necessary in this portion of the narrative. (588)

The footnote refers to Walter's first discussion with Pesca about the brotherhood, before Pesca begs him not to put his life at risk, and well before Walter does precisely that in giving the letter, with full address, to M. Rubelle. But the editorial footnote should only raise questions in the mind of a discerning reader. Have we not just heard the same promise in virtually the same words? Most immediately, we might remember something very much like it a dozen pages earlier, when Walter tells us why he has left not only Pesca in the background until now but also his mother and sister. The opening of the novel has shown us a faithful son and brother in Walter, the family picture completed by the arrival of his "quaint little friend, Professor Pesca" (579). Now, however, we learn that both his mother and sister had been put by "till they had learnt to do justice to my wife." He refers to their "jealous affection" for him and to their concern. But Walter airily acknowledges here yet more alteration and suppression: "all these little domestic occurrences have been left unrecorded, because they were not essential to the main interest of the story." He dismisses the ways they may have increased his "anxieties and embittered [his] disappointments," then waves them off as irrelevant (579).

A few pages before this admission, Walter tells us that for Laura's sake he has also, of course, used a feigned name for her first husband. Worse, "for her sake, still, I tell this story under feigned names" (556). Every name, we thus learn well in advance of a footnote commenting on a single alteration done only because it is a matter of life and death, every name in the entire text has been altered.

And fewer than three pages after this footnote and its claim of first and last concealments, we find that not only are people and their names altered but so, too, are critical things, images, devices: "I abstain from describing the device which the brand represented. It will be sufficient to say that it was circular in form, and so small that it would have been completely covered by a shilling coin" (592). Once we recognize Walter's deviousness, whatever his stated moral reasons, we are forced to realize what has been going on in front of us, like a clever shell game, throughout the novel.

I have described the gradual breakdown of Walter's clarity of purpose, even his clarity of mind, as the novel moves toward his encounter with Count Fosco. Whereas Walter manages to remain clearheaded and strong throughout his dealings with Sir Percival, he grows more anxious—for his own safety, for Laura's—as he recognizes how much more dangerous is Fosco. The danger clouds his thinking; at times it even leads him to betray those who have most trusted him, such as Pesca; at other times he rationalizes not following through on what he feels to be an act of justice (such as punishing Fosco). And it is during this same period, as we approach the end of the novel, that we find an increasing number of contradictory statements, each suggesting that this is the one and only place where, for whatever reason, Walter finds it necessary to disguise information or withhold it from the reader. Yet when Walter is more comfortably himself he still glosses over the ways in which he takes in information, and does so with such consummate certainty and ease that we tend to ignore the possible implications of distortion in the facts he records. For example, Hester Pinhorn, Fosco's cook, is illiterate. She gives her statement to Walter to take down and he reads it back to her, so that all seems in order. But the possibilities of misunderstanding under such circumstances are myriad.

More than misunderstanding may affect Mrs. Catherick's account as it is given, in great anger and with great distaste, to Walter. We assume it to be correct in general but perhaps significantly distorted in certain particulars, through anger and bitterness that may be guessed at but not fully understood, certainly not completely corrected. Finally, Laura's father remains a malignant cipher right to the end of the novel, a man whose philandering has brought on so much of this story's distress and yet one who remains essentially unblamed—and unknown.

Far more serious is the way in which Walter will attempt to record something remembered after considerable time has passed, essential events that are remembered vaguely and piecemeal, as Marian is only able to remember some of what happened to her. Other memories that are proved incorrect, such as those of Laura, Walter may only defend: who would not forget and distort under similar pressures and nightmarish experiences? And elsewhere, Walter, who vows to do anything and everything necessary to establish Laura in her rightful place, is suddenly crippled by scruples he neither can explain nor cares to explain. Approaching closer to the world of professional spies, Walter, ever the upright Englishman, suddenly discovers the idea of adopting a disguise "repellent . . . so meanly like the common herd of spies and informers in the mere act of adopting a disguise—that I dismissed the question from consideration, almost as soon as it had risen in my mind" (492–93).

At other points, Walter simply refuses to discuss a significantly charged period of time when it affects him too strongly. Thus he begins The Third Epoch: "I open a new page. I advance my narrative by one week." He has just seen the dead come alive: Laura herself stares at him over her own grave. But while we may appreciate how powerfully he was affected by her appearance, it only contributes to a growing sense that, as a reliable editor, he leaves a great deal to be desired. His reasons for skipping a week? "The history of the interval which I thus pass over must remain unrecorded. My heart turns faint, my mind sinks in darkness and confusion when I think of it. This must not be, if I who write, am to guide, as I ought, you who read. This must not be, if the clue that leads through the windings of the story is to remain from end to end untangled in my hands" (420). And while he is accurate in his account of his own emotional turmoil and confusion, it renders him incapable of including a most significant period in the novel. He thus concludes by simply reasserting what he has decided, owing to his own sensibilities and emotional difficulties, to skip: "I left my narrative in the quiet shadow of Limmeridge church: I resume it, one week later, in the stir and turmoil of a London street" (420).

Walter always manages to sound so reasonable, to find a rational or seemingly rational explanation for all the various ways in which he in effect continually distorts the narrative and at times directly contradicts himself. We often come across descriptions that, entirely because of context, strike us as reasonable. In a modern work, such as a novel by Alain Robbe-Grillet, precisely the same words become a deliberate way of stretching the literary context and authorial assumptions of all writing. Thus when Walter asserts that Laura has passed through her vague memories and now has recollections "(of which Lady Glyde was certain)" (433), we, in turn, assume Walter is truthful and her recollections are clear and correct. But what follows is virtually, word for word, the kind of description that occurs repeatedly in Robbe-Grillet's *La Maison de Rendez-Vous*. From *The Woman in White*: "They entered the house, and went upstairs to a back room, either on the first or second floor" (434). From *La Maison de Rendez-Vous*: "She climbs to the second floor without seeing anything, or to the third."[23] In Robbe-Grillet's "New Novel" the uncertainty is deliberate, a commentary about inevitable subjective uncertainty. In Collins's novel, it simply *is*, a fact or a mistake made in passing, without remark.

The recurrent theme of the dead returned to life is frequently employed in Collins's novels and shorter pieces. William H. Marshall puts the matter succinctly, describing the early, short work *Sister Rose* (1855):

> That Rose is saved marks an emerging characteristic
> in Collins' work, which, for better or worse, was to be
> exploited in a number of ways—the return to life of those
> presumed by someone to be dead. . . . In each instance
> revival is essential for the furtherance of the narrative
> beyond a specific point; in *Sister Rose* the return to life
> and freedom of those presumed to have died becomes the
> central point on which all action and the resolution of
> the narrative must rest.[24]

In his concluding chapter, Marshall again comments on how frequently Collins was to use this device throughout his life, both in his full-length works and shorter pieces:

> the theme of the resurrection of the seeming dead
> contributes to the pleasure in sensationalism sought by
> the public sensibility and to the symbolic representation
> of reaffirmation and psychological rebirth contemplated
> by the more thoughtful in Collins' generation.
> In some of the narratives, particularly the novels,
> certain objects are significant as a means both of motivat-
> ing the action and of judging characters by the response
> that they make to these objects as symbols. . . . Of the
> lute Antonina makes a symbol of continuing identity,
> of her own emotional survival in the dark house of her
> father. Valentine Blyth . . . most unsuccessfully an artist,
> turns back to life, with love and understanding for all
> men, and makes of it an art.[25]

In general, Marshall offers a balanced view of this theme, whether with people or objects, noting at times that Collins pandered to a sensational cliché and at other moments made use of such themes in a most original way. In *The Woman in White* and *The Moonstone*, in particular, as in the last four novels of Dickens, Collins makes a most powerful use of a device far older than the sensational.[26] In these later novels, particularly in *Our Mutual Friend*, there is a modernist strand that has invariably been overlooked. Dickens's last complete novel is a mystery where we are never sure who the criminals are or exactly how the crime was committed, something we are far more likely to find today than we are in the nineteenth century.[27] Collins may seem even less likely than Dickens to provide us with a modern or open-ended work, but that is precisely what he does. What I am saying about *The Woman in White*, because it grows from a private and not a self-conscious or literary device on Collins's part, may give us a work that has been read in a single way for one hundred and forty years and now offers us the possibility of reading it in two very different ways—accepting both readings at once or insisting on one reading or the other.[28]

Collins and Fosco

In a letter written to his brother Charles in 1853, Wilkie Collins confesses with some glee that he "must not forget to say that Charles Iggulden—the pattern goodboy who used to be quoted as an example to me—has married a pretty girl without his parents' consent." We have all grown up with such figures as the obscure Charles Iggulden, acquaintances made odious to us in direct proportion to our parents' praise; and we may all have taken some small delight in their later fall from grace. Collins seems to have taken more delight than most young men, a fact that may tell us something about his feelings toward his heroes. Certainly on close examination Walter Hartright appears to grow weaker and more inconsistent through the course of the novel. In his delight, Collins cannot resist spreading even more gossip about the unfortunately named Mr. Iggulden: "[he] has married a pretty girl without his parents' consent—is out of the banking business in consequence—and has gone to Australia to make his fortune as well as he can. I was rather glad to hear this, as I don't like 'well-conducted' young men! I know it is wrong! But I always feel relieved and happy when I hear that they have got into a scrape."[29]

But this is schoolboy stuff. As Collins grew up, and grew more and more eccentric, it seems increasingly clear from the letters and biographies we have that he quite enjoyed being a bad boy, more Fosco than Walter.[30] When Collins and Dickens went off to Paris, they indulged quite fully in all that city had to offer.[31] It was certainly one reason why Collins ultimately replaced the stodgier Forster as Dickens's closest friend and confidant. Fred Kaplan, for example, writes in his biography of Dickens that in 1856, while living in Paris and working on *Little Dorrit,* Dickens felt under tremendous strain. Still at an early stage in the novel and characteristically placing himself under immense pressure, Dickens, according to Kaplan, began "to feel desperate. His pace through *Little Dorrit* revealed his usual writing rhythms, periods of uncertainty, depression, and intense restlessness." He found at least a partial solution in bringing Collins over to Paris, securing an apartment for his friend on the same street where he was living. Macready, Lemon, and James White also visited. And with male companionship, Dickens relieved a great deal of pressure by exploring "the strange places" of Parisian night life: "Late one night he paid three francs to go into a dance hall, where dance partners and prostitutes were for hire."[32] This pattern was true for much of his career, as reflected in his infamous invitation beckoning Collins to join him for a night of "Haroun Alraschid" behavior.[33] Collins was much less likely to balk over leading a double life, given his remarkably understanding mother and his companionship with the more bohemian artists and actors of the time. Dickens, in fact, typically dined with Collins and his mistress but made it clear that propriety would not allow for the reverse.

Given what we know of Wilkie Collins's life, then, it should hardly come as a surprise that from early on he should have enjoyed giving his heroes an occasional comeuppance while particularly enjoying some of his villains, especially the ones who so enjoyed themselves, such as Count Fosco. Godfrey Ablewhite, an absolute moral hypocrite, was an anathema to Collins—something like a cross between Charles Iggulden and the devil. By contrast, Fosco was not only fun—as we have seen—but someone whose thoughts, and to some degree whose behavior, Collins could enjoy expounding and even experiencing. Early in the novel, leaving plenty of time for the discussion to have become a vague memory for most of his serial readers by the last installment, Collins has Fosco goad Laura by referring to wise men who are wise criminals:

> "It is easy to turn everything into ridicule," said
> Laura, resolutely; "but you will not find it quite so easy,
> Count Fosco, to give me an instance of a wise man who
> has been a great criminal."

The Count shrugged his huge shoulders, and smiled on Laura in the friendliest manner.

"Most true!" he said. "The fool's crime is the crime that is found out, and the wise man's crime is the crime that is *not* found out. If I could give you an instance, it would not be the instance of a wise man. Dear Lady Glyde, your sound English common sense has been too much for me. It is checkmate for *me* this time, Miss Halcombe—ha?"

"Stand to your guns, Laura," sneered Sir Percival, who had been listening at his place at the door. "Tell him, next, that crimes cause their own detection. There's another bit of copy-book morality for you, Fosco. Crimes cause their own detection. What infernal humbug!" . . .

"It is truly wonderful," he said, "how easily Society can console itself for the worst of its shortcomings with a little bit of clap-trap. The machinery it has set up for the detection of crime is miserably ineffective—and yet only invent a moral epigram, saying that it works well, and you blind everybody to its blunders, from that moment. Crimes cause their own detection, do they? And murder will out (another moral epigram), will it? Ask Coroners who sit at inquests in large towns if that is true, Lady Glyde. Ask secretaries of life-assurance companies if that is true, Miss Halcombe. Read your own public journals. In the few cases that get into the newspapers, are there not instances of slain bodies found, and no murderers ever discovered? Multiply the cases that are reported by the cases that are *not* reported, and the bodies that are found by the bodies that are *not* found, and what conclusion do you come to? This. That there are foolish criminals who are discovered, and wise criminals who escape. The hiding of a crime, or the detection of a crime, what is it? A trial of skill between the police on one side, and the individual on the other. When the criminal is a brutal, ignorant fool, the police, in nine cases out of ten, win. When the criminal is a resolute, educated, highly-intelligent man, the police, in nine cases out of ten, lose. If the police win, you generally hear all about it. If the police lose, you generally hear nothing. And on this tottering foundation you build up your comfortable moral maxim that Crime causes its own detection! Yes—all the crime *you* know of. And what of the rest?" (*The Woman in White*, 235–37)

Second only to the impossible notion of Madame Fosco's writing her husband's posthumous biography, this discussion is critically important for understanding the possibility of a double story and a double ending. The fact that it occurs less than a third of the way through the novel allows Collins to set out a position without making it obvious that he may believe it, or that Fosco may enact it. The logic of what Fosco says has been echoed so many times over the past hundred years in books on crime, detection, "victimology," and serial murder that it is by now a truism. Yet once again, put these words in the mouth of the villain, and it is relatively easy for an audience, already inclined to take the moral high road, to dismiss Fosco's thinking out of hand.

The Brotherhood

Italians who espoused revolution, who joined secret societies (*brotherhood* was a generic term for such groups), and who, above all, wished to unite the widely disparate states that would eventually constitute Italy, found a most welcome home in England. No other country had laws as generally conducive to free thought, no other country in Europe, certainly, approached the ideals of democracy and republicanism as did England. Accordingly, several generations of Italian exiles fled to England.[34] Collins's notion of a secret brotherhood to which Pesca and Fosco belonged was a mix of different ideas from different parts of a divided Italy. The creation of Fosco was like the work of a great chef, reducing to their essence dozens of ingredients, until a single, central character emerged, a prototype of the revolutionary turned spy.

Where we have no absolute proof, indeed no story but only negative proof and the likely negation of the story of the end, we may only guess that on betraying his oath and commitment to the brotherhood, Fosco became a spy, almost certainly for France. (There was nothing, however, to prevent spies from selling information to any of several countries—Spain, France, Austria, Russia—each of which had a great deal at stake in keeping Italy from uniting.) It is equally possible that Fosco broke his oath for very characteristic reasons— because it was more in his financial or personal interests to turn spy than to remain loyal to the brotherhood. Marian notes that he always wanted to know of any other Italians in any neighborhood to which he moved, and that he often received official looking, sealed documents, one of which seemed to have come from France.

France played a critical role, first siding with Italian nationalists when the French Revolution of 1848 seemed to be a revolution of Republicanism. It was not long, however, before France's political interests inevitably took over. France subsequently helped to partition Italy, along with Austria, and to use that much-divided nation as a presumed source for European stability. France also attempted to annex parts of Italy closest to its borders. Thus, by the mid-1850s, the contempt Italians had for Napoleon III was extreme. In turn, France became more and more invested in maintaining a divided Italy as a means of securing, even increasing, its own power. Repeated attempts to assassinate Napoleon III failed, but that monarch insistently saw all such attempts originating in England. Throughout the Continent, England was thought of as a breeding ground for bomb-throwing revolutionaries, a haven for every violent Italian found guilty of crimes in his home nation. London was considered a large urban factory for the making of bombs. Even though it was clear that one attempt on Napoleon III was not by Mazzini, the "little Napoleon" insisted throughout his life that it was, and that Mazzini had been directly aided by the British.[35]

In every way England found itself opposed to French interests. These French interests clashed with British feelings about dictatorship and oppression as much as they clashed with England's political self-interest in keeping France weak. Thus, for most Italians who had been condemned to prison or death—and there were a great many—England was the most convenient place to stay while they waited for some form of popular overthrow at home. America was too far away, and almost all of the other countries surrounding Italy had their own interests in opposing revolution. And those countries not in opposition, countries that even held principles similar to the British, were not strong enough to resist pressure from their neighbors. Mazzini, for example, spent several years in Switzerland and left most reluctantly. But the Canton in which he lived, like the country as a whole, was not strong enough to resist the external pressures to have him deported or exiled.[36]

The result of a regular flow of Italians into England was manifold. They were often, as young men of principle who had been condemned to death, figures of romance. And for the exiled Italians, marriage to an Englishwoman had numerous attractions, not the least of which was a firm connection to the country of their chosen exile, and of financial security. Some Italians grew so enamored with England and the women who inhabited it that they claimed not only to find Italian women uninteresting, but their very speech impossible to listen to after having heard the sweet language of the British![37]

Fosco's Fate

Although I have described Fosco finding a way to escape death I have deliberately not been specific. To do so, especially early in this essay, would defeat the very point I make about readers creating their own stories based on the details of narration as they emerge during a reading of the novel. I am more struck by those aspects of the work that make it unlikely, if not impossible, that the ending as it has commonly been interpreted cannot be accurate. Yet in proposing this view I am invariably asked to account for what did happen, or for what Fosco might have done. And here I am only able to offer my own speculations. What still remains more interesting to me is that once the reasons for not believing Walter are seen, Collins provides the opportunity, indeed the necessity, for each reader to create an alternate reading, a new ending, a new view of what Fosco has done and may proceed to do.

Given what is Fosco's apparent connection to France (the letters he receives, as well as his two French assistants, the Rubelles), his immediate decision to escape at once to Paris, when he sees the position Walter and the man with the scar have placed him in, seems to be an action taken by someone who is, to use the count's own words, "an intelligent criminal": he retreats to the place where he is strongest. As an intelligent criminal who knows that one day he may well face the deadly vengeance of the brotherhood he has betrayed, he would have taken precautions of his own. He would have thought through, in advance, the possibility of discovery and the best means of dealing with it; certainly we would not expect someone such as Fosco to ignore that possibility and allow himself to be surprised by it, indeed to be murdered because of it. First, he would disguise himself. But necessarily he would have to disguise himself so that he, in turn, could look very much like the person he had selected. In return, and if the time came, someone could then be substituted for a disguised Fosco, or Fosco disguised into his own double, and murdered. Hence all of the theatrical or stage business about size.

With the help of whatever network or assistance he has in Paris as well as his own ability to seek out what he needs, Fosco would have marked out someone with distinct features, ones he would most easily be able to imitate and which would, in turn, be most easily distinguished and remembered. For, when the time came, he must not simply escape, but find someone to take his place among the dead. Otherwise, the brotherhood would send yet another person to kill him. That is why Fosco returns to Paris, and why he adopts the dress of an artisan, for it must have been an artisan who most strikingly resembled the Fosco we see throughout the book. If Fosco actually possesses the power to preserve the dead in a state of perfect resemblance to the living, we might assume he has sealed up his double somewhere, to be called upon when needed. Much more likely, however, is that Fosco returns to Paris, takes on the clothing and traits of his preselected double, then kills that unsuspecting victim. The man is thrown into the Seine where he will soon be found and brought up for display in the Morgue. Fosco's victim has no reason to suspect he will be the target of foul play, hence there is no sign of a struggle. But Fosco takes care to use the "T" to obliterate what may have been—but almost certainly was *not*—on the upper inside of the man's arm.

Having faked his own death, Fosco would need to dispose of the man sent to kill him. And since he has several French people working for him, it would seem most likely that he sets a trap for this would-be assassin in Paris, kills him, and disposes of him. Perhaps his body, too, has been thrown into the Seine and will be seen at the Morgue—simply not seen by Walter nor reported to us—and his death duly recorded; or he may have been disposed of in a more permanent way. In either case, what can the brotherhood think, given the information about a dead Fosco and either a dead agent or no word from their agent, but that both men died in a struggle to the death?

Safely buried at Père Lachaise for more than a year, and safely resettled in the country he has served as a spy, Fosco may now feel secure enough to bring out his own biography—all the while living under an assumed name, looking like an entirely different person. Fanciful? Hardly any more fanciful than most of the sensational details of the plot so far. And in Collins's very next novel, *No Name*, Captain Wragge is also remarkably adept at assuming false identities. In a letter to Magdalen Vanstone, who herself plays out an assumed identity to acquire her inheritance, he writes:

> My books—I hope you have not forgotten my Books?—
> contain, under the heading of *Skins to Jump Into*, a list
> of individuals retired from this mortal scene, with whose
> names, families, and circumstances, I am well acquainted.
> Into some of those Skins I have been compelled to Jump,
> in the exercise of my profession, at former periods of my
> career. Others are still in the condition of new dresses,

and remain to be tried on. The Skin which will exactly fit us, originally clothed the bodies of a family named Bygrave. I am in Mr. Bygrave's skin at this moment—and it fits without a wrinkle.[38]

Captain Wragge quite openly engages in the activity that Fosco must apparently undertake more clandestinely, because while Wragge is simply a con artist, Fosco's very life is at stake. Moreover, this scenario of Fosco's jumping, Wragge-like, into a new skin has the appeal of creating a parallel set of disappearances, false deaths, and resurrections. Just as Laura disappears into Anne Catherick and is resurrected, so Fosco disappears and brings himself back to life. By doing so at the end of the book his resurrection completes the novel with a perfect, if quite unexpected, symmetry.

But the specifics of how Fosco lives or continues to live are finally irrelevant. What matters are the numerous indications that this story makes far more sense if we see him as appearing to die but in fact remaining alive, like so many of Collins's fictional figures. And in this case, my suspicion is that he does so entirely for Collins's pleasure, personal and aesthetic, and not necessarily as a plot twist to be perceived by the reader—certainly not by Victorian readers. Yet in every way such a false death and resurrection creates a perfectly balanced structure for this remarkable story. Fosco's name is itself derived from the Italian for that which is murky, dark, unclear, obscure (oscuro); Laura Fairlie's name, on the other hand, with a host of positive meanings, includes as an essential definition that which is clear, distinct, plain, direct.[39] We see, as we expect to see, the heroine rightly returned to her place and rank, and married to the man she loves. But in the world of obscurity in which Fosco dwells, so cunningly and with such self-delight, we should recognize the survival and continued work of a highly intelligent criminal. The intelligent criminal in this case may be reduced to more elaborate means of seeming to be dead, but he remains every bit as alive, and is every bit as successful, as when Fosco first propounds his theory of intelligent crimes and stupid crimes.

The Dramatization

Whatever Collins may have had in mind, when we compare the novel with the play he wrote and produced ten years later, everything is changed in the worst possible ways. To some degree this is a problem generic to the Victorian theater, which had not yet discovered the oblique, the unstated. Everything had to be clear to the audience for a play to find acceptance. The results we find in the dramatized version of *The Woman in White* are frequently horrifying. If it is possible to make a character as one dimensional as Sir Percival even more so, Collins succeeds, employing a dialogue that frequently sounds like two children tormenting one another in a schoolyard. In the opening scene, for example, Sir Percival wants to alter the record of his birth but finds Anne Catherick sitting in the church; the conversation is terse, banal in its brevity:

> *Sir P. (to himself).* What is the crazy fool doing there? If I don't get rid of her she will see me open the vestry-door. *(He advances, and calls to her.)* Anne! Anne Catherick!
> *Anne (turning towards him).* You know my name? *(She rises.)* I know yours. Sir Percival Glyde.
> *Sir P.* What are you doing in the churchyard?
> *Anne.* Thinking of the dead.
> *Sir P.* Suppose you try a change. Take a walk in the village, and think of the living.[40]

Collins will leave nothing to chance when it comes to Fosco. From the beginning, Fosco is doomed (Pesca receives two letters, one for Walter confirming his job at Limmeridge, the second with instructions for killing Fosco). What does remain constant is that Marian is absolute in her desire for revenge, whereas Walter wavers as he does in the novel. And Fosco still appears to be attracted to Marian. Everything in the play is otherwise shaped in such a way that it starts with Fosco's death warrant and concludes with his unmistakable murder. The play closes as Fosco dismisses Walter and, illuminated by moonlight, goes to feed his birds. Two assassins appear and stab Fosco:

> *The first man, at a blow, stabs him to the heart. He sinks with a low cry on the man who holds him by the throat. The man, aided by his accomplice, lays the dead body on the floor of the ante-chamber. This done, the two men, lifting their daggers in their left hands, join their right hands solemnly over the corpse—stand, for a moment, in that position—and then disappear. . . . The body of Fosco lies in the moonlight. For a moment or two there is silence. Then a knock is heard at the door on the right. After another pause, the voice of Madame Fosco is audible outside, saying—"Count! may I come in?"*

The Curtain Falls.
THE END. (*Drama*, 88)

What the play demonstrates, beyond the obvious weaknesses of Victorian theater compared with Victorian fiction, is that Fosco is now without question at the center of the story. The love story of Walter and Laura, although present, is so subordinated to the story of revenge that it is virtually nonexistent. And the revenge plot, so rich in its fictional form, is here allowed no space at all for the development of Fosco's complexity or for the audience's imagination. Not one but two men attack him unexpectedly. There is no doubt either about the centrality of revenge nor about the death of Fosco himself.

The need to turn seven hundred pages of fiction into an eighty-page play requires immense reduction, just as it risks being reductive. And the theatrical conventions of the period demand an obviousness of dialogue and plot that the complex novel of multiple narration so effectively avoids. The very complexity of perspective and richness of a character such as Fosco is sacrificed to an overly clear plot. And that which makes the novel so full of possibility is here reversed, emphasizing in its obviousness and simplicity the power of the serial novel of multiple narrators—and in particular this serial novel with one of the most interesting and complex villains in the history of fiction.

Psychoanalysis, Reading, and Resurrection

Although psychoanalysis was, from its inception, closely linked with literature, analysts have been very slow to see the therapeutic possibilities of literary and narrative studies. Freud's first major prize was the Goethe Prize (for writing), and his most famous early theories drew heavily on his extensive reading, frequently attaching to the classics particular complexes or forms of neurotic behavior—such as the Oedipus Complex. In turn, many psychological studies, particularly those on children and the uses of play therapy, have connected reading, writing, and mental health. Too often, however, the problem with most psychological studies, especially of adults, is that, in order to qualify as empirically respectable and accurate, they are extremely limited in what they set out to do, even more so in what they achieve.

I have noticed in my own clinical practice that one of the most consistent signs of the early onset of depression is the inability to read fiction. Patients who lose interest in reading fiction usually do not consider themselves depressed, but gradually their difficulty in imaginative reading and the demands of imaginative literature begin to extend as well to the pleasure they may have previously taken in reading nonfiction, until eventually they find themselves unable to read or uninterested in reading at all. After this point they will start to show clinical signs of the early onset of depression ("lack of interest in things around them," "inability to feel pleasure"). But from the point at which these symptoms are manifest, the depression may well be so severe that it will take a good deal more therapy, and often some form of medication, to bring them out of their depressive episodes.[41]

In working on this article, however, I have come to understand the same problem in a new way. Rather than beginning from a therapeutic perspective and looking for neuroses, I have been moved by Collins's rich imagination and his playfulness to focus first on health and pleasure. The playfulness of all of Collins's work, particularly what I see as the private and public playfulness combined and disguised in *The Woman in White,* has made me most aware of the powerful, interactive possibilities of serial publication, or of any work that depends on narrative subjectivity. When we read works that are both limited and redefined by the limiting subjectivity of their narrators, we, as readers, are brought most fully into fiction as process: we should recognize that, particularly in a Collins novel, we are dealing with a form somewhere between fiction and theater.

If my conjectures are correct about the ways people who begin to suffer from depression first withdraw from works of art that stimulate and even insist on interaction, then why not reverse this perspective? Would it not, for example, be helpful in treating patients who show these very early forms of depression to make use of fiction, and in particular the fiction I have been describing in this study? More generally, would it not be reasonable to assume that reading fiction itself is not an indulgence, but a valuable and even necessary way of re-creating oneself throughout adult life?

The Woman in White, like many of the works of Collins and Dickens, maintains a steady interest in the theme of resurrection. It is easy enough for us to denigrate this theme as one of the great clichés of sensation fiction—as indeed it sometimes was. But when it begins to define, so thoroughly, the late work of Dickens and, I believe, the best work of Collins, we are not dealing with a common or overused cliché of nineteenth-century sensation writing. On the contrary, the function of resurrection in these works most closely resembles a form of humanistic magic, of faith and belief that fully allow for change through recreation. And in the case of Collins, we are able to see that such terms need not be ones of high seriousness or literary pretension, just as we enjoy their application, above all, to the villain of the piece.

Rebirth, resurrection, the movement through a form of death into a new and more vibrant existence is far older and more meaningful than a motif of Victorian sensation writing. At its best, as in the works I have described here, it comes closest to the magic of Shakespeare's late romances. And in order to engage playfully and fully with these texts, to enjoy them most completely and gain as much as possible from them, we must do as Paulina instructs all the characters—and the audience—to do in the final act of *The Winter's Tale*. It is necessary that we awake our faith.

Notes

As this paper continued to expand, so, too, did my reliance on colleagues, students, and friends. I wish particularly to thank Raymond Soto, The King Of Humanities Bibliographers, Eric Jager and Michael Colacurcio, Maria Paul and Alan Chiu, as well as UCLA's Special Collections for all their help, and the UCLA Committee on Research, whose grant has made possible much of my research. This essay is dedicated to Murray Baumgarten and Max Novak, two friends who have given so much and whose collegial support over twenty-five years has been as unstinting as it remains inspirational.

1. See Kenneth Robinson, *Wilkie Collins: A Biography* (New York: Macmillan, 1952), 149.

2. One reviewer, for example, stated that the novel was "by common consent, Mr Collins's best book" (Review of *The Woman in White*, by Wilkie Collins, *Morning Advertiser* [20 Aug. 1860], 3). The reviewer for *The Spectator* called it "by many degrees, the best work of an author who had already written so many singularly good ones" (Review of *The Woman in White*, by Wilkie Collins, *The Spectator* 33 [8 Sept. 1860]: 864).

3. See Julian Symons, introduction to *The Woman in White* (London and New York: Penguin, 1998), 16. Symons naturally simplifies in this brief introductory essay, devoting a page to the critical reception of *The Woman in White* as well as to reviews of later works. "The reviews," he asserts, "became steadily harsher, of course with occasional exceptions, during the rest of his career" (16). For a more thorough and balanced account of reactions to *The Woman in White* and Collins's other works, see particularly Sue Lonoff, *Wilkie Collins and His Victorian Readers: A Study in the Rhetoric of Authorship* (New York: AMS Press, 1982), and William H. Marshall, *Wilkie Collins* (New York: Twayne Publishers, 1970). *Wilkie Collins: The Critical Heritage*, ed. Norman Page (Boston: Routledge and Kegan Paul, 1974) usefully provides the reviews themselves or excerpts from them. An overview of Collins's works, with some reference to contemporary reactions

and a good deal of commentary by the author is to be found in Kirk H. Beetz, *Wilkie Collins: An Annotated Bibliography* (Metuchen, N.J.: Scarecrow Press, 1978). An excellent article dealing with critical response as part of a larger argument about *The Woman in White* is David Blair, "Wilkie Collins and the Crisis of Suspense," in *Reading the Victorian Novel: Detail into Form,* ed. Ian Gregor (London: Vision Press, 1980), 32–50. Always interesting, witty, and provocative is Jerome Meckier, "Wilkie Collins's *The Woman in White*: Providence Against the Evils of Propriety," *Journal of British Studies,* 22, no. 1 (1982): 104–26. Because Meckier's article offers one of the best readings of the novel, it also offers one of the best readings against which to test my own argument.

4. See Edmund H. Yates, "Mr. Wilkie Collins in Gloucester Place," in *Celebrities at Home,* 3d ser. (London: Office of *The World,* 1879), 145–56, and Wilkie Collins, "How I Write My Books: Related in a Letter to a Friend," in Wilkie Collins, *The Woman in White,* ed. Kathleen Tillotson and Anthea Trodd (Boston: Houghton Mifflin Co., 1969), 511–14. First published in *The Globe,* 26 Nov. 1887.

5. For information on Mazzini, see Dennis Mack Smith, *Mazzini* (London and New Haven: Yale Univ. Press, 1994). Foscolo is greatly admired in Italian literature and still relatively unknown outside Italy. Mazzini felt that one of his many missions was to make at least some of Foscolo's works available in translation and to publish critical essays on him. Foscolo is sometimes thought to be the originator of the modern Italian novel, with his *Ultime Lettere di Jacopo Ortis* (1802). Foscolo constantly emphasized the need to mobilize literature and political philosophy into action, and Mazzini trumpeted the importance of two of his literary heroes, Byron and Foscolo, when he was forced out of Italy into France.

6. For more information on Vidocq and the various ways in which his life seemed to parallel numerous aspects of Fosco's life and accomplishments, I have relied on Vidocq's *Mémoires* (Paris: Tenon, 1828), and the *Supplément aux Mémoires de Vidocq* (Paris: Librairie Centrale de Boulland, 1830), which completed the first volume of 1828; M. Froment, *Histoire de Vidocq* (Paris: Robert Laffont, 1829); François Vidocq, *Memoirs of Vidocq: The Principal Agent of the French Police* (Philadelphia: T. B. Peterson and Brothers, 1859); Samuel Edwards, *The Vidocq Dossier: The Story of the World's First Detective* (Boston: Houghton Mifflin, 1977); and Philip John Stead, *Vidocq: A Biography* (New York: Staples Press, 1953). Vidocq was indeed an extraordinary and original man who developed a number of techniques used again, and much later, by the police in France and elsewhere (see J. Peuchet, *Mémoires Tirés Des Archives de la Police de Paris* [Paris: Bourmancé, 1838] and Froment). Although largely self-taught, he was adept at science, particularly chemistry, and is presumed to have been the first person to attempt to introduce fingerprinting into police work. He made significant use of acids to distinguish among blood types. When he was finally forced out of the Sûreté for the last time,

he went on tour (1845), demonstrating his skill at disguise not merely by dress but also by making himself seem taller and, far more remarkably, shorter, as well as fatter.

Deborah Wynne points out that the republication of Vidocq's *Mémoires* in 1859 adds to its likely importance for Collins's novel (1860), as for that of his reading public. She also notes, and attributes to Vidocq, Fosco's theories on the nature of undiscovered crime by intelligent criminals ("Vidocq, the Spy: A Possible Source for Count Fosco in Wilkie Collins's *The Woman in White*," *Notes and Queries* 44 [1997]: 342).

Finally—and most important—Vidocq was a master at changing sides as well as faking and recovering from his own supposed deaths. Vidocq used these reports of false deaths for convenience when he was in danger or simply needed to disappear. Collins had a copy of Peuchet's *Mémoires* in his library; see William Baker, *Wilkie Collins's Library: A Reconstruction* (Westport, Conn.: Greenwood Press, 2002), 137.

7. Nuel Pharr Davis, *The Life of Wilkie Collins* (Urbana: Univ. of Illinois Press, 1956), 218.

8. D. O. Maddyn, for example, called the novel "almost revolting" and "unwholesome" (Review of *Basil* by Wilkie Collins, *The Athenaeum*, no. 1310 [4 Dec. 1852]: 1322–23; rpt. in Page, 47–48).

9. The Paris Morgue was rebuilt at the beginning of the nineteenth century, using the wrecked, two-story edifice of something like a mall of former butcher shops. It was situated on the Quai Marché Neuf, right by the Saint Michel bridge, where a stairway brought one to look onto the level of the river bank and to view drowned corpses. These corpses were laid out on black marble, their clothes hung above them. This morgue became so disease ridden and caused so many deadly infections that a new morgue, constructed at the end of the Île de la Cité, was built in 1864 ("Morgue," in *La Grande Encyclopédie: Inventaire Rasionné Des Sciences, Des Lettres et Des Arts,* ed. A. Betholot [Paris: H. Lamirault et cie, 1886–1902]). This newer morgue became most famous in Paris, a so-called monument to science. However, at the time Collins's novel took place or indeed at any time when he might himself have viewed a corpse before the publication of *The Woman in White,* he would have been led through the old, renovated, sixteenth-century pavilion of butcher shops, up a stairway, with only limited ways of viewing the cadaver. The same, of course, would have been true for Walter.

Walter's description of seeing Fosco at the morgue had to have been completely inaccurate. At that time, he would have viewed the body set out in one of two tiers of corpses, placed on a slight incline. Later, and in other cities, special arrangements were made for family members to view a body for purposes of identification. But the morgue in Paris was as much as anything a tourist attraction, busiest in the early morning, and frequented by the middle and upper classes after an evening of dining out and, possibly, debauchery: Paris's explicit version of *momento mori.* Not until later in the century were people allowed to approach a corpse and view it closely—and from different angles.

10. Virtually every pronouncement by the count, certainly anything official or written, reaffirms his own exceptional powers as well as his insight and correctness, usually subordinating others, even principles or groups or nations, to the power of his individual perceptions. Walter cites the final sentence of the biography, which is not only Fosco in style but in deviousness: "His life was one long assertion of the rights of the aristocracy and the sacred principles of Order, and he died a martyr to his cause" (*The Woman in White*, ed. John Sutherland [Oxford: Oxford Univ. Press, 1999], 641. Hereafter cited in the text as *The Woman in White*). It seems clear enough that he betrayed the brotherhood for money and position, and logical enough that he would ultimately insist on seeing himself as an aristocrat, an exceptional man among men. But most deft is Fosco in not only including the word *order* but also capitalizing it (as he could have done, but did not, with *aristocracy*). This surely is the same Fosco who talks of intelligent criminals who win nine times out of ten. Self-important as he is, tempted as he might have been to inflate further the close of his own biography, he is smart enough not to insist on something that he shows, throughout the novel, he never believed. The issue for Fosco was opportunism, and intelligence in its performance. Order and its principles are to be used by a cunning criminal, such as Fosco, to control the vast and foolish population who believe in such cant. But even without that touch, and the self-important (and false) martyrdom and equally false implication that he always stood by what he believed, no one anywhere in this novel shows a style close to this—even as it is demonstrated here in a single sentence.

11. Under other conditions I might find considerable support from Collins's detailed correspondence with his friend and literary mentor, Charles Dickens. But Dickens went to great trouble to burn his letters on two different occasions, as Collins himself would later burn much of his own adult correspondence, so that direct corroboration through the letters of Collins and Dickens remains limited.

12. *The Woman in White* began its serialization in *All the Year Round*, 29 Nov. 1859.

13. *Re-creational* in this sense stems from the oldest form shown in the OED. Still the most intelligent and useful writer on this subject is the psychoanalyst D. W. Winnicott, in books such as *Playing and Reality* (London: Tavistock Publications, 1971), and *The Child, the Family, and the Outside World* (Harmondsworth: Penguin, 1964). I have discussed this issue very briefly in an article on Winnicott ("Poetry in Psychoanalysis: Hopkins, Rossetti, Winnicott," *International Review of Psychoanalysis* 9 [1982]: 303–16).

14. This is not intended as an anti-intellectual statement or a negative comment about fiction that self-consciously plays with such issues. But it is my belief that when the reader is most entertained and engrossed in the story and least aware of the metastory, the impact of such creative expansion is natural, stronger, and, generally, greater.

15. *Wilkie Collins: A Critical and Biographical Study,* ed. E. R. Gregory (Toledo, Ohio: Friends of the Univ. of Toledo Libraries, 1977), 86. For other comments by Sayers, see her introduction to *The Omnibus of Crime* (New York: Harcourt Brace, 1929), 21–24.

16. Sayers, 86–87.

17. Algernon Charles Swinburne, "Wilkie Collins," *Fortnightly Review,* n.s. 275 (1 Nov. 1889): 589–99; rpt. in Page, 253–64. Swinburne becomes Sayers's arbiter of balance, a moral high ground he too often tried to claim for himself. He demands of Collins a more judicious and less extreme novelist than Collins could have been at this early point in his career. But during the same period as his review of Collins, for much of Collins's life in fact, Swinburne himself was nothing but extreme. He worshipped Italian revolutionaries, Mazzini in particular, whom he felt to be a political reincarnation of Christ. His personal behavior, however extreme, cannot disqualify him from effectively evaluating the work of others. But Swinburne's review of Collins and particularly his subsequent comments about *The Woman in White,* a novel that often parodies Italians, and manipulates, even denigrates, the Italian brotherhoods through which a great deal of their revolutionary energy was channeled, might well suggest a conflict for Swinburne the reviewer. In addition, the arbitrary nature of his judgment seems to impair his ability to read Collins's texts, particularly *The Woman in White*—not unlike Sayers herself. For Swinburne's attitude about Mazzini, see Harry W. Rudman, *Italian Nationalism and English Letters* (New York: Columbia Univ. Press, 1940), 129.

18. According to Sayers: "The truth is that in *Basil* two Collinses were inharmoniously at work together. One of them—the Collins who was arrested in his development—was trying to write a realistic tale about a love-affair; the other, the Collins who was eventually to achieve greatness, was clumsily trying to put together a melodramatic plot about vengeance and horror. It was this second Collins who ruined the story and falsified its tone by making the wicked paramour a person with a long-cherished grievance against Basil's father, thus reducing the plain tale of passion to an unconvincing revenge-drama" (Sayers, *Wilkie Collins,* 87). Were *The Woman in White* similarly to be reduced to a plain tale of passion and its revenge-drama eliminated—we see Walter contemplating such an action—it would reduce a great novel to a mediocre piece of sensation writing. It would, in effect, eliminate the essential presence of the count. I am of course aware that Sayers was fascinated by both Collins and his work and referred to him as creating the first great mystery novels. It is precisely because of her sometimes very

high regard for Collins that her extremely limited reading and magisterial judgments of his work elsewhere become all the more striking.

19. "Unlike Dickens," writes U. C. Knoepflmacher, "who would later urge his friend to respect the sensibilities of his Victorian audience, Collins never disguised his fascination with the amorality of the counterworld" ("The Counterworld of Victorian Fiction and *The Woman in White*," in *Wilkie Collins*, ed. Lyn Pykett [New York: St Martin's Press, 1998], 60). Knoepflmacher's seminal essay was originally published in 1975 and has established a modern reading that permits us to see just how thoroughly Collins enjoyed his villains and at times identified with them. In his conclusion to this essay he comments that "Collins has given a fuller hearing than any of his English predecessors to the antisocial voice of the Rebel" (Knoepflmacher, 66). In these final pages he makes a strong argument for the dominance of Fosco's views, although finally he will allow them to be undermined just as he, too, assumes Fosco must be punished and killed.

20. Collins, undoubtedly influenced here by Dickens, who was an accomplished mesmerist, was himself greatly interested in mesmerism. He found the sensational possibilities of mesmerism—of remembering and forgetting—particularly interesting, and would use them quite brilliantly as a way of creating and then solving the central mystery of *The Moonstone*.

21. Speed, grace, and noiseless movement are all unlikely characteristics for an obese man, even for a man of ordinary size unless he is extraordinarily athletic. The implication is once again of a disguise of obesity, beneath which the real Fosco is quite normal, perhaps even lightweight, and, indeed, athletic.

22. If we required any further proof of how determined Walter is to treat Laura like a child and to keep her that way, we have only to examine this passage closely. Disconsolate, Walter sits down across from Laura and begs to know what is bothering her. She answers with a weary and hopeless sigh, telling Walter that he and Marian work and get money, while there is nothing she can do: "You will end in liking Marian better than you like me." Spoken like a petulant five-year old! But Walter loves it. Having come up with his plan and delighting in her response, he sets aside "a little weekly tribute" from his limited earnings as the price presumably paid by strangers "for the poor, faint, valueless sketches of which I was the only purchaser. It was hard sometimes to maintain our innocent deception, when she proudly brought out her purse to contribute her share towards the expenses, and wondered with serious interest, whether I or she had earned the most that week." As a parent does with a small child, Walter keeps and still has all those "hidden drawings" in his possessions: "they are my treasures beyond price—the dear remembrances that I love to keep alive" (*The Woman in White*, 490).

23. Alain Robbe-Grillet, *La Maison de Rendez-Vous*, trans. Richard Howard (New York: Grove Press, 1966), 45.

24. Marshall, 42.

25. Ibid., 132–33.

26. In my summary of supporting arguments I have listed Dickens's last four novels and offered a very brief sense of the centrality of rebirth or resurrection in all four. The only novel where the case may be doubtful for some is that of *Great Expectations,* and I have elsewhere tried to make an argument for precisely the wonder of Pip discovering himself again, as he does at the beginning of the final chapter, through a process of rebirth that begins, appropriately, in water, moves through salvation, and leads to the conclusion of the novel. See Albert D. Hutter, "Crime and Fantasy in *Great Expectations,*" in *Psychoanalysis and Literary Process,* ed. Frederick Crews (Cambridge, Mass.: Winthrop, 1970), 25–65.

27. See specifically *Our Mutual Friend,* bk. 2, chap. 13, "A Solo and a Duett." While John Harmon comes to know, in a vague way, what had happened to him on landing, he remains unsure of precise action and people. Once more, the language reads like a much more modern novel as he tries to puzzle out the central mystery of who tried to kill him, then threw him in the river and left him for dead:

> "Thus much I know," he murmured. "I have never been here since that night, and never was here before that night, but thus much I recognize. I wonder which way did we take when we came out of that shop. We turned to the right as I have turned, but I can recall no more. Did we go by this alley? Or down that little lane?"
>
> He tried both but both confused him equally, and he came straying back to the same spot. [He remembers poles pushed out of windows, drying clothes, a public house, the sound of a fiddle and dancing feet coming from a narrow passage.] But here are all these things in the lane, and here are all these things in the alley. And I have nothing else in my mind but a wall, a dark doorway, a flight of stairs, and a room.
>
> He tried a new direction, but made nothing out of it; walls, dark doorways, flights of stairs and rooms, were too abundant. And, like most people so puzzled, he again and again described a circle, and found himself at the point from which he had begun. (*Our Mutual Friend,* ed. Stephen Gill [Harmondsworth: Penguin, 1971], 421–22.)

    Even had Dickens never called attention to these details, I cannot think of a nineteenth-century novel that would not, before the end, have cleared up such inconsistencies and confusions and turned the circle into a straight narrative line leading from clues to solution to ending. But while Dickens makes a great deal of Harmon's confusion, nowhere in the novel does he resolve these questions.

28. Between 1850 and 1900 there were a number of writers whose very style seemed to remove them from the more common novels driven by plot, or sensational writing, but rather characterized at once by the abstract

and demanding. The very way in which these authors wrote lends itself to recent approaches such as that of deconstruction and postmodernism, particularly because these works remained ambiguous, often open-ended. A writer such as Melville evoked from the beginning extreme reactions in reviews both in the United States and England.

Perhaps the most consistently questioned and reinterpreted fictional work of the nineteenth century is Henry James's novella *The Turn of the Screw* (1900). For nearly thirty years it was accepted as a ghost story. When Edmund Wilson and others suddenly recognized that the entire tale could also be read as a psychological thriller in which the deranged governess kills Miles by scaring him to death, we discovered a text which had been read in only one way for three decades and which was now perceived in two radically different ways. Sometimes, indeed often, its readers now prefer to understand it in its two radically different ways.

29. Collins to Charles Collins, Rome, 13 Nov. 1853 (*The Letters of Wilkie Collins*, ed. William Baker and William C. Clarke, 2 vols. [New York: St. Martin's Press, 1999], 1:114–15).

30. By allowing Fosco to become the author of sensation fiction, an experienced professional writer, Collins's identification with his villain appears to be complete. When Fosco writes out for Walter the required information, he is described as preparing a number of narrow "slips," the technical term used by writers of the time. When Collins allows Fosco to become an author of sensation fiction, he uses his villain to question the hero's ability to narrate (or edit) in such a demanding style:

> The Count walked to a writing-table near the window, opened his desk, and took from it several quires of paper and a bundle of quill pens. He scattered the pens about the table, so that they might lie ready in all directions to be taken up when wanted, and then cut the paper into a heap of narrow slips, of the form used by professional writers for the press. "I shall make this a remarkable document," he said, looking at me over his shoulder. "Habits of literary composition are perfectly familiar to me. One of the rarest of all the intellectual accomplishments that a man can possess is the grand faculty of arranging his ideas. Immense privilege! I possess it. Do you?" (*The Woman in White*, 612)

31. Fred Kaplan, *Dickens: A Biography* (New York: William Morrow, 1988), 340.

32. Ibid., 341.

33. Dickens to Wilkie Collins, Paris, 12 Dec. 1855, in *The Letters of Charles Dickens*, vol. 7, ed. Graham Storey, Kathleen Tillotson, and Angus Easson (Oxford: Clarendon Press, 1993), 762.

34. See Rudman, 179–248. Several studies on Italian secret societies and revolutionary groups proved central in defining a historical phenomenon,

particularly in its relation to *The Woman in White*. Charles William Heckethorn, *The Secret Societies of All Ages and Countries* (London: R. Bentley and Son, 1875) was completely revised in 1897, so that its section on the Italians provides both a historical overview and something close to a contemporary argument. *Secret Societies,* ed. Norman MacKenzie (London: Aldus Books, 1967) offers a collection of essays from the popular and sensational to the scholarly. Stephen Knight's *The Brotherhood* (London: Granada, 1984) is somewhat more recent and more focused than these others, particularly on the Italians. Thomas R. Forstenzer's *French Provincial Police and the Fall of the Second Republic: Social Fear and Counterrevolution* (Princeton: Princeton Univ. Press, 1981) has been remarkably useful not only for specifics but also, as the second half of the title implies, for more general attitudes and fears, individual and national.

35. The assassination attempt was by Orsini, who quarreled with Mazzini in 1857 because he found the latter too timid.

36. According to Smith, "In June 1836, responding to continued foreign pressure, the Swiss federal authorities ordered Mazzini's expulsion" (Smith, 20). He fled from Switzerland to England.

37. Cavour was probably the most outspoken on this matter, but it was an amusing subtext of gossip among the young, Italian expatriates. Mazzini loved, throughout his life, a woman from his native town, and Garibaldi married an Italian. But none of them was above taking advantage of the patina of revolutionary glamour and a dashing Italian style.

38. Wilkie Collins, *No Name,* ed. Virginia Blain (Oxford: Oxford Univ. Press, 1986), 235.

39. In Italian, *fosco* is currently in use as an adjective meaning "dark, dull, obscure," pertaining to color or night or day, a dark color, black night, overcast day. Referring to a mood it suggests sadness, gloom, darkness; figuratively it implies that which goes into shadow and darkness, that is, "the unknown." According to the *OED, fair* as in "clean" and "clear" were original meanings that lasted through the nineteenth century, so that the term did not simply connote beauty but also something closer to the metaphorical and moral opposite of Fosco's "unknown" and "obscure."

40. Wilkie Collins, *The Woman in White. A Drama. In a Prologue and Four Acts. (Altered from the Novel for Performance on the Stage.)* (London: Published by the Author, 1871), 5–6. Hereafter cited in the text as *Drama*.

41. I have been studying the relationship between various forms of reading fiction and the nature of depression. To use an old-fashioned term from Marshall McLuhan, my work so far shows quite conclusively that the "hotter" (more demanding) the medium, the more quickly someone first going into a depression finds it difficult, even unpleasant, to engage in the normally pleasurable activity of reading fiction. I hope to establish this on a scale that includes the practice of psychoanalysis in America

and the West, but also extends beyond Western culture. It would then enable therapists to note one of the earliest warnings of a possible depression, using a patient's growing inability to read, or to read in forms that demand more active imaginative participation. Difficulty with, or changes in patterns of, reading become markers for the possible severe onset of a major depressive episode. Such markers will enable therapists to see patterns and make interpretations earlier—intervening more immediately and most effectively. Over the past ten years in particular, cognitive psychologists and psychoanalysts have begun to work together, looking at the ways in which people read as well as the responses elicited by fiction. In 1999, The American Academy of Psychoanalysis held a symposium on this subject, from which a number of interesting studies have emerged. Keith Oatley and Alison Kerr, who have worked in this field for a decade, presented a paper entitled "Memories Prompted by Emotions—Emotions Attached to Memories: Studies of Depression and Reading Fiction." They asked subjects to record specific responses to specific works, using what they called "Emotion Diaries." Because of the empirical style of their writing and the limits and nature of their findings, it is difficult for me to appreciate the full clinical implications of these studies. They have, nevertheless, built an impressive body of work. Perhaps most interesting to those of us in literature, they are making a concerted effort to bridge experimental and behavioral studies with a more broad-based, psychoanalytic theory. They draw, for example, on Thomas J. Scheff, *Catharsis in Healing, Ritual, and Drama* (Berkeley: Univ. of California Press, 1979), and Deanne Bogdan, *Re-educating the Imagination: Toward a Poetics, Politics, and Pedagogy of Literary Engagement* (Portsmouth, N.H.: Boynton-Cook, 1992). While I have often cited Sue Lonoff on other matters, and sometimes disagreed with her, the spirit of her work, particularly in the chapter "Collins at Play" (Lonoff, 108–36) comes very close to what I am talking about here, without either using the jargon of psychoanalysis or speculating as far as I have on the nature and meaning of imaginative recreation.

The movement from which such speculative thinking originates in psychoanalysis begins with D. W. Winnicott, as I have mentioned above, and in literary studies with the enormously productive Norman Holland, starting with his book *5 Readers Reading* (New Haven: Yale Univ. Press, 1975).

The combination of literary studies and psychoanalysis—used in both directions—offers two new and important ways to understand the significance of reading fiction. I am indebted to a number of writers, especially those just mentioned, for clarifying ways in which we may combine these fields, while I present throughout this essay a new way to read *The Woman in White*. But I am also suggesting that we apply narrative theory, and what Frank Kermode calls a *sense of an ending*, that we use our sense of fiction in general, and of complex narrative fiction in particular, to anticipate the onset of a major depressive episode. My own clinical experience (combined with research and an informal survey of more than a hundred colleagues) suggests that therapists may rely on a patient's statements about increased difficulty in reading fiction, or reading in general, or that therapists may want to raise questions about a patient's reading or similar recreational activities whenever they are concerned about the possibility of depression.

References

Baker, William. *Wilkie Collins's Library: A Reconstruction*. Westport, Conn.: Greenwood Press, 2002.

Beetz, Kirk H. *Wilkie Collins: An Annotated Bibliography*. Metuchen, N.J.: Scarecrow Press, 1978.

Betholot, A., ed. *La Grande Encyclopédie: Inventaire Raisonné Des Sciences, Des Lettres et Des Arts*. Paris: H. Lamirault et cie, 1886–1902.

Blair, David. "Wilkie Collins and the Crisis of Suspense." In *Reading the Victorian Novel: Detail into Form*, ed. Ian Gregor, 32–50. London: Vision Press, 1980.

Bogdan, Deanne. *Re-educating the Imagination: Toward a Poetics, Politics, and Pedagogy of Literary Engagement*. Portsmouth, N.H.: Boynton-Cook, 1992.

Collins, Wilkie. *The Letters of Wilkie Collins*. Ed. William Baker and William C. Clarke. 2 vols. New York: St. Martin's Press, 1999.

———. *No Name*. Ed. Virginia Blain. Oxford: Oxford Univ. Press, 1986.

———. *The Woman in White*. Ed. John Sutherland. Oxford: Oxford Univ. Press, 1999.

———. *The Woman in White*. Ed. Julian Symons. London and New York: Penguin, 1986.

———. *The Woman in White*. Ed. Kathleen Tillotson and Anthea Trodd. Boston: Houghton Mifflin Co., 1969.

———. *The Woman in White. A Drama. In a Prologue and Four Acts. (Altered from the Novel for Performance on the Stage.)* London: Published by the author, 1871.

Davis, Nuel Pharr. *The Life of Wilkie Collins*. Urbana: Univ. of Illinois Press, 1956.

Dickens, Charles. *The Letters of Charles Dickens*. Vol. 7. Ed. Graham Story, Kathleen Tillotson, and Angus Easson. Oxford: Clarendon Univ. Press, 1993.

———. *Our Mutual Friend*. Ed. Stephen Gill. Harmondsworth: Penguin, 1971.

Edwards, Samuel. *The Vidocq Dossier: The Story of the World's First Detective*. Boston: Houghton Mifflin, 1977.

Forstenzer, Thomas R. *French Provincial Police and the Fall of the Second Republic: Social Fear and Counterrevolution*. Princeton: Princeton Univ. Press, 1981.

Froment, M. *Histoire de Vidocq*. Paris: Robert Laffont, 1829.

Heckethorn, Charles William. *The Secret Societies of All Ages and Countries*. London: R. Bentley, 1875.

Holland, Norman. *5 Readers Reading*. New Haven: Yale Univ. Press, 1975.

Hutter, Albert D. "Crime and Fantasy in *Great Expectations*." In *Psychoanalysis and Literary Process*, ed. Frederick Crews, 25–65. Cambridge, Mass.: Winthrop, 1970.

———. "Poetry in Psychoanalysis: Hopkins, Rossetti, Winnicott." *International Review of Psychoanalysis* 9 (1982): 303–16.

Kaplan, Fred. *Dickens: A Biography*. New York: William Morrow, 1988.

Knoepflmacher, U. C. "The Counterworld of Victorian Fiction and *The Woman in White*." In *Wilkie Collins*, ed. Lyn Pykett, 58–69. New York: St. Martin's Press, 1998.

Knight, Stephen. *The Brotherhood*. London: Granada, 1984.

Lonoff, Sue. *Wilkie Collins and His Victorian Readers: A Study in the Rhetoric of Authorship*. New York: AMS Press, 1982.

MacKenzie, Norman, ed. *Secret Societies*. London: Aldus Books, 1967.

[Maddyn, D. O.]. Review of *Basil*, by Wilkie Collins. *The Athenaeum*, no. 1310 (4 Dec. 1852): 1322–23.

Marshall, William H. *Wilkie Collins*. New York: Twayne Publishers, 1970.

Meckier, Jerome. "Wilkie Collins's *The Woman in White*: Providence Against the Evils of Propriety." *Journal of British Studies* 22, no. 1 (1982): 104–26.

Page, Norman, ed. *Wilkie Collins: The Critical Heritage*. Boston: Routledge and Kegan Paul, 1974.

Peuchet, J. *Mémoires Tirés Des Archives de la Police de Paris*. Paris: Bourmancé, 1858.

Review of *The Woman in White*, by Wilkie Collins. *Morning Advertiser*, 20 Aug. 1860, 3.

Review of *The Woman in White*, by Wilkie Collins. *Spectator* 33 (8 Sept. 1860): 864.

Robbe-Grillet, Alain. *La Maison de Rendez-Vous*. Trans. Richard Howard. New York: Grove Press, 1966.

Robinson, Kenneth. *Wilkie Collins: A Biography*. New York: Macmillan, 1952.

Rudman, Harry W. *Italian Nationalism and English Letters*. New York: Columbia Univ. Press, 1940.

Sayers, Dorothy. *The Omnibus of Crime*. New York: Harcourt Brace, 1929.

———. *Wilkie Collins: A Critical and Biographical Study*. Ed. E. R. Gregory. Toledo, Ohio: Friends of the Univ. of Toledo Libraries, 1977.

Scheff, Thomas J. *Catharsis in Healing, Ritual, and Drama*. Berkeley: Univ. of California Press, 1979.

Smith, Dennis Mack. *Mazzini*. London and New Haven: Yale Univ. Press, 1994.

Stead, Philip John. *Vidocq: A Biography*. New York: Staples Press, 1953.

Vidocq, François Eugène. *Mémoires*. Paris: Tenon, 1828.

———. *Memoirs of Vidocq: The Principal Agent of the French Police*. Philadelphia: T. B. Peterson and Brothers, 1859.

———. *Supplemént aux Mémoires de Vidocq*. Paris: Librairie Centrale de Boulland, 1830.

Winnicott, D. W. *The Child, the Family, and the Outside World*. Harmondsworth: Penguin, 1964.

———. *Playing and Reality*. London: Tavistock Publications, 1971.

Wynne, Deborah. "Vidocq, the Spy: A Possible Source for Count Fosco in Wilkie Collins's *The Woman in White*." *Notes and Queries* 44 (1997): 342.

Yates, Edmund H. *Celebrities at Home*. 3d ser. London: Office of *The World*, 1879.

Outlandish English Subjects
in *The Moonstone*

Timothy L. Carens

ILKIE COLLINS WROTE *THE MOONSTONE*
(1868) DURING A PERIOD IN WHICH FEW
VICTORIANS QUESTIONED THE LEGITIMACY
of imperial rule in India. At that time it was
widely believed that Indians were instinctual,
impulsive, and fanatic; in other words, they supposedly lacked the mechanisms of self-control
that guarantee sound government at the level of
self and society alike.[1] The 1857 rebellion
known in England as the Mutiny confirmed for
many the passionate volatility of "the Indian
character" and its general antipathy to law and
order.[2] Although Collins does not directly dis-
pute prevailing assumptions about Indians, he
does question the extent to which "the English
character" differs from its ungovernable colonial
counterpart. In his novels, regulatory forces that
supposedly prevail within the civilized self—
rationality, morality, Christian faith—routinely
fail to exert their hold. English characters are

overmastered by their own "dark" and irrational obsessions, inordinate desires, unruly aggressions, and self-abasing idolatries. In *The Moonstone,* this uncanny irony subverts accepted oppositions between those who inhabit India, which Betteredge dismisses as one of the "outlandish places of the earth,"[3] and those who inhabit the presumed "center" of empire. Indeed, the mysterious gem, coveted by Indian and English characters alike, exerts a profoundly decentering power, drawing forth into the light "outlandish" impulses that brood beneath the surface of purportedly civilized subjectivity. This "first and greatest of English detective novels," as T. S. Eliot called *The Moonstone,*[4] not only detects a stolen diamond; it also detects a sustaining illusion at the center of imperial ideology, the belief that savage passions exist at a comfortable remove, the unique possessions of racially other colonial subjects.

By disclosing an ungovernable "darkness" native to the English self, Collins anticipates insights developed by Freud in "The Uncanny" (1919). In this classic essay, Freud studies the origin of disconcerting feelings provoked by certain experiences (or representations of such) perceived as strange. The sense of strangeness is, he argues, superficial and deceptive, for the ego has sought to protect the conscious mind from knowledge of primitive impulses by translating them into forms that *appear* to be foreign to the self. The uncanny, he argues, "is in reality nothing new or alien, but something which is familiar and old-established in the mind and which has become alienated from it only through the process of repression."[5] The distressing eeriness of uncanny experiences indicates not a confrontation with otherness, but rather a veiled encounter with strategically estranged aspects of the self.

Collins shows how imperial ideology functions as a repressive mechanism of the cultural mind, alienating ungovernable passions by projecting them onto the "lower races" who inhabit colonial territory.[6] He reveals how Victorian culture attempts to distinguish the civilized English subject from its colonial counterpart in India and how, ironically, the distinctions it draws fall into doubt. For, in *The Moonstone,* as in Freud's model, the repressive mechanism functions imperfectly. The susceptibility of English characters to the influence of the diamond demonstrates the fragility of their own self-command when embattled by "native" passions. The most fearful aspect of the "Oriental strangers" (*The Moonstone,* 197) who pursue the diamond, Collins knows, is the secret familiarity of their impulses and behavior. The novel dismantles conventional distinctions between Oriental and

English, between savage colonial other and well-regulated imperial self. Collins constructs what is, as Franklin Blake terms it, a "strange family story" (7), a narrative that uncovers the forgotten strangeness that inhabits the familiar, the imperfectly repressed savagery that lives on in the family.

Approaching *The Moonstone* as an uncanny text of imperial culture has two advantages. In the broad context of postcolonial criticism, it heeds a call for readings attuned to the features of narratives that destabilize the dichotomies naturalized by imperial ideology. Edward Said, who largely initiated postcolonial studies by exposing those dichotomies, defines Orientalist discourse as a "political vision of reality whose structure promoted the difference between the familiar (Europe, the West, 'us') and the strange (the Orient, the East, 'them')."[7] Yet theorists who have followed Said have argued that such clear-cut differences remain elusive even within the discourses that proclaim them. As Sara Suleri observes, "colonial facts" and, by extension, the representation of those facts, "fail to cohere around the master-myth that proclaims static lines of demarcation between imperial power and disempowered culture, between colonizer and colonized."[8]

Freud's discussion of the uncanny helps to account for the faulty construction of these "lines of demarcation" between familiar imperial culture and its strange Oriental colony. Early in his essay, Freud observes that the German words *unheimlich*, uncanny or strange, and *heimlich*, homely or familiar, are not so distinct as their antithetical construction implies. His etymological research discovers that, in addition to meaning "what is familiar and agreeable," *heimlich* also signifies "what is concealed and kept out of sight," while, according to one definition, *unheimlich* means that which "ought to have remained secret and hidden but has come to light."[9] Like Said, Homi Bhabha appreciates that imperial discourses set in opposition the "*heimlich* pleasures of the hearth" and the "*unheimlich* terror of the space or race of the Other."[10] Yet Bhabha also perceives, as his use of Freud's terms suggests, the instability of the distinction. He asserts, indeed, that the "'other' is never outside or beyond us."[11] Exposing this distressing truth as well, *The Moonstone* shows that the familiar pleasures of the English hearth and home, relying as they do on a dynamic of repression and projection, are sustainable only so long as native English passions remain hidden in the dark.

This approach also enables a constructive synthesis of two persuasive lines of analysis that have been applied to *The Moonstone*. A long-accepted reading of the novel decodes its symbolic structure as a psychosexual drama in which Blake's theft of Rachel's jewel figuratively enacts a sexual violation. "What is stolen from Rachel," as Albert Hutter argues, "is both the actual gem and her symbolic virginity."[12] This interpretation helped to establish Collins's fascination with the disruptive force of repressed impulses on codes of propriety meant to restrain them. Another line of inquiry turns its focus toward the novel's concern with imperial politics. John R. Reed, who initiated this perspective, treats the diamond as a reference to "England's imperial depredations," a "symbol of a national rather than a personal crime."[13] The novel, according to Reed, inverts the moral scheme of the civilizing mission by depicting the Hindu priests as "heroic figures, while the representatives of Western Culture are plunderers."[14] Ian Duncan concurs with Reed that the novel exposes the false pretenses of imperial authority but takes issue with the notion that it simply redistributes moral authority to India. *The Moonstone,* he argues, more disturbingly inverts the distribution of power while continuing to align India with moral depravity. Playing upon the "imperialist panic" generated by the Mutiny, Collins subjects his readers to the "nightmare of a devilish India," depicting "another world triumphant in its darkness."[15] While Duncan offers a more compelling reading of Collins's representation of India, he, like Reed, emphasizes an opposition that the novel in fact calls into question. Jaya Mehta similarly claims that *The Moonstone* "counterposes colonial terror to domestic romance," invoking the "nationalist mythology of a quintessentially placid English domesticity as a foil to colonial Indian violence."[16] Arguments that position India as England's other, however, whether victimized and plundered or nightmarish and vengeful, miss the extent to which the novel challenges such antithetical constructions.

The novel does so by focusing attention on forces that erupt from the dark otherworldly terrain of English subjectivity, where dwell impulses fully as irrational, violent, and passionate as those projected onto India. The novel's depiction of English subjectivity is thus itself a response to the imperial cultural moment. As Patrick Brantlinger observes, Mutiny narratives propagate a view of colonial insurgents as "wholly irrational, at once childish and diabolic," while aligning British colonial authority with rational order.[17] In *The Moonstone,* this racial polarization of subjective faculties, a cornerstone of imperial ideology, falls into disarray. The successful foray of the Hindu priests no doubt enacts, as Lillian Nayder argues, a "reverse colonization of England" in symbolic retaliation for imperial exploitation.[18] But the more striking irony is that irrational and diabolic forces need not colonize the imperial nation, because they are already indigenous inhabitants. Collins offsets the depiction of Indian subjects in Mutiny narratives by representing the mutinous instincts and impulses that disrupt the rational government of the English mind.

Persistent Affiliations

If the "master-myth" of Victorian imperial ideology attempted to enforce "lines of demarcation" between colonizer and colonized, contemporary religious and secular theories also existed that provided a basis, at least, for a skeptical critique of such dichotomies. Both evangelical Christianity and Victorian evolutionary anthropology, for example, promoted a universalist approach to human subjectivity that eroded clear-cut racial differences. To be sure, both movements were themselves shaped by, and in notable ways reconfirmed, British imperial power. In its paternalistic mission to convert the benighted heathen, evangelical Christianity supplied an ethical justification for empire.[19] Although evolutionary anthropologists sought to study, rather than convert, colonial subjects, they were not cultural relativists. Rather, they assumed that colonial subjects represented primitive stages in the line of human development that reached its apex in northern Europe.[20]

Still, both movements manifested a strong commitment to the common origin of mankind and consequently perceived "the savage" not as essentially different or wholly alien, but rather as a distant relative of the civilized self. Adhering to the biblical account of creation, evangelical Christians held that all humans descended directly from Adam and Eve. Those with darker skins, they believed, had simply indulged unregenerate human nature to a greater extent. As a result, Christian faith had degenerated into abject idolatry and its ethical system had succumbed to unrestrained instincts. Also asserting the common ancestry of different races, Victorian evolutionary anthropologists explained cultural and racial differences as the outcome of unequal progress from a common state of bestial wildness. From their perspective, the "savage races" had, rather than degenerating into savagery, lagged behind European cultures in the emergence from it.

Despite their evident biases, then, both disciplines maintained a theoretical commitment to the existence of a single "human family," as Betteredge terms it (*The Moonstone*, 82). This belief prepares the ground for uncanny reminders of family ties. For Freud, again, the uncanny accounts for instances in which the conscious mind registers, if only in its unease, an ancestry held in common with the irrational, unrestrained "other" that, ironically, continues to inhabit the self. Evangelical Christianity and evolutionary anthropology similarly trace the genealogy of the modern English subject back to a point of origin preceding racial and cultural differentiation, to a period when the savage other *was* the self. Crucially, both disciplines also then expose the lingering presence of this "primitive" entity in supposedly civilized English subjects. According to evangelical doctrine, Christian subjects harbored the same degenerate propensities given freer rein in tropical climes. Even as Protestant denominations established missionary societies to convert the heathen abroad, they detected "heathen" tendencies at home.[21] Evolutionary anthropologists believed that even the most progressive cultures retained, in modified and hidden forms, primitive practices and beliefs. Just as biological organisms furnished vestigial evidence of earlier formations, so too did modern civilization disclose surviving relics of its savage past.[22]

By no means a rigorous student of either discipline, Collins nonetheless absorbed their broadly disseminated ideas. He was particularly intrigued by the notion that the supposedly civilized modern English self harbored primitive impulses antagonistic to the religious and ethical dictates of Victorian culture. In *The Moonstone,* he shows slight sympathy for the evangelical movement itself, which was by the 1860s a waning cultural force. He satirizes its rhetoric in the person of the self-righteous Miss Clack, who remains ever-conscious of the need to "discipline the fallen nature which we all inherit from Adam" (191). The comic shadow cast on Clack's piety, however, obscures the extent to which Collins justifies her vigilance. His novels in general confirm her understanding of the ongoing internalized conflict between the forces of self-command and an intractable natural element. Sir Patrick, a principal character of *Man and Wife* (1870), translates Clack's spiritual struggle into a secular code of ethical development that bears the imprint of contemporary evolutionary assumptions. Articulating one of the chief didactic messages of the novel, he excoriates the national obsession with athleticism for catering to the "inbred reluctance in humanity to submit to the demands" of "moral and mental cultivation."[23] Those who exercise their muscles alone, he believes, find themselves at the mercy of the "savage instincts latent in humanity—the instincts of self-seeking and cruelty that are at the bottom of all crime" (*Man and Wife,* 213). While Clack and Sir Patrick express very different points of view, both understand the modern English self as a precariously balanced governmental structure.

The authority in power, aligned with spiritual discipline and ethical/intellectual cultivation, struggles to maintain its rule over rebellious instincts, aligned with an original yet persistent element perceived from the evangelical perspective as "fallen nature," from the anthropological view as "savage instincts."

Confirming this understanding of subjectivity throughout his work, Collins contests imperial dichotomies by questioning the ability of the modern English self to control the eruption of its primitive instincts and impulses. The notion that civilized subjects share a "fallen nature" and "savage instincts" with colonial others holds subversive potential in relation to the imperial "master-myth." Collins might have contained that potential by applauding the English for disciplining their primitive instincts and impulses more effectively than their colonial counterparts. He might have suggested that only the aberrant criminal few at the center of empire lack the capacity for self-restraint. Yet he emphasizes instead a broad unreliability of self-control. His novels continually replay the "outbreak" (a favorite term) of what he calls in *No Name* "original wildness," or what he labels "naked nature" in *The Evil Genius*.[24] They cultivate an anxiety about the irrepressibility of English savagery that the criminalization of certain particularly unrestrained individuals does not allay. The conviction that "our ancestor the savage" lurks within all English subjects wears the distinction between civilized and savage in the modern imperial world dangerously thin (*The Evil Genius*, 264).

Clack's evangelical perspective affords her partial insight into this disturbing fact. Attempting to extract an edifying moral from the incident in which the Hindu priests subject her hero Godfrey Ablewhite to an ignominious search, she exclaims, "How soon may our own evil passions prove to be Oriental noblemen who pounce on us unawares!" (*The Moonstone*, 198). The Indian rebellion, in which "Oriental noblemen" took British colonial authority "unawares," offers a precedent for the "outrage" committed on Ablewhite in the streets of London. More disturbingly still, it offers a precedent for surprise attacks committed by what Clack calls "our own evil passions." There is indeed, as Clack observes, a "dark conspiracy" at work "in the midst of us" (198). The fact that she describes the passions with terms drawn from the lexicon of peripheral otherness suggests a vain effort to preserve a sense of the foreignness of desires and rages that disrupt the government of the imperial self. Collins insists, rather, that "dark" passions are as much "native" to the heart of empire as to the "outlandish places of the earth."

The Foreign Face of Passion

The significance of the novel's representation of India and its native subjects emerges in light of this irony. Collins certainly demonstrates familiarity with conventional depictions of India as the nightmarish antithesis of orderly domestic life in England. Yet the disconcerting irony is that the English home, inspected closely, fails to oppose itself to strange colonial otherness. The novel's representation of India and its natives deserves close attention because it establishes habits of mind that recur, in muted ways, in England. The most explicitly "foreign" elements of the novel provide keys to the most familiar.

The prologue represents India as the native ground of rapacious violence and fanatical idolatry, characteristics that, particularly after 1857, were typically associated with the colony. According to the unnamed Herncastle cousin who relates the history of the Moonstone, the gem is for many centuries worshipped as an integral part of a Hindu idol that resides in a temple in Somnauth.[25] In the early eighteenth century, however, the Mogul emperor unleashes "havoc and rapine" against his Hindu subjects. During this period, a Mohammedan "officer of rank" steals the diamond from a shrine in Benares, where the idol had been transported for protection. A succession of three Hindu priests then devote their lives to the service of the deity, pursuing the diamond as it passes "from one lawless Mohammedan hand to another" until it becomes the possession of Tippoo, Sultan of Seringapatam. Unable to use "open force" against their oppressors, they instead await an opportunity to recapture the gem "in disguise" (*The Moonstone*, 3). Before they do so, of course, John Herncastle steals the diamond and removes it to England.

This "wildest" of legends extracted from the "native annals of India" is propelled by a conflict between varieties of unrestrained Indian subjectivity (1). The synecdoche of the "lawless Mohammedan hand" indicates unrestrained desire, subjectivities abandoned to the pleasures of brutal acquisition. In the Hindu priests, the self-indulgence of the Oriental despot gives place to dutiful self-renunciation. Their pursuit of the Moonstone exemplifies unrestrained devotion, subjectivities governed by zealous idolatry. To the Mohammedan, the diamond is treasure, valuable for its beauty and monetary value. To the Hindu idolaters, the diamond is sacred talisman, valuable because it belongs to the deity before whose will they bow.

If the Moonstone's history offers a stereotypical portrait of unrestrained Indian subjectivities, Collins also shows how such portraits are eagerly accepted as evidence of the foreignness of passionate excess. The reception of information supplied by Murthwaite, the Orientalist traveler recently returned from the "wild places of the East," provides a case in point (65). On the evening when Rachel first wears the diamond, he informs her, "I know a certain city, and a certain temple in that city, where, dressed as you are now, your life would not be worth five minutes' purchase." The Ablewhite sisters, who "burst out together vehemently, 'O! How interesting!'" enact the unquestioning attitude that assumes the veracity of "interesting" pictures of strange and distant locales (66). Although Betteredge disdains their enthusiasm, he also relies on Murthwaite's expertise as he constructs the foreignness of India and its subjects. "[C]lever as the Hindoo people are in concealing their feelings," Murthwaite penetrates the disguise of the priests when they appear at the dinner party (79). They turn on him, Betteredge reports, with "tigerish quickness," briefly revealing their murderous impulses before reassuming their "polite and snaky way" (70). This scene confirms that the Hindu priests are violent, deceptive, and unreservedly devoted to their idol, but it also shows how Betteredge intensifies the otherness of those he fears. To his mind, the Hindu priests, with their "tigerish" manner and "snaky" indirection, represent dangerous tropical animality that has encroached upon the temperate and familiar regions of English country life.

Such clear-cut dichotomies between the familiar nation and its strange bestial others rely on a naive ethnocentric mind-set exemplified most clearly by Betteredge, the character most leery of the "outlandish places of the earth": "[H]ere was our quiet English house," he exclaims, "suddenly invaded by a devilish Indian Diamond" (33). The "Indian Diamond" broadly signifies for Betteredge an infernal world in which the antithesis of all that is good, proper, rational, well ordered, and English prevails. "Who ever heard the like of it," he wonders, "in the nineteenth century, mind; in an age of progress, and in a country which rejoices in the blessings of the British constitution?" (33). This devoted servant of the "quiet English house" articulates several striking tributes to the progress and stability of his nation and its subjects. Unlike mutinous Indians and Continental revolutionaries, the English are, Betteredge asserts, "an easy people to govern, in the Parliament and in the Kitchen" (58). Just as he guards the circumference of the estate to secure it against the intrusive ploys of the Indians, so too does

Betteredge patrol the ideological borders of the imperial nation, defending them against rebellious otherness.

But sometimes, as Freud indicates, disturbing secrets are hidden in apparently quiet houses. *The Moonstone* undercuts Betteredge's naive ethnocentrism by disclosing what appear to be disruptive alien passions within the "quiet English house." Those who inhabit the imperial nation and its domestic spheres fail to offer uniquely tractable or well-governed alternatives to volatile colonial subjects. Mutinous English passions may be more deeply repressed and their forms of expression more cleverly hidden, but they nonetheless become visible over the course of the narrative. As they erupt within the familiar social realm, they expose the artificiality of the racial oppositions that sustain the imperial project.

In the Shivering Sands, Collins constructs a symbol that both acknowledges and repudiates the tendency to estrange disruptive passions by projecting them onto racial others. Inspiring intermingled horror and fascination in those who gaze upon it, the Shivering Sands is one of the novel's focal points of uncanny intensity. Its disturbing power emanates from the knowledge it discloses about the structure of human subjectivity in England as well as in India. While the surface of the quicksand appears relatively benign, at certain moments it heaves and ripples, indicating the "spirit of terror" that "live[s] and move[s] and shudder[s] in the fathomless deeps beneath" (304–5). Collins describes the surface as the "false brown face" (304), adopting a phrase that certainly recalls the deceptive Hindu priests, whose "polite" demeanor briefly reveals their terrifying intentions. But Collins does not arbitrarily locate the quicksand in Yorkshire, deep in the heart of the imperial nation and notably adjacent to the "quiet English house." This juxtaposition suggests that "quiet English" subjects, no less than their colonial counterparts, conceal volatile passions in their "fathomless deeps."

Collins associates the Shivering Sands most explicitly with Rosanna Spearman, the "silent" maidservant who is "troubled occasionally" by shudders of repressed desire for unattainable Franklin Blake (21–22). She reinforces the symbolic import of the Shivering Sands by sinking herself and her confession in its unquiet depths. Her death, however, leads Betteredge to a broadly relevant insight about the nature of the self and its repressed passions. He reflects that "we learn to put our feelings back into ourselves, and to jog on with our duties as patiently as may be" (159). Although Betteredge assumes that members of the upper classes can afford to indulge their feelings, his insight is not restricted to a particular class, gender, or race. The comment forges a connection between "quiet English" characters and the Hindu priests, noted for their "patience" and adept at "concealing their feelings" (71–72). The Shivering Sands bears a sign of racial difference on its "brown face," but only those who read superficially may convince themselves that the knowledge it symbolically conveys applies only to strangers.

Family Ties

The prologue of the novel foregrounds not just the outlandishness of India, but also its forceful appeal to a character invested with imperial authority. John Herncastle, an officer in the imperial army, proves easily susceptible to irrational and passionate impulses associated with the colony. As the British force prepares for the assault on Seringapatam, the "fanciful story of the Moonstone" awakens his acquisitive desire and volcanic ire (3). A man of "unlucky temper," Herncastle vows in an "angry outbreak" to capture the jewel for himself (3, 5). Ironically entrusted to "enforce the laws of discipline" after the conquest of the city, Herncastle succumbs to an aggressive "frenzy" in which he seizes the diamond, murdering the Indians who guard it (5). This first English chapter in the story of the Moonstone notably extends a motif established by events that precede the intervention of the purportedly civilized nation. Herncastle is but another "officer of rank" in a conquering force who grasps the diamond in his "lawless hand."

Back in England, the Herncastle family takes decisive action to disavow their unsavory relative. On the strength of testimony given by Herncastle's cousin, the rest of the family repudiates him as well: "He came back" from India, Blake remembers, "with a character that closed the doors of all his family against him" (30). This version of events suggests that Herncastle has acquired a "character" he did not formerly have, that he has been contaminated in India by essentially alien passions. Yet the effort to ostracize the wayward son, to close the family doors against him, suggests fearful complicity as much as disapproval. The Herncastles repudiate John because he extravagantly indulges impulses that they still attempt to hide. If he possesses a more liberal "dash of the savage" (30) than they, he differs from them in degree only. His sister Lady Verinder shares his volatile anger, possessing her own "dash . . . of the family temper" (32). The similar structure of these phrases suggests that "the savage" and "the family temper" might be read synonymously. Rachel exhibits her own "dash" of the family temper when her diamond is stolen, acting "wild and angry" and speaking to Blake "savagely" in an "outbreak of ill-will" (86, 101).

Nor is this dash of savagery limited to blood relatives of Herncastle. Irritated by Rachel's decision to break off her engagement to his son, the senior Mr. Ablewhite denounces the Herncastle family, implicitly representing his own line as superior. As he does so, however, he ironically gives vent to savage anger: "[B]ecoming purple" with anger, he looks "backwards and forwards from Rachel to Mr. Bruff in such a frenzy of rage with both of them that he didn't know which to attack first" (257). This "outbreak" recalls the "frenzy" that possesses Herncastle, who of course actually attacks multiple opponents in India (4). Collins indicates that even Ablewhite, a "remarkably good-natured man," verges at times on violent fury (253). The "self-registering thermometer" of Ablewhite's complexion grows a "shade deeper" as his rage intensifies, suggesting the emergence of his racially "foreign" self (255). The most distressing "family secret" of the novel is that upper-middle-class English characters share much in common with members of the "human family" they would like to hold at a distance.[26]

Never less than detestable, Herncastle does perceive the hypocrisy of those who bar their doors against passions already lodging comfortably within. That knowledge perhaps provokes his sardonic laugh "*into* himself" (32) when turned away from Rachel's birthday celebration. By this point on terms of joking familiarity with the family savage who abides within, Herncastle anticipates with cruel pleasure the spectacle of foreign passions unleashed by the Moonstone within the "quiet English house."

English Idolatry

When the diamond arrives in the Herncastle home as a birthday gift to Rachel, the superstitious regard it enjoys begins to indicate the fragility of the distinction between those allotted opposing positions on imperial lines of demarcation. When Betteredge bemoans the fact that the "cursed Moonstone ha[s] turned us all upside down," he attributes agency to the diamond itself, which is ironic for multiple reasons (82). Most notably, he exemplifies the tendency to "alienate" the sources of disturbance by blaming the "devilish Indian Diamond" (33). But his attempt is amusingly self-defeating, for by attributing "devilish" agency to the gem, Betteredge invests the object with supernatural power. He thus duplicates the kind of "outlandish" belief system he elsewhere dismisses as "hocus-pocus" (49). His first reaction to the diamond compounds this irony:

> Lord bless us! it *was* a Diamond! As large, or nearly,
> as a plover's egg! The light that streamed from it was like
> the light of the harvest moon. When you looked down
> into the stone, you looked into a yellow deep that drew
> your eyes into it so that they saw nothing else. It seemed
> unfathomable; this jewel, that you could hold between
> your finger and thumb, seemed unfathomable as the
> heavens themselves. . . . No wonder Miss Rachel was
> fascinated: no wonder her cousins screamed. The
> Diamond laid such a hold on *me* that I burst out with
> as large an "O" as the Bouncers themselves. (61–62)

The gem erodes barriers and distinctions that Betteredge elsewhere invests with much importance. He finds himself, as he admits, helplessly expressing the giddy enthusiasm of the Ablewhite sisters. His fascination, shared by his young mistress, transects the class divisions that structure the household. Through a symbolic connection, it also links him to Rosanna, the reformed urban criminal whom he admonishes for her morbid obsession with the "fathomless deeps" of the Shivering Sands. His hypothetical speculation "that you could hold" the diamond "between your finger and thumb" suggests an awakening in him of the acquisitive desire that governs John Herncastle.

But most strikingly, Betteredge swoons into a mind-set analogous to those held by the "influence of Oriental religions" and superstitions (39). Murthwaite later asserts, "We have nothing whatever to do with clairvoyance, or with mesmerism, or with anything else that is hard of belief to a practical man" (282). Yet the novel indicates that "practical" English subjects are as prone to fanatic obsessions and irrational superstitions as "Oriental strangers." The ethnocentric steward, another apostle of English common sense, quickly succumbs to the mesmeric grip of the Oriental talisman. It lays "such a hold" on him, drawing his "eyes into it so that they saw nothing else." In the spirit of exposing a hypocrisy (rather than admonishing a sin), Collins appropriates the evangelical habit of unveiling forms of idolatry that have crept into Christian culture. In *Practical Christianity,* Wilberforce defines "idol" broadly as whatever "draws off the heart from [God], engrosses our prime regard, and holds the chief place in our esteem and affections."[27] In this sense, Clack justifiably refers to Betteredge as a "heathen old man" (193). His "prime regard" is easily engrossed by the Moonstone and, of course, by Defoe's sacred text.

Collins is particularly concerned to indicate that habits of mind triggered by the foreign diamond precede its arrival. The appearance of the Moonstone only provides a new occasion for the exhibition of impulses "old-established in the mind." Early in his account, Betteredge memorably asserts, "I am not superstitious," only then to confess his superstitious regard for *Robinson Crusoe,* the text from which he draws clairvoyant readings of the future (8). After describing a search for guidance within its pages he remarks with relief, "I saw my way clear" (12). Long before the devilish Oriental diamond appears, Betteredge practices his own heathen cult, worshiping as his divine oracle, no less, a story that narrates the civilizing genius of the English hero.[28] As he holds the novel in his hands, searching the pages for esoteric wisdom, he represents merely an older version of the "sensitive" English boy who, employed as medium by the Hindus, reads the future in "the ink in the hollow of his hand" (18). The distinction between Betteredge's homely reading and their outlandish ritual is, as it were, paper thin.

The English "fascination" for the Moonstone does not therefore mark a reverse colonization of the imperial nation by Oriental superstition. Rather, it reveals purportedly "foreign" modes of idolatry already in place, although unacknowledged, in England. The displacement of the diamond from Indian to English culture exposes the artificiality of racial distinctions sustained by imperial rhetoric.[29] The effort to estrange the variety of mind subject to the "influence" of the mysterious and valuable jewel, already problematic after John Herncastle's violent "frenzy," becomes increasingly untenable as more English characters fall under its spell.

Heathen Idolatry and Savage Self-Seeking at Home

The Moonstone's experience in England uncannily repeats its history in India because presumably alien habits of mind secretly inhabit Victorian domestic culture.[30] Long before the intervention of the British Empire, the diamond graces the figure of a Hindu idol regarded as "the inviolate deity" by its worshippers (*The Moonstone,* 2). The deity is then violated by a Mohammedan officer who values the diamond as a material rather than a sacred object. In revenge for the hypocrisy of his family, Herncastle sets in motion a process that reveals the full extent to which the English domestic sphere harbors the same instincts and impulses that determine the diamond's stormy history in India. Specific forms of idolatrous worship and lawless acquisition change to reflect their unique shape in Victorian culture. The Hindu cult of the Moon god gives way to the English cult of domesticity. Mohammedan despot transmutes into materialistic scoundrel. Yet these parallels expose the persistent presence of heathen idolatry and savage self-seeking "at home."

Recent critics have argued that the theft of the jewel from Rachel exposes a similarity between patriarchal authority in the middle-class domestic sphere and British imperial authority in India. Nayder observes, for example, that in "his dual role of protector and thief, Blake illuminates the paradox of Victorian guardianship, in both its patriarchal and its imperial guises."[31] While the novel does align Rachel with colonial savagery and perhaps implicitly positions Blake as her colonial governor, it gives even more reason to perceive an uncanny correspondence between English heterosexual relationships and Oriental idolatry. This link largely confirms Nayder's point about the paradox of male guardianship, since even those who bow before the domestic deity and her talisman insist upon possessing the objects they worship.

On the verge of marriage, Rachel has attained the status of a powerful goddess in the Victorian cult of domesticity. Both before and after the theft of the diamond, men in her circle approximate the idolatrous service exemplified by Indian devotees. Blake expresses his "devotion" by renouncing cigars when she mentions her dislike of their odor (55). Her word is also law for Bruff, who affirms the innocence of Ablewhite on the strength of her unsupported testimony. The "practical" lawyer abandons rules of evidence when the English deity speaks. Betteredge, who confesses himself "an average good Christian" only when "you don't push [his] Christianity too far," exhibits the fierce loyalty of those in thrall to "Oriental religions" (165). Irritated by Cuff's effort to implicate Rachel in the theft, his heathen passion "break[s] out," provoking him to grab the Sergeant by the throat and pin him against the wall (133). Holding "on like death to [his] belief in Miss Rachel," Betteredge reveals a liberal "dash" of the ferocity that drives the Hindu priests to smother Ablewhite (151). Collins suggests that those Victorians who perceive their culture untainted by the fanaticism of heathen religions may find evidence to the contrary in the chivalric code that structures sexual relations in the middle-class cult of domesticity.

Ablewhite, who secretly despises this sacred cult, violates the deity in the manner of his Mohammedan predecessors. In his culture, of course, it is the religious cult that holds power and legitimacy, and this forces him to practice subterfuge like the Hindu priests. Ablewhite plays the role of mild philanthropist and seems to adhere with special devotion to Victorian chivalric codes. He is the gracious assistant to multiple "Ladies' Charities" and pays homage to Rachel in affectionate birthday verses (55). This sensitive facade conceals varieties of acquisitive desire conventionally associated with Mohammedan despotism. In a secret villa, Ablewhite indulges the opulent lifestyle of an Oriental potentate, supporting his sensual gratifications with appropriated wealth. The gentle consideration he shows for women masks the sexual appetite of the stereotypical Sultan. Although Ablewhite keeps only a single mistress, his villa includes "a conservatory of the rarest flowers" and "jewels which are worthy to take rank with the flowers" (448). Given the associations of female sexuality with flowers and jewels (a particularly resonant metaphor in this novel), the villa takes on the symbolic character of an English harem.

Ablewhite regards both Rachel and her diamond as loot to plunder from the temple of domesticity. He views the diamond as a financial resource with which to sustain his sensual life and sees Rachel herself as yet another flower for his conservatory. His desire is not as apparent as his financial chicanery, but Betteredge does at one point catch him "ogling" the heiress (62). In her analysis of nineteenth-century imperial discourse, Inderpal Grewal observes that the image of the "woman 'caged' in the harem, in purdah, becomes the necessary Other for the construction of the Englishwoman presumably free and happy in the home."[32] Skeptical of such oppositions, Collins intimates that an Englishwoman may well find herself caged within a marriage that replicates the power structure of the harem.

Yet Collins perceives that the English cult of domesticity also limits the freedom and independence of women. Language that links Rachel to the diamond itself clarifies both the sources of her authority over her idolaters and the restrictions placed upon it by them as well. She becomes the "centre-point towards which everybody's eyes [are] directed" because she, like the diamond, has great worth and great beauty (64). Her vast wealth and multifaceted beauty help to explain the mysterious influence she wields over those men who succumb to her "charming" and "irresistible" power (47, 270). The sad case of Rosanna, who lacks her mistress's "handsome income" as well as her physical advantages, highlights the point that only beautiful women of a certain socioeconomic position might expect to win the idolatrous regard of men in Victorian England (249). Rachel, however, pays a significant price for the power she wields. She embodies the symbolic instability of the diamond, which is always, even within the framework of the sacred cult, simultaneously sacred talisman and desirable possession. The patriarchal cult in England, like its colonial counterpart, must own the object of its adoration. It is a sanctified variety of acquisitive desire that Blake expresses in his need to see and to possess, to have and to hold, the idol he serves. It is particularly ironic that Collins discloses the operation of primitive possessive impulses within the cult of domesticity, for many Victorians believed that the status afforded middle-class women marked one of the essential distinctions between their culture and savagery. It is this popular assumption that John Stuart Mill treats with scorn in *The Subjection of Women* (1869). To his eye, as to Collins's, relations between the sexes in supposedly civilized England carries the "taint of brutal origins."[33]

The theft of the diamond, the crime committed at dead of night in the "quiet English house," thus represents a twofold outbreak of primitive possessiveness, implicating both Blake, the idolatrous servant, and Ablewhite, the lawless thief. Collins introduces the tantalizing possibility that Rachel will reject both forms of outlandish authority that her cousins represent. The Moonstone's mysterious flaw corresponds to what Betteredge calls the single "defect" in the character of "this charming creature," her "independence" or "self-will" (52–53). The history of the diamond suggests that it possesses a maddening "independence" as well, tending as it does to wander away from those who desire to possess it (35). Rachel exerts her independence after witnessing the symbolic assertion of ownership by her chief devotee. She resigns her post as deity, abandoning the temple and retreating into inscrutable silence. Just as the Hindu cult recaptures its talisman, however, the English cult of domesticity eventually reclaims Rachel. Victorian England clings to its forms of heathen worship as tenaciously as India.

Face to Face with Strangers

As the romantic and criminal story lines draw to a close, Collins offers no sense of a triumphant transcendence of imperial dichotomies. Both plots continue to emphasize the strength of Victorian cultural investment in the otherness of heathen idolatry and savage self-seeking. Yet both plots also ensure that the complicity of English characters in outlandish modes of thought and behavior at least comes to light. And both plots continue to erode, through very different mechanisms, lines of demarcation between colonizer and colonized.

The happy ending of the romantic plot reflects the result of a sympathetic relationship that bridges the social divide between the English lovers and Ezra Jennings. In the context of England's self-proclaimed mission to enlighten the dark places of the earth, it is deeply ironic that the solution of the mystery in England, the "toilsome journey from the darkness to the light," depends on this racially hybrid colonial subject (329). Jennings has been treated recently with a degree of asperity for placing himself in the role of colonial servant and for thus countenancing British imperial rule.[34] Yet Jennings himself has a position of authority; throughout the final section, Blake agrees to be "guided implicitly by [his] advice" (384). Indeed, Jennings usurps the presumed role of British civilizing authority in India and reverses the path of reform by correcting injustice and diffusing refined sentiment in outlandish England. While English characters inflict passionate violence on India in the "storming" of Seringapatam, Jennings "enter[s] to us," as Blake phrases it, "quietly" (1, 319). The peaceful intervention of the racial hybrid counteracts the conventional polarization of racial identities.

The fact that Jennings is a physician suggests that he offers a healing curative for a culture sickened by racial dichotomies. The remedy he offers, the capacity to perceive arbitrarily drawn "lines of demarcation" and to tolerate their dissolution, is inscribed in and on his body. As the child of an English man and a woman indigenous to "one of our colonies," Jennings subverts in his biological heritage the barrier dividing colonizer and colonized (366).[35] The code of his weird appearance further calls that barrier into doubt. His most notable feature, his "piebald" hair, opposes black and white "without the slightest gradation of grey" (319). Collins emphasizes the abnormality of this stark division, referring to it as an "extraordinary contrast" that has occurred only through "some freak of nature." The ideological separation of racial identities is, he suggests, as fully "capricious" as the principle that has divided the colors of Jennings's hair. It is further remarkable that the dividing "line between the two colors," preserves "no sort of regularity. At one place, the white hair ran up into the black; at another, the black hair ran down into the white" (319). Those who gaze upon Ezra Jennings confront a symbolic text that graphically illustrates the construction and inevitable confusion of antithetical racial categories.

Because he unsettles imperial dichotomies, Jennings calls forth the intense dread of the uncanny. A servant at the Verinder estate experiences "downright terror" in his presence (410). Mrs. Merridew, Rachel's chaperone, "utter[s] a faint little scream at the first sight of [his] gipsy complexion and [his] piebald hair" (412). Jennings inspires, as he ruefully observes, near universal "dislike and distrust" (393). His ostracism is tragic because, unlike the novel's other uncanny symbols, he demonstrates the universality of human nature by exemplifying certain of its most admirable qualities. While the Moonstone awakens and intensifies acquisitive desire and idolatrous obsession, the colonial hybrid kindles sympathy and compassion. Revealing the precious associations he holds for "little hedgeside flowers," Jennings speaks in the voice of a Wordsworthian persona who taps into the great fund of human feeling by projecting significance onto the "meanest flower that blows" (366). Both Blake and Rachel find it possible to look beyond his deceptively foreign appearance to appreciate such familiar sentiments. Although Rachel is at first taken aback by his aspect, she refuses to treat him "like a stranger" (410). As Blake repeatedly comes "face to face with Ezra Jennings," he begins to sense the "inscrutable appeal to [his] sympathies" emanating from the "strange man" (364, 365). Collins rewards them for overcoming the "terror" inspired by hybridity by reuniting them within the fold of tenderness over which Jennings presides. Notably, both first express their love for each other to Jennings.

If Jennings shows that strangers possess familiar sentiments, his detective work correspondingly discloses the unfamiliar terrain of the English self. He counteracts the projection of criminal instincts and savage impulses onto racial others by guiding Blake toward a degree of self-knowledge. On the morning following the theft of the diamond, Blake confidently asserts that the "Indians have certainly stolen the Diamond" (80). Even after he discovers evidence that implicates himself, he remains at a loss to explain his motivations. Jennings surmises that opium, secretly administered by Dr. Candy, impels Blake "to possess [him]self of the Diamond, with the purpose of securing its safety" (389). The experiment he devises to prove this supposition repeats and exposes the process of alienating possessive idolatry. As Blake drops into an opium-induced trance, Jennings recalls to his mind the "unexpected appearance of the Indians at the house" (418). It is, ironically, fear of the Hindu priests that provokes Blake to mimic their effort to possess themselves of the jewel. As they prowl outside the house, intending to secure the safety of their deity's jewel, he unconsciously performs a parallel act of idolatrous service within. Although Blake owns his actions, he never self-consciously perceives the extent to which he shares the idolatrous tendencies of those he scapegoats. Such self-consciousness might in turn have triggered the recognition that, after all, the Moonstone belongs to their deity, not to his. The experiment is, as Jennings admits, only "partially successful" (424).

The conclusion of the criminal plot forcefully demonstrates the inevitable return to the English self of impulses projected onto the racial other. The "noticeably dark complexion" Ablewhite assumes to avoid detection while spiriting the diamond away yet again throws criminal suspicion onto colonial subjects (430). From one perspective, the disguise indicates the extent to which Ablewhite has fallen into line with the lawless Mohammedan hands that have preceded him. At the same time, it deprives Victorian culture of the consoling affiliation of self-seeking and cruelty with racial otherness. The "swarthy complexion" is a disguise, but then so too is the white face of benevolent philanthropy (444). Surface colors, such as the "false brown face" of the Shivering Sands, are ultimately less accurate guides to the nature of character than the variety of passions that seethe beneath the surface.

The unmasking of Ablewhite dramatizes the terror provoked by the realization that the familiar English philanthropist has all along concealed lawless acquisitive desire. Significantly, Blake is able to gaze with grim distaste upon the body of a dark criminal. His nerves, however, are simply "not strong enough to bear it" when Cuff reveals the "livid white" skin beneath the "swarthy complexion." Cuff is more stoic, but the task of stripping away the swarthy disguise etches "horror in his face" (444). The intensity of these reactions indicates the extent to which Victorian culture is repelled by the knowledge that the "savage instincts" of "self-seeking and cruelty" do not remain "latent," even in the most apparently able and white of English subjects.

The scene of Ablewhite's unmasking emblematically captures the larger symbolic and thematic structure of *The Moonstone*, which strips the foreign disguise from the face of familiar passions. The uncanny logic of the novel repeatedly subverts prevailing assumptions about differences between English selves and Indian others. The irrational superstitions, idolatrous obsessions, and acquisitive desires that Victorians associate with the volatile colony come spilling back across the lines of demarcation, ironically arising within the "quiet English house" itself.

Notes

I would like to thank Peter Chapin and Terence Bowers for their insightful comments on a draft of this essay.

1. This basic assumption surfaces in justifications of British rule in India in many distinct imperial discourses throughout the nineteenth century. Charles Grant, a missionary who wrote an influential treatise on the character of the "people of Hindostan," described them in 1797 as "a race of men lamentably degenerate and base . . . governed by malevolent and licentious passions" (qtd. in Eric Stokes, *The English Utilitarians and India* [Oxford: Oxford Univ. Press, 1959], 31). In 1833, Thomas Babington Macaulay represents the administration of the East India Company, despite its serious flaws, as the advent of the government of reason: "I see that we have established order," he definitively states, "where we found confusion" (*"Government of India," in Prose and Poetry*, ed. G. M. Young [Cambridge: Harvard Univ. Press, 1970], 704). In 1888, John Strachey, a member of the Viceroy's council, anticipates a return to "confusion" should the British leave India: "We cannot foresee the time in which the cessation of our rule would not be the signal for universal anarchy and ruin, and it is clear that the only hope for India is the long continuance of the benevolent but strong government of Englishmen" (qtd. in Stokes, 284).

2. For a survey of literary responses to the Mutiny, see Patrick Brantlinger, "The Well at Cawnpore: Literary Representations of the Mutiny of 1857," in *Rule of Darkness: British Literature and Imperialism, 1830–1914* (Ithaca: Cornell Univ. Press, 1988), 199–224. In her reading of Mutiny narratives, Jenny Sharpe focuses on a specific motif that indicates the tendency to locate the cause of colonial uprisings in the presumed passionate volatility of colonial subjects. She traces an obsessive concern for the rape of white women by native men, which functions to translate a "struggle for emancipation" into an "uncivilized eruption that must be contained" (*Allegories of Empire: The Figure of Woman in the Colonial Text* [Minneapolis: Univ. of Minnesota Press, 1993], 7).

3. Wilkie Collins, *The Moonstone,* ed. John Sutherland (Oxford: Oxford Univ. Press, 1999), 74. Hereafter cited in the text as *The Moonstone*.

4. T. S. Eliot, "Wilkie Collins and Dickens," in *Selected Essays, 1917–1932* (New York: Harcourt, Brace and Co., 1932), 377.

5. Sigmund Freud, "The 'Uncanny,'" in *An Infantile Neurosis and Other Works*, vol. 17, *The Standard Edition of the Complete Psychological Works of Sigmund Freud*, ed. James Strachey (London: Hogarth Press, 1955), 241.

6. Collins witnessed this process in reactions to the Mutiny, which, as Sue Lonoff suggests, "firmly established" in the minds of many of his contemporaries a picture of Indians as "an alien, mysterious, and potentially violent people" (*Wilkie Collins and His Victorian Readers* [New York: AMS

Press, 1982], 178). Collins himself published a response to the Mutiny—
"A Sermon for Sepoys"—in *Household Words* 17 (27 Feb. 1858):
244–47, which strikes a comparatively restrained note by attempting to
discover common ground in the moral and ethical systems of the two
cultures. Anthea Trodd, in the introduction to her edition of *The
Moonstone*, refers to his essay as a "reminder, ostensibly to Moslems but
really to his readers, of the virtues inherent in the Muslim faith" (introduction to *The Moonstone* [Oxford: Oxford Univ. Press, 1998], xvii).

7. Edward Said, *Orientalism* (New York: Pantheon, 1978), 43.

8. Sara Suleri, *The Rhetoric of English India* (Chicago: Univ. of Chicago
Press, 1992), 3.

9. Freud, 224–25.

10. Homi K. Bhabha, "Introduction: Narrating the Nation," in *Nation and
Narration,* ed. Homi K. Bhabha (New York: Routledge, 1990), 2.

11. Ibid., 4.

12. Albert D. Hutter, "Dreams, Transformations, and Literature: The Implications of Detective Fiction," *Victorian Studies* 19 (1975): 242. See also
two additional psychosexual readings of the novel: Lewis A. Lawson,
"Wilkie Collins and *The Moonstone*," *American Imago* 20 (1963): 61–79,
and Charles Rycroft, "A Detective Story: Psychoanalytic Observations,"
The Psychoanalytic Quarterly 26 (1957): 229–45. Feminist accounts that
interpret Blake's sexual "conquest" as broadly indicative of Rachel's sub-
ordination to patriarchal power have developed the standard psychosexual interpretation. Tamar Heller argues, for example, that the diamond
"signifies not merely [Rachel's] virginity but what Bruff calls her 'self-
dependence' as well" (*Dead Secrets: Wilkie Collins and the Female Gothic*
[New Haven: Yale Univ. Press, 1992], 146).

13. John R. Reed, "English Imperialism and the Unacknowledged Crime of
The Moonstone," *Clio* 2, no. 3 (1973): 286.

14. Ibid., 283. For a more recent account that compellingly reads the novel
as a critique of British imperial practices, see Lillian Nayder, *Wilkie
Collins* (New York: Twayne Publishers, 1997), 115–25. This line of
argument is contested by Ashish Roy, who claims that the novel is a
"prototypical imperialist text exhibiting imperialist rule and a justification of that rule within a single narrative strategy" ("The Fabulous
Imperialist Semiotic of Wilkie Collins's *The Moonstone*," *New Literary
History* 24, no. 3 [1993]: 676).

15. Ian Duncan, "*The Moonstone,* the Victorian Novel, and Imperialist
Panic," *Modern Language Quarterly* 55 (1994): 305.

16. Jaya Mehta, "English Romance: Indian Violence," *The Centennial Review*
39 (1995): 612. Although I disagree with this thesis, Mehta's account is
historically informative, sophisticated in its close readings, and often persuasive in its claims. The thesis is balanced by the observation that

Collins "draws attention to the crosscutting of race and class . . . and the arbitrariness of racial identity" (623).

17. Brantlinger, 222.

18. Nayder, 101.

19. Gauri Viswanathan argues that the Clapham Sect, a group of influential evangelicals, "played a key role in the drama of consolidation of British interests in India . . . supplying British expansionism with an ethics of concern for reform and conversion" (*Masks of Conquest: Literary Study and British Rule in India* [New York: Columbia Univ. Press, 1989], 36). Also see Stokes, 28–36.

20. George W. Stocking provides a lucid review of the different intellectual strands of Victorian anthropology. In the discussion that follows, I rely heavily on his analysis of pre- and post-Darwinian views and the impact of anthropological inquiry on the understanding of the relationship between civilization and savagery. Particularly see his chapter "The Darwinian Revolution and the Evolution of Human Culture" in *Victorian Anthropology* (New York: Free Press, 1987), 144–85. I should clarify that my use of the term *anthropology* is somewhat anachronistic, since those who subscribed to the single origin thesis and embraced the evolutionary paradigm generally belonged to the Ethnological Society of London (founded 1843). In the early 1860s, those who believed that the different races were actually different species split off to form the Anthropological Society of London. In 1871, the two factions rejoined in the Anthropological Institute. See Stocking, 248–54.

21. William Wilberforce, one of the principal architects of the Anglican missionary movement in India and Africa, perceived his own culture as only slightly more enlightened. In a book that remained popular throughout the first half of the nineteenth century, Wilberforce implores his English readers to acknowledge that "sensual gratifications and illicit affections have debased our nobler powers" (*A Practical View of Christianity*, ed. Kevin Charles Belmonte [Peabody, Mass.: Hendrickson, 1996], 18). He rails against those for whom the title of Christian "implies no more than a sort of formal, general assent to Christianity in the gross, and a degree of morality in practice, but little if at all superior to that for which we look in a good Deist, Mussulman, or Hindoo" (Wilberforce, 77).

22. The central expositors of sociocultural evolution subscribed in one form or another to a doctrine of "survivals," the notion that contemporary culture comprehends practices that, if examined closely, reveal previous evolutionary states. In *The Origin of Civilization and the Primitive Condition of Man* (1870), for example, John Lubbock asserts that "among the most civilized nations there are traces of original barbarism" (qtd. in Stocking, 154). Although Freud primarily uses the uncanny to explain the reemergence of the individual's primitive self, he also applies it to the survival of culturally primitive habits of mind. Commenting upon the

animistic belief in the "omnipotence of thoughts," for example, he observes that "We—or our primitive forefathers—once believed that these possibilities were realities, and were convinced that they actually happened. Nowadays we no longer believe in them, we have *surmounted* these modes of thought; but we do not feel quite sure of our new beliefs, and the old ones still exist within us ready to seize upon any confirmation" (Freud, 247).

23. Wilkie Collins, *Man and Wife*, ed. Norman Page (Oxford: Oxford Univ. Press, 1998), 211. Hereafter cited in the text as *Man and Wife*.

24. See Wilkie Collins, *No Name*, ed. Virginia Blain (Oxford: Oxford Univ. Press, 1986), 474, and Wilkie Collins, *The Evil Genius*, ed. Graham Law (Peterborough, Ontario: Broadview Press, 1994), 264. Hereafter cited in the text as *The Evil Genius*.

25. Collins does not name the Hindu idol, and critics have advanced readings of the novel based on different assumptions about its identity. William M. Burgan, who provides a detailed source study of texts Collins relied upon for information about Hindu mythology, identifies the deity as Siva, god of destruction and generation ("Masonic Symbolism in *The Moonstone* and *The Mystery of Edwin Drood*," in *Wilkie Collins to the Forefront: Some Reassessments,* ed. Nelson C. Smith and R. C. Terry [New York: AMS Press, 1995], 101–48). Mark M. Hennelly alternatively identifies the deity as Vishnu ("Detecting Collins' Diamond: From Serpentstone to Moonstone," *Nineteenth-Century Fiction* 39 [1984]: 25–47). Both interpretations argue that the novel's symbolic and thematic structure reflects the duality of these mythological figures.

26. Elisabeth Rose Gruner also argues that *The Moonstone* undermines the conventional Victorian ideal of the upper-middle-class family as a safe and secure "sphere" that excludes disreputable elements, although she emphasizes its connection to sordid crime rather than to colonial savagery. "For Collins," she argues, "the Victorian family, far from protecting one from the increasingly complex and dangerous public world, is itself the source of many of its own complexities and dangers" ("Family Secrets and the Mysteries of *The Moonstone*," *Victorian Literature and Culture* 21 [1993]: 128).

27. Wilberforce, 86.

28. Arguing that *The Moonstone* "takes large comfort" from *Robinson Crusoe,* the "workmanlike myth of colonial enterprise," Ashish Roy conflates the novel with Betteredge and misses the irony of his clairvoyant readings (Roy, 657).

29. The enforced removal from India of the famous Koh-i-noor diamond, one of the Moonstone's several historical precedents, complements this point. After annexing the Punjab in 1849, Governor-General Dalhousie demanded that Maharaja Dalip Singh cede the Koh-i-noor to Queen Victoria, who added it to the stock of crown jewels. In an interesting

analysis of this transaction, Mehta observes that the "incorporation of loot from the conquered into imperial regalia has ancient and primitive antecedents; at once magical and metaphorical, it performs a kind of visual cannibalism" (Mehta, 616). If the acquisition of the Koh-i-noor demonstrated imperial power, it also ironically reveals the survival of primitive impulses and rituals within Victorian culture.

30. Hennelly argues that the diamond's "travels in both India and England apparently serve to locate thematic values in either one or the other culture. But the actual point is the reverse—namely, that such an identification of national characteristics is too reductive and narrow-minded and that the insular Victorians, especially, must integrate what they see as Indian (or lunar) values into their own petrified culture" (Hennelly, 42). While the novel confirms his point about the dangers of reductive national identities, I would argue that it does so not by *advocating* the integration of "foreign" values, but rather by documenting the extent to which they are already integrated.

31. Nayder, 122; see also Heller, 144.

32. Inderpal Grewal, *Home and Harem: Nation, Gender, Empire, and the Cultures of Travel* (Durham: Duke Univ. Press, 1996), 54.

33. John Stuart Mill, *The Subjection of Women,* in *On Liberty and Other Essays,* ed. John Gray (New York: Oxford Univ. Press, 1991), 476.

34. Nayder, 122–23.

35. In *The Races of Men* (1862), an anthropological study that provided theoretical support for apologists of empire by disputing the assumption of common origins, Robert Knox represents the racial hybrid as a "degradation of humanity . . . rejected by nature" (qtd. in Robert J. C. Young, *Colonial Desire: Hybridity in Theory, Culture and Race* [New York: Routledge, 1995], 15). Collins emphasizes the fact that the hybrid is rejected by human communities rather than by nature. In the symbolic text of Jennings's hair, analyzed below, it is the "capricious" division of black and white that is described as a "freak of nature."

References

Bhabha, Homi K., ed. *Nation and Narration.* New York: Routledge, 1990.

Brantlinger, Patrick. *Rule of Darkness: British Literature and Imperialism, 1830–1914.* Ithaca: Cornell Univ. Press, 1988.

Burgan, William. "Masonic Symbolism in *The Moonstone* and *The Mystery of Edwin Drood.*" In *Wilkie Collins to the Forefront: Some Reassessments,* ed. Nelson C. Smith and R. C. Terry, 101–48. New York: AMS Press, 1995.

Collins, Wilkie. *The Evil Genius.* Ed. Graham Law. Peterborough, Ontario: Broadview Press, 1994.

————. *Man and Wife*. Ed. Norman Page. Oxford: Oxford Univ. Press, 1998.

————. *The Moonstone*. Ed. Anthea Trodd. Oxford: Oxford Univ. Press, 1998.

————. *The Moonstone*. Ed. John Sutherland. Oxford: Oxford Univ. Press, 1999.

————. *No Name*. Ed. Virginia Blain. Oxford: Oxford Univ. Press, 1986.

————. "A Sermon for Sepoys." *Household Words* 17 (27 Feb. 1858): 244–47.

Duncan, Ian. "The Moonstone, the Victorian Novel, and Imperialist Panic." *Modern Language Quarterly* 55, no. 3 (1994): 297–319.

Eliot, T. S. *Selected Essays, 1917–1932*. New York: Harcourt, Brace and Co., 1932.

Freud, Sigmund. *An Infantile Neurosis and Other Works*. Vol. 17, *The Standard Edition of the Complete Psychological Works of Sigmund Freud*, ed. James Strachey. London: Hogarth Press, 1955.

Grewal, Inderpal. *Home and Harem: Nation, Gender, Empire, and the Cultures of Travel*. Durham: Duke Univ. Press, 1996.

Gruner, Elisabeth Rose. "Family Secrets and the Mysteries of *The Moonstone*." *Victorian Literature and Culture* 21 (1993): 127–45.

Heller, Tamar. *Dead Secrets: Wilkie Collins and the Female Gothic*. New Haven: Yale Univ. Press, 1992.

Hennelly, Mark M. "Detecting Collins' Diamond: From Serpentstone to Moonstone." *Nineteenth-Century Fiction* 39 (1984): 25–47.

Hutter, Albert D. "Dreams, Transformations, and Literature: The Implications of Detective Fiction." *Victorian Studies* 19, no. 2 (1975): 181–209.

Lawson, Lewis A. "Wilkie Collins and *The Moonstone*." *American Imago* 20, no. 1 (1963): 61–79.

Lonoff, Sue. *Wilkie Collins and His Victorian Readers: A Study in the Rhetoric of Authorship*. New York: AMS Press, 1982.

Macaulay, Thomas Babington. *Prose and Poetry*. Ed. G. M. Young. Cambridge: Harvard Univ. Press, 1970.

Mehta, Jaya. "English Romance: Indian Violence." *The Centennial Review* 39 (1995): 611–57.

Mill, John Stuart. *On Liberty and Other Essays*. Ed. John Gray. Oxford: Oxford Univ. Press, 1991.

Nayder, Lillian. *Wilkie Collins*. New York: Twayne Publishers, 1997.

Reed, John R. "English Imperialism and the Unacknowledged Crime of *The Moonstone*." *Clio* 2, no. 3 (1973): 281–90.

Roy, Ashish. "The Fabulous Imperialist Semiotic of Wilkie Collins's *The Moonstone*." *New Literary History* 24 (1993): 657–81.

Rycroft, Charles. "A Detective Story: Psychoanalytic Observations." *The Psychoanalytic Quarterly* 26, no. 2 (1957): 229–45.

Said, Edward. *Orientalism*. New York: Pantheon, 1978.

Sharpe, Jenny. *Allegories of Empire: The Figure of Woman in the Colonial Text*. Minneapolis: Univ. of Minnesota Press, 1993.

Stokes, Eric. *The English Utilitarians and India*. Oxford: Oxford Univ. Press, 1959.

Stocking, George W. *Victorian Anthropology*. New York: Free Press, 1987.

Suleri, Sara. *The Rhetoric of English India*. Chicago: Univ. of Chicago Press, 1992.

Viswanathan, Gauri. *Masks of Conquest: Literary Study and British Rule in India*. New York: Columbia Univ. Press, 1989.

Wilberforce, William. *A Practical View of Christianity*. Ed. Kevin Charles Belmonte. Peabody, Mass.: Hendrickson, 1996.

Young, Robert J. C. *Colonial Desire: Hybridity in Theory, Culture and Race*. New York: Routledge, 1995.

"Blue Like Me"

Collins, *Poor Miss Finch,* and the Construction of Racial Identity

———◆———

Lillian Nayder

Were we racists or were we not? That was the important thing to discover. Black men told me that the only way a white man could hope to understand anything about this reality was to wake up some morning in a black man's skin. I decided to try this in order to test this one thing. In order to make the test, I would alter my pigment and shave my head, but change nothing else about myself. I would keep my clothing, my speech patterns, my credentials, and I would answer every question truthfully.

—John Howard Griffin
"What's Happened Since *Black Like Me,*" 1977

ETERMINED TO TEST AND DOCUMENT THE REALITY OF RACISM IN THE LATE 1950S, JOHN HOWARD GRIFFIN DARKENED HIS SKIN color, shaved his head, and passed as a black man in the Deep South of the United States. Recording his experience of racism in *Black Like Me* (1961),[1] Griffin showed that "the same man" received very different treatment solely because of a change in his pigmentation, becoming "not even . . . a second-class citizen, but . . . a tenth-class one" (*Black Like Me,* 5, 47). In a book that many readers continue to see as a "classic exposé of racism,"[2] Griffin testified to the injustice of racial discrimination first-hand, helping to inspire the civil rights movement. Transforming himself into a "black" man, he sought to question essentialist notions of racial identity and difference, and to prove that a man's character and worth have nothing to do with the "accident" of skin color: what he terms "this least important of all qualities, the skin pigment" (120).

In recent years, a number of critics have questioned the "liberalism" of *Black Like Me* and its formulations of racial identity, arguing that Griffin reinscribes the very categories he sets out to dismantle, reinforcing conceptions of white authority. While acknowledging Griffin's "'good intentions,'" for example, Gayle Wald finds him "unequipped to imagine black people elaborating their own ontology of blackness or voicing their own opposition to segregation." As Wald points out, Griffin bases his "ethno-journalistic experiment" on "a false opposition between the white researcher's theoretical apprehension and the black subject's . . . non-consciousness."[3] Despite the "unresolved contradictions" that inform the book, however, *Black Like Me* is generally praised as "groundbreaking."[4] Translated into more than a dozen languages and published in a Braille edition, it has sold more than twelve million copies since 1961.

Yet Griffin's tale of darkening skin color was anticipated by nearly a century in a book that remains considerably more obscure than *Black Like Me:* Wilkie Collins's novel *Poor Miss Finch* (1872), in which the Caucasian hero, Oscar Dubourg, turns dark blue as a result of the medical treatment he receives for epilepsy. Treating Oscar's change in pigmentation as if it were a transformation in race, Collins considers the ways in which racial identity is socially constructed in Victorian culture while also suggesting that racial difference is a disfigurement of sorts. Uniting his dark-blue hero with a blind, white heroine who must overcome her irrational aversion to dark-skinned people in order to marry the man she loves, Collins calls attention to the blindness of racial prejudice, despite what we might consider his own short-sightedness on the subject, and represents, albeit in displaced form, what most Victorians were unwilling to imagine—the interracial marriage of an Anglo-Saxon bride and a dark-skinned groom.

By October 1871, when *Poor Miss Finch* began its serialization in *Cassell's Magazine,* Collins's interest in racial passing was already well established. In the epilogue to *The Moonstone* (1868), for example, Mr. Murthwaite, a British "expert" on India who is "lean enough and brown enough to make it no easy matter to detect [his] European origin," passes as "a Hindoo-Boodhist" in the region of Kattiawar and witnesses the restoration of the plundered Hindu diamond to its shrine.[5] As Murthwaite describes it, the return of the sacred Moonstone to its proper place underscores the criminal means by which the British first gained possession of the gem and associates their colonial possessions with stolen goods that ought to be restored to their rightful owners. At the same time, however, Murthwaite's infiltration of Hindu culture suggests Collins's ambivalence about Britain's empire building—his desire to defend as well as to criticize it. As Jaya Mehta and others note, Murthwaite functions as an undercover policeman of sorts, an agent of empire whose ability to cross racial boundaries seems to be an English prerogative.[6] Whereas Murthwaite successfully disguises his racial origins, the leader of the Brahmins who reclaim the Moonstone cannot. Indeed, his attempt to pass as a European in England is immediately detected by the solicitor Mathew Bruff. The "mysterious client" who consults him is "carefully dressed in European costume," Bruff explains: "But his swarthy complexion, his long lithe figure, and his grave and graceful politeness of manner were enough to betray his Oriental origin to any intelligent eyes that looked at him" (The Moonstone, 275).[7]

In Collins's melodrama Black and White, the implications of racial passing are more subversive than they are in The Moonstone, in part because the "native" hero in the play is the one who successfully performs this masquerade, although he does so unwittingly.[8] Written in collaboration with Charles Fechter, Black and White was first performed at London's Adelphi Theater in March 1869. Set on the island of Trinidad in 1830, four years before the slaves in the British West Indies were emancipated by an act of Parliament, the play centers on the misadventures of a French aristocrat, the Count de Layrac, who visits Trinidad and becomes engaged to Emily Milburn only to discover that he is the son of a slave woman and a white plantation owner, long since dead, and hence himself a slave. Warned by his dying mother that "the master who bought [him] can claim [him] again," de Layrac heroically refuses to deny his connection to the woman who bore him just as Miss Milburn heroically marries de Layrac although he is pronounced a slave, hoping to buy her husband at an auction.[9] Instead, de Layrac is privately purchased by his hateful rival, Stephen Westcraft; but he is ultimately liberated by the discovery of a paper of manumission signed by his dead father.

Creating a hero whose racial identity is repeatedly redefined over the course of three acts, and whose status as a slave or an aristocrat depends on his geographical location rather than his character or "nature," Collins uses Count de Layrac to suggest the arbitrary and shifting grounds of "whiteness" and "blackness," and to collapse the distance between them. He uses de Layrac's mother, the "quadroon" Ruth, to the same end; more "white" than "black," she is a slave nonetheless. At a time in which racial differences were often represented as absolute, and used by the British to justify their imperial rule over dark-skinned peoples, Collins blurs the distinction between "white" and "black" and reveals that racial boundaries are not fixed by human biology but change according to changing cultural definitions and economic needs. He develops much the same argument in *Poor Miss Finch*, although through different means—by literally changing the skin color of his hero.

Set in 1858–59, in the retired English village of Dimchurch, *Poor Miss Finch* is narrated by Madame Pratolungo, a Frenchwoman and widow of the "celebrated South American patriot," Doctor Pratolungo, whose dedication to the revolutionary cause led to the couple's exile and impoverishment.[10] Madame Pratolungo serves as companion to Lucilla Finch, a beautiful young Englishwoman blind since her first year, who lives with her father (the rector), her stepmother, and their many children, including Lucilla's half-sister "Jicks," known as "the wandering Arab of the family" (*Poor Miss Finch*, 129) because of her tendency to roam about the countryside. Lucilla soon falls in love with a stranger living in the village—a young English gentleman who assumes the name "Oscar Dubourg" after he is acquitted of a murder charge in Exeter. Oscar is acquitted through the detective efforts of his twin brother, Nugent, who proves that he could not have committed the crime. Within weeks, Oscar and Lucilla become engaged, but their marriage is postponed indefinitely after Oscar is badly beaten during a robbery and develops epilepsy as a result of his head injuries. Determined to cure his epilepsy and marry Lucilla, Oscar chooses to ingest silver nitrate, a treatment that ends his seizures, yet permanently turns his skin a dark blue. Only after this transformation does Oscar learn of Lucilla's irrational loathing of dark colors and dark-skinned peoples, a trait common to the blind, we are told.

Nugent Dubourg complicates matters when he returns to England from the United States, secretly falls in love with Lucilla, and arranges to have her examined by medical experts in the hope of restoring her vision. Oscar struggles to tell his fiancée of his darkened complexion but fails to do so, identifying Nugent rather than himself as the blue-skinned brother. When Lucilla's sight is restored by the German surgeon, Herr Grosse, she mistakes Nugent for Oscar, at whom she recoils, and the treacherous twin makes the most of Lucilla's error by assuming his brother's identity. Struck by her lack of feeling for the man she believes to be Oscar, a change that she attributes to her regained vision, Lucilla suffers a relapse into blindness yet is relieved to have lost her sight. By the time Madame Pratolungo exposes Nugent's plot and helps reunite Oscar and Lucilla, the sightless heroine has overcome her *real* blindness—her color prejudice—and come to value Oscar as she should, regardless of his dark hue.

Victorian reviewers of *Poor Miss Finch* failed to note the social implications of Oscar's changing skin color. Described in *The Athenaeum* as "a sensation novel for Sunday reading," the "proper" *Poor Miss Finch* was contrasted with the subversive *Armadale,* for example,[11] and Oscar's "blue face" dismissed as an incidental if startling plot device introduced solely "for the purpose . . . of confusion,"[12] and suggesting the pointlessness of Collins's novel. "For what is the aim of this story?" a reviewer in *The Nation* asked: "That the blind should marry the dark-blue? There is then an excellent opening for some novelist, distracted for a plot, to write about the love of the color-blind for the jaundiced."[13] In one of the few essays on *Poor Miss Finch* to be published in recent years, Catherine Peters argues for the novel's literary merit but, like the *Athenaeum* reviewer, sees it as a strikingly apolitical story. "In marked contrast to much of the work of his later years," she asserts, "*Poor Miss Finch* . . . is exceptionally free from calls for reform of the law or society."[14] Peters points out that Collins researched his medical subjects thoroughly, and she confirms that silver nitrate "was still being used in the 1850s as a treatment for epilepsy" despite "its serious and permanent effect on the skin colour of the patient." Yet she dismisses this effect as one of those "superficial absurdities" that are responsible for the critical neglect into which the novel has fallen.[15]

However, Oscar's dark blue skin color is neither an absurdity nor is it incidental to what Peters identifies as Collins's "central concerns" in *Poor Miss Finch:* the theme of vision and blindness.[16] Rather than serving as an improbable plot device, Oscar's darkening hue is carefully connected to a racial subtext in which blindness and racism become indistinguishable. Once we recognize this subtext and its political implications, the ties between *Poor Miss Finch* and Collins's more pointedly "reformist" fiction become clear.

The action of the novel begins in 1858, at a time when the Victorians were preoccupied with race relations. This was the second year of the Indian Mutiny, in which Hindu and Muslim sepoys rebelled against and murdered their English officers, killing English women and children as well. Although Victorians often attributed the Mutiny to the allegedly "treacherous nature" of Orientals,[17] the origins of the revolt were political and economic, as both Karl Marx and Benjamin Disraeli argued; for all their political differences, Marx and Disraeli agreed that the rebels were reacting to oppressive colonial practices on the part of the British.[18] The rebellion was caused, most immediately, by the sepoys' belief that the Enfield rifle cartridges they had to bite before loading were greased with pig and cow fat—in effect, that the British were forcing them to commit sacrilege. Collins was familiar with such details about the Indian rebellion and its causes, having collaborated with Dickens on a story loosely based on the Mutiny and published as the Extra Christmas Number of *Household Words* in 1857 ("The Perils of Certain English Prisoners"), and having written an article on the subject for Dickens's periodical the following year, entitled "A Sermon for Sepoys."[19] As critics note, Collins's attitude toward the Indians was considerably more sympathetic than that of many contemporaries, Dickens in particular, who defined "low, treacherous, murderous, tigerous . . . Hindoos" against heroic Englishmen, and wished to "exterminate the [Oriental] Race from the face of the earth."[20] Their collaboration on "The Perils of Certain English Prisoners" is characterized by striking discrepancies in tone and subject matter, which point to their differing views on the Mutiny and its origins, on the problem of race relations in the colonies, and on the veracity of racial stereotypes.[21]

By 1858, when *Poor Miss Finch* opens, the British had largely regained control of India, and their brutal reprisals against the sepoys were gaining notoriety in the press. In January 1858, Sir Colin Campbell had marched to Lucknow and retaken the city, which was looted and reduced to ruins by British troops in March. In *Poor Miss Finch,* however, the only military campaign to which Collins refers is "the battle of Solferino," fought during the war of "France and Italy against Austria" in 1859 (*Poor Miss Finch,* 379–80). Sending Oscar to help nurse the Italian wounded in a hospital near Turin, Collins acknowledges their struggle against the Austrian empire, and clearly supports their desire for independence (386), but he fails to mention the contemporaneous struggle of the sepoys against the British. Nonetheless, his novel is full of references to British India, to its army officers, and to the Indians themselves, a number of whom fall victim to racial prejudice in England.

Of the many characters in Collins's novel, only one leaves England for India in the course of the story: the "Dimchurch doctor" who treats

Oscar with silver nitrate and who departs for the colony soon afterward, having "obtained an appointment . . . which offered great professional advantages to an ambitious man" (129). But one does not need to leave England to meet Indians, Lucilla quickly discovers. At a dinner party at the London home of her Aunt Batchford, she is introduced to "a Hindoo gentleman . . . to whom [her] aunt ha[d] taken a great fancy," and she describes her encounter with him in a letter to Oscar, recounting a scene in which Collins broaches the subject of race relations and the problem of racial prejudice:

> While the maid was dressing me, I unluckily inquired if
> she had seen the Hindoo—and, hearing that she had, I
> still more unfortunately asked her to tell me what he was
> like. She described him as being very tall and lean, with
> a dark brown complexion and glittering black eyes. My
> mischievous fancy instantly set to work on this horrid
> combination of darknesses. Try as I might to resist it,
> my mind drew a dreadful picture of the Hindoo, as a kind
> of monster in human form. I would have given worlds to
> have been excused from going down into the drawing-
> room. At the last moment I was sent for, and the Hindoo
> was introduced to me. The instant I felt him approaching,
> my darkness was peopled with brown demons. He took
> my hand. I tried hard to control myself—but I really
> could not help shuddering and starting back when he
> touched me. To make matters worse, he sat next to me
> at dinner. In five minutes I had long, lean, black-eyed
> beings all round me; perpetually growing in numbers,
> and pressing closer and closer on me as they grew. It
> ended in my being obliged to leave the table. When the
> guests were all gone, my aunt was furious. I admitted
> my conduct was unreasonable in the last degree. (118)

Ostensibly, Lucilla's "unreasonable" reaction to the Hindu gentleman, and the panic in which she peoples "[her] darkness" with a horde of "brown demons," are marks of her pathology as a blind person—symptoms of a diseased imagination. Her reaction to the dark-skinned Hindu resembles that of the "daughter of an Indian officer," a little girl "blind from infancy like Lucilla" (226). The girl's behavior is recalled by the eye specialist Mr. Sebright, who tells Oscar of her revulsion from the Indian nurse whom she sees for the first time. In a conversation with Madame Pratolungo, Oscar reviews the details of the case:

After operating successfully, the time came when [Mr. Sebright] could permit his patient to try her sight. . . . Among the members of the household assembled to witness the removal of the bandage, was an Indian nurse who had accompanied the family to England. The first person the child saw was her mother—a fair woman. She clasped her little hands in astonishment, and that was all. At the next turn of her head, she saw the dark Indian nurse—and instantly screamed with terror. Mr. Sebright owned to me that he could not explain it. The child could have no possible association with colours. Yet there nevertheless was the most violent hatred and horror of a dark object (the hatred and horror peculiar to the blind) expressing itself unmistakably in a child of ten years old! . . . My first question was, "Did the child get used to the nurse?" I can give you his answer in his own words. "In a week's time, I found the child sitting in the nurse's lap as composedly as I am sitting in this chair." (226)

What is most surprising about these two case histories is not that a young English girl and a young English woman would be terrified by their contact with Indians, for whom they express "the most violent hatred and horror," but that anyone in England could possibly be surprised at their reaction. Indeed, after 1857, such horrified responses to Indians were considered the *norm* rather than the exception, particularly on the part of Englishwomen, whose revulsions from Hindu and Muslim men were fueled by the rape narratives in which the political history of the Indian Mutiny was recast. As Nancy Paxton explains in her analysis of these narratives, the sexual lawlessness of lascivious Indian men eager to rape Englishwomen served as a central theme of Mutiny literature and "performed specific ideological work," justifying British rule in India while also reinforcing traditional images of female vulnerability and dependence.[22] Lucilla's response to the "Hindoo gentleman" in her aunt's home suggests that she has been reading these narratives, since her vision of "perpetually growing . . . numbers" of "brown demons . . . pressing closer and closer on [her]" is likely informed by a fear of interracial gang rape, a staple of Mutiny novels (118).

Rather than justifying the English heroine's sexual panic, as the writers of Mutiny fiction so often did, Collins expresses surprise at a reaction *expected* of Englishwomen in 1858, one commonly represented as "only natural." By identifying this reaction as "unreasonable in the last degree"—a "hatred and horror peculiar to the blind"—Collins effectively pathologizes the racist norm (118, 226). He develops this critique by charting the education of Lucilla, who learns to love a dark-skinned man, and by replacing the familiar Mutiny story of interracial rape with one that implicitly condones interracial marriage.

It might be objected that Oscar is not a "Hindoo gentleman" but a Caucasian one, his "blackish blue" skin (117) an unfortunate side effect of his medical treatment, not a sign of his racial difference. Yet Oscar relates the story of the Hindu gentleman to Madame Pratolungo because he feels that it has bearing on his own relationship to Lucilla, and Collins gives racial significance to Oscar's altered skin color. He does so, in part, through Madame Pratolungo's alarmed reaction to the first dark-blue man she sees—like Oscar, an epileptic cured by ingesting silver nitrate. Demonizing this unnamed European, "an object of horror" (110) in her eyes, Madame Pratolungo responds to him in a way that mirrors Lucilla's reaction to the "horrid" Hindu: a "brown demon" and a "monster in human form," in Lucilla's view (118). Describing her encounter with "the blue man in Paris" (109), Madame Pratolungo recalls her "involuntary act of rudeness" toward him: "The man's face, instead of exhibiting any of the usual shades of complexion, was hideously distinguished by a superhuman—I had almost said a devilish—colouring of livid blackish *blue!* He proved to be a most kind, intelligent, and serviceable person. But when we first confronted each other, his horrible colour so startled me, that I could not repress a cry of alarm" (105).

Originally "white," the Parisian speaks of himself as "discoloured" rather than colored, and tells Madame Pratolungo that his "people" (that is, the "discoloured") number in the "hundreds." Although a much less populous "race" than others governed by the British, and dispersed over "the various parts of the civilised world" (105), the "blackish *blue*" are linked to the Indian by means of yet another medical case—that of a "black-blue" English officer visiting Ramsgate with his family after retiring from the service in India.

On the beach with Nugent, whom she mistakenly believes to be Oscar, Lucilla observes "a lady . . . with two lovely children, and with a tall man at her side":

> My eyes, looking first at the lady and the children, found
> their way next to the gentleman—and saw repeated in his
> face, the same black-blue complexion which had startled
> me in the face of Oscar's [that is, Nugent's] brother, when
> I first opened my eyes at the rectory! For the moment I

felt startled again—more, as I believe, by the unexpected repetition of the blue face in the face of a stranger, than by the ugliness of the complexion itself. At any rate, I was composed enough to admire the lady's dress, and the beauty of the children, before they had passed beyond my range of view. (339–40)

Describing this "black-blue" gentleman as "a retired Indian officer" rather than as an Englishman retired from the Indian service (340), Collins purposely obscures his racial identity. The account of this character and his family that is provided by "a nice old lady" on the beach plays on this ambiguity; referring to the "blue face" of the Indian officer, the woman speaks of his marriage as if it were an interracial one. "It don't matter much, after all," she confides to Lucilla: "There he is, as you see, with a fine woman for a wife, and with two lovely children. I know the landlady of the house where they lodge—and a happier family you couldn't lay your hand on in all England" (340).

In conceiving of the "blackish blue" characters of *Poor Miss Finch*, Collins probably drew on Thomas Watson's *Lectures on the Principles and Practice of Physic,*[23] a medical text that describes the treatment of epilepsy with silver nitrate, with its "'disfiguring effect'" on the skin.[24] But Collins may also have drawn from a second source, a journal article identifying those who are "blackish blue" as the children of interracial marriages—the so-called "half-castes" of British India. Written by John Lang, and published in *Household Words* in 1856, shortly after Collins became one of Dickens's staff members, "Black and Blue" describes the marriage of a renegade English aristocrat, Francis Gay, and "a young Mahommedan girl," converted to Christianity before their wedding.[25] Their child, a black-skinned boy with "light blue eyes," is christened "Ernest Augustus George Francis Frederick Gay" after his English father and uncles, but called "Chandee" by his parents. Later, he is renamed "Black and Blue" by the abusive English officers he comes to serve ("Black and Blue," 278–79). After his father is murdered by robbers, Chandee forgets his Anglo-Saxon lineage, becoming a peddler in Delhi. But when the early deaths of his paternal uncles leave him the heir to an earl's estate and title, he follows the advice of an attorney and travels to England to claim his rights. Soon afterward, he disappears, apparently kidnapped or murdered by his English relations.

In "Black and Blue," Lang treats the "half-caste" with some sympathy, underscoring the moral hypocrisy of the English general who discourages Francis Gay from marrying a native woman while the general himself keeps Indian mistresses in his own house and criticizing the English officers who physically abuse Chandee when he comes to sell them his wares. Although these officers give Chandee his nickname after "the colour of his eyes and skin," "Black and Blue" also refers to the bruises they inflict on him. As Chandee himself reminds his English customers when they knock off his turban and burn him with their cigars, "God make us all—black and white; all equal right up above" (277, 279). In spite of the equality of the races in the eyes of God, however, Lang clearly intends his article as a warning against interracial unions, which deprive the sons of Englishmen of their place in the "civilized" world. When he chooses to, Francis Gay can assimilate into Indian culture, passing as the Muslim trader "Mustapha Khan" (278), yet his half-caste son cannot pass as an Englishman; in "Black and Blue," as in *The Moonstone*, passing is the white man's prerogative: "In his snow-white muslin dress, his pink turban, and his red slippers covered with gold embroidery, Black and Blue had looked an aristocratic native, notwithstanding he was so very black. . . . But, in his black trowsers, black waistcoat, black surtout coat, white neckcloth, black beaver hat, and Wellington boots, poor Black and Blue looked truly hideous" (282).

Ernest Gay/Chandee is defined as Other by his skin color, whatever his class identity, and "no . . . European girl of respectability . . . [would] have wedded the black heir to the title and estates of the Earl of Millflower," Lang assures us: "Not in India could his sable lordship have found a virtuous white woman to accept his hand!" (281). A white aristocrat of dubious morals may marry an Indian woman, Lang suggests, but no respectable and virtuous "white woman" will marry a "sable lordship."

In *Poor Miss Finch*, Lucilla sets such rules at defiance, at least implicitly, marrying a "blackish blue" gentleman who fears that the woman he loves "is a woman forbidden to [him]" (*Poor Miss Finch*, 111). Despite her own union with a man of "brown complexion" (2), Madame Pratolungo feels a "shock" when she sees "the two faces [of Lucilla and Oscar] together . . . her fair cheek laid innocently against the livid blackish blue of *his* discoloured skin" (121). Braving such reactions, Lucilla embraces a blindness that differs from her first: an ability to disregard appearances and "see . . . [Oscar] as [he] really [is]" (225), whatever his skin color.

"*Never look at a white woman—look down or the other way. What do you mean, calling a white woman 'darling' like that, boy?*" (*Black Like Me*, 72). Repeating the lesson taught to the "black" man in a racist culture, as well as the accusation leveled at those who fail to accept it, John Howard Griffin describes his own inability to write to his "white" wife during his tenure as a "black" man:

> I tried to write my wife—I needed to write to her, to give her my news—but I found I could tell her nothing. No words would come. She had nothing to do with this life, nothing to do with the room in Hattiesburg or with its Negro inhabitant. It was maddening. . . . My conditioning as a Negro, and the immense sexual implications with which the racists in our culture bombard us, cut me off, even in my most intimate self, from any connection with my wife.
>
> I stared at the letter and saw written: *Hattiesburg, November 14. My darling,* followed by a blank page.
>
> The visual barrier imposed itself. The observing self saw the Negro . . . write "Darling" to a white woman. The chains of my blackness would not allow me to go on. (71–72)

As Kate Baldwin points out in her critique of *Black Like Me,* in this scene Griffin is "chained" by his "whiteness"—by his "conditioning . . . as a Southern gentleman"—rather than by his presumed "blackness," as he claims. "Griffin cannot bear the thought of a black man contacting his white wife," Baldwin argues: "Thus, despite his intentions to break the color barrier, Griffin finds himself—a white Southerner—policing that very line he presumably set out to sever."[26] In Baldwin's view, Griffin performs such acts of "policing" throughout *Black Like Me* as he reinforces the racial categories he seeks to question. Because Griffin begins and ends his book with accounts of his "real" life and identity, Baldwin notes, "his 'whiteness' always persists in framing his blackness," and his "passing produces a continual 'error' of identity that the reader . . . is always intended to register," shoring up our sense of "the necessary difference between white and black."[27] While Griffin describes skin color as superficial and insignificant, his project promotes a racial double standard in which whiteness seems "invisible" and "transparent," and only blackness can be "discerned visually."[28] To Wald, similarly, Griffin seems aware of "the theatricality of his own racial identity," yet "posits the liberal white male researcher 'passing' as a universal, neutral subject."[29]

Like Griffin, Collins qualifies what seems most radical about his narrative by reinscribing prevailing assumptions about racial difference.

In his more subversive moments, Collins questions the universal "standard" of whiteness and, by implication, the attribution of certain moral qualities to specific shades of skin, anticipating Mr. Fielding's "scandalous" remark in *A Passage to India* "that the so-called white races are really pinko-grey."[30] Like Forster, Collins reminds us that his Caucasian characters are in no sense actually "white"; rather, their hue is continually shifting. Lucilla's "colour change[s] from pale to red—from red to pale" (*Poor Miss Finch,* 182), just as Nugent repeatedly "change[s] colour" (330, 343, 348). In such passages, whiteness appears no more fixed or absolute than blackness. Yet the logic of Collins's analogy between the "blackish blue" and the South Asian—between "discoloured" whites and Indians—also identifies racial difference as a "disfigurement" (105), an unfortunate if necessary deviation from the healthy white norm. Furthermore, Collins's displaced representation of interracial marriage, which he figures as the union of a white bride and a "discoloured" groom, allows him to sidestep the volatile issue raised in Lang's "Black and Blue"—the consequences of what was termed miscegenation. Although Lucilla and Oscar have children, their sons and daughter are not racially mixed like Chandee but "rosy-face[d]" as well as "blue-eye[d]" (426), and their position in English society is thus assured.

Since the early 1980s, some critics have questioned Collins's reputation as a Victorian radical, pointing to the "strategies of indirection" that characterize his social criticism as well as his tendency to "contain" or qualify the more subversive elements of his fiction.[31] His displaced approach to the subject of race relations in *Poor Miss Finch* lends force to such readings. In assessing Collins's reticence as a social critic, however, we also need to consider the conservative bent of his publishers and readers, and the realities of what would and would not be printed in a magazine like *Cassell's,* renamed *Cassell's Family Magazine* after 1874. Writing in the decades following the Indian Mutiny, Collins may well have felt that the members of his audience would only read a novel "about" interracial marriage if the subject were conveyed subtextually, or by means of a comic subplot far removed from England's shores. Thus Madame Pratolungo brings Collins's novel to its close by voicing her amusement at the latest news from the Finch family, now living in a "distant colon[y]," with Lucilla's transgressive half sister making explicit what Lucilla's own story only *suggests:* that marriage with a "native" is possible for a white Englishwoman: "On my table is a letter from Mrs. Finch, dated from one of our distant colonies—over which Mr. Finch (who has risen gloriously in the world) presides pastorally as bishop. . . . 'Jicks' is in her element among the aboriginal members of her father's congregation: there are fears that the wandering Arab of the Finch family will end in marrying 'a chief'" (426).

Defining "Jicks" against Lucilla, and dividing his story into text and subtext, Collins produces a novel that can pass as "proper"—"a sensation novel for Sunday reading," as the *Athenaeum* reviewer puts it.[32] Yet in so doing, Collins himself reminds us of the compromises required of reformers who pass as Other, and not only subvert but reinforce the social status quo.

Notes

1. John Howard Griffin, *Black Like Me* (2d ed. Boston: Houghton Mifflin, 1977), 179. Hereafter cited in the text as *Black Like Me*. The epigraph is from Griffin's epilogue.

2. Review of *Man in the Mirror: John Howard Griffin and the Story of Black Like Me,* by Robert Bonazzi, *Kirkus Reviews* 65 (1 Aug. 1997): 1172.

3. Gayle Wald, "'A Most Disagreeable Mirror': Reflections on White Identity in *Black Like Me*," in *Passing and the Fictions of Identity,* ed. Elaine K. Ginsberg (Durham: Duke Univ. Press, 1996), 154. Placing Griffin's book in the context of the Cold War, and considering the ways in which it meets the political needs of American nationalism in the late 1950s and early 1960s, Kate Baldwin develops a similar argument about Griffin's book in "Black Like Who? Cross-Testing the 'Real' Lines of John Howard Griffin's *Black Like Me*," *Cultural Critique* 40 (fall 1998): 103–43. Eric Lott considers the importance of "imaginary racial transformation" to the idea of white American manhood, which depends on and "internalizes" racist fantasies about sexualized black men ("White Like Me: Racial Cross-Dressing and the Construction of American Whiteness," in *Cultures of United States Imperialism,* ed. Amy Kaplan and Donald E. Pease [Durham: Duke Univ. Press, 1993]). Lott argues that Griffin criticizes the uses to which whites put conceptions of blackness while remaining "complicitous with the racial designs [his book] sets out to expose" (476, 485). For a more appreciative discussion of Griffin and his racial experiment, see Robert Bonazzi, *Man in the Mirror: John Howard Griffin and the Story of Black Like Me* (Maryknoll, N.Y.: Orbis Books, 1997).

4. Wald, 155.

5. Wilkie Collins, *The Moonstone,* ed. John Sutherland (Oxford: Oxford Univ. Press, 1999), 464. Hereafter cited in the text as *The Moonstone*.

6. Jaya Mehta, "English Romance: Indian Violence," *The Centennial Review* 39 (1995): 611–57.

7. Mehta discusses this "racial asymmetry" and argues that Murthwaite is "part of an imperial literary and historical tradition of secret agents in

native disguise that leads eventually to figures such as Kipling's Kim and Lawrence of Arabia. It is part of this colonialist tradition that whereas the Englishman can easily 'pass' as a native among natives, no Indian can 'pass' amongst Englishmen." With his "virtuosity" in passing, Mehta asserts, Murthwaite can make the "minute ethnological observation[s] so integral to British science and surveillance" (638). As Wald notes in discussing Griffin's experiment with passing, "white people (especially white men) traditionally have enjoyed a greater liberty than others to play with racial identities and to do so in safety, without permanent loss or costs," acting under the assumption that, whereas whiteness is "universal and invisible . . . black identity . . . can be put on or taken off at will" (162–63).

8. As Baldwin observes, however, the ability of a "native" to pass as white is not necessarily subversive: "While purportedly disrupting the hegemony of whiteness through infiltration, blackness in its lightest form, its passing form, served to support the very racial boundaries it sought to sever" (109).

9. Wilkie Collins and Charles Fechter, *Black and White: A Drama, in Three Acts* (London: C. Whiting, 1869), 24, 41.

10. Wilkie Collins, *Poor Miss Finch,* ed. Catherine Peters (Oxford: Oxford Univ. Press, 1995), 1. Hereafter cited in the text as *Poor Miss Finch.*

11. [D. E. Williams], *The Athenaeum* (17 Feb. 1872): 202–3. Rpt. in *Wilkie Collins: The Critical Heritage,* ed. Norman Page (London and Boston: Routledge and Kegan Paul, 1974), 191–95.

12. *Canadian Monthly and National Review* 1 (May 1872): 477–79. Rpt. in Page, 200.

13. *The Nation* 14 (7 Mar. 1872): 158–59. Rpt. in Page, 198–99.

14. Catherine Peters, introduction to *Poor Miss Finch,* vii.

15. Peters, xii, xvi.

16. Ibid., xvi.

17. Patrick Brantlinger discusses this racist "explanation" in his chapter on the literary works generated by the Mutiny, noting that "treachery serves as a reductive synecdoche for the entire rebellion" in many British accounts, "one that is its own instant explanation, transforming politics into crime and widespread social forces into questions of race and personality" (*Rule of Darkness: British Literature and Imperialism, 1830– 1914* [Ithaca: Cornell Univ. Press, 1988], 203).

18. Ibid., 202.

19. *Household Words* 17 (27 Feb. 1858): 244–47.

20. Charles Dickens to Emile de la Rue, 23 Oct. 1857, *The Letters of Charles Dickens,* Pilgrim Edition, vol. 8, ed. Graham Storey and Kathleen Tillotson (Oxford: Clarendon Press, 1995), 473. For a discussion of

Collins's attitudes toward empire, see my review of recent criticism devoted to the subject ("Wilkie Collins Studies: 1983–1999," *Dickens Studies Annual* 28 [1999]: 257–329).

21. For a discussion of the counterpoint between Dickens and Collins in "The Perils of Certain English Prisoners," see Lillian Nayder, *Unequal Partners: Charles Dickens, Wilkie Collins, and Victorian Authorship* (Ithaca: Cornell Univ. Press, 2002), 115–280.

22. Nancy L. Paxton, "Mobilizing Chivalry: Rape in British Novels About the Indian Uprising of 1857," *Victorian Studies* 36, no. 1 (fall 1992): 6.

23. Fourth ed. (London: J. W. Parker and Son, 1857), 659–60.

24. Qtd. in Peters, xii.

25. [John Lang], "Black and Blue," *Household Words* 14 (4 Oct. 1856): 277. Hereafter cited in the text as "Black and Blue."

26. Baldwin, 127–28.

27. Ibid., 114.

28. Ibid., 119.

29. Wald, 153, 156. Wald also considers the ways in which Griffin examines and confronts "his own whiteness" (165) and argues that he abandons his essentialist notions of white and black over the course of his "experiment."

30. E. M. Forster, *A Passage to India* (1924; New York: Harcourt Brace Jovanovich, 1984), 65.

31. Richard Barickman, Susan MacDonald, and Myra Stark, *Corrupt Relations: Dickens, Thackeray, Trollope, Collins, and the Victorian Sexual System* (New York: Columbia Univ. Press, 1982), 112; Tamar Heller, *Dead Secrets: Wilkie Collins and the Female Gothic* (New Haven: Yale Univ. Press, 1992), 8.

32. *The Athenaeum* (17 Feb. 1872). Qtd. in Page, 191.

References

Baldwin, Kate. "Black Like Who? Cross-Testing the 'Real' Lines of John Howard Griffin's *Black Like Me*." *Cultural Critique* 40 (fall 1998): 103–43.

Barickman, Richard, Susan MacDonald, and Myra Stark. *Corrupt Relations: Dickens, Thackeray, Trollope, Collins, and the Victorian Sexual System*. New York: Columbia Univ. Press, 1982.

Bonazzi, Robert. *The Man in the Mirror: John Howard Griffin and the Story of Black Like Me*. Maryknoll, N.Y.: Orbis Books, 1997.

Brantlinger, Patrick. *Rule of Darkness: British Literature and Imperialism, 1830–1914*. Ithaca: Cornell Univ. Press, 1988.

Collins, Wilkie. *The Moonstone*. Ed. John Sutherland. Oxford: Oxford Univ. Press, 1999.

———. *Poor Miss Finch*. Ed. Catherine Peters. Oxford: Oxford Univ. Press, 1995.

Collins, Wilkie, and Charles Fechter. *Black and White: A Drama, in Three Acts*. London: C. Whiting, 1869.

Dickens, Charles. *The Letters of Charles Dickens*. Vol. 8. Ed. Graham Story and Kathleen Tillotson. Oxford: Clarendon Press, 1995.

Forster, E. M. *A Passage to India*. 1924. New York: Harcourt Brace Jovanovich, 1984.

Griffin, John Howard. *Black Like Me*. 2d ed. Boston: Houghton Mifflin, 1977.

Heller, Tamar. *Dead Secrets: Wilkie Collins and the Female Gothic*. New Haven: Yale Univ. Press, 1992.

[Lang, John]. "Black and Blue." *Household Words* 14 (4 Oct. 1856): 276–82.

Lott, Eric. "White Like Me: Racial Cross-Dressing and the Construction of American Whiteness." In *Cultures of United States Imperialism*, ed. Amy Kaplan and Donald E. Pease, 474–95. Durham: Duke Univ. Press, 1993.

Mehta, Jaya. "English Romance; Indian Violence." *The Centennial Review* 39, no. 4 (fall 1995): 611–57.

Nayder, Lillian. *Unequal Partners: Charles Dickens, Wilkie Collins, and Victorian Authorship*. Ithaca: Cornell Univ. Press, 2002.

———. "Wilkie Collins Studies: 1983–1999." *Dickens Studies Annual* 28 (1999): 257–329.

Page, Norman. *Wilkie Collins: The Critical Heritage*. London and Boston: Routledge and Kegan Paul, 1974.

Paxton, Nancy L. "Mobilizing Chivalry: Rape in British Novels About the Indian Uprising of 1857." *Victorian Studies* 35, no. 1 (fall 1992): 5–30.

Review of *Man in the Mirror: John Howard Griffin and the Story of Black Like Me*, by Robert Bonazzi. *Kirkus Reviews* 65 (1 Aug. 1997): 1172.

Wald, Gayle, "'A Most Disagreeable Mirror': Reflections on White Identity in *Black Like Me*." In *Passing and the Fictions of Identity*, ed. Elaine K. Ginsberg, 151–77. Durham: Duke Univ. Press, 1996.

Plain Faces, Weird Cases

Domesticating the Law in Collins's *The Law and the Lady* and the Trial of Madeleine Smith

Karin Jacobson

N 1857, MADELEINE SMITH, AGED TWENTY-ONE, WAS ACCUSED OF POISONING, WITH ARSENIC, PIERRE EMILE L'ANGELIER, A SHIPping clerk who turned out to have been not only her secret fiancé but also her lover. One of the most infamous trials of the Victorian period, Madeleine Smith's story, as Richard Altick claims, "has everything: sex, a setting in well-to-do Scottish society, abundant echoes of contemporary conventions and prejudices, and, not least, more reverberations among high literary folk of the Victorian era than were called forth by any other immediately contemporary murder."[1] One of the "high literary folk" who capitalized on Smith's notoriety was Wilkie Collins in his novel *The Law and the Lady* (1875).[2] Based loosely on the trial,[3] Collins's story charts the history of Eustace Macallan, accused of the arsenic poisoning of his first wife, Sara Macallan, and vindicated by the sleuthing of his second wife, Valeria

Woodville/Macallan; in fact, the story can only be recovered by recourse to "the lady," who uncovers the evidence missed by the legal authorities. In both the Smith case and Collins's text, the defense counsel argues that the arsenic was purchased in order to improve a bad complexion. Both trials end with the uniquely Scottish verdict of "not proven," leaving the defendants, Madeleine Smith and Eustace Macallan, legally free but morally condemned. Dougald MacEachen, elucidating the similarities between the Smith trial and Collins's novel, writes that the "not proven" verdict was suggested by the trial but then concludes that there are "no close parallels between this historical case and Collins's fictional one except that in both cases the victim dies from arsenic that has been bought ostensibly for cosmetic purposes."[4] But the "not proven" verdict carries more significance than MacEachen suggests.

Henry James, whose family had avidly followed the Smith trial, writes: "I can still see the queer look of the 'not proven,' seen for the first time, on the printed page of the newspaper."[5] The "queerness" noted by James indicates not only the unfamiliarity of this Scottish verdict to an American or English audience but also further announces the improbability or the "weirdness" of both cases, a factor which links them more firmly than MacEachen suggests. Specifically, the "not proven" verdict introduces an element of "queerness" into the supposedly unambiguous realm of the law, a "queerness" associated with women. Justice does not prevail, as the defendant is left in a morally ambiguous position—neither hanged nor vindicated. In her discussion of canonicity in law and literature, Susan Sage Heinzelman elucidates the differences among "hard," "easy," and "weird" cases.[6] While in "easy" cases, the language of the law "speaks for itself," in "hard" cases the judge must "actively interpret the language of the relevant rule, statute or legal opinion in order to resolve the conflict."[7] Through the system of precedent, "hard" cases act as fathers to future legal conflicts, providing an established and recognized guide by which "hard" legal language becomes "easy," that is, unambiguous, clear. Existing beyond the recognized language of the law, "weird" cases are so wildly counterfactual that "even the clearest language breaks down," leaving them with no predictive or normative value and nothing to say. In order to become "hard," the weirdness must be extricated from these cases; that is, they must be "domesticated" so that they can set a precedent and father future laws. Ironically, to be good fathers, "weird" cases require a good mother.[8]

Valeria Woodville/Macallan is such a good mother in *The Law and the Lady*, ferreting out information denied to the legitimate authorities. By becoming a good mother, Valeria attempts—though she does not suc-ceed—to mediate the excess and control the passion that constitutes the "weirdness" of both trials: Madeleine's letters to L'Angelier provide evidence of an excessive desire, and both Sara Macallan and her suc-cessor, Valeria, contract extravagant attachments to Eustace Macallan. Valeria also uncovers the sexual secrets hidden by the veneer of middle-class respectability and thus discovers that the domestic itself is inex-tricable from the "weird." Heinzelman wonders if "domestication" negates "that which cannot be canonized,"[9] rather than creating a space for the weird within the canon of "hard" cases. While the novel's happy ending apparently supports Heinzelman's theory, I argue that Sara's suicide letter is never disciplined, never incorporated into the letter of the law. Remaining as a keepsake for the Macallan's first-born son, Sara's letter memorializes the law's failure to fathom women's stories and functions as a reminder of the excessive passions that ren-der the domestic itself uncanny. In the second section of this essay, I consider the relationship of ladies and law: how were women legally represented? How does Valeria interact with the legal authorities to uncover Sara's secret? Finally, I analyze the relationship of masquerade and the uncanny. Like Collins's novel, Freud's discussion of the uncanny reminds us that the domestic, the seemingly secure and comfortable, necessarily contains uncomfortable, uncanny elements. Just as Freud wanders the dangerous routes of the unconscious to complete his the-ories of human behavior, Valeria investigates uncannily "devious paths"[10]—rather than the "straight path of the law," advocated by Macallan's legal counsel during his first trial—to find the truth about Sara Macallan's death. Not only must Valeria venture into London's odd suburbs to interrogate Misserimus Dexter, but she must also assume multiple identities to elicit evidence from suspicious witnesses. In the course of her investigations, Valeria becomes identified with the mur-dered woman, with the masquerading Dexter, and with her own pseu-donym, Mrs. Woodville, identifications that differentiate her from the model of the detached detective. Both the Smith trial and *The Law and the Lady* suggest that woman's sexuality is not easily translated into recognizable legal discourse and, in particular, that the law's attempts to exclude weirdness only emphasize its own participation in the spec-tacular. In the course of both investigations, the law becomes entwined with the sensational narratives it seeks to make "plain," breaking the boundaries between legal and emotional discourses, between law and ladies, between the plain and the ornamental, and, finally, between the domestic and the uncanny.

Law, Letters, Hysteria

The trial of Madeleine Smith provides a useful companion text to the novel, elucidating Valeria's position in relation to the law, showing the use of women's textual productions and self-presentations within the courtroom, and also foregrounding the "uneven"[11] ideological position of female sexuality within Victorian representations of women. In both the Smith case and Collins's text, the relationship of law and women hinges on the difficulty of letters—hidden or missing in some cases, in others, too apparent. The most damning evidence against Madeleine Smith was self-produced: letters she wrote to L'Angelier. Indeed, the entire course of their affair can be traced through hundreds of letters, generally signed, "thy ever-loving and ever-devoted Mimi, thine own wife."[12] Recognizing that she had "put on paper what I should not," Madeleine Smith requested that L'Angelier return her letters. He refused. Instead, he threatened to blackmail her by revealing the illicit words to Madeleine's father. When L'Angelier died suddenly, hundreds of her letters were found in his bedchamber and office, making her what she most dreaded, "the public scandal."[13] In *Famous Trials of the Century* (1899), J. B. Atlay reports that the reading of Madeleine's letters in court was the only moment in which she lost her composure: "when her terrible letters were being read she covered her face with her hands."[14] Madeleine's response suggests the reciprocity between women's bodies and women's writing: the words evoke a visceral response—Madeleine's body becomes legible when her letters are read. Although they do not leave a scar to mark Madeleine's difference, the words still have a physical impact—they leave an emotional trace on her body, and in doing so they reveal a truth about women's desire that should have remained hidden. Jane Carlyle, writing of the case, applauds Miss Smith for "giving the death-stroke to testimonials."[15] Her comment suggests that the emotions documented by Madeleine were more common than we might have thought, while also hinting at the problematic bodily uncontrollability invoked by "testimonial" writings.

The following passage, taken from one of Madeleine's letters, suggests that women's writing introduced an unwelcome, even incongruous, element into the Victorian courtroom: an image of woman's desire: "It was a punishment to myself to be deprived of your *loving me,* for it is a pleasure, no one can deny that. It is but human nature.

Is not every one that *loves* of the same mind? Yes, I did feel so ashamed after you left of having allowed you to see (any name you please to insert)."[16] While Madeleine explains woman's desire as "human nature," the legal system refuses to recognize her emotions as natural. One judge, commenting on Madeleine's "licentious" letters declared that this passage, in particular, was written "in terms which I will not read, for perhaps they were never previously committed to paper as having passed between a man and a woman." Later, this same judge wrote, "Certainly such a sentence was probably never before penned by a female to a man."[17] Not only is Madeleine on trial for the murder of her lover, she also stands accused of bringing "weirdness" into the courtroom, bringing what has not been written between men and women into the written language, a new mode of discourse which Freud calls *un chat un chat*.[18] While Freud obscures his sexual discussions with French phrases, simultaneously revealing and concealing feminine desire, Madeleine's sexual/bodily language is partially hidden under a mask of euphemism—for "menstruation," she writes that she was "ill"; for "intercourse," she substitutes the underlined word "love."[19] Still, her language is considered too suggestive for the Victorian courtroom in that it would allow women's bodies to enter the reasonable realm of legal decision-making. Madeleine's love letters break down the barriers between the respectable lady and the painted lady, as well as the boundary between male and female sexuality: enjoying sex, Madeleine argues, is "but human nature," and "everyone" that loves is "of the same mind."[20]

The judge does not object to sexual relations between men and women; he is incensed, though, that Madeleine has "committed" such intercourse to paper. His fear suggests that Madeleine's language, which linguistically covers the underlying organ, is a recognizable language for the female audience. Ironically, by disallowing Madeleine's most sexually suggestive letters as evidence, the judge unintentionally allows sexual intercourse and the specter of women's genital organs to enter the courtroom under the veil of silence—the judge's concealment creates a cleft; in the gaps produced by Madeleine's missing correspondence, the imaginative audience member could substitute her own fantasies. Much of the perceived danger of the Smith case hinged on the belief that a female audience was too capable and willing to fill in those gaps.

Commenting on the trial, *The Glasgow Sentinel,* for example, argues that Madeleine was "as much the seducer as the seduced. And when once the veil of modesty was thrown aside, from the first a very frail and flimsy one, the woman of strong passion and libidinous tendencies at once reveals herself."[21] Madeleine's explicit expression of her illicit passion will unveil the sexuality barely concealed under the makeshift garment of Victorian modesty. The press accuses the crowd of thousands, mostly women, of having "dishonoured their sex" by "eagerly drinking in that filthy correspondence."[22] Producing an intoxication ("eagerly drinking") into the supposedly rational boundaries of the courtroom, Madeleine's letters endanger the female spectators of the trial. Words and body intertwine; language elicits a physical reaction that rends legal discourse. Making apparent the spectacular origins of law, a narrative pleasure from which the law cannot separate itself,[23] Madeleine's letters reportedly produce an "overwhelming excitement"[24] in the courtroom, parallel to that which her body produces in L'Angelier. Her letters introduce an intoxication, a *jouissance,* which the court dismisses as evidence. Freud, too, tries to clothe female sexuality in scientific metaphors, but instead unveils it with his jarring use of French, divulging the irrational language of desire that underwrites both psychoanalytic and legal discourse.[25] The Madeline Smith trial makes evident the "weirdness" that underlies even the hardest cases. In attempting to erase the specter of sexuality from the courtroom, arguing that it cannot become part of legal discourse, the question of sex, ironically, becomes the most potent question in the case.

Uncovering the truth of a woman's story, writing a desire that has never been written, Madeleine Smith's trial begins to embody the gap that has traditionally constituted women's sexuality. Sara Macallan's missing letter to Eustace, the mystery around which *The Law and the Lady* turns, creates a parallel link between women's writing and sexuality. While Madeleine's letters are simultaneously visible and hidden, Sara Macallan's letter is invisible until the end of the novel. Recognizing that the note reveals his double guilt in betraying both Eustace and Sara—in showing Eustace's diary to Sara and thus leading Sara to suicide—Dexter shreds the letter and tosses the fragments into a gluey wastepaper basket from which they are thrown into a dust-heap. Although Sara had intended her letter to be read publicly in order to vindicate Eustace of her death, the letter remains dangerously private. Even after it has been recovered, the letter is never fully reconstructed.

Valeria's discovery of the existence of this letter, revealed through Dexter's madness and his cousin Ariel's insistence on a story, provides insight into the problematic relationship between women and narrative. A woman's writing is buried deep within a rousing tale that viscerally affects both author and audience. When Valeria arrives at Dexter's house to discover the extent of his knowledge about Sara Macallan's death, she hopes to learn "just the facts," declaring, "We don't want the story" (*The Law and the Lady*, 335). Dexter's companion and cousin, Ariel, on the other hand, advocates a more roundabout and, paradoxically, more effective route to the truth: a story, "Puzzle my thick head. Make my flesh creep. Come on. A good long story. All blood and crimes." Dexter is intrigued with Ariel's demand for narrative— "You don't understand a word of my stories, do you?"—"And yet I can make the flesh creep on your great clumsy body" (332). Ariel's requirements are not for intellectual truth, not for a rational interpretation, but rather for an emotional response to the tale. The stories told in the courtroom are expected to be related dispassionately and then subjected to endless, rational, repetitive interpretations in order to uncover "hard" meanings. Ariel, however, demands the "weird and fanciful" bodily pleasures provided when, in the words of Heinzelman, "the clearest language breaks down,"[26] leaving a residual bliss created by the pure sound of the words, "nothing but the repetition, the endless mechanical repetition" (336). But Ariel's demands also show the imbrication of fact and flesh—"facts" have an emotional component. Necessarily, the audience at Madeleine's trial, like Ariel, is intoxicated by the tale. Drunk on words, and on Dexter's "kingly Burgundy," Royal Clos Vougeot, Ariel embodies the sound of the words: "Look at Ariel! Her flesh creeps; she shudders audibly" (336, 338). Although her repetitive demand reveals the dangerously visceral effect of narrative on the female audience, it equally makes visible the location of Sara's secret letter—hidden in a wayward narrative, "stolen" by a man whose storytelling ability allows him to compete with the legal authorities.[27] So the legalistic attempt to separate the visceral and rational realms cannot be satisfied because it creates a false dichotomy. The novel emphasizes the narrative, spectacular origins of the law; because the law refuses its origins, ignores or never attempts to uncover this viscerally affecting story, the legal authorities are unable to discover Sara's missing letter. Similarly, the judges' refusal to admit many of Madeleine's letters as evidence restricts their ability to discover the truth in her case. Again, the law's attempts to distance itself from its own sensational origins signals the limits of its own access to truth. Both trial and novel show the institutionally imposed boundaries on legal "truth," which is formed in a particular socially constructed space and is, therefore, shaped and restricted by the contours of that space. As the Madeleine Smith trial indicates, nineteenth-century judges erased the evidence of female sexuality from their courtrooms, thereby eliminating the possibility of constructing Smith as a sexually motivated subject, and, consequently, of convicting her in L'Angelier's murder.

Rejecting the limitations of legal truth, Valeria digs below the meaning constructed by the courts, ferrets out the evidence missed by the authorities, and determines—viscerally and rationally—the adequacy of the evidence she uncovers. She is passionate enough to recognize Dexter as the source of truth and reasonable enough to interpret correctly his enigmatic message, labeled incorrectly by Benjamin, Valeria's elderly male Watson, as "jibberish." Like Benjamin, Valeria initially questions the value of narrative as a mode to legal truth but eventually becomes "as eager as Ariel to hear the story," because "Dexter's memory of the true events might show itself reflected in the circumstances of the fiction" (337). Ariel listens for pure sensual satisfaction, Valeria for the "snares," for meaning. Thus, Valeria's relation to narrative combines pleasure with profit; like Ariel, she is "excited" by the tale; like a good lawyer, she notices the gaps in the sensational narrative. Valeria reads fiction for "truth"—emotional and factual truth—in order to uncover Sara's letter and vindicate Eustace. Invoking Ann Cvetkovich's language, I claim this female detective must utilize her emotional responses in order to forge familial bonds, while diffusing any excessive displays of emotion that might rend those same bonds. Cvetkovich theorizes emotion's contradictory role—a source of social stability and instability—in Victorian society:

> A discourse about affect represented marriage and the
> family as the product of natural affective bonds and
> individual self-expression. The construction of affect
> as natural, however, also meant that it might be uncon-
> trollable. . . . This contradiction is embodied in the figure
> of the middle-class woman, whose capacity for emotional
> expression at once exemplifies the domestic ideal and
> represents the threat of transgression.[28]

Cvetkovich argues that emotional or affective ties are necessary to forge strong familial bonds, yet emotion has the potential to become excessive, hysterical. Woman, traditionally associated with emotion, brings strong emotion into the family and, therefore becomes the source of a possible hysterical contagion. How can domestic emotional levels be kept within a reasonable range? In texts such as Collins's it becomes the role of the female domestic detective (Valeria) to contain excessive emotion and reestablish the family within acceptable emotional boundaries.

Extending Cvetkovich's argument, I would suggest the discourse of affect also influenced representations of law. In *The Law and the Lady* truth cannot be found without recourse to Dexter's "morbid sensibilities," to his emotional excess; while the law distances itself from the sensational crimes it investigates, tries, and convicts, the novel emphasizes that this separation limits the law's effectiveness. Only by placing herself in a vulnerable position—as the occasional double of both Sara and Dexter—does Valeria uncover the story secreted under the official narrative. In order to uncover the "truth" in the Smith trial and the Macallan case, the law must investigate the sexual excess of both Smith and Sara Macallan—by refusing to acknowledge Smith's sexually explicit letters and by neglecting to recognize Sara's abusive marriage, however, the law will be a second-rate source of truth.

Both trials imply that passions born in the drawing room threatened to escape into the courtroom. Confirming that Sara was found hidden before their marriage in Eustace's bedchamber "by some bachelor friends who came to visit him," Lady Brydehaven's testimony "produced a strong sensation among the audience, and had a marked effect on the minds of the Jury" (154–55). Following Lady Brydehaven's testimony, Sara Macallan's letters were read aloud in court, causing Eustace to lose "all control over his feelings. In piercing tones which rang through the Court, he protested against the contemplated violation of his own most sacred secrets and his wife's most sacred secrets" (156). While the unveiling of Madeleine's secret correspondence produced an excessive emotional response only in the female members of the audience, the revelation of Sara's secrets results in a more widespread infection—the reading of her letters produces an overwhelming physical excitement in Eustace, an excitement which her body could never produce. Eustace's "want of composure" is counted as evidence in his favor: "Self-possession, in his dreadful position, signified to their minds, the stark insensibility of a heartless and shameless criminal, and afforded in itself a presumption—not of innocence—but of guilt" (127). The specter of Sara's writing allows Eustace to atone for his earlier, "unnatural," lack of passion for her and prevents his "dreadful position"—as a man who was not excited by his wife's body—from being revealed in the courtroom. His current excitement allows him to cover the evidence of his earlier apathy.

While Eustace's lack of self-control counts in his favor, Madeleine Smith's complete self-composure saves her. A *Spectator* reporter noted her "perfect self-possession," her "fashionable" clothes, and her "most attractive appearance,"[29] along with her lighthearted attitude as she "stepped up the stair into the dock with all the buoyancy with which she might have entered the box of a theatre." Men are rewarded for private chastity and public display, women for public chastity and private display. The sight of a man making a spectacle of himself is "indescribable. Some of the women present were in hysterics" (156). Hysteria spreads. As the foundation of a group hysteria that circulates from the courtroom and into the streets, Eustace's emotional outburst produces an overblown and misinformed mob mentality that threatens to preempt the verdict of the legal authorities:

> As usual in such cases, the excitement in the Court
> communicated itself to the crowd outside in the street.
> The general opinion here—led, as it was supposed, by
> one of the clerks or other inferior persons connected
> with the legal proceedings—was decidedly adverse to
> the prisoner's chance of escaping a sentence of death.
> "If the letters and the Diary are read," said the brutal
> spokesmen of the mob, "the letters and the Diary
> will hang him." (157)

A member of the legal elite has spread the rumor, supporting Diana Fuss's argument that the "law's production of the hysterical symptom works in the manner of a *letter opener* that permits the law to sustain itself through the introduction and management of its own breaches and resistances."[30] While the trials of both Smith and Macallan literally open disturbing letters that produce and function as hysterical symptoms, I question the law's management of resistance in these cases. Because of the hysterical situation during the Macallan trial, the judges read "extracts" from the letters of Sara's friends and from Eustace's diary. Since the entire letter would cause too much emotion in an already overly affective courtroom, the letters of Sara's friends are read as fragments. To limit the breach of legal control, the authorities create a false context for the reading of these words. Though originally written as part of a dialogue between Sara and her friends, the letters are presented out of context; in the courtroom we hear her friends' responses to Sara's words but never Sara's voice. To maintain its control, the court erases Sara's voice; the victim becomes a shadow. While Madeleine Smith is more problematically represented as victim, the judges in her trial also limit the hysterical outbreak by erasing her most sexually explicit letters, the letters that would most clearly indicate the contradictions within female identity in nineteenth-century England. In addition, they rewrite her language as "impossible," as never having passed from male to female, and, therefore, as too "weird" for the courtroom.

But the best attempts of the legal authorities to exclude certain types of evidence do not prevent the outbreak of hysteria in court. While Fuss argues that institutions chisel their own chinks, she also indicates that group hysteria may result disturbingly in uncontrollable, political resistance: "Nevertheless, the spectacle of group hysteria can be read, at the same time, as a clear act of resistance. At least to Freud, group hysteria is far more disturbing than seemingly isolated cases such as Dora's, simply because it holds out the unsettling possibility of collective or even *organized* resistance."[31] Similarly, in the courtroom scenes investigated here, we see cases of hysterical identification— "eager" intoxication on the drama presented in the courtroom—that extend beyond the boundaries of the law. But, as Fuss also asks, "To what extent can prohibited identifications and the desires they produce be considered a form of social resistance?"[32] Answering her own question from a Foucauldian perspective, Fuss argues that the institutional scene of hysterical resistance is important:

> Both the hospital and the school are sites of social classification, disciplinary spaces organized for the observation, regulation, and supervision of their subjects. The function of these two institutions is to produce subjects whose progress can be isolated, individualized, examined, charted, measured, and systematically classified. But these institutions also *produce* the identities they are socially instituted to manage, installing at the center of the disciplinary project their own resistances.[33]

Like the hospital or the schoolroom theorized by Fuss, the courtroom is obviously another institutional space whose goal is the production of certain types of subjects. In the cases of both Smith and Macallan, though, the law refuses to accept certain types of evidence, refuses to sanction certain subjects; it refuses to create Madeleine Smith as a sexual subject, despite the overwhelming evidence of her sexual pleasures, or to present Sara as an abused wife, contrary to the fragmented evidence presented at the trial. Both trial and novel show the legal limits to allowable "types" of female subjects or to acceptable female discourse. Of course, the law's attempts to keep sexual narratives from circulation only create further contagion. Group hysteria in both instances is an important source of resistance, because it shows the spread of a dangerous desire despite the best attempts of the legal authorities to halt its circulation. In both cases, "weirdness" exceeds the control of legal authority.

Law and Ladies

While the law's attempts to delimit female subjectivity only emphasize its socially constructed boundaries and its foundation in sensational narrative, both cases also reveal that domesticity is itself tainted with a weirdness that disallows "domestication" as a civilizing force. Both Madeleine Smith and Sara Macallan, apparently proper English ladies, have moved beyond the space of acceptable affect and into an uncanny realm of violent and uncontrolled emotion: a phrenologist's analysis of Madeleine's personality suggests "more than usual force of character, owing to large combativeness, self-esteem, love of approbation, and firmness, powerful affections . . . a warm, sanguine temperament";[34] Sara Macallan has a "poetic" temperament that is linked with her "headstrong and violent" tendencies (128). Before sneaking into Macallan's bedchamber, Sara "pined away visibly; neither medical help nor change of air and scene did anything for her" (154). Even the female detective, Valeria, is infected with Dexter's—that is, Sara's—viscerally powerful narrative; in fact, as I suggested earlier, Valeria uncovers Sara's secrets partially because of her identification with the dead woman. Like Sara, Valeria is overwhelmed by physical desire for Eustace: "we forgot our breeding as lady and gentleman; we looked at each other in barbarous silence," and, after a secret assignation with Eustace, "I could not breathe; I could not think; my heart fluttered as if it would fly out of my bosom—and all this for a stranger" (14–15). As Cvetkovich suggests, emotion occupies an ambiguous position in the Victorian family as signifier both of proper ladyhood and of transgressive desire. Sara's sexual passion for Eustace, for example, is born in the bosom of the family, the consequence of "perfectly innocent intercourse" (154)—nights in the drawing room playing the piano and reading books. Not only the "fast young ladies"[35] of the period displayed this excessive emotion, but also respectable women who displayed it only to advertise their *control* of it.

In order to be considered a serious candidate for patroller of the dangerously passionate Victorian household, Valeria must therefore display both passion and control. While the Smith trial and Collins's novel both clearly indicate the difficulty women had in controlling the audience of their texts and the dangerous connection between women's writing and their bodies, they equally question the adequacy of the interpretations of women's words provided by a traditional economy of criticism. Dexter's tale, for example, produces such overwhelming affect in Ariel that she cannot properly interpret the subtext, while Valeria, who is emotionally and intellectually invested in Dexter's story, creates a "correct" interpretation, one that allows her to discover Sara's missing letter. Though the novel suggests the original can never be fully recovered—the fragments of Sara's letter are found but never completely reconstructed—Valeria's investigation of Eustace's secret provides her with insight into her own identity. Thus, the novel stages what Smith's trial never does: woman's role in the transformation of transgressive, weird tales into precedent-setting laws able to father future cases. The novel rewrites the Smith case as "hard" and therefore expands the repertoire of representations of women in a way the trial cannot. While the novel suggests that affect impairs analysis, it also offers a forum in which an emotional story can be properly interpreted, supporting the theories of Heinzelman and Wiseman, who argue that novels, unlike male-dominated courtrooms, often function both as an outlet for the representation of transgressive, "illegal" female stories and as an "authorization of those stories, presenting them as "credible and realistic."[36]

Though many of Madeleine's letters were erased from the official court case, they have gained meaning through repeated narrative rehearsals of the trial. Many of her words could not be read in court but were later published in the official British Trials series, though even this edition did not include a complete set of Madeleine's letters. Subsequent readers of the trial have published ever more complete versions of it. In *Victorian Murderesses,* Mary Hartman writes that additional material, "including several previously unpublished letters by Madeleine Smith, is contained in Peter Hunt . . . and in Nigel Moreland. . . . Hunt's is the best full account of the case."[37] A similar puzzle presents itself in the reconstruction of Sara Macallan's suicide note. From the clues hidden in Dexter's meandering and cyclical story of "a Mistress and a Maid" (337), "snares" whose meaning escapes both Ariel and Benjamin, Valeria discovers the letter buried "deep" in a mound of trash. The lawyer, Mr. Playmore, and Benjamin painstakingly excavate, unglue, and finally refabricate Sara's words in a manner analogous to Benjamin's weekly "Enigma" puzzles (370). As the dismissal of Madeleine's writing from the courtroom suggests, women's stories must be pieced together on the border between public/legal and private/domestic discourse, because the law provides no plausible

Karin Jacobson

295

context for interpretation—no precedent exists to "father" women's words, to make them "hard" precedent; they are viewed as too weird, "never having passed from a woman to a man." Since many of the original pieces of the letter have been lost, Benjamin and Playmore have "reconstructed certain sentences, declaring, in the plainest words, that the arsenic which Eustace procured was purchased at the request of his wife" (385). Despite Benjamin's assurances that Sara's words have been "plainly" recovered, the nervous footnotes placed by Playmore in the text of the letter suggest otherwise; he states that the first pages of the letter were "a scattered wreck," but, like Benjamin, he believes that "the utmost pains" have been taken "to supply the deficiency in exact accordance with what appeared to be the meaning of the writer" (395, 390).

While the methods used by the representatives of the law to uncover Sara's "deplorable and shocking" (385) letter are instructive, Valeria's explication of the contents of the letter reveals her own conflicting motivations. She prefaces her introduction of Sara's "confession" by reminding her forgetful readers of the scandalous beginning—verified, she emphasizes, in "the sworn testimony of respectable witnesses" (386)—of her husband's first marriage. In distinguishing herself from Sara, the first Mrs. Macallan, Valeria assumes a contradictory position in relation to the law, accepting the courtroom-produced interpretation of Sara's conduct but rejecting the judicial analysis of Eustace's involvement in Sara's death. Just as the legal authorities in the Smith case dismiss some of the evidence in order to limit the outbreak of group hysteria, Valeria underplays Eustace's role in Sara's suicide in order to redeem her husband's reputation. According to Diana Fuss, violence exists at the center of identification: "All active identifications, including positive ones, are monstrous assassinations: the Other is murdered and orally incorporated before being entombed inside the subject." To become Mrs. Macallan, Valeria must resurrect Sara Macallan, then violently erase her. But, as Fuss also recognizes, identification "travels a double current, allowing for the possibility of multiple and contradictory identifications coexisting in the subject at the same time."[38] Sara's letter affects Valeria viscerally, as does Dexter's tale: "As soon as I could dry my eyes and compose my spirits, after reading the wife's pitiable and dreadful farewell, my first thought was of Eustace—my first anxiety was to prevent him from ever reading what I had read" (395). First, Valeria incorporates the letter into herself, allowing Sara's "pitiable and dreadful farewell" to affect her emotionally; as a personal revelation between two women, the letter,

Valeria vows, must be kept secret from Eustace and the public. Despite her recognition of the letter's powerful testimony against Eustace, Valeria, the first-person narrator of the novel, still includes its full restoration in her text. Thus, the letter and Valeria's preface are evidence of her ambivalent identification with Sara: not only does she wish to include this remembrance of the first "dear wife," but Valeria also needs to vilify Sara so that she can replace her as Mrs. Macallan.

Just as Benjamin and Playmore glue together the fragmented bits of Sara's letter in order to attain a "plain" copy, Valeria pieces together a "plain" version of Sara in order to understand the "truth" of her identity; this subjectivity is never singular, but continually contradicting, as fragmented as the trashed suicide note. The female detective forages through the debris of Dexter's "wayward" tale in order to uncover Sara's story, and, equally, her own. Valeria's detective work both discloses her identity, separate from Eustace, and uncovers the existence of the first wife and her secret letter—the letter the law could never discover. The law's failure to recognize Sara Macallan as an individual,[39] in particular, as a multiply constructed individual, leaves it unable to uncover her secret suicide or to excise the "spectre of the poisoned woman" (112). But this abused and unloved first wife must be vindicated before Valeria can properly become "Mrs. Macallan." "What the Law has failed to do for you, your Wife must do for you" (116), says Valeria to Eustace; equally, what the law has failed to do for Valeria, which is recognize her as a legal entity, she must do for herself. What the law has failed to do for Sara, which is allow her a voice, Valeria must do with the publication of Sara's letter in her rendition of "The Trial of Eustace Macallan." Indeed, Playmore freely acknowledges his debt to Valeria, arguing "you have opened an entirely new view to my mind. . . . Here is the client leading the lawyer" (274). Cvetkovich suggests that the growing need for detectives in Victorian society resulted both from the law's failure to understand the family and from the perceived inappropriateness of outside assistance in the resolution of domestic disputes: "In an age before psychoanalysis, the detective, the new professional required by the law's intrusion into the family, sought out the family's tensions, its sexual undercurrents, its madwoman (the hysteric's precursor). . . . The conversion of lawyers into detectives disguises a new form of social control, allowing for a deinstitutionalized, private, and resolvable inquiry into the family."[40]

The Law and the Lady creates a family-based detective—the mother as analyst—whose job specifically is to root out sexual and emotional excesses in order to establish a stable domestic space. In Collins's novel, the family has become the scene of tension and conflict—Valeria's uncle comments that there is "something under the surface in connexion with Mr. Woodville, or with his family" (20). It was an "abyss in the shape of a family secret" (34)—as well as the progenitor of supposedly inappropriate sexual impulses. Both Madeleine and Sara prove that the threat of uncontrolled feminine sexuality has invaded the middle-class home; not only does Madeleine write "licentious" letters, she also sneaks her lover into the house and makes love in the grass behind the family's summer home. While both the trial and novel make plain the dangerous desire infecting the domestic sphere, they equally emphasize the law's inability to decipher signs of female sexuality. Although Valeria makes Sara's letter "plain," giving Sara back her voice, even Valeria cannot control readers' interpretations of the letter, as it resists a clear, singular translation.

Implicitly, the text grants Valeria access to a new form of writing that refuses the sexual and emotional excesses of Madeleine and Sara. In his interactions with Valeria, Playmore briefs her on traditional legalistic mechanisms and also allows her to watch him write: "There shall be no professional mysteries between you and me. . . . You will see what is passing in my mind, if you see what I write" (275). While Misserimus Dexter taught Valeria the importance of narrative, of reading below the surface, of looking for the gaps in the story, Playmore and Ogilvie's Imperial Dictionary teach her legal discourse: "[T]he Law and the Lady have begun by understanding one another. In plain English, I have looked into Ogilvie's Imperial Dictionary" (116). She understands both Dexter's "wayward" text and the "plain English" of legal discourse, both weird, uncanny narratives and "hard" fathering texts. The goal of Valeria's sleuthing is a discovery of a hidden woman, a voice lost in the courtroom. But will Valeria ultimately reduce Sara to the "plain English" that Benjamin and Playmore use to describe Sara's reconstituted letter and that is now used by Valeria to describe her reading of legalese?

As my discussion of Dexter's story suggests, this novel argues that fact and emotion, plain and wayward texts, cannot be separated—there are no pure, emotion-free "facts," and "plain" English is just a fiction. Valeria's methodology continually breaks down these dichotomies in the manner of contemporary feminists such as Jane Gallop[41] who advocate "impertinent questions" as a proper mode of feminist discourse; Valeria says, "I shall ask all sorts of questions which grave lawyers might think it beneath their dignity to put" (121). However, Playmore reminds Valeria of the need for intuition combined with fact, "plain evidence which can alone justify anything like a public assertion of his guilt" (279). Valeria's attempt to maintain a balance between her view of the case and the legal one again invokes Gallop, whose belief in the necessity of paying attention to small details and to localizing theory[42] provides an antidote to the "masculine" inclination of universalizing. Equally, this feminist approach provides insight into contemporary complaints about Collins's "knot-tying." According to one reviewer, "He can tie knots that are almost as ingenious as the knot of Gordius, and can form a puzzle that would be no discredit to a Chinaman. Untying knots and unravelling puzzles is at best but very dull work, though to people of a sluggish mind it would seem to be as pleasant as any other occupation."[43] Not surprisingly, the playfulness—the multiplicity of identity necessary for solving mysteries and asking "impertinent" questions—becomes the domain of women and foreigners. The critics' depiction of Valeria's investigations as unnecessary work, used to solve an uninteresting case, suggests women's problematic alienation from the law: they are not taken seriously either as agents of the law or as subjects of legal discourse.

Valeria's appropriation of legal methodologies was not well-received. Early reviewers of the novel implicitly question Collins's juxtaposition of women and law by belittling a plot centered on a woman's writing. *The Saturday Review* claims that the secret of *The Law and the Lady* is not one which "altogether repays the trouble of getting at it." Additionally, this reviewer questions the woman's role in investigating crime, particularly a crime based on a woman's sexual secrets: "Here was a pretty mystery in which to involve a young bride." But the state of marriage depicted in both Sara's burial and Valeria's displacement suggests that questioning their husbands' secrets is exactly what "young brides" must do.[44]

The secret of *The Law and the Lady* is certainly not that of a woman sneaking into a man's chambers. After all, Sara Macallan's passionate excesses were revealed in the courtroom. The secret, however, is that of a woman's suicide because of her husband's lack of love, of a plain woman's attempts to be attractive for her husband. Ultimately, the result of Valeria's investigation of Eustace's past is not the salvation of a passive and uninteresting husband, but the recovery of a woman's secret letter and a resuscitation of a woman's emotionally deadening marriage. These are the "deplorable and shocking" truths this text insists must not remain hidden from the law nor buried in a woman's fragmented suicide note. Despite Valeria's careful sleuthing, Sara Macallan remains forever excluded from the legal sphere, her suicide note never becomes a "hard" legal document or enters the court. Nor does Valeria. Although she works in conjunction with Playmore, and, in fact, arrogates his authority by discovering a solution to the case, she is never allowed to enter the courtroom. Instead, most of her work is conducted in the drawing rooms of Major Fitz-David and Misserimus Dexter. The threat Valeria poses to the established systems of justice is apparent in her criticism of Eustace's lawyer, Playmore. In her assessment of Playmore, Valeria describes him as "[k]ind, genial, clever—but oh, how easily prejudiced, how shockingly obstinate in holding to his own opinion" (290–91). More damningly, her entire sleuthing enterprise is premised on the law's failure to defend Eustace adequately, primarily because of its failure to recover the secret of Sara's letter: as Playmore tellingly praises Valeria, "The light which the whole machinery of the Law was unable to throw on the poisoning case at Glenninch, has been accidentally let in on it, by a lady who refuses to listen to reason and who insists on having her own way" (277). The lawyer's reference to Valeria's unreasonable techniques— often echoed in Valeria's self-assessments, as, for example, when she states, "I alone refuse to listen to reason"—tacitly refers to a growing critique of the legal profession's overly convoluted rhetoric (241).[45] Beyond this growing bureaucratic bungling, women had every right to be suspicious of legal assistance, given the law's continued nonrecognition of married women as legal subjects.

Plain Women, Plain Texts

Both texts suggest that women need to assume a mask, to masquerade, when confronting the law. Despite overwhelming evidence against her, the jury presented a verdict of "not proven" against Madeleine because of their inability to reconcile her ladylike appearance with the cunning and cruelty necessary for murder (xix). Henry James writes: "And what a pity she was almost of the pre-photographic age— I would give so much for a veracious portrait of her *then* face."[46] James was desperate for the image of Madeleine, a woman who did not fit within the boundaries of proper womanhood. The male critic's fascination with the sight of the female criminal, and with her supposed sexual voraciousness, continues one hundred years later in the work of Richard Altick:

It was also rumored—though supposedly not in print—
that Madeleine, doubly blessed in that the judge was
reputed to be not wholly unsusceptible to feminine
charms and that the crinoline of the day facilitated the
shy revealment thereof, took care that he should now
and then be granted a glimpse of her neat foot and
ankle. But so banal an embellishment, though probably
inescapable under the circumstances, is unworthy of a
place in a classic chronicle; even truth must be rejected if
its vulgarity blemishes the artistic effect. More disturbing
is the fact that such likenesses of Madeleine as survive
do not reassure us of her comeliness.[47]

Altick's gossipy invocation of the "shy revealment" of crinoline and of
a less than unbiased judge, suggests that excessive passion was a problem not merely for innocent bystanders; indeed, women's presence in
the courtroom infects the basic premise of impartial justice. Madeleine,
in particular, is accused of deliberately using her sexuality in a variety
of ways: demure and domestic for the jury, a coy sex kitten for the
judge. But Altick's attempts to banish the "vulgar" from the tableau
vivante of Madeleine's trial suggest that he, like the jurors, is more
interested in maintaining the artistic effect produced by an unsullied
vision of Victorian ladyhood than in discovering the truth about the
murder. More problematic, in his opinion, than the image of
Madeleine's vulgarity is the question of her comeliness. A vulgar
woman is one thing; an unattractive one, something else. The tale of a
woman using her sexuality as a tool is acceptable, but that of an unattractive woman inciting male desire is implausible. Like the judge who
had earlier rejected pieces of Madeleine's story that did not confirm the
proper intercourse between men and women, Altick rejects parts of the
story that do not create a sufficiently artistic impression. "More disturbing," Madeleine was "not necessarily a ravishing beauty."[48] Both
Madeleine and Sara are shockingly plain. Again, Altick's comments
suggest the jarring truth women's presence in the courtroom makes
apparent: truth equals beauty, there is no difference between these concepts where a woman is concerned. By satisfying the demands of
"beauty" and "aesthetic wholeness," the demands of "truth" or "justice" are implicitly met. Obviously, Madeleine's management of her
image was effective—as a perfect image/reflection of the lady,
Madeleine was safe from the law's vengeance, but still subject to the

beauty rating scales of critics such as Altick. Both cases are premised on women's looks—both gazes and beauty. This is the weirdness that can neither be erased nor accounted for. Madeleine becomes the image, providing a safe distance from herself, as that "self" was reflected in the letters she wrote to L'Angelier.

Madeleine's looks reveal the gap between the "truth" of feminine sexuality and the appearance of proper Victorian womanhood, a gap that is not so clearly revealed in her writings—or in her plain face. How does a woman's plainness—both Madeleine and Sara are accused of being plain—disrupt clear reading? Why is a plain face more difficult to decipher than a beautiful one? Madeleine's less than "ravishing" appearance disrupts Altick's trial tableau; Sara's murky complexion leads to suicide, following a fatal dose of her (and Madeleine's) beauty elixir, arsenic. The hidden passion of the supposedly plain woman creates a problem while legal discourse supposedly reveals the truth; just as plainness signals asexuality, the hidden depths behind the plain face refuse interpretation. Similarly, weirdness cannot be eradicated from legal discourse. The sensational narrative that founds the legal case can be encased in proper English, just as feminine desire is sheathed in proper dress. But, to paraphrase *The Glasgow Sentinel*'s analysis of the Smith trial, once the veil of legalese is thrown aside, from the first a very frail and flimsy one, the narrative of strong passion and libidinous tendencies upon which the law is founded at once reveals itself.[49] By making Sara's story "plain," Valeria actually adds complexity to the case as recorded in the "British Trials" series; more important, this "plainness" does not vindicate Eustace; his treatment of Sara is still abusive.

While Sara Macallan's attempts to hide the flaws of her complexion under an arsenic veil reveal the sinister side of cosmetics,[50] Collins's text additionally argues that masquerade may be usefully deployed by women. The novel is filled with images of women using masquerade for their own benefit. For example, Helena Beauly switches places with her maid in order to attend a masked ball for "Ladies of doubtful virtue . . . and gentlemen on the outlying limits of society" (*The Law and the Lady*, 267), and in doing so, Helena's playful masquerade creates a position for her outside of the control of the judgmental male gaze. In attempting to glean important evidence from Major Fitz-David, one of her husband's oldest friends, Valeria also resorts to masquerade. She allows the chambermaid to fetch a "box of paints and powders" in order to make up Valeria's face:

I saw, in the glass, my skin take a false fairness, my cheeks a false colour, my eyes a false brightness—and I never shrank from it. No! I let the odious deceit go on; I even admired the extraordinary delicacy and dexterity with which it was all done. "Anything" (I thought to myself, in the madness of that miserable time), "so long as it helps me to win the Major's confidence! Anything so long as I discover what those last words of my husband's really mean!" (57)

This quotation is reminiscent of Sara's "anything" in order to win her husband's love, including arsenic poisoning; it equally argues the utility of masquerade in order to uncover masculine meaning that is similar to Madeleine Smith's impersonation of a proper lady during her trial in order to prevent male penetration. Following the transformation of her face, Valeria "seemed in some strange way to have lost [her] ordinary identity—to have stepped out of [her] own character" (57–58). The change in her appearance elicits a parallel change in her personality: while her temperament was usually nervous and anxious, she now feels self-confident. In fact, Valeria's new look also creates confidence in the other: "What would Oliver's report of me have been, if I had presented myself to him with my colourless cheeks and my ill-dressed hair." Valeria thus recognizes that "[a]ppearances are not always to be trusted" (59, 80). She assumes a feminine role deliberately, and in the process becomes that role, though, like Madeleine Smith, she is never subject to it: both women are always in control of their self-representations.[51]

The difficulty posed by masquerade, though, is apparent: identity becomes multiple, capable of infinite transformation so that, finally, there is no difference between self and other. By naming Dexter the most multiplicitous, the most often masked character, the novel implicitly labels masquerade a dangerous pastime. Assuming masquerade as a technique of detection, Valeria becomes implicitly linked with Dexter. In her introduction to the novel, Jenny Bourne Taylor writes that Dexter "overturns all rational and coherent ways of making sense of him, and thus acts out the investigation of the boundaries of consciousness at work in the novel in his continual transformations. . . . At the same time he provides a self-conscious commentary on the processes of representation and story-telling that are at work throughout" (xxii). Because "nature" has committed a "careless" and "cruel" mistake in creating him, Dexter feels no compassion for nature's supposed laws.

Instead, he believes everything is story, that all representations are subject to revision. Thus, he ironically names his clumsy, clodding, Caliban-like cousin, Ariel. Dexter and Ariel break gender dichotomies, suggesting that sexuality resides in the imagination and that "nature" is pure, cruel artifice. Dressed in pink and green silk as he sits embroidering, Dexter reminds us that gender dichotomies are sheer masquerade, as are the truths that seemingly guide the law. He provides Valeria with an alternative view of the law, reminding her that in most situations there are at least two interpretations: "One on the surface, and another under the surface" (297). Dexter's emphasis on narrative reminds us again of the sensational origins of the law and argues that "truth" belongs to the best storyteller.

Dexter's playful manipulation of his self-representation aligns with Luce Irigaray's theory of masquerade as a playfully subversive act:

> One must assume the feminine role deliberately. Which
> means already to convert a form of subordination into
> an affirmation, and thus to begin to thwart it. . . . To
> play with mimesis is thus, for a woman, to try to recover
> the place of her exploitation by discourse, without allowing
> herself to be simply reduced to it. It means to resubmit
> herself—inasmuch as she is on the side of the "percep-
> tible," of "matter"—to "ideas," in particular to ideas
> about herself, that are elaborated in/by a masculine
> logic, but so as to make "visible," by an effect of playful
> repetition, what was supposed to remain invisible. . . .
> It also means "to unveil" the fact that, if women are
> such good mimics, it is because they are not simply
> resorbed in this function.[52]

Irigaray's insistence on "playful repetition" as a route to the revelation of truth echoes throughout Collins's text: Ariel's repetitive demand for a story guides Valeria to Sara's hidden letter and, as Sara's double, Valeria can play with her own identity in order to uncover another woman's secret.

Irigaray's invocation of a "playful repetition" that reveals "what was supposed to remain invisible," also mirrors Freud's language in his description of the uncanny. The *unheimlich* (or "unhomey") is the name for everything that ought to have remained hidden and secret but that has become visible, everything that is both too close for comfort and too weird. Both masquerade and the uncanny reveal, through repetition, "what should remain hidden"; masquerade reveals the artificiality of the construction of femininity, while the uncanny, as the reappearance of something that has been "disavowed," reveals the woman who is veiled and hidden away behind the "homey" appearance of the middle-class "lady." "Painted women" stare out of the center of Freud's work on the uncanny, an image of female sexuality Freud never acknowledged in his essay. In her rereading of Freud's essay, Jane Marie Todd argues that two motifs are regularly pushed aside by Freud: "[T]he central figure of woman in many of his examples and the related theme of seeing and being seen. The last example, the view of female genitals that some men find *unheimlich,* is by no means incidental. However, Freud failed to see the implications of his own evidence—the underlying motif that would unify the randomness of his examples."[53] In theorizing the uncanny, Freud wanted to uncover the difference between the ideas of the *heimlich* and the *unheimlich.* Instead, he continually discovers the congruence of the two terms, such that the uncanny has become indistinguishable from the domestic, the homely housewife shades into the eye-catching painted lady.[54] Todd argues that the uncanny is, at bottom, a fear of castration linked to the gaze of the "painted," the sexually desiring, woman. Freud's text reveals the position opened up for the "painted woman"—she becomes the owner of the gaze, she sees while also being seen. In masquerading, women become "double-visioned": they are the source and the site of the gaze.

Combining the analyses of Irigaray and Todd, I argue that masquerade creates a necessary space for women, providing protection from masculine mastery and allowing women to gaze. As Todd shows, the audacious gaze at the root of the uncanny is not gendered masculine, but is presented as the look of the sexually desiring woman. By using masquerade as a technique in her investigation, Valeria discovers what the law missed, namely Dexter's secret desire for Sara, as well as Sara's rejected passion for Eustace. In illuminating their desires, Valeria creates a space for the representation of a sexually desiring woman, and the desire for a "plain" woman, and, implicitly, sanctions the representation of herself as sexually passionate for Eustace. Both Madeleine Smith's trial and *The Law and the Lady* suggest that women's writing is dangerous because of its close proximity to the body—not only did this writing implicitly invoke women's bodies and sexuality, but it also overwhelmingly affected its readers. Women's writing, by gazing directly at sexuality, could not be admitted directly into the Victorian courtroom. When it was, its effect was hysteria. Unlike the letters in these texts, which created an implausible image of female sexuality for Victorian readers, masquerade imagines a uniform identity and a clear meaning. While plain women are impossible to read, just as their "plain English" cannot be interpreted within legal discourse, women in drag represent explicit, unambiguous meaning. Masquerade paints a woman who can be bluntly read by a male audience such as the jury and press at Madeleine's trial. In addition, masquerade opens woman's eyes, allowing her to use her looks in order to look.

The locus of her gaze is the uncanny underside of Victorian respectability. A world of deformed, ambiguously gendered beings, such as Ariel and Dexter, provides Valeria with more help than the legal authorities. Thus, while Heinzelman argues that the transformation of weird cases into hard law eradicates the noncanonical, these texts suggest not only that the weird cannot be erased, but that the "natural" is premised on the uncanny, that the "hard" depends on the "weird." Madeleine Smith's trial, for example, with its "not proven" verdict, is always suspect. "High literary folk" continued to speculate about her future life, suggesting that the literary community, unlike the legal counsel, was not as easily duped by her conservative appearance. George Eliot, for example, writes that "since she is acquitted it is a pity Palmer [a convicted poisoner] is not alive to marry her and be the victim of her second experiment in cosmetics—which is too likely to come one day or other."[55] To overcome the blinkered vision of the law, Valeria reads "wayward" narratives along with legal documents. She recovers Sara's tragic agency and subjectivity, but Sara's subversiveness is never erased. Instead, Valeria's search reveals the multiplicity of Sara's identity and equally proves the indeterminacy of Valeria's subjectivity, as the double of every other woman in the novel. By playfully repeating their identities, Valeria recovers Sara's letter and proves Eustace's legal innocence, though he remains morally culpable. Eustace's passivity is never reversed in this story, so no strong male rends woman's authority. The roles of wife and mother, along with the absence of strong male characters, counter the traditional heterosexual romance that seemingly domesticates the ending of the novel. These texts present an uncanny view of women as sexual creatures— not women who roam the streets, but Victorian "ladies." Finally, these texts uncover the multiplicity of Victorian female identities, dangerous identities because they cannot be plainly read, because the stories of these women, which are ultimately fictions, cannot be translated into "plain English." The "plain" face masks the most violent passions; the plain text, the most complex narratives.

Notes

1. Richard D. Altick, *Victorian Studies in Scarlet* (New York: Norton, 1970), 175.

2. Wilkie Collins, *The Law and the Lady*, ed. Jenny Bourne Taylor (Oxford: Oxford Univ. Press, 1992). Hereafter cited in the text as *The Law and the Lady*.

3. The connection between the two cases has been noted by a number of critics, including Jenny Bourne Taylor, introduction to *The Law and the Lady*, vii–xxvi; Dougald MacEachen, "Wilkie Collins and British Law," *Nineteenth-Century Fiction* 5 (1950): 121–39; and Julian Symons, *Bloody Murder: From the Detective Story to the Crime Novel*, 3d rev. ed (New York: Mysterious Press, 1992), 52. For background on the Smith trial, see Mary S. Hartman, *Victorian Murderesses: A True History of Thirteen Respectable French and English Women Accused of Unspeakable Crimes* (New York: Schocken, 1977), 51–84; F. Tennyson Jesse, ed., *The Trial of Madeleine Smith* (New York: Day, 1927); Peter Hunt, *The Madeleine Smith Affair* (London: Carroll and Nicholson, 1950); Nigel Morland, *That Nice Miss Smith* (London: Muller, 1957); and Altick, 175–90.

4. MacEachen, 136.

5. Qtd. in Altick, 189.

6. Susan Sage Heinzelman, "Hard Cases, Easy Cases and Weird Cases: Canon Formation in Law and Literature," *Mosaic* 21, no. 2 (1988): 59–72. Heinzelman draws the terms *hard, easy,* and *weird* from an article by Fred Schauer entitled "Easy Cases," *Southern California Law Review* 58 [1985]: 399–440. She argues that this terminology is "familiar to scholars and practitioners of the law" (60).

7. Heinzelman, 60.

8. Ibid., 60–61. As an example of a weird case that has become hard, Heinzelman offers the Baby M case. Heinzelman discovers "weird irony" in this case in which "the woman who could not biologically be a mother is declared a mother, whereas the woman who biologically could conceive is declared not a mother" (62). To eradicate this weirdness and make the case one of hard precedent, the judge transformed it into an issue of contract law, thereby negating the weird, gendered issues of power and of reproductive rights that necessarily underlie it (63).

9. Ibid., 70.

10. Freud associates the uncanny with a devious walk through the streets of Vienna. Masquerade, feminine sexuality, and repetition are all important components of Freud's devious walk ("The 'Uncanny,'" in *An Infantile Neurosis and Other Works*, vol. 17, *The Standard Edition of the Complete Psychological Works of Sigmund Freud*, ed. James Strachey (London: Hogarth Press, 1955), 237. Hereafter cited as "The Uncanny."

11. Mary Poovey suggests the "unevenness" within the construction and deployment of mid-Victorian representations of gender, and of women in particular, in *Uneven Developments: The Ideological Work of Gender in Mid-Victorian England* (Chicago: Univ. of Chicago Press, 1988), 4.

12. Jesse, 329.

13. Hunt, 107.

14. Qtd. in Altick, 178.

15. Ibid., 188.

16. Jesse, 336.

17. Ibid., 295.

18. Sigmund Freud, *Fragment of an Analysis of a Case of Hysteria*, vol. 7, *The Standard Edition of the Complete Psychological Works of Sigmund Freud*, ed. James Strachey (London: Hogarth Press, 1955), 48. Hereafter cited as "Dora."

19. Jesse, 353, 295.

20. Ibid., 336.

21. Qtd. in Douglas MacGowan, *Murder in Victorian Scotland: The Trial of Madeline Smith* (Westport, Conn.: Praeger, 1999), 151. This comment is reminiscent of Freud's defense of his use of sexually explicit language in his analysis of adolescent women: "No one can undertake the treatment of a case of hysteria until he is convinced of the impossibility of avoiding the mention of sexual subjects, or unless he is prepared to allow himself to be convinced by experience. The right attitude is: 'Pour fair une omelette il faut casser des oeufs.' The patients themselves are easy to convince; and there are only too many opportunities of doing so in the course of treatment. There is no necessity for feeling any compunction at discussing the facts of normal or abnormal sexual life with them. With the exercise of a little caution all that is done is to translate into conscious ideas what was already known in the unconscious" ("Dora," 49).

22. *Daily Express*, 11 July 1857.

23. The law's connection with entertainment and narrative is not new in the nineteenth century. As Foucault vividly shows, public hangings and other graphic punishments were a popular source of entertainment until well into the eighteenth century. Also, the narrative potential of the law's stories becomes apparent in the eighteenth-century publications of criminals' lives, which are seen by many theorists of the novel as ancestors of the novel (Michel Foucault, *Discipline and Punish: The Birth of the Prison*, trans. Alan Sheridan [New York: Vintage, 1979], 3–69).

24. *Daily Express*, 11 June 1857.

25. Making a similar point, Diana Fuss writes, "The letter of hysterical speech and the letter of symbolic prohibition follow an identical path of transmission, reminding us that in our present cultural symbolic the language of desire *is* the language of prohibition" (*Identification Papers* [New York: Routledge, 1995], 133–34). Fuss argues that the law itself orchestrates the

production of hysterical discourse in order to "sustain itself through the introduction and management of its own breaches and resistances" (134). Based on my reading of Collins's *The Law and the Lady*, though, I question how well the law actually manages these resistances. I argue here that the law cannot control the breach introduced by Madeleine's sexuality or by Sara's suicide.

26. Heinzelman, 60.

27. Because of his vivid storytelling techniques, Dexter competes with the power of the law: "The cross-examination resolved itself, in substance, into a mental trial of strength between the witness and the Lord Advocate; the struggle terminating (according to the general opinion) in favour of the witness" (178). This quotation makes apparent the danger of "storytelling" in the courtroom; as the law is based primarily in stories, the master tale-teller will win the case. Dexter also speaks the language of the law, asking the judges, "Am I here to declare theories, or to state facts?" (178).

28. Ann Cvetkovich, *Mixed Feelings: Feminism, Mass Culture and Victorian Sensationalism* (New Brunswick: Rutgers Univ. Press, 1992), 6.

29. Qtd. in Hartman, 399.

30. Fuss, 134.

31. Ibid., 118.

32. Ibid., 119.

33. Ibid., 119.

34. Jesse, 409.

35. According to Mary Hartman, "fastness" generally designated women who were "brash, self-assertive and flirtatious" and reflected the reality of a growing wealthy upper middle class that could "create a distinguishable group of leisured young women in search of diversion" (61). See also C. Willert Cunnington, *Feminine Attitudes in the Nineteenth Century* (London: Heinemann, 1935).

36 Susan Sage Heinzelman and Zipporah Batshaw Wiseman, *Representing Women: Law, Literature, and Feminism* (Durham: Duke Univ. Press, 1994), 251.

37. Hartman, 276.

38. Fuss, 34.

39. The common-law practice of coverture, whereby a woman was "covered" by her husband because the interests of husband and wife were assumed to be the same, left the wife "nonexistent" in the eyes of the law. Sara's letter, fragmented and deeply buried beneath a pile of trash, is an apt image of the "covered" state of women under common law. The novel begins with the Marriage Service of the Church of England, which emphasizes women's erasure within marriage: "For after this manner in the old time the holy women also, who trusted in God, adorned themselves, being in subjection unto their own husbands; even

as Sarah obeyed Abraham, calling him lord" (*The Law and the Lady*, 8). Perhaps it is not surprising that Valeria signs her married name, rather than her maiden name, on her marriage certificate, signifying a married woman's immediate erasure by English law. For more on women's position within nineteenth-century marriage, see Mary Poovey and Mary Shanley, *Feminism, Marriage, and the Law in Victorian England, 1850–1895* (Princeton: Princeton Univ. Press, 1989).

40. Cvetkovich, 52.

41. Jane Gallop, *The Daughter's Seduction: Feminism and Psychoanalysis* (Ithaca: Cornell Univ. Press, 1982).

42. According to Gallop, "the gesture of paying attention to small details is not simply some external methodological device, but is the very stuff of what I am trying to advance as a psychoanalytic, feminist reading"; "attention to context, to materiality, which refuses the imperialistic, idealizing reductions that have been solidary with a denigration of the feminine-material, localized, at home, *in situ*—in favour of the masculine-active, ideal, in movement, away from the home" (92–93).

43. Review of *The Law and the Lady,* by Wilkie Collins, *The Saturday Review* 39 (13 Mar. 1875): 357. Hereafter cited as *The Saturday Review*. Qtd. in Norman Page, *Wilkie Collins: The Critical Heritage* (London and Boston: Routledge and Kegan Paul), 203.

44. *The Saturday Review,* 357.

45. For a further exploration of the nineteenth-century critique of legal procedures and rhetoric, see Lynne M. DeCicco, "Uneasy Alliances: Women and Lawyers in the Mid-Nineteenth-Century English Novel" (Ph.D. diss., Columbia Univ., 1992).

46. Qtd. in Altick, 189.

47. Altick, 178.

48. Ibid.

49. *The Glasgow Sentinel* writes that Madeleine was "as much the seducer as the seduced. And when once the veil of modesty was thrown aside, from the first a very frail and flimsy one, the woman of strong passion and libidinous tendencies at once reveals herself" (qtd. in MacGowan, 151).

50. That arsenic was viewed as a proper "technology" of female beauty can be seen in a spate of articles on "arsenic-eating" that appeared in Victorian journals. The article, "The Narcotics We Indulge In," *Blackwood's* (Dec. 1853), states that arsenic could be used for "freshness of complexion and plumpness of figure" (Jesse, 395). The article "The Poison-Eaters," *Chambers's Journal* (Dec. 1851), called arsenic "the woman's secret," arguing that only "the confessional or the deathbed . . . raises the veil from the terrible secret" (Jesse, 392).

51. Recent feminist theorists of masquerade show the difficulty of deciding whether it works for or against women. In a well-known essay "Womanliness as a Masquerade," Joan Riviere theorizes that intellectual women

may put on a mask of womanliness to avert anxiety and the retribution feared from men ("Womanliness as a Masquerade," in *Psychoanalysis and Female Sexuality*, ed. Hendrick M. Ruitenbeck [New Haven: College and Univ. Press, 1966], 209–20). Although Riviere's theory provides insight into Valeria's anxieties as she usurps male authority, it does not capture the feeling of freedom or confidence that masquerade allows her. Emily Apter, however, sees more to critique than to praise in masquerade. She asks "why one would want to retain such a theory. With its language of veils, masks, and sexual travesty, the discourse of the masquerade seems always to participate in the very obfuscation of femininity that it seeks to dispel" (*Feminizing the Fetish: Psychoanalysis and Narrative Obsession in Turn-of-the-Century France* [Ithaca: Cornell Univ. Press, 1991], 90). While I agree with Apter's critiques of Riviere, I still believe that masquerade provided nineteenth-century women with a useful antidote to theories of female passivity. Switching identities gives Valeria pleasure. In masquerading as her maid, Mrs. Beauly, similarly, can defeat Eustace's moralizing.

52. Luce Irigaray, *This Sex Which is Not One*, trans. Catherine Porter (Ithaca: Cornell Univ. Press, 1985), 76.

53. Jane Marie Todd, "The Veiled Woman in Freud's '*Das Unheimliche*,'" *Signs* 11 (1986): 521.

54. In "The Uncanny," Freud writes: "Once, as I was walking through the deserted streets of a provincial town in Italy which was strange to me, on a hot summer afternoon, I found myself in a quarter the character of which could not long remain in doubt. Nothing but painted women were to be seen at the windows of the small houses, and I hastened to leave the narrow street at the next turning. But after having wandered about for a while without being directed, I suddenly found myself back in the same street, where my presence was now beginning to excite attention. I hurried away once more, but only to arrive yet a third time by devious paths in the same place. Now, however, a feeling overcame me which I can only describe as uncanny, and I was glad enough to abandon my exploratory walk and get straight back to the piazza I had left a short while before" ("The Uncanny," 237).

55. Qtd. in Altick, 187.

References

Altick, Richard D. *Victorian Studies in Scarlet*. New York: Norton, 1970.

Apter, Emily. *Feminizing the Fetish: Psychoanalysis and Narrative Obsession in Turn-of-the-Century France*. Ithaca: Cornell Univ. Press, 1991.

Collins, Wilkie. *The Law and the Lady*. Ed. Jenny Bourne Taylor. Oxford: Oxford Univ. Press, 1992.

Cvetkovich, Ann. *Mixed Feelings: Feminism, Mass Culture and Victorian Sensationalism*. New Brunswick: Rutgers Univ. Press, 1992.

DeCicco, Lynne M. "Uneasy Alliances: Women and Lawyers in the Mid-Nineteenth-Century Novel." Ph.D. diss., Columbia Univ., 1992.

Foucault, Michel. *Discipline and Punish: The Birth of the Prison.* Trans. Alan Sheridan. London: Allen Lane, 1977.

Freud, Sigmund. *The Standard Edition of the Complete Psychological Works of Sigmund Freud.* Ed. James Strachey. 24 vols. London: Hogarth Press, 1953–74.

Fuss, Diana. *Identification Papers.* New York: Routledge, 1995.

Gallop, Jane. *The Daughter's Seduction: Feminism and Psychoanalysis.* Ithaca: Cornell Univ. Press, 1982.

Hartman, Mary S. *Victorian Murderesses: A True History of Thirteen Respectable French and English Women Accused of Unspeakable Crimes.* New York: Schocken, 1977.

Heinzelman, Susan Sage. "Hard Cases, Easy Cases and Weird Cases: Canon Formation in Law and Literature." *Mosaic* 21, no. 2 (1988): 59–72.

Heinzelman, Susan Sage, and Zipporah Batshaw Wiseman, eds. *Representing Women: Law, Literature, and Feminism.* Durham: Duke Univ. Press, 1994.

Hunt, Peter. *The Madeleine Smith Affair.* London: Carroll and Nicholson, 1950.

Irigaray, Luce. *This Sex Which is Not One.* Trans. Catherine Porter. Ithaca: Cornell Univ. Press, 1985.

Jesse, F. Tennyson, ed. *The Trial of Madeleine Smith.* New York: Day, 1927.

MacEachen, Dougald. "Wilkie Collins and British Law." *Nineteenth-Century Fiction* 5 (1950): 121–39.

MacGowan, Douglas. *Murder in Victorian Scotland: The Trial of Madeline Smith.* Westport, Conn.: Praeger, 1999.

Morland, Nigel. *That Nice Miss Smith.* London: Muller, 1957.

Page, Norman. *Wilkie Collins: The Critical Heritage.* London and Boston: Routledge and Kegan Paul, 1974.

Poovey, Mary. *Uneven Developments: The Ideological Work of Gender in Mid-Victorian England.* Chicago: Univ. of Chicago Press, 1988.

Riviere, Joan. "Womanliness as a Masquerade." In *Psychoanalysis and Female Sexuality,* ed. Hendrick M. Ruitenbeck, 209–20. New Haven: College and Univ. Press, 1966.

Shanley, Mary. *Feminism, Marriage, and the Law in Victorian England, 1850–1895.* Princeton: Princeton Univ. Press, 1989.

Symons, Julian. *Bloody Murder: From the Detective Story to the Crime Novel.* 3d rev. ed. New York: Mysterious Press, 1992.

Todd, Jane Marie. "The Veiled Woman in Freud's 'Das Unheimliche.'" *Signs* 11 (1986): 519–28.

Collins, Race, and Slavery

Audrey Fisch

HE WRITINGS OF WILKIE COLLINS PROVIDE
AN UNEXPECTED AND UNDEREXAMINED
EXCEPTION TO THE REPRESENTATION OF
black and mixed-race people in Victorian England. In *Armadale* (first published in *The Cornhill Magazine*, 1864–66), *Black and White* (a
play written by Collins with Charles Fechter and
produced in 1869), *Miss or Mrs?* (published in
the *Graphic Illustrated Newspaper*, 1871), and
The Guilty River (published in 1886), Collins
unabashedly presents Victorian readers and audiences with protagonists, heroes, and heroines
descended from either American or English colonial slaves, and his representations provide a
sharp contrast to the caustic bigotry that characterized the popular rhetoric and the major historical events of his time (the Indian Mutiny, the
Jamaica Rebellion, etc.).

Collins's politics were not in fact totally
different from those of Dickens and Carlyle, with
their cruelly blithe imagination of the elimina-
tion of Indians and blacks.[1] Like his peers, Collins

saw black, mixed-race, and other nonwhite characters as a potentially disruptive problem for English society; that Collins shared in the mainstream attitudes of his day is evidenced in texts such as *The Moonstone* and *Ioláni*. It strikes me thus as perfectly logical that Collins could collaborate with Dickens on "The Perils of Certain English Prisoners."[2] Unlike his peers, however, Collins seems to have been interested in a slightly different problem: the legacy for England of slavery and colonialism. And he seems to have identified this legacy as a pathology within white Englishness, particularly white English masculinity. What seems to follow is a new sort of logic about the penetration of mixed-race characters into Victorian society. In the works examined here, this penetration for Collins is not cause for hysteria, as it was for his peers, but an opportunity for the English to detoxify a contaminated past of slavery and colonialism. Incorporating mixed-race people into traditional English society allows Collins to reimagine his world and restore Victorian values.

Miss or Mrs? is the simplest and starkest example of how Collins's work differs from his contemporaries. Natalie Graybrooke, the heroine of *Miss or Mrs?*, is the daughter of a white English sea captain and a woman of "a mixture of Negro blood and French blood," yet she is peacefully assimilated into mainstream English society.[3] Natalie's character initially seems to conform to nineteenth-century stereotypes about the sexualized, doomed, tragic mulatta, as seen in Harriet Beecher Stowe's Cassy, whose sexual abuse is practically predicted by her exotic beauty, and in James Fenimore Cooper's Cora in *The Last of the Mohicans,* whose tint of skin and genealogical origins predict death, not marriage, etc.[4] Natalie is exotically beautiful and prematurely developed—"At fifteen years of age . . . she possessed the development of the bosom and limbs, which in England is rarely attained before twenty" (*Miss or Mrs?,* 9–10). The heroine's sexuality, or so the reader is led to expect, will be central to this tale of sensational intrigue.

And, undeniably, there is a sensational plot in this typically Collinsian story. Natalie secretly weds her cousin to avoid the marriage to an old acquaintance her dimwitted father has arranged; this acquaintance turns out to be a criminal who seeks only her dowry, attempts to kill her father, and threatens to rape her. But the plot line of this story refuses the developments typically concomitant to such a racialized heroine; Collins insists that Natalie is not different from her lighter-skinned counterparts—her "remarkable bodily development was far from being accompanied by any corresponding development of character. Natalie's manner was the gentle innocent manner of a young girl" (*Miss or Mrs?*, 10)—and the story bears out the fact that Natalie is a faithful representation of passive, submissive Victorian womanhood. Black West Indian blood briefly differentiates and exoticizes Natalie, but Collins's successful marriage plot, in which Natalie is rewarded by marriage (to a white man), love, parental approval, and wealth, negates the idea that Natalie's difference from other lighter-skinned Victorian heroines should influence her story.

Miss or Mrs? obviously stands in sharp contrast to "The Perils"; the idea that a mixed-race woman can marry a white man and live happily ever after in England was radical. But Collins was not generally so sanguine about such assimilation. In *Black and White*, a farcical "Love Story" (the subtitle of the play) set in Trinidad in 1830, just before the abolition of colonial slavery, the challenges to the mixed-race character are greater than those that Natalie faces in *Miss or Mrs?* and, more specifically, located around racism and slavery.

Maurice de Layrac, a French gentleman, has come to the West Indian island in pursuit of an heiress, Miss Emily Milburn, whom he met and courted in France. Arriving in Trinidad, he encounters Ruth, a slave on the island, who reveals that she is his mother, that his father was a white planter, and that he was secretly adopted by a white French nobleman, the Count de Layrac, as a baby. Although Maurice is a free man according to English law outside the West Indies, he forfeits that freedom when he returns to the West Indies, and Maurice is now legally a slave. Stephen Westcraft, a West Indian planter who was engaged to Emily before her affections were stolen by Maurice, decides to take his revenge by buying Maurice, the slave. This tragedy is avoided by the discovery of a document written by Ruth's master freeing her (and her offspring), that had been mislaid by the jealous wife of Ruth's master. At last, all ends happily, with Maurice and Emily's impending marriage assured.

Written after the demise of colonial slavery, Collins's retrospective play reflects mid-Victorian England's ideological investment in the moral and national rightness of the decision to abolish colonial slavery.[5] Maurice voices this rhetoric most obviously when he speaks of how his adoptive parents took him to England: "They took me to a free country—they made me citizen of a great nation. Mother! on the day when I set foot on the soil of England, I was free!"[6] Slavery, personified by Westcraft with his "violent temper," his "rough manner, and . . . rude voice" (*Black and White*, 7, 29), is depicted as unmannered, ungenteel, and outmoded, a corrupting and degrading influence on whites such as Westcraft.

If this play's endorsement of intermarriage can be explained in part by contemporary disapproval of colonial slavery,[7] the play's perspectives on race, power, and the rights of black West Indians are more surprising and more complicated. Specifically, the play insists that Maurice's heritage is not shameful. Questioned about his birth and parentage, Ruth hesitates about telling Maurice that she is his mother. But Maurice insists, "Be she who she may, my mother is sacred to me!" Then, according to Collins's stage directions, *The truth suddenly flashes on* [Maurice]. . . . [H]*e falls on his knees at the bedside* [of his mother], *and opens his arms,*" beseeching "'Oh, my mother, kiss me! oh, my mother, bless me!'" (21). Likewise, when asked by the Provost Marshall about his background for the purposes of determining whether he is indeed a slave, Maurice embraces his past: "come what may of it—I'll not deny the mother who bore me! I am the son of Ruth the Quadroon." His honesty and courage are rewarded by the commendation of the Provost Marshall—"I respect you"—and by the hand of Emily—"He shall see that I can appreciate him too! Slave, or free, Maurice, take the hand I promised you; and make me your wife!" (51). And, of course, the ultimate reward for Maurice's honesty is the play's happy ending, which grants him freedom, marriage, and fortune.

The play does not pretend that racial prejudice does not exist. In fact, Emily is at first repulsed by Maurice when she learns that his mother is Ruth, "that poor old Quadroon" (5). When Maurice kisses her: "(*The action causes an instantaneous revulsion of feeling in her. She sees the position in its true light—and breaks away from him, with a cry of horror.*) 'What have I done? Am I mad?' (*She covers her face with her hands.*) 'Oh, the shame of it! the shame of it!'" (27).

The shame, as she explains to Maurice, is that "[i]n this island, sir, a lady is degraded if a slave's hand touches her. A slave's lips had touched mine" (27–28). But Emily decides to follow her heart, to forswear the judgment of society, and to marry Maurice, even if he is a slave. It is her contrary instincts about her lover's position, dictated by the norms of white Trinidadian society—"In this island, sir"—that prove shameful within the context of the play and not his racial identity itself.

Certainly this enlightened view of relations between a black slave and a white woman is aided in no small measure by the fact that Maurice is very light skinned (the son of a quadroon and a white man), very well educated (in manners, languages, etc.), and the adoptive son of and heir to a count. Finally, the death of Ruth renders Maurice's ties to slavery both abstract and abstruse. (Natalie's links to her black past are similarly weak because her mother has died many years before *Miss or Mrs?* begins.) In this sense, Collins is able to validate his protagonist's black heritage while liberating Maurice from the familial as well as the social and legal ties of that heritage.

If *Black and White* entertains the idea that a black heritage is honorable (even if the play works to erase the traces of such a past), the play even more radically allows West Indian blacks a voice of power, anger, and intelligence through the character of Plato. A free black, Plato engages in a kind of Socratic dialogue with Michaelmas, a white servant. Through the sarcastic double-speak of Plato, Michaelmas learns of the portending upheaval in Trinidad and discovers the political savvy and anger of the blacks.

The discussion begins with Michaelmas's remarks on Plato's name and of the names of Plato's friends: "Mr. Socrates; Mr. Homer; Mr. Virgil; Mr. Shakespeare; Mr. Milton." Michaelmas asks "how you six black gentlemen came by the[se] names," and Plato responds, "We took 'em, sar. . . . . [W]e don't see why de dam white man should hab all de 'lustrious names to himself!" (14). The veiled hostility inherent in this appropriation of white patriarchy is writ large in Plato's discussion of the two political parties of the island. While the division of the population into conservative blacks and liberal blacks mirrors the two-party political system back home in England, the objects of these parties are quite different. Plato explains:

> We hab but one object, sar—de sacred right ob freedom.
> And we hab two ways ob getting at it. De Liberal way is
> de easiest, I admit. De Liberal way is to get up early one
> morning, and kill all de whites. . . . De Conservative way
> is de most peaceable and de most proper. De Conservative
> way is to found a nigger club. Little by little, sar, dis club
> will unite all de blacks in one great conspiracy to learn no
> lessons, and to do no work. What is de necessary conse-
> quence? De dam white man (saving your presence) leaves
> de island. (15–16)

We might be tempted to see Plato as a comic buffoon or a dangerous savage, in either case aping the names and social strategies of the white man; certainly, the awkward construction of dialect in his speech gives credence to such a reading. The pointedness of his sarcasm, however, suggests not mindless mimicry but rather the triumph of the black man at the white man's own game.

In contrast to *Miss or Mrs?*, which Collins describes as having been "fortunate enough to find its way at once to the favour of an unusually large circle of readers" (355), *Black and White* enjoyed only mild success at the Adelphi Theatre,[8] and it did not achieve the run Collins and Fechter anticipated. Collins had his own theory for the lack of interest in the play:

> We [Collins and Fechter] had completely forgotten the popular mania of seventeen years before, satirised by the French as *Oncle Tommerie*. Almost every theatre in Great Britain had, in those days, provided an adaptation of *Uncle Tom's Cabin*. It mattered nothing that the scene of *Black and White* was laid far away from the United States, in the island of Trinidad, and that not one of the persons of the drama recalled the characters of Mrs. Stowe's novel in the slightest degree. Mrs. Stowe's subject was slavery and our subject was slavery; and even the long-suffering English public had had enough of it.[9]

The suggestion that the public had somehow tired of the subject of slavery seems insufficient to account for the lack of interest in Collins's play. The 1860s did mark a shift away from *Uncle Tom's Cabin* and related products of American abolition that had been so vastly popular in England.[10] But, as Collins himself notes, *Black and White* only dimly resembles *Uncle Tom's Cabin* and thus would have been in a poor position to capitalize on "Tom-mania" even had it been produced during the height of the popularity of American abolitionism. Moreover, the play's depiction of black people as vengeful and angry at their treatment by white people bears no resemblance to the overall passive, martyrology of Stowe's novel. A brief review in *The Illustrated London News* describes *Black and White* as a play in which "[t]he blacks and whites are shown in antagonism," not a comment apt to be made about Stowe's novel.[11] Similarly, the play's depiction and celebration of intermarriage between a descendent of colonial slavery and a plantation owner, with its suggestion that some blackness can be amicably incorporated into proper English identity, steers far from the course of emigration that Stowe employs to keep American national identity unsullied by any blood of black slaves.

Indeed, while Stowe's novel, which strives to keep black and white populations firmly separate, is ultimately conservative on the question of how blacks will be integrated into mainstream white society, Collins, more radically, seems to undertake seriously the question of assimilation. He offers two competing models. In one, represented by Plato, blacks mimic and transform English colonial politics; they are angry and potentially violent. In the other, represented by Maurice in *Black and White* and Natalie in *Miss or Mrs?*, colonialism leaves its mark on the colonized black population in the form of a mixed-race progeny who eventually can be assimilated into white society with no other change in the status quo. Collins seems to begin each of these works with the assumption that slavery and colonialism are fully inter-twined in English identity (even foregrounding the connection in his title, *Black and White*), and that therefore black and white have and must inevitably come together and mix in one way or another. Collins's solution to the dilemma of how this union will happen seems to be to offer his audience the peaceful assimilation of mixed-race characters into white society over and against the more dangerous and threatening specter of black alienation and/or rebellion.

This peaceful assimilation of black within white, however, is a tenuous solution because of degeneration, not within the mixed-race characters, as we might expect, but within the white characters. It is Natalie's white father in *Miss or Mrs?* who is irresponsibly blind to the white predator after Natalie and her dowry; Natalie's father, in other words, is pathetically unable to play his proper role as white patriarch. White Stephen Westcraft, the spurned lover in *Black and White,* is the cruel and violent one, not the gentle and honorable Maurice. These two texts begin to define white English identity, particularly white English masculinity, as pathological: passive and ineffective, on the one hand, and brutal, on the other.

The final two texts I want to consider, *The Guilty River* and *Armadale,* take up this issue of white male degeneration even more directly, and, perhaps for this reason these two texts are less sanguine about the possibility for peaceful assimilation of mixed-race people into English society. In these two texts, the mixed-race characters are called on to sacrifice themselves to restore a degraded white society to its rightful position.

The white hero of *The Guilty River,* Gerard Roylake, is the product of a degenerated society. His father was "a bad man," his "mother's worst enemy," a man whose "jealousy, foully wronged the truest wife, the most long-suffering woman that ever lived."[12] When this angelic, suffering English wife dies, Gerard's father takes a new wife without even telling his son. Returning after his father's death, Gerard meets his stepmother and encounters her and her society's fascination with "rank and riches, entirely for their own sake," and finds himself a gentleman and heir to a "large landed property," utterly estranged from the material values of his "own country people" (*The Guilty*

River, 246, 248). He mistakes one of his own servants for a stranger and a peer, treats English social institutions (such as luncheon and other social occasions) with "contempt," and even fails to be interested in English women of his own class and society" (284, 286). Gerard is thoroughly estranged from his English identity, in part because he has been educated abroad in Germany, but mainly because English society has become estranged, in its focus on fortunes as illustrated by the character of his stepmother, from the decent English values of loyalty and family.

Gerard's reassimilation into English society is made possible through his encounter with a dark double, a rival who loves a country woman, Cristel. This man, the "Lodger," whose real name the reader, like Gerard, never learns, is deaf from a midlife illness. Like Gerard, he is a gentleman, but his love for Cristel is returned on her part only by contempt, fear, and loathing. The Lodger's jealousy of Gerard eventually causes him to attempt both to poison Gerard and to spirit Cristel away from the protection of her family and friends. He fails in both attempts. In the end, trading his life for the temporary three-weeks' restoration of his hearing, the dying Lodger, exiled in Genoa, reveals all his machinations to Gerard and effects the reunification of the lovers.

For most of the story, the Lodger is referred to by a nickname of his own choosing, "The Cur": "I come of a mixed breed . . . Call me The Cur" (257). H. L. Malchow has described the "demonized dog" or "half-wolf" as "a common trope for the threatening half-breed in the nineteenth century," and Collins's "The Cur" seems to fit this pattern.[13] The Lodger is descended on one side from a mother who was "[b]orn of slave-parents . . . [and] sold [before she had "reached her eighteenth-year"] by auction in the Southern States of America" to a man who eventually freed her on his deathbed (261). Overcoming this dubious background—with its unstated suggestion that she was sold as a concubine but eventually freed by that lover/master—the Lodger's mother subsequently met and married his white English father.

Contrary to the stereotype, however, the Lodger's descent from an American slave does not mar his life; his childhood and early life are fortunate. After schooling with a "head master [who] was more nearly a perfect human being than any other man that I have ever met," he attends Cambridge. Then, after "three years of unremitting study at one of the great London hospitals," he embarks on a budding career as a surgeon; after fortuitously serving a nobleman in an accident, he "enjoyed the confidence and goodwill of a man possessing boundless social influence" (261–62). Even after he becomes deaf, the

Lodger is unrestrainedly welcomed in society: "privileged victims of hysterical impulse [that is, rich women] . . . wrote me love-letters, and offered to console the 'poor beautiful deaf man' by marrying him" (267). If the Lodger's name, "The Cur," might in some sense mesh with his mixed-race background, his loving description of his ex-slave mother—"no better wife and mother ever lived" (261)—as well as the success of his life and of his integration into English society negate any association of that background with shame.

Mixed together with black blood in the Lodger's breeding is his white English father's genealogy, and the associations derived from the blood of this side of the family offer another explanation for the Lodger's self-description. After the deaths of his parents, the Lodger discovers the secrets of his father's side of the family: his grandfather was a murderer, hanged on the scaffold; his uncle, a captain in the army, cheated at dice and was killed in a duel by a fellow officer; and his own father, the only one to escape punishment, had in his youth deceived a young girl who subsequently drowned herself and their child. In this sense, then, while the Lodger's father is not literally a sexually abusive American slaveholder, he is clearly the figurative equivalent of the white man who degraded the Lodger's mother.

The inheritance of white criminality on one side and black blood and a heritage of slavery on the other battle for the content of the Lodger's character. Yet, for him, it is always clear that his morality is drawn from his black heritage. The Lodger asks: "What wholesome influences had preserved me, so far, from moral contamination by the vile blood that ran in my veins?" And his answer, "resembling my good mother physically, I might hope to have resembled her morally" (264), once more affirms his own understanding of the honor of his "blackness."

The Guilty River, then, insists that the Lodger's racial heritage is no issue, that his blackness, like Natalie or Maurice, can be fully assimilated into Englishness. Yet the inseparability of the Lodger's black heritage from its violent counterpart, his white English criminal heritage, stands in the way of his happy future. And it is the restoration of this white heritage, ultimately, that requires the Lodger's death.

While the Lodger cannot reform his white father, he can and does enable the white hero of *The Guilty River* to be restored to the English identity from which he has become estranged. The Lodger makes Gerard's restoration possible through the character of Cristel. Society, personified by Gerard's stepmother, Mrs. Roylake, is horrified by Gerard's attachment to and interest in the poor and simple Cristel, whom Mrs. Roylake suggests is "a little coarse and vulgar" (285). The Lodger's attempt to kidnap her, however, serves as the catalyst for Cristel's decision to run away to her wealthy uncle's house. Here, her "improvement" is undertaken by her aunt, and when she eventually marries Gerard, she "is a mistress who is worthy of her position at Trimley Deen" (353). It is therefore the Lodger who restores Cristel and ultimately Gerard (with his now proper English wife) to their positions in English society. That this honorable marriage of two such good, young people is underwritten by love and not money restores English society to its "true" values.

The sacrifice of the mixed-race character in favor of the white male finds its implicit critique near the end of the narrative as the Lodger returns to the subject of his name and remarks: "does it strike you that The Cur is a sad cynic? . . . Perhaps I am in one of my tolerant humours to-day; I see nothing disgraceful in being a Cur. He is a dog who represents different breeds. Very well, the English are a people who represent different breeds: Saxons, Normans, Danes. The consequence, in one case, is a great nation. The consequence, in the other case, is the cleverest member of the whole dog family" (319). Having identified himself as "The Cur," the Lodger alludes to Africans (those most likely in the language of the day to be characterized in the animal language of breeds) who, in addition to the Saxons, Normans, and Danes, make up the English people.[14] At the same time, the Lodger references the English erasure of those Africans from the history of English "breeding," that is to say, from genealogy. While Collins's plot works to eliminate the Lodger from his novel so as to make room for Gerard, the Lodger's comments remind us of his necessary presence as a foil and of the unseen contribution of black people to English society. Indeed, the Lodger suggests, elliptically at least, that blackness is already within Englishness; that the English are the mixed breed, the real "Cur"; and that it is this mixing that creates the greatness of the nation.

In two important ways, then, *The Guilty River* hints at the violence inherent in the project of reconstructing a society after slavery. Going a step further than *Black and White*, which leaves unexamined the role of the white colonialist (as rapist?) in the production of mixed-race Maurice and locates only potential violence in the characters of the slave, Plato, and the slaveholder, Westcraft, *The Guilty River* comes closer to representing both the violent origins of a mixed-race society and its historical legacy. Indeed, the Lodger's criminal instability stems from his white heritage, a heritage tainted by precisely the kind of corruption and sexual brutality bred *in whites* during slavery (a guilty river of genealogy?). If the story begins to uncouple blackness and violence by identifying the disease in his white roots, however, it nonetheless exploits the Lodger, killing him off for the purpose of elevating his white double.

If Gerard and the Lodger are in some senses racialized doubles, *Armadale*, the most critically acclaimed and well known of the Collins texts that I am considering here, plays out this dynamic of racial doubling quite literally. As in the cases of *The Guilty River*, the novel centers upon two men, one black, one white, their intertwined fates, and the intertwined fates of their fathers. (Both fathers and both sons are christened Allan Armadale. To avoid confusion, I'll simply refer to the sons by the names they use, Armadale and Midwinter, and to the fathers as Armadale's father and Midwinter's father.) As in the case of Maurice in *Black and White* and the Lodger in *The Guilty River*, the mixed-race protagonist of *Armadale*, known by the pseudonym Ozias Midwinter, is the son of a West Indian planter and "a woman of the mixed blood of the European and the African race."[15] Midwinter's father spent his formative years in the West Indies in "idleness and self-indulgence, among people—slaves and half-castes mostly," and his adulthood was similarly "a wild life and a vicious life" (*Armadale*, 31, 14). Like white Gerard in *The Guilty River*, Midwinter's father was thoroughly estranged from the life, including education and socialization, suitable to a young white Englishman. As Midwinter's father concludes about himself, "I doubt if there is a gentleman of my birth and station in all England, as ignorant as I am at this moment" (31). And for Midwinter's father, as is not the case for Gerard, this estrangement is explicitly linked with colonial slavery.

Notwithstanding this dubious background, upon inheriting the estates of his godfather, Midwinter's father is set up for marriage with a beautiful, white English woman, Miss Blanchard. The marriage is foiled, however, by the father of the white protagonist, Allan Armadale. Armadale's father is the disinherited son of the godfather of Midwinter's father. Having been disinherited, Armadale's father comes to Barbados to seek revenge. He drugs Midwinter's father with a "negro-poison," impersonates him, and succeeds in marrying Miss Blanchard under false pretenses. The two men leave the islands on board a yacht and are caught in a storm. Meanwhile, Midwinter's father is saved by an "old black nurse" who administers "the known negro-antidote" (35). Midwinter's father reaches the troubled yacht at sea and saves his intended bride. But Midwinter's father locks his foe, Armadale's father, into the cabin of the vessel and leaves him to drown, effectively murdering Armadale's father.

The drama of the novel focuses on the relationship between the sons of these two men. The mixed-race protagonist, Midwinter, knows his history. The white protagonist, Allan Armadale, born after his father's murder, lives in ignorance of his past. In other words, while both share a criminal inheritance born of the corruption of West Indian slavery on their white fathers, Armadale lives in complete ignorance. The mixed-race Midwinter is aware of and needs to do psychological battle with his inheritances: black blood on one side and white criminality on the other. His self-description recalls "The Cur": "there was I, an ill-conditioned brat, with my mother's negro blood in my face, and my murdering father's passions in my heart" (105). And this battle, figured in the novel as "his hereditary superstition" (124), shapes his life. The novel, in other words, makes clear that both protagonists share in a corrupt inheritance, a legacy they inherit through their fathers' connections with colonial slavery. Yet the guilt and responsibility for that inheritance rest only on the mixed-race Midwinter's shoulders.

In the end, this feeling of responsibility leads Midwinter to substitute himself for his white namesake in the chamber of a sanatorium, where he suspects a culmination of the foul play that structures the novel. Miss Gwilt, a white woman whose depravity can be traced back to Barbados, where she participated in the plot against Midwinter's father, seeks her revenge on Miss Blanchard's son, Allan Armadale. Switching rooms with Armadale so as to place himself in the chamber "in which the danger lay" (796), Midwinter thinks only of what might happen to his friend. Through this ruse Midwinter makes possible Armadale's escape from danger and by extension his eventual happy marriage and life, but Midwinter is poisoned and barely escapes. Literally, the mixed-race character takes the poison for the white one here and, in so doing, enables the white man's continued success.[16]

Accounted as "no common man" (811), Midwinter is not killed off, yet he remains alive only as a marginal figure. While the white Armadale gets the traditional happy ending of wife and wealth, the novel suggests only that Midwinter takes "to Literature" (814), with the suggestion that he may become a writer. The history of colonial treachery that has troubled the relationship between the two and sparked the intrigue of this sensation novel is never written, however, since Midwinter insists on "silence" (814), and thus the secrets of his past are never revealed to the white hero.

The novel closes with the suggestion by Midwinter "that out of Evil may come Good" and that the two men "will never be divided again" (815). These statements reflect the idea enacted in *Black and*

White and *The Guilty River* that colonialism is indeed a guilty, evil heritage, but one productive, nonetheless, of the great nation that England is now. Moreover, *Armadale* insists that black and white remain intertwined and inseparable, like white Armadale and mixed-race Midwinter, even as they still do not share equally in the responsibilities of that colonial heritage. The fact that Midwinter's real name is Allan Armadale and that both men's fathers were christened Allan Armadale literalizes the inseparability of their individual identities and of the colonial worlds they each represent.

In *Race and Empire in British Politics,* Paul B. Rich writes that "Victorian racialism represented a complex amalgam of competing ideologies and interests and developed a set of stereotypes towards blacks that portrayed them as both savage and bestial figures who needed to be controlled at all costs and as passive and helpless beings in need of missionary care and protection."[17] This brief excursion through some of his work suggests that blackness figured in Collins's imagination as something slightly different from evil, dangerous savagery or pathetic, stunted development. If anyone is bestial or passive in Collins's works, it is the white Englishman.[18]

The deficiencies of the white men in these texts are apparent: Natalie's father, the pathetic white sea captain in *Miss or Mrs?* who is blind to the white predator after his daughter and her dowry; Stephen Westcraft, the piggish and vengeful spurned lover, on the one hand, and the adulterer/rapist who is Maurice's anonymous white plantation father, on the other, in *Black and White*; the Lodger's father and white family, murderers, thieves, and scoundrels, in *The Guilty River;* Midwinter's white father, a murderer, and Allan Armadale's white father, a deceitful imposter and a poisoner who attempts murder, in *Armadale;* and the pliable white Gerard and Allan Armadale, who wander through their own stories under the control of their mixed-race counterparts. These texts seem to define white English identity as pathological and white English masculinity as criminal or passive. If anxiety over imperialism and the end of slavery are integral to Victorian conceptions of blackness, what emerges through an examination of these texts is that this anxiety is also central to Victorian conceptions of whiteness.

While Collins gestures toward a sickness at the heart of white English identity, he closes these stories with the insistence that all is still well in England. Natalie's white father in *Miss or Mrs?* is pitifully unable to play his proper role as white patriarch, but she is still able to achieve a successful marriage to a white man. In *Black and White,* the loathsome Stephen Westcraft's plans are swiftly overcome, and Maurice marries his white bride and lives happily ever after. If neither the Lodger nor Midwinter achieves happiness, the endings of *The Guilty River* and *Armadale* restore the more important white hero to his rightful social position. Moreover, while the disease within white identity is identified explicitly in *Black and White, The Guilty River,* and *Armadale* and implicitly in *Miss or Mrs?* with the corruption of slavery, the abolition of colonial slavery, and of slavery in the United States, ensures that this infection of white identity by slavery is a thing of the past.

Meanwhile the texts insist that the mixed-race legacy of that past will either be absorbed into white England, as is the case with Natalie and Maurice, or be shouldered single-handedly by the mixed-race characters who will happily sacrifice themselves to restore their white peers, as is the case with the Lodger and Midwinter. Working with mixed-race characters whose relationship to black society is attenuated at best, Collins can suggest that the colonial project, symbolized by these characters who are the literal progeny of England's colonial endeavors, need not disrupt English normalcy.

Notes

Research and time for writing this essay was made possible by a grant from the Huntington Library in coordination with the North American Conference on British Studies and by a senior research fellowship at the Center for Humanities at Wesleyan University. An earlier version of this essay was presented at Wesleyan, and I am grateful to the university community there and the other fellows at the center for their comments and encouragement, particularly Laurie Lewis and Richard Ohmann. Thanks also to Elise Lemire and Lisa Botshon for their thoughtful criticism of this piece.

1. See Patrick Brantlinger, *Rule of Darkness: British Literature and Imperialism, 1830–1914* (Ithaca: Cornell Univ. Press, 1988). Reacting to the Sepoy Rebellion, Dickens had written in a letter that were he a "Commander in Chief in India" he would do his "utmost to exterminate the Race . . . to blot it out of mankind and raze it off the face of the Earth" (qtd. in Brantlinger, 206–7). Dickens, like Carlyle in his "On the Nigger Question" (1849), approved of, as Patrick Brantlinger puts it, "imperial domination and even, if necessary, of the liquidation by genocide of 'niggers' and 'natives'" (207).

2. Collins and Dickens collaborated on this story that focused on "the native question"; it appeared in the *Household Words* Christmas number in 1857.

3. Wilkie Collins, *Miss or Mrs?*, in *Miss or Mrs?, The Haunted Hotel, The Guilty River,* ed. Norman Page (Oxford: Oxford Univ. Press, 1999), 9. Hereafter cited in the text as *Miss or Mrs?*

4. On this issue in Cooper, see Elise V. Lemire, *"Miscegenation": Making Race in America* (Philadelphia: Univ. of Pennsylvania Press, 2002).

5. David Turley, *The Culture of English Antislavery, 1780–1860* (New York: Routledge, 1991).

6. Wilkie Collins and Charles Fechter, *Black and White: A Love Story* (London: C. Whiting, 1869), 23. Hereafter cited in the text as *Black and White*.

7. See Douglas A. Lorimer, "Bibles, Banjoes and Bones: Images of the Negro in the Popular Culture of Victorian England," in *In Search of the Visible Past: History Lectures at Wilfrid Laurier University, 1973–1974*, ed. Barry M. Gough (Waterloo, Ontario: Wilfrid Laurier Univ. Press, 1975), 31–50.

8. Robert Ashley, *Wilkie Collins* (London: Arthur Barker, 1952), 80.

9. Qtd. in William M. Clarke, *The Secret Life of Wilkie Collins* (Chicago: Ivan R. Dee, 1988), 119.

10. See Audrey Fisch, *American Slaves in Victorian England: Abolitionist Politics in Popular Literature and Culture* (Cambridge and New York: Cambridge Univ. Press, 2000).

11. "The Theatres," *The Illustrated London News*, 3 Apr. 1869, 343.

12. Wilkie Collins, *The Guilty River* in *Miss or Mrs?, The Haunted Hotel, The Guilty River*, ed. Norman Page (Oxford: Oxford Univ. Press, 1999), 247. Hereafter cited in the text as *The Guilty River*.

13. H. L. Malchow, *Gothic Images of Race in Nineteenth-Century Britain* (Stanford: Stanford Univ. Press, 1996), 181.

14. Peter Fryer suggests there were some ten thousand blacks living in England at the beginning of the nineteenth century (*Staying Power: The History of Black People in Britain* [London: Pluto Press, 1984], 235).

15. Wilkie Collins, *Armadale*, ed. Catherine Peters (Oxford: Oxford Univ. Press, 1989), 23. Hereafter cited in the text as *Armadale*.

16. Lillian Nayder argues that Collins "emphasizes the Creole's [Midwinter's] racial otherness and repeatedly suggests that the part-African character brings the dangers of native insurrection to England's shores" (*Wilkie Collins* [New York: Twayne Publishers, 1997], 113). I would argue instead that Midwinter's character represents not the dangers of native insurrection and of the racial other, per se, but the battle, writ small *within* Midwinter, between racial other and white colonial oppressor. In the end, Midwinter's nobly sacrificial character emerges out of his racial heritage, not his white criminal background.

17. Paul B. Rich, *Race and Empire in British Politics* (Cambridge: Cambridge Univ. Press, 1986), 12.

18. Although there may also be an argument to be made about how slavery corrupts the white female characters as well. Lydia Gwilt, in *Armadale*, certainly suffers from a corresponding gender dysphoria that results in

her unnatural criminality, overt sexuality, and unfeminine aggressiveness of mind and spirit (Nayder, 110–15). See also Jonathan Craig Tutor, "Lydia Gwilt: Wilkie Collins's Satanic, Sirenic Psychotic," *University of Mississippi Studies in English* 10 (1992): 37–55.

References

Ashley, Robert. *Wilkie Collins*. London: Arthur Barker, 1952.

Brantlinger, Patrick. *Rule of Darkness: British Literature and Imperialism, 1830–1914*. Ithaca: Cornell Univ. Press, 1988.

Clarke, William M. *The Secret Life of Wilkie Collins*. Chicago: Ivan R. Dee, 1988.

Collins, Wilkie. *Armadale*. Ed. Catherine Peters. Oxford: Oxford Univ. Press, 1989.

———. *Miss or Mrs?, The Haunted Hotel, The Guilty River*. Ed. Norman Page. Oxford: Oxford Univ. Press, 1999.

Collins, Wilkie, and Charles Fechter. *Black and White: A Love Story*. London: C. Whiting, 1869.

Fisch, Audrey. *American Slaves in Victorian England: Abolitionist Politics in Popular Literature and Culture*. Cambridge and New York: Cambridge Univ. Press, 2000.

Fryer, Peter. *Staying Power: The History of Black People in Britain*. London: Pluto Press, 1984.

Lemire, Elise V. *"Miscegenation": Making Race in America*. Philadelphia: Univ. of Pennsylvania Press, 2002.

Lorimer, Douglas A. "Bibles, Banjoes and Bones: Images of the Negro in the Popular Culture of Victorian England. In *In Search of the Visible Past: History Lectures at Wilfrid Laurier University, 1973–74*, ed. Barry M. Gough, 31–50. Waterloo, Ontario: Wilfrid Laurier Univ. Press, 1975.

Malchow, H. L. *Gothic Images of Race in Nineteenth-Century Britain*. Stanford: Stanford Univ. Press, 1996.

Nayder, Lillian. *Wilkie Collins*. New York: Twayne Publishers, 1997.

Rich, Paul B. *Race and Empire in British Politics*. Cambridge: Cambridge Univ. Press, 1986.

"The Theatres." *The Illustrated London News*, 3 Apr. 1869, 343.

Turley, David. *The Culture of English Antislavery, 1780–1860*. New York: Routledge, 1991.

Tutor, Jonathan Craig. "Lydia Gwilt: Wilkie Collins's Satanic, Sirenic, Psychotic." *University of Mississippi Studies in English* 10 (1992): 37–55.

Yesterday's Sensations
Modes of Publication and Narrative Form in Collins's Late Novels

Graham Law

HIS ESSAY CONCENTRATES ON WILKIE COLLINS'S LATER FICTION, ALMOST ALL OF WHICH, AFTER MORE THAN A CENTURY OF neglect, is now once again readily accessible to the general reader. While I do not intend to take issue with the widely held view that the last decades of Collins's career witnessed a marked decline in the quality of his literary output, I would argue that the decline was less precipitate and more uneven than is sometimes assumed. A variety of personal causes have been put forward to explain this falling off, from the ravages of illness and pain-killing drugs to Collins's overwhelming sense of loss over the deaths of his mother (always a confidante) and his mentor, Dickens. My purpose is not to detract from or add to these explanations, but rather to map the weaknesses of Collins's later writings both against developments in the fictional genres available to Victorian authors in the 1870s and

1880s and against the changing print media through which they were made available to the reading public. In placing the late novels in relation to their public and material context of production, I argue that Collins became increasingly uncertain of his status and his audience in the rapidly changing late Victorian literary marketplace. The fault lines in the later novels can thus be read as symptoms not only of the growing divide between romantic and professional views of authorship, and between "gentlemanly" and "commercial" modes of fiction production, but also of Collins's growing confusion as to which side of the divide he was on. Indeed, the seeds of this uncertainty can even be traced back to the era of his great sensation novels.

The alarm caused in the early 1860s by the fashion for "sensation" novels such as Collins's *The Woman in White* (1860) or Mary Elizabeth Braddon's *Lady Audley's Secret* (1862), which set scandalous and mysterious events within respectable domestic environments, has generally been explained by the fact that these novels transgressed conventional boundaries of gender and class. They did so, it is argued, not only by portraying women in aggressively active social and sexual roles but also by inserting what were perceived as the proletarian themes of violence, infidelity, and insanity into bourgeois settings.[1] While all this is evidently true, it does not offer any clue as to why the storm of protest arose quite when it did. As Braddon pointed out wittily in *The Doctor's Wife* (1864), such transgressive narratives had been current for some time before the term of disapprobation was coined: "That bitter term of reproach, 'sensation,' had not been invented for the terror of romancers in the fifty-second year of this present century; but the thing existed nevertheless in divers forms, and people wrote sensation novels as unconsciously as Monsieur Jourdain talked prose."[2] Indeed, Collins's *Basil* (1852) has as good a claim as any to be seen as a forerunner of the sensation boom. What particularly distinguished the melodramatic novels of the early 1860s, however, is that they transgressed not only in their ideological content but also in their form of publication, by encouraging the middle classes to participate in the proletarian mode of weekly serialization, with its powerful manipulation of enigma and suspense. In his scathing critique in the *Quarterly Review*, H. L. Mansel used the term "the Newspaper Novel" to describe the fashion for sensation fiction, indicating that material more appropriate to the popular Sunday crime-and-scandal journals was finding its way into publications aimed at the bourgeoisie.[3] Braddon and other sensation novelists had succeeded in "making the literature of the kitchen the favourite reading of the

Drawing-room," as Fraser Rae put it,[4] while a review of Collins's *Armadale* (1866) in the *Westminster Review* saw "Sensational Mania" as a "virus . . . spreading in all directions, from the penny journal to the shilling magazine, and from the shilling magazine to the thirty shillings volume."[5]

Although *Basil* appeared first as a triple-decker library novel from the house of Bentley, from *The Dead Secret* (1857) onward, all Wilkie Collins's novels were published initially in serial form. Until the end of the 1860s, every novel apart from *Armadale* made its debut in Dickens's family weeklies. As early as 1858, Collins discussed the extensive proletarian readership of the "penny-novel-journals" (that is, of *Reynolds's Miscellany, Family Herald, London Journal,* and their lesser competitors) and predicted that "the readers who rank by millions will be the readers who give the widest reputations, who return the richest rewards, and who will, therefore, command the service of the best writers of their time."[6] Nevertheless, Collins clearly felt no immediate temptation to encounter such a broad social audience, although around this time other sensation writers were prepared to take the risk of appearing in the cheapest weekly miscellanies. Charles Reade's *The Double Marriage,* for example, was first published in serial form under the title "White Lies" in the *London Journal* as early as 1857. In 1863, Braddon's *Lady Audley's Secret* and *Henry Dunbar* (under the title "The Outcasts") also appeared there, in addition to half a dozen "penny dreadfuls" written especially for the *Halfpenny Journal* between 1861 and 1865. From 1868, even the aging melodramatist Harrison Ainsworth began to issue his serials regularly in John Dicks's *Bow Bells,* the new penny miscellany aimed especially at female readers and which had quickly overtaken *Reynolds's Miscellany* in popularity.[7]

Indeed, Collins's article "The Unknown Public" as a whole reveals a curious social embarrassment at the prospect of a plebeian audience. The tone is chiefly comic, but the laughter is directed not so much at the serial stories in the penny-novel-journals, which are dismissed swiftly for their dullness and sameness, but rather at "the social position, the habits, the tastes, and the average intelligence of the Unknown Public," as inferred from the columns devoted to "Answers to Correspondents."[8] The authorial first person plural asserts a yawning social divide between the readers of the penny journals and the "known reading public," that is, the subscribers to Dickens's twopenny miscellany: "We see the books they like on their tables. We meet them out at dinner, and hear them talk of their favourite authors."[9] Yet, by this time many of the penny journals had already begun to target a lower middle-class family audience that must have overlapped to some extent with that of *Household Words,* which claimed in an advertisement for its opening number to be "designed for the instruction and entertainment of all classes of readers."[10] In fact, in the year before Collins's piece appeared, the editorship of the *London Journal,* still the best-selling of the penny journals but now owned by Herbert Ingram of *The Illustrated London News,* was taken over briefly by Mark Lemon, founder of *Punch* and Collins's fellow actor in Dickens's amateur theatricals. It is then perhaps not surprising that Collins's later encounters with the emerging mass audience were often uncomfortable, being tainted with the complex forms of snobbery seen in "The Unknown Public."

In what follows, I analyze Collins's reaction to three key "moments" of change in narrative form and mode of publication in the later 1870s and 1880s: "The moment of *Jezebel's Daughter*" (the decline of sensationalism in the newspaper serial), "The moment of *The Evil Genius*" (the challenge of naturalism to the triple-decker library edition), and "The moment of *The Guilty River*" (the emergence of the best-selling single-volume thriller).

The Moment of
Jezebel's Daughter

At some point in the first half of 1873 an original deal was struck between W. F. Tillotson, a Liberal newspaper proprietor in the cotton town of Bolton, Lancashire, and John Maxwell, Braddon's companion, publisher, and literary representative. For the sum of £450 Maxwell sold to Tillotson and Son the initial serial rights to Braddon's latest novel, *Taken at the Flood,* and the story appeared simultaneously between August 1873 and April 1874 in a dozen local newspapers, including Tillotsons's own *Bolton Weekly Journal.* This was by no means the first instance of the publication of fiction in the Victorian provincial press. Immediately after the repeal of the penny newspaper tax in 1855, serial novels had begun to appear with regularity in weekly news miscellanies, first in Scotland and soon in northern and western England and Wales. The Scottish melodramatic novelist David Pae, most notably, arranged for around fifty of his tales to be serialized repeatedly in a wide range of country journals, beginning with "Jessie Melville; or, the Double Sacrifice" in the Edinburgh *North Briton* in the second half of 1855, and he could thus claim to be one of the most widely read novelists in mid-Victorian Britain.[11] However, there is no doubt that the deal between Maxwell and Tillotson was innovative—it created the first systematic syndicate of British provincial newspapers that not only covered virtually the whole of the country but also concerned new work by an author with a reputation already established in the metropolitan literary world. It thus set a trend that would come to dominate the serial fiction market for much of the final quarter of the nineteenth century. Rival fiction syndication agencies quickly sprang up both in the provinces, such as the two Sheffield firms of Leaders and Lengs, and in the metropolis, Cassell's or the National Press Agency; but Tillotsons long remained the market leader.

It has been calculated that the number of subscribers to all the newspapers carrying Braddon's *Taken at the Flood* must have reached at least a quarter of a million. By the mid-1880s, well-constructed provincial syndicates for works by popular authors could approach half a million sales, since by then a number of major city weeklies featuring serial fiction, such as the *Liverpool Weekly Post* and *Glasgow Weekly Mail,* individually commanded circulations in excess of 100,000 copies.[12] Such circulations were comfortably in advance of the readership of the most successful penny-novel-journals, whether the more respectable *Family Herald* or the racier *London Journal.* The social range of the readership reached by the provincial syndicators was also broader. The variety of editorial and advertising material found in Tillotsons's client newspapers shows that they often circulated among the solid middle class as well as further down the social scale and appealed fairly equally to women and men.[13] Tillotsons's client authors were also noticeably of higher literary standing than those featured in the penny-novel-journals. To begin with, most were protégés of John Maxwell, such as the sensation novelists Dora Russell and Florence Marryat, though a few were maverick adventurers like the aging Mayne Reid or the young Joyce Muddock. Both followed David Pae in regularly selling melodramas directly to provincial papers, but also on occasion offered their wares to the Bolton firm.[14] By the later 1870s, however, Tillotsons had established a reputation in London literary circles and had begun to purchase fiction regularly from a new group of well-known metropolitan authors, many of whom had been taken up by the progressive publishing firm of Chatto and Windus, which issued its first catalog in 1874. These new clients gradually came to include not only masters of mystery and suspense such as James Payn and Charles Reade, but also more leisurely exponents of domestic and regional subjects, including Margaret Oliphant, William Black, and even Thomas Hardy.

Nevertheless, there is no doubt that Braddon herself remained Tillotsons's leading author until nearly the end of the 1880s, when Maxwell abruptly switched allegiance to the Leng agency in Sheffield.[15] By this time he had sold a dozen of her latest works to the Bolton firm. As during the 1860s, when Braddon simultaneously supplied both penny dreadfuls to the cheapest weekly journals and triple-deckers for the middle-class monthlies and circulating libraries, so virtually throughout the following two decades she was engaged in writing two novels at once. One was generally a more "serious" work aimed at the metropolitan magazines, with pretensions to realism, generally along French lines, and often with an exotic or historical setting, the other a more "popular" effort exploiting the mechanics of mystery and suspense written for the provincial newspapers. However, the gulf between the two narrative modes was by no means so great as during the first decade of Braddon's literary career, and both types later appeared uniformly not only in expensive three-volume first editions for library subscribers but also as cheap yellowback reprints for the railway market. All the novels Braddon wrote for Tillotsons's "Fiction Bureau," as it became known, still rely to some extent on the sensation formula, though her transgressive heroines tend by then to be rather more introspective than in the days of Lady Audley and Aurora Floyd. Being allowed more fully to enter the consciousness of such female protagonists, to understand the motives behind their gestures of defiance, must have encouraged in Braddon's readers a greater degree of empathy. Notable among such novels would be not only *Taken at the Flood* but also *An Open Verdict* (1878), which was running in the *Bolton Weekly Journal* when Collins signed his first contract with the Fiction Bureau.

In early 1867, at the first signs of a downturn in his sales, Collins had played with the idea of reprinting his most successful sensation works in the penny-novel-journals, and even of writing a new novel for them based on melodramatic stage pieces such as *The Red Vial* (1858). Though nothing seems to have come of these plans,[16] two of his serials were to appear in *Cassell's Magazine* in the early 1870s, alongside Reade's *A Terrible Temptation* (1871). But Collins discussed the idea of syndication in country papers enthusiastically with Mayne Reid and Joyce Muddock around the same time,[17] and the first novel he sold to Tillotsons, *Jezebel's Daughter* (1879), indeed proved to be a recycling of the plot of *The Red Vial*. Collins had transferred the volume publication of his new novels entirely to Chatto as early as

1874, and he was clearly the most famous, and one of the earliest, of the Chatto authors to sign up with Tillotsons. The contract he signed on 11 July 1878 was by far the longest drawn up by the Fiction Bureau in its early years, being full of particular publication restrictions imposed by the author.[18] By contrast, agreements were made with Braddon not in formal contracts but by means of a simple exchange of letters between John Maxwell and Willie Tillotson.[19] Collins's Tillotsons contract specified payment of £500, the same sum received for *An Open Verdict,* though that novel was stipulated to be in thirty-three weekly installments as opposed to the twenty of *Jezebel's Daughter.* The length of the installments of Collins's contribution was specified as "10 manuscript pages equal to that contained in chapters 9 & 10 of 'An Open Verdict' recently published in Bolton Weekly Journal."[20] Since both narratives hinge on death by poisoning, there is a useful basis for comparing the respective generic affiliations of these two serials written for Tillotsons.

Collins's original play, *The Red Vial,* had been hooted off the stage when it ran in London at the Olympic Theatre, and Collins thereafter refused to allow it to be performed or printed. However, the review of the first performance in *The Times* describes the story in detail, noting that it "does not much differ in kind from the plot of an old-fashioned melodrama."[21] The setting is the house of a Frankfurt merchant in the 1820s, and the two leading roles are those of his housekeeper and servant. The former is the widow of an eminent physician, who attempts to use the contents of her husband's medicine chest to murder her employer because he opposes her daughter's marriage to the son of a partner. The latter doggedly tries to protect his master, who has rescued him from a lunatic asylum, and fortuitously administers an antidote found in the same medicine chest, which, however, brings on the appearance of death. The final act thus takes place in the Frankfurt dead-house, where the supposed corpse comes back to life to the delight of the maniac and the horror of the would-be murderess, who becomes the accidental victim of her own poisonous preparations. Written twenty years later, the Tillotsons serial *Jezebel's Daughter* preserves both the outline and detail of this simple melodrama of murder and madness but adds a further narrative layer through which Collins can express the propagandist impulses that underlie many of his later fictions. The Frankfurt business is now merely the branch office of a larger English firm, and the narrator is a young Englishman whose aunt takes over the running of the firm on her husband's death. She uses her position to promote two missions—not only rescuing lunatics from the cruelties of the madhouse but also saving young women from more disreputable occupations by introducing them as clerks into the family business. This sets up a potentially interesting clash between two powerful mature women, a devil driven by maternal instincts and an angel espousing feminist causes. Collins develops this theme only perfunctorily, however, and instead, as so often in the later novels, devotes most of his attention to evoking sympathy for the various "friendless creatures" in need of salvation.[22] The narrative thus ends with the businesswoman taking on the role of second mother to the soft and yielding daughter of Jezebel as she marries the heir to the family firm.

In contrast, Braddon's Tillotsons serial focuses most consistently on the contrasting characters and fortunes of two young women and explores the dramatic interplay of their acts of transgression and submission. Beatrix Harefield is a wealthy heiress deprived of human warmth by a strict and jealous father who drives his wife to desertion and an early death and forces his daughter Beatrix into unwilling rebellion. Beatrix's sole friend from childhood has been the impetuous Bella Scratchell, whose poverty forces her to earn money as a morning governess and companion. Both are attracted by the hero, the grave young socialist clergyman Cyril, but when Beatrix's father dies of poisoning, Bella's jealous actions bring suspicion of murder on Beatrix. Beatrix recoils into saintlike self-sacrifice and Bella into greed and sensuality. The latter's profligacy leads to her death in a riding accident, while the former's patient service is finally rewarded by reconciliation and marriage with Cyril. Despite their dichotomies, both women are presented at once as victims and victors and fairly share authorial sympathy, in marked contrast to the noble hero who comes across as something of a prig. While Braddon is not averse to exploiting the mechanics of mystery and suspense (often at the close of the weekly installment), and a number of minor roles are familiar stereotypes from stage melodrama (notably Beatrix's self-made and self-satisfied manufacturer husband or her rakish seducer complete with military mustache), the sensationalism of the narrative is counterbalanced by a strong impulse toward social and psychological realism. The main setting of *An Open Verdict* is in the north of England in the 1850s, and the novel attempts to imagine tension in the industrial city as well as among the village squirearchy. In its treatment of social and religious problems the narrative seems consciously to emulate the Kingsley of *Alton Locke* (1850), while the relationship emerging between the two heroines, and the satire on provincial Grundyism, pay clear tribute to the George Eliot of *The Mill on the Floss* (1860) or *Middlemarch* (1872).

The extremity of the contrast between the forms of these two novels is seen most clearly in their treatment of death by poisoning and their use of a Borgia motif. In *Jezebel's Daughter,* the housekeeper's physician husband has been left the formulae of a number of the infamous but supposedly lost Borgia poisons by a mysterious Hungarian master in chemical science. The husband has devoted his life to recomposing these with the aim of discovering effective antidotes that would allow their safe use in small doses in therapeutic medicine. The climax of the novel is then the description of "the deliberate progress of the hellish Borgia poison, in undermining the forces of life," of the would-be murderess and the "nervous shudderings" that precede her remorseless death (*Jezebel's Daughter,* 410). In *An Open Verdict,* the poison proves to be merely the commonplace painkiller laudanum, used as a narcotic by both wife and daughter to find relief from abuse by the tyrannical husband and father, and the fatal overdose is self-administered when he is brought face to face with the consequences of his oppression. This information is immediately made available to the reader but is hidden from both the protagonists and the coroner's inquiry. The community is quick to point the finger of suspicion at the long-suffering daughter, but Braddon insists on more than one occasion that the true venom is in the slanderous tongues of the local gossips, their imaginations fed on a diet of popular melodrama: "There was a general idea that Mr. Harefield's death was a very mysterious affair . . . that Beatrix, being of Italian origin on the mother's side, was likely to do strange things. In support of which sweeping conclusion the better informed gossips cited the examples of Lucretia Borgia, Beatrice Cenci, and a young woman christened Bianca, whose surname nobody was able to remember."[23]

Neither serial was presumably considered a failure by the Bolton agency, as both Braddon and Collins continued to be in great demand among the proprietors of weekly news miscellanies all over the country and attracted increasingly higher rewards for their newspaper novels, but there is little doubt which of the two pays greater respect to, or makes greater demands on, the sensibility and intelligence of the provincial newspaper reader.

The Moment of *The Evil Genius*

In June 1883, when George Moore's first novel, *A Modern Lover* (1883), was published in three volumes by Tinsleys, the house that had made its fortune from *Lady Audley's Secret* in the early 1860s, the firm was facing hard times. Moore had spent much of the 1870s in

Paris, where he had latterly become an advocate of the latest theories in art and literature, particularly Manet's impressionism and Zola's naturalism.[24] Set between London and Paris, and between the bohemian and bourgeois worlds, *A Modern Lover* is the story of a handsome but impoverished artist who climbs the ladder of social success by casually betraying three women who sacrifice themselves for him. There are a number of parallels with Maupassant's later *Bel-Ami*,[25] and *The Spectator* was quick to note that Moore's intention was to "imitate the methods of Zola and his odious school."[26] William Tinsley had published the novel only on the condition that the author reimburse his losses should the major circulating libraries refuse to take up the novel because of its provocative title and theme. Smith's and Mudie's, in fact, purchased only a few copies of the novel and kept it under the counter to be issued only if specifically requested by a subscriber. Fortuitously, a fire at a warehouse destroyed the many unwanted but insured copies and saved the author from having to write a check for forty pounds to honor his publishing contract.[27]

There is no doubt that, at this point, the major metropolitan circulating libraries exercised virtually hegemonic control over the material form and ideological content of new volumes of British fiction. The library vogue had begun as early as the mid-eighteenth century, though the custom of borrowing reading matter, rather than purchasing it for private use, was greatly encouraged by the inflated price of books in the first quarter of the nineteenth century. However, it was not until after the midcentury, when prevailing economic conditions encouraged a shift to the mass production of copyright works, that the library market came to be dominated by Charles Edward Mudie, who had set up shop in 1842. As the adjective suggests, Mudie's Select Library was particular both about the social standing of its clientele and the "moral" status of the works it approved for rental. The basic annual subscription was a guinea, which allowed only a single volume to be borrowed at a time, but the most popular was the two-guinea subscription, which permitted borrowing four volumes simultaneously and was geared to the form of the multivolume novel.[28] Thus the market for new novels remained dominated by the form of publication in which Walter Scott's Waverley novels had appeared in the 1820s—the "triple-decker" at the prohibitive retail price of a guinea and a half. First editions therefore normally numbered in the hundreds rather than the thousands, of which the bulk would go to the circulating libraries at large discounts, since only the wealthiest individuals were in a position to purchase. If this system guaranteed a small but stable return to conservative publishers at a time of rapid change, and a living to marginal talents, it also severely limited the potential readership and rewards of established writers and strangled social or aesthetic experiment in fiction with the dead hand of Grundyism.

Being the quixotic individual that he was, and certainly not satisfied with the luck that left him with only forty pounds in pocket after the fire that destroyed most copies of the unsuccessful *A Modern Lover*, Moore set about tilting against the system of library censorship itself. He seems to have started out by going in person to shout at at least one of the proprietors in question,[29] and, as we shall see, went on to publish vitriolic attacks on the circulating libraries on more than one occasion. But his most important move was to join forces with the aging bohemian publisher Henry Vizetelly to issue his next novel, *A Mummer's Wife,* in a single volume at six shillings. The *Spectator* review of *A Modern Lover* had suggested (erroneously) that, in Moore's case, "the faith of a Christian and the instincts of a gentleman" had prevented him from going quite as far as "M. Zola or any of the hogs of his sty."[30] So, with the encouragement of Vizetelly, in *A Mummer's Wife* (1884) Moore set about proving that he could "go the whole hog." The novel describes the inner life of Kate Ede, the wife of a linen draper. She is seduced by her lodger, a traveling actor, deserts her husband, and takes to the stage with her lover. She is divorced and remarries but gradually recoils from bohemian freedom; allowing her child to die of neglect, she descends into alcoholism and psychosis and dies alone. This psychological drama unfolds against a background of relentless physical description—the grim streets, shops, and factories of the Potteries town of Hanley, the sordid lifestyle of the provincial theater troupe, the draper's initial chronic attack of asthma, and Kate's terminal bout of delirium tremens.

As intended, this narrative was banned outright by both Smith and Mudie. Moore immediately sent a lengthy letter to the London evening paper the *Pall Mall Gazette,* containing a blistering attack on the high-handedness of the circulating libraries.[31] But *A Mummer's Wife* received reviews that were far from entirely unsympathetic and achieved a *succès de scandale*, going into a fourth edition within the year of publication. At this point Moore issued a pamphlet, entitled *Literature at Nurse; or, Circulating Morals,* which savagely mocked Mudie's policy of "selection." What was most at issue was the writer's freedom to choose the form of the narrative. Moore records that Mudie, the personification of "the British Matron," states that "he did not keep naturalistic literature—that he did not consider it 'proper.'"[32]

Thus, the pamphlet attempted to show that many fashionable sensation novels actively promoted by Mudie (such as Florence Marryat's latest) were considerably more salacious than *A Mummer's Wife,* which had been judged "an immoral publication which the library would not be justified in circulating."[33] Each indictment ended with the sardonic refrain: "*tell me, Mr. Mudie, if there be not in this doll just a little too much bosom showing, if there be not too much ankle appearing from under this skirt? Tell me, I beseech you.*"[34]

Unlike the "quite witless and quite *h*-less" Tinsley,[35] Vizetelly was a well-read man who was well aware of the cultural issues involved. He had been a pioneer in pictorial journalism from the 1840s and had acted as Paris correspondent of *The Illustrated London News* for almost a decade from the mid-1860s, where he had acquired a reputation as an authority on contemporary French literature. He understood it was no coincidence that, not long after the midcentury, France had allowed progressive publishers such as Michel Lévy to throttle its circulating libraries by slashing the price of the best new works of fiction and had been rewarded with the flourishing of social and psychological realism. Meanwhile, Britain had allowed Mudie to remain in control and was trapped in a seemingly endless cycle of sensation and sentiment. Moore's *A Mummer's Wife* was marketed as the third in the series of "Vizetelly's One-Volume Novels," preceded by a translation of Daudet's *Numa Roumestan* (1884) and followed by works from Flaubert and Maupassant. Earlier, Vizetelly had started to issue a series of Zola's work in cheap single volumes, beginning with *L'Assomoir* and *Nana* in 1884 and succeeded by *Germinal* and *Pot-Bouille* in 1885. There were thus more than a dozen Zola titles in print by 1888, when, notoriously, Vizetelly was prosecuted and eventually imprisoned for publishing "obscene libels" in the form of translations of Zola's *La Terre,* among other titles. On the other hand, it would be naive not to recognize that, like those of the inveterate attention-seeker Moore, Vizetelly's motives in the matter were mixed. As the comments in the *Spectator* make clear, Zola's popular reputation in London in the 1880s was unambiguously that of a pornographer.[36] Vizetelly was thus not above increasing his sales by advertising the novels prominently as "without abridgement," by issuing *Pot-Bouille* under the appetizing title of *Piping-Hot! A Realistic Novel,* or by selling the serial rights to his translation of *Nana* to the pornographic weekly *Town Talk,* where it ran from late 1883 to mid-1884 alongside a lively, extensive, and doubtless largely fictional correspondence on the subject of "Indecent Whipping."[37]

Though Moore broke new ground in taking direct action to claim the freedoms long enjoyed in Paris, he was, of course, very far from being the only or the first Victorian author to attack Mudie. In an 1880 article in the *Fortnightly Review,* as august a voice as that of Matthew Arnold had praised Michel Lévy and cheap books, condemning the library system as "eccentric, artificial, and unsatisfactory in the highest degree."[38] Even Henry James had struck a glancing blow at the libraries in his "The Art of Fiction" (1884), in response to Walter Besant's earlier lecture under the same title. Their respective positions were representative of a much more widespread argument in the mid-1880s, where the extreme positions were represented by Andrew Lang's defense of romance and William Dean Howells's support of naturalism.[39]

Wilkie Collins's disgust at the conservatism of the library owners was obviously of considerably longer standing. As early as 1853 Collins had offered his support to Richard Bentley in a (finally abortive) plan to circumvent the library market by bringing out triple-deckers at half a guinea for the complete set rather than merely a single volume.[40] In *Armadale,* Lydia Gwilt was used as a mouthpiece to mock "the commonplace rubbish of the circulating libraries,"[41] while in 1871 the author told George Smith that the monopolies they wielded were "anomalies in a commercial country" and predicted "a revolution in the publishing trade" in the near future.[42] Twice during the 1870s his fascination with the figure of the reformed prostitute made Collins fall foul of Mudie, who wanted the title of *The New Magdalen* (1873) changed and refused to handle *The Fallen Leaves* (1879) altogether.[43] In the dedication to the triple-decker edition of *Jezebel's Daughter,* he had had to explain that this was not the projected sequel to *The Fallen Leaves,* which was deferred (permanently, as it turned out) until the original should receive the seal of approval of "the great audience of the English people" with the appearance of the novel as a cheap single volume (*Jezebel's Daughter,* 5). In early 1885, in a letter to George Bentley, he was still in favor of "hastening the end of the dying system of the Circulating Libraries."[44] That same month, Collins began to write the opening of a novel that was eventually to be given the title *The Evil Genius* (1886), though he had already divulged to a friend the previous autumn the detailed plot of a new story centering on the themes of adultery, desertion, and divorce.[45] The novel was once again syndicated by Tillotsons and appeared in newspapers both in the provinces and overseas between the autumn of 1885 and the spring of 1886, though the publication in volume form was put off until the autumn of that year because of political uncertainty on account of the Irish situation.[46] Given that *The Evil Genius* weighed in at little over 100,000 words, compared to not much less than 150,000 for *A Mummer's Wife,* it clearly required considerable generosity in the way of white space to stretch Collins's text out to fill three volumes.[47] We should also note that at this time Collins's publishers Chatto and Windus were among those beginning to issue new full-length novels by both major and minor authors in cheaper single-volume format, such as Robert Louis Stevenson's *Prince Otto* (1885) or Tighe Hopkins's *'Twixt Love and Duty* (1886). In these circumstances, it seems pertinent to consider why Collins did not follow the trail blazed by Moore and issue *The Evil Genius* so that it would bypass the library system.

Though Collins had been a frequent visitor to Paris from his youth, spoke French with some fluency, and kept hundreds of volumes in that language in his library,[48] he was almost wholly antipathetic to developments in French fiction after the midcentury. He did, though, admire the early explorations in realism of Balzac even more than the melodramas of Sue or the romances of Dumas *père*. Writing to Flaubert's English translator in 1886, he claimed to have been "deeply impressed" by *Salammbô* when he read it on publication in 1862 but curiously categorized the author with the elder Dumas as a disciple of Walter Scott.[49] There seem to be no specific comments on Zola,[50] but in 1877 he claimed to read modern French novels "by dozens" while traveling and to find them without exception to be "Dull and Dirty": "The 'Nabob' by Daudet (of whom I once hoped better things) proved to be such realistic rubbish, that I rushed out (it was at Dijon) to get something 'to take the taste out of my mouth,' as the children say. Prosper Merimée's delicious 'Columba' appeared providentially in a shop window—I instantly secured it, read it for the second time, and recovered my opinion of French Literature."[51]

It thus seems clear that Collins had no sympathy with the naturalist project and would have recoiled from any association with Moore.[52] Nevertheless, the common themes of adultery, desertion, and divorce—by no means unusual ones in the mid-1880s, as witness Meredith's *Diana of the Crossways* (1885) or Hardy's *The Mayor of Casterbridge* (1886), most famously—invite comparison between *The Evil Genius* and *A Mummer's Wife.*

The outline of his new story, which Collins sketched to William Winter in October 1885, ran as follows:

The central notion is . . . a divorced husband and wife, who (after a lapse of a few years) regret their separation. *He* finds that the woman who has seduced him is in no sense worth the sacrifice—and becomes a miserable man. She (passing in the world as a widow) has an offer from a sincerely religious man—hesitates (being a good woman) to marry him under false pretences—decides on telling him the truth—and is rejected with horror by her lover, who remembers his New Testament, and dare not marry a divorced woman. But these same religious principles urge him to bring the separated pair together, in the interests of their eternal welfare. He is innocently assisted by the child of the marriage.[53]

In composing the novel itself, Collins makes two significant departures from this plan. Firstly, he recasts the worthless seducer as a vulnerable young governess more sinned against than sinning and thus permits a convincing account of the mutual affection and respect that survives the conflict of interest of the two women, who form an interesting variation on the old theme of the dark and fair sisters. At the same time, he balances pathos with comedy, not merely at the dénouement but throughout the narrative, in large part through the interventions of the stereotypical figure of the wife's mother. This is the figure who gives the book its title and whom Collins had recently used in a remarkably similar way in a novel that also glances at the theme of desertion and separation, *The Black Robe* (1881). As I have argued in detail elsewhere,[54] in *The Evil Genius* Collins's general inclination is to support the move away from the patriarchal concept of matrimony as a device for the preservation of property and the male line and toward the liberal view of the marriage union as an equal partnership. The issue of the day was that of child custody, and the drift of the narrative is to offer imperative psychological evidence in support of the wishes of the mother and, most notably, the welfare of the child.[55] However, in the face of the demands of comic closure, Collins gets himself into the curious position of overtly supporting the double standard on adultery of English law, which then condoned "sexual frailty" on the part of the husband only. In contrast, when the Matrimonial Causes Act of 1857 was debated, Collins had been forthright in his condemnation of the "senseless prejudice . . . [against] any project for obtaining a law of divorce which shall be equal in its operation on husbands and wives of all ranks who cannot live together."[56]

In *A Mummer's Wife*, the divorce itself is treated in such a casual, ordinary, inevitable fashion that it comes as something of a surprise to learn that "[d]ivorce was still largely out of the reach or even imagination of the poor" at this time, when the divorce rate was still only 0.007 percent of all married couples.[57] Collins is obviously much more concerned than Moore to explicate the intricacies of family law, to demonstrate the importance of social disapprobation in discouraging divorce proceedings, and to exploit the dramatic possibilities of differences between the English and Scottish legal systems, as he had done previously in *Man and Wife* (1870) and *The Law and the Lady* (1875). On the other hand, Collins's choice of setting in the remote Scottish highlands makes the social issues unnecessarily distant. Moore's naturalistic methods clearly offer a much more profound understanding of the causes and consequences of infidelity, and we are left in little doubt that sexual "frailty" is by no means an exclusive male prerogative.

The contrast between the forms of these two novels is seen most clearly in their respective references to their own narrative form. While at work on *A Mummer's Wife* in Dublin, Moore wrote to Zola that he was engaged in "digging a dagger into the heart of the sentimental school."[58] This he attempted not only by describing in such stark detail the material circumstances determining Kate's subjection, but also by showing repeatedly that her very dreams of escape are shaped by the sentimental fiction that has fed her imagination since childhood. She is shown to have progressed from the fairy stories of the nursery, through the Gothic romances in the *Family Herald*, and finally to the sensational school of Braddon. The novels Kate keeps in a trunk under her bed and turns to in times of distress are not difficult to identify.[59] One, which must be *Aurora Floyd*, relates to "the love of a young lady in the awkward predicament of not being able to care for anyone but her groom," while Kate's favorite romance, clearly *The Doctor's Wife*, has as its heroine the wife of a country physician who "used to read Byron and Shelley to the gentleman who went to India in despair" (*A Mummer's Wife*, 108). This is curious, particularly because Moore's characterization of the novel as a "grotesque mixture of prose and poetry, both equally false" (42) is a travesty of Braddon's work. As Lyn Pykett has recently shown, *The Doctor's Wife*, influenced in part by Flaubert's *Madame Bovary* (1856), is less a sensation novel than a self-conscious investigation into the psychological needs the form meets.[60] It is curious also because, on more than one occasion in his memoirs, Moore was to recall that Braddon's was the voice that awakened him in childhood to the call of literature, singling out *The Doctor's Wife* as the source of his love of Shelley and Byron.[61] Clearly the dagger needed also to be driven into the heart of the author's own romantic urges.

In *The Evil Genius,* by contrast, Collins's consciousness of narrative form is more simply reactionary. Through the mouth of the governess, who makes the money needed to advertise her services in the newspaper by selling a manuscript to an editor, Collins is able to express his old prejudice against the penny-novel-journals, dismissing more contemptuously than Moore the "feeble and foolish" romances they offer, and the sensibility of their readers who are satisfied "so long as the characters [a]re lords and ladies, and there [i]s plenty of love in it." But at the same time, through the mouth of the wife's mother, he can poke fun at "the new school of novel writing"—the realists who offer little in the way of story and no drama, but only a "masterly anatomy of human motives" that is so dull as to be soporific.[62] This sweeping rejection of both romance and realism leaves the novelist little option but the most conservative form of comedy. It is thus unsurprising that neither Mudie's nor Smith's found anything to object to in *The Evil Genius.*

The Moment of
The Guilty River

Fred Fargus had joined the family auctioneering business in Bristol as a junior partner at the age of twenty on his father's premature death in 1868 but decided to sell when his uncle retired in the summer of 1884.[63] By then Fargus was far more widely known as the author Hugh Conway. Under that pseudonym, by the early 1880s he had already published a slim volume of verse, the lyrics to a number of romantic songs, and a handful of short tales of mystery and the supernatural. The stories had appeared not only in the *Bristol Times* and other local publications but also in metropolitan magazines such as the weekly *Chambers's Journal* and the monthly *Blackwood's.* The short novel, which appeared in November 1883 as a paperback Christmas annual (issued by J. W. Arrowsmith), unexpectedly became the publishing sensation of the season and brought Conway sudden national and international fame.[64]

Only around half of the initial edition of six thousand of *Called Back,* as the novella was entitled, had sold by the end of 1883, but in the new year sales picked up, the story was reissued as a shilling volume in Arrowsmith's Bristol Library, and a total of thirty thousand copies were cleared by March 1884. At the same time, in collaboration with J. Comyns Carr, the author rapidly created a dramatic version that was to enjoy long runs in both provincial and metropolitan theaters. This sudden turn of events seems to have stemmed in large part from an enthusiastic notice in Henry Labouchere's widely read London society weekly *Truth* of 3 January 1884:

> Who Arrowsmith is and who Hugh Conway is I do not
> know, nor had I ever heard of the Christmas Annual of
> the former, or of the latter as a writer of fiction; but, a
> week or two ago, a friend of mine said to me, "Buy
> Arrowsmith's Christmas Annual, if you want to read
> one of the best stories that have appeared for many a
> year." A few days ago, I happened to be at the Waterloo
> Station waiting for a train. I remembered the advice,
> and asked the clerk at the bookstall for the Annual. He
> handed it to me, and remarked, "They say the story is
> very good, but this is only the third copy I have sold." It
> was so foggy that I could not read it in the train as I had
> intended, so I put the book into my pocket. About 2 that
> night, it occurred to me that it was nearing the hour when
> decent, quiet people go to bed. I saw the Annual staring
> me in the face, and took it up. Well, not until 4.30 did
> I get to bed. By that time I had finished the story. Had
> I not, I should have gone on reading. I agree with my
> friend—nay, I go farther than him, and say that Wilkie
> Collins never penned a more enthralling story.[65]

According to the original agreement, Fargus ceded the entire copyright of *Called Back* to Arrowsmith for only eighty pounds. However, on the success of the book, this was canceled by mutual consent and a royalty was paid for a period of six years. By summer 1887, more than 350,000 copies of the book had been sold throughout the British Empire.[66] A much larger number were undoubtedly printed in various cheap and unauthorized editions in the United States, and the story was quickly translated into all the major European languages. Many contemporary commentators, such as the *Truth* reviewer or Margaret Oliphant in *Blackwood's*,[67] tended to compare the story to Collins's sensation novels of the 1860s, but readers are now more likely to recognize Fargus's tale as one of the first examples of the modern bestselling thriller.

Free of his duties as an auctioneer and inundated with commissions, Fargus turned out a vast amount of new fiction material in the year following the success of *Called Back*. He wrote a full-length serial for Lengs for £1,200 and received a further £200 for a trio of short stories for Tillotsons, in addition to contributing regularly to metropolitan periodicals. Among these contributions was *A Family Affair*, which was serialized in Carr's monthly *English Illustrated Magazine* from October 1884, before appearing as a triple-decker from Macmillan the following year. It is generally considered the young Fargus's best work and an indication of considerable literary potential.[68] However, Fargus's most popular and remunerative efforts were undoubtedly the two further thrillers for Arrowsmith, *Dark Days* and *Slings and Arrows,* which appeared as the Christmas annuals for 1884 and 1885 respectively.[69] However, many of these narratives appeared in volume form only posthumously. Perhaps the excess of literary labor led to physical exhaustion, for early in 1885 Fargus showed symptoms of tuberculosis and was advised to seek rest and recuperation in a warmer climate. While in the Riviera in the spring, following visits to Milan, Florence, and Rome in search of copy, he was diagnosed as suffering from typhoid fever. When convalescent, he caught a chill, suffered a relapse, and died at Monte Carlo on 15 May 1885.

Like almost everyone else in England, Collins was well aware of Hugh Conway's brief moment of glory. Around a month after the writer's death, he wrote to his agent A. P. Watt suggesting that, in order to copyright the title of his new story so that it could not be stolen by pirates if used in advance publicity, he should adopt the method pioneered by "Poor Fargus" with *Dark Days*.[70] This was to issue a "bogus" story of a half-dozen pages or so under the same title, a practice that was in fact adopted with both *The Evil Genius* and *The Guilty River*.[71] Indeed, it seems more than likely that *A Family Affair*, which combines sensationalism with delicate social comedy in treating the themes of adultery and illegitimacy, was an influence on the form of Collins's *The Evil Genius*. It is then perhaps not surprising that when J. W. Arrowsmith approached Collins after Fargus's death to see if he would take over the Bristol author's role for the Arrowsmith's Christmas annual for 1886, Collins was happy to agree to write a story "equal in length to 'Called Back.'"[72] The result was *The Guilty River*, though it failed notably to achieve the popular and commercial success of Fargus's three efforts. When Watt wrote to Bristol on Collins's death to settle the royalty account, Arrowsmith informed him that he still had 25,000 unwanted copies of the Bristol Library Edition of the story on his hands.[73] By then Fargus's mantle had already passed to Walter Besant, who wrote all the Arrowsmith's annuals from 1887 to 1890, presumably with greater financial success than Collins.[74] In the 1890s many of the annuals were produced by the rising young stars of imperial mystery and suspense, including Arthur Conan Doyle with *The Great Shadow* (1892), Anthony Hope with *The Indiscretion of the Duchess* (1894), and H. Rider Haggard with *The Wizard* (1896), all of which were also reissued as short shilling romances in the Bristol Library.

Since *The Guilty River* and *Called Back* have more in common than simply their length, we have grounds for comparing their narrative contents and strategies. Both center on a love triangle, where one of the male rivals is suddenly handicapped by sensory deprivation, where the rejected suitor attempts or commits murder, and where the result is a transgressive but finally happy union. In *The Guilty River*, the young landowner Gerard Roylake falls in love with Cristel Toller, the brown, buxom daughter of his tenant, the miller. To achieve fulfillment, however, he has to counter not only the social disapproval of his stepmother and the neighboring gentry but also the extreme jealousy of the miller's mysterious and nameless Lodger, a physician of great beauty and promise who has lost both his hearing and his sanity on discovering that homicide runs in the family. In *Called Back*, the rich and independent Gilbert Vaughan hastily marries the pale willowy beauty Pauline March, the half-English daughter of an Italian patriot, only to discover at leisure that she is an amnesiac with the mental and emotional capacities of a child. Thus, before the union can be consummated, the husband needs to assume the role of detective in order to remove the veil from his wife's past. In doing so, he simultaneously comes to understand a mysterious and melodramatic incident in his own youth, at a time when he was struck temporarily by blindness. The villain of the piece is the stiletto-wielding Macari, whose desire for Pauline led him to murder her brother in a traumatic scene strangely witnessed by both Gilbert and Pauline, then unknown to each other but finally happily united.

Although we are told that Collins's hero has been educated on the Continent and his villain's mother was a New World slave, *The Guilty River* is set uniformly and claustrophobically in the gloomy woods crowding the banks of a murky river in middle England, one of those heavily symbolic landscapes familiar from the author's early sensation novels.[75] At the same time the social issues raised are deeply embedded in class prejudice. In contrast, *Called Back* is keener to exploit stereotypes of national and racial identity. Though revolutionary politics are not themselves a serious issue, political conspiracy in Italy and political exile in Siberia provide an exotic background, so that the narrative can switch from Turin to Moscow in jet-setting James Bond style, or indeed travel from London's West End to Old Town Edinburgh on a shrieking express train that looks forward to John Buchan.

The pacing of the two narratives is also markedly different. Fargus had written *Called Back* in less than six weeks,[76] but the aging and ailing Collins got into serious difficulties when he attempted to work to a similar schedule. Publication of *The Guilty River* was arranged for 15 November 1886, with a simultaneous appearance in New York in Harper's Handy Series. Collins had been late finishing *The Evil Genius* in March, only a month or so ahead of the newspaper serialization, and was seriously ill for some time afterward, so that he only set to work on the Arrowsmith story in August, and it was still less than half finished in early October. He was forced into working twelve hours a day from the beginning of November to complete the story, and even then unrevised proofs had to be sent to New York to meet the publication deadline.[77] Fargus's tale in fact gets off to a rather slow and laborious start, but, after the murder scene, increases the grip of suspense inexorably until the release of the dénouement. Collins, in contrast, has a strong opening sequence underlining the doppelgänger relationship between hero and villain, but after the failed murder attempt the narrative loses its way and ends in bathos and confusion. The tale "was spoilt for want of room" as Collins put it in a postscript to a letter to William Winter.[78]

Perhaps the greatest contrast, however, is in narrative tone, as evidenced by the following climactic scenes where both heroes are forced to imbibe an unknown liquid. Collins's hero is made to swallow the antidote to the poisoned tea he has naively drunk, by his lover who is quicker to divine the intentions of the villain:

> "Drink it," she said, "if you value your life!"
>
> I should of course have found it perfectly easy to obey her, strange as her language was, if I had been in full possession of myself. Between distress and alarm, my mind (I suppose) had lost its balance. With or without a cause, I hesitated.
>
> She crossed the room, and threw open the window which looked out on the river.
>
> "You shan't die alone," she said. "If you don't drink it, I'll throw myself out!"

I drank from the tumbler to the last drop.

It was not water.

It had a taste which I can compare to no drink,
and to no medicine, known to me. I thought of the other
strange taste peculiar to the tea. At last, the tremendous
truth forced itself on my mind. The man in whom my
boyish generosity had so faithfully believed had
attempted my life.[79]

Stumbling in his blindness on the scene of the murder, Fargus's hero is
made to drink a narcotic by the murderer and his fellow conspirators
before he is restored to freedom:

Presently a curious odour—that of some drug was
perceptible. A hand was laid on my shoulder and a
glass full of some liquid was placed between my fingers.

"Drink," said the voice—the only voice I had heard.

"I will not," I cried, "it may be poison."

I heard a short harsh laugh and felt a cold metallic
ring laid against my forehead.

"It is not poison; it is an opiate and will do you no
harm. But this," and as he spoke I felt the pressure of the
little iron circlet, "this is another affair. Choose!"

I drained the glass and was glad to feel the pistol
moved from my head. "Now," said the spokesman, taking
the empty glass from my hand, "if you are a wise man,
when you awake tomorrow you will say, 'I have been
drunk or dreaming.' You have heard us but not seen
us, but remember we know you."[80]

Though neither tale can bear great claims to enduring literary significance, there is little doubt that Fargus's use of language is here crisper,
more concise, more modern. In sum, though Collins attempts inter-
mittently to reproduce the light romance of Fargus's thriller, he is constantly seduced by the attractions of heavy Gothic.

Although *Called Back* represented a key intervention in the
market, Arrowsmith was not the only progressive house to explore the
economic possibilities of publishing new shorter romances in single volumes at a fraction of the price of a triple-decker. The best-selling tales
of adventure that established the reputations of both Stevenson and
Haggard appeared as five-shilling volumes from Cassell's (*Treasure Island*

[1883] and *King Solomon's Mines* [1885]) or Longmans (*Doctor Jekyll and Mr. Hyde* [1886] and *She* [1887]), while Doyle's first Sherlock Holmes story, *A Study in Scarlet,* appeared from Ward, Lock at only a shilling as *Beeton's Christmas Annual* for 1887. Specialist metropolitan periodical publishers were also happy to use the thriller to wrest back power in the serial market from provincial syndicators such as Tillotsons. In the mid-1880s, sixpenny illustrated weeklies such as the *Graphic* and *The Illustrated London News* regularly devoted their special holiday numbers not to a series of seasonal tales, but to complete romances of novella length, and these commonly reappeared quickly in cheap single-volume format.[81] Shortly after, the new style of penny weekly miscellany—George Newnes's *Tit-Bits,* the Lengs's *Weekly Telegraph,* or *Cassell's Saturday Journal*—began regularly to serialize short thrillers by the likes of Grant Allen, E. P. Oppenheim, and Frank Barrett. And by the 1890s there was also a new generation of sixpenny illustrated monthlies, notably Newnes's *Strand Magazine* and *Pearson's Magazine,* which prominently featured series of detective stories by Conan Doyle, Arthur Morrison, and others. As I have argued elsewhere,[82] this restoration of metropolitan dominance in the serial market contributed to a much more rapid and unambiguous process of commodification of fictional form than had taken place under the provincial syndicators. There is no doubt that, in the long run, Mudie's and the multivolume novel were hit less by the ideological threat of naturalism than by the economic threat of the cheap thriller.

The only new fiction Collins seems to have read with much enthusiasm during the last years of his life were the adventure stories of Haggard and Stevenson. The former was also a client of A. P. Watt's at this stage, and when Collins's agent sent him copies of the Cassell's editions of *King Solomon's Mines* or *Kidnapped,* he responded with uncharacteristic animation.[83] However, the failure of *The Guilty River* seems to have discouraged him from any further attempts at writing thrillers himself. While Collins was struggling to complete his assignment for Arrowsmith, Watt was asked whether the author would also write a short romance of the same type for J. & R. Maxwell, the publishing house now run by John Maxwell's two sons. Collins replied that, though he might be "tempted by a five shilling series," if the offer involved "a shilling or two shilling series, then no."[84] *The Legacy of Cain* and *Blind Love,* Collins's last two novels, both exercises in old-fashioned sensationalism, thus duly appeared as old-fashioned triple-deckers from Chatto and Windus.

The works published late in Collins's life offer at best a halfhearted attempt to engage with new narrative forms and thus provide only a very occasional challenge to prevailing bourgeois values in the later Victorian decades. This theme could obviously be pursued further by analyzing the increasingly reactionary aspect of Collins's thinking toward the end of his life in matters of religion, gender, and politics. For this there is ample evidence not only in the private correspondence but also in the published fiction—for example, in the gradual retreat into sentimental Christianity in *Heart and Science,* the mockery of American feminism at the end of *The Legacy of Cain,* or the caricature of Irish nationalism in the prologue to *Blind Love.* But, of course, scholars such as Ann Cvetkovich, Tamar Heller, and Lillian Nayder[85] have demonstrated that, even at the height of the 1860s sensation boom, the radical gestures of writers like Collins and Braddon were already compromised and contested by retreats into conformity. In order to speak convincingly about what is ideologically and aesthetically challenging in Collins's work, we need to be clear about what is not.

Notes

1. The following have argued this case in a variety of contexts: Winifred Hughes, *The Maniac in the Cellar: Sensation Novels of the 1860s* (Princeton: Princeton Univ. Press, 1980), 9–18; Kate Flint, *The Woman Reader, 1837–1914* (Oxford: Clarendon Press, 1993), 277–78; Lyn Pykett, *The "Improper" Feminine: The Women's Sensation Novel and the New Woman Writing* (London: Routledge, 1992), 73–82; and Ann Cvetkovich, *Mixed Feelings: Feminism, Mass Culture, and Victorian Sensationalism* (New Brunswick: Rutgers Univ. Press, 1992), 15–19.

2. Mary Elizabeth Braddon, *The Doctor's Wife,* ed. Lyn Pykett (Oxford: Oxford Univ. Press, 1998), 11.

3. [H. L. Mansel], "Sensation Novels," *Quarterly Review* 113 (Apr. 1863): 261.

4. [W. Fraser Rae], "Sensation Novelists: Miss Braddon," *North British Review* 43 (Sept. 1865): 198.

5. [J. R. Wise], "Belles Lettres," *Westminster Review,* n.s. (July 1866): 270.

6. Wilkie Collins, "The Unknown Public," *Household Words* 18 (21 Aug. 1858): 222. Hereafter cited as "The Unknown Public."

7. Louis James, "The Trouble with Betsy: Periodicals and the Common Reader in Mid-Nineteenth Century England," in *The Victorian Periodical Press: Samplings and Soundings,* ed. J. Shattock and M. Wolff (Leicester: Leicester Univ. Press, 1982), 358–59.

8. "The Unknown Public," 218.

9. Ibid.

10. Cited in Andrew Gasson, *Wilkie Collins: An Illustrated Guide* (Oxford: Oxford Univ. Press, 1998), 49.

11. See Graham Law, *Serializing Fiction in the Victorian Press* (London: Palgrave, 2000), 44–50. Hereafter cited as *Serializing Fiction*.

12. Ibid., 127–37.

13. This is especially so in the case of those weeklies published as independent journals with an integral news service, like the Tory *Nottinghamshire Guardian* or Tillotsons's own *Bolton Weekly Journal*, rather than as weekend companions to daily papers, such as the *Sheffield Weekly Independent* or the *Sheffield Weekly Telegraph*. See *Serializing Fiction*, 143–46.

14. I should perhaps note that Tillotsons also occasionally took work from regular contributors to the *Family Herald* such as Mary Cecil Hay and less distinguished "adventurers" such as James Skipp Borlase. See *Serializing Fiction*, 67–68.

15. *Serializing Fiction*, 80–84.

16. Catherine Peters, *The King of Inventors: A Life of Wilkie Collins* (Princeton: Princeton Univ. Press, 1991), 279.

17. J. E. P. Muddock, *Pages from an Adventurous Life* (London: T. Werner Laurie, 1907), 107–10.

18. These restrictions included limiting publication to twelve newspapers to be named by the publisher and approved by the author, with no more than one journal either based in London or owned by the same proprietor. Only the summary of this contract seems to have survived. See "Abstract of Agreements between W. F. Tillotson Esquire and Authors" (*Bolton Evening News* archive, item 4, folder 4).

19. Graham Law, "'Engaged to Messrs. Tillotson and Son': Letters from John Maxwell, 1882–88," *Humanitas* (Waseda University Law Society) 37 (1999): 1–42.

20. *Bolton Evening News* archive, item 4, folder 4.

21. Review of *The Red Vial*, by Wilkie Collins, at the Olympic Theatre, *The Times*, 12 Oct. 1858, 10.

22. Wilkie Collins, postscript to *Jezebel's Daughter* (New York: Collier, 1900), 416. Hereafter cited in the text as *Jezebel's Daughter*. Compare the discussion of *Heart and Science* in terms of the elision of the treatment of cruelty to animals and to women in Lillian Nayder, *Wilkie Collins* (New York: Twayne Publishers, 1997), 136–39.

23. Mary Elizabeth Braddon, *An Open Verdict* (London: Simpkin, Marshall, Hamilton, Kent, n.d.), 163.

24. Adrian Frazier, *George Moore: A Biography, 1852–1933* (New Haven: Yale Univ. Press, 2000), 27–66.

25. Richard Allen Cave, *A Study of the Novels of George Moore* (Gerrards Cross, Bucks: Colin Smythe, 1978), 29–30.

26. Review of *A Modern Lover,* by George Moore, *Spectator,* 18 Aug. 1883, 1069. Hereafter cited as Review of *A Modern Lover.*

27. Joseph Hone, *The Life of George Moore* (London: Victor Gollancz, 1936), 98.

28. Guinevere L. Griest, *Mudie's Circulating Library and the Victorian Novel* (Bloomington: Indiana Univ. Press, 1970), 38–39.

29. Compare Hone, 95, and Frazier, 93. The details of this encounter are inevitably tentative because in his own various articles and memoirs, Moore is clearly a partial and unreliable witness.

30. Review of *A Modern Lover,* 1069.

31. George Moore, "A New Censorship of Literature," *Pall Mall Gazette* 40 (10 Dec. 1884): 1–2. The article gave rise to a lengthy and animated correspondence, to which George Gissing was among the contributors. See P. J. Keating, *The Haunted Study: A Social History of the English Novel, 1875–1914* (London: Secker and Warburg, 1989), 255–66, and Frazier, 114–15.

32. George Moore, *Literature at Nurse, or Circulating Morals* (London: Vizetelly, 1885), 18. Hereafter cited as *Literature at Nurse.*

33. Ibid., 5.

34. Ibid., 9.

35. George Moore, *Confessions of a Young Man* (New York: Brentano's, 1906), 184.

36. Compare, for example, Andrew's Lang comments on *L'Assomoir* and *Nana* in his otherwise surprisingly restrained article "Emile Zola," *Fortnightly Review* 31 (June 1882): 451–52.

37. *Town Talk* had been a society paper owned by John Maxwell in 1858–59, but the title was taken over by Adolphus Rosenberg in 1878 for a magazine of a rather different character. Interestingly, *Germinal* appeared in serial from November 1884 in a number of popular but perfectly respectable Tory newspapers, notably the London *People* and the *Sheffield Telegraph.* See *Serializing Fiction,* 106–7.

38. Matthew Arnold, "Copyright," *Fortnightly Review,* n.s., 27 (Mar. 1880): 327.

39. See *Serializing Fiction,* 211–13.

40. Gasson, 179.

41. Wilkie Collins, *Armadale,* ed. Catherine Peters (Oxford: Oxford Univ. Press, 1989), 594.

42. Collins to George Smith, London, 23 Oct. 1871, in *The Letters of Wilkie Collins,* ed. William Baker and William M. Clarke (London: Macmillan, 1999), 2:349. Hereafter cited as *Letters.*

43. Gasson, 109.

44. Collins to Bentley, 6 Jan. 1885, Berg Collection, New York Public Library. Unrealistically, in the same letter to Bentley, Collins saw the best means of achieving this end as the widespread (and illegal) importation through the parcel post of cheap editions of English novels from the Leipzig house of Tauchnitz.

45. Concerning the title, see Collins's letter to A. P. Watt (7 Sept. 1885, Pembroke College Library, University of Cambridge) and, concerning the plot, see Collins's letter to William Winter, Ramsgate, 5 Oct. 1884 (*Letters*, 2:473–74).

46. On this occasion, the serial was sold to Tillotsons not directly by the author but through his agent A. P. Watt, who had personally arranged the newspaper syndication of Collins's previous two novels, *Heart and Science* and *I Say No*. For a detailed discussion, see Steve Farmer and Graham Law ("'Belt-and-Braces' Serialization: The Case of *Heart and Science*," *Wilkie Collins Society Journal*, n.s., 2 [1999]: 62–72). On the delay in volume publication, see Collins's letter to Charles Kent, 11 May 1886, Harry Ransom Humanities Research Center, Univ. of Texas, Austin.

47. W. F. Tillotson had received complaints from his client newspapers in the United States that many of the twenty-six installments were well below the promised minimum of five thousand words, and in his own "Lancashire Journals" series of newspapers, led by the *Bolton Weekly Journal*, had issued the novel over only twenty weeks. See *Serializing Fiction*, 174.

48. Gasson, 63.

49. Collins to Mary French Sheldon, London, 11 Apr. 1886 (*Letters*, 2:520–21).

50. The only direct mention of Zola that I have found in Collins's writings is a passing comment on a "dull" article on the French author in a letter to Harry Quilter of 18 May [1888], Henry E. Huntington Library, San Marino, Calif. The reference is probably to Frank T. Marzials, "M. Zola as Critic," *Contemporary Review* 51 (Jan. 1887): 57–70.

51. Collins to Nina Lehmann, London, 28 Dec. 1877 (*Letters*, 2:409).

52. Collins was also antipathetic to parallel developments in American realism. Compare his late letter to A. P. Watt: "My idea is that these American magazines all stand committed to the new American school of fiction and that my way of writing represents the abomination of desolation in their eyes" (28 June 1887, Pembroke College Library).

53. Collins to William Winter, Ramsgate, 5 Oct. 1884, *Letters*, 2:473.

54. See Graham Law, introduction to *The Evil Genius*, by Wilkie Collins (Peterborough, Ontario: Broadview Press, 1994), 9–14.

55. The Guardianship of Infants Act, which rejected the common-law presumption of the paramountcy of the father's claims in matters of child

custody and asserted the equal importance of the mother's wishes and the child's welfare, was passed in 1886.

56. Wilkie Collins, "Bold Words by a Bachelor," *Household Words* 14 (13 Dec. 1856): 507.

57. Lawrence Stone, *Road to Divorce, England, 1530–1987* (Oxford: Oxford Univ. Press, 1990), 387 and table 13.1.

58. Cited and translated in Hone, 101.

59. George Moore, *A Mummer's Wife* (New York: Brentano's, 1917), 108. Hereafter cited in the text as *A Mummer's Wife*.

60. See Pykett, introduction to *The Doctor's Wife*, vii–xxv.

61. *Confessions of a Young Man*, 2–3.

62. *The Evil Genius*, 97, 89. For good measure, in his attack Collins added a sideswipe at the quantity and quality of novels being written by women (340). In fact these were old jokes that Collins had used only a few years earlier in *The Black Robe*. Compare the dialogue between the mother and daughter there:

> "let us go on with our reading. Take the first
> volume—I have done with it."
> "What is it, mama?"
> "A very remarkable work, Stella, in the present
> state of light literature in England—a novel that
> actually tells a story. It's quite incredible, I know.
> Try the book. It has another extraordinary merit—
> it isn't written by a woman." (Wilkie Collins, *The
> Black Robe* [New York: Collier, 1900], 327–28)

63. For a brief biography of Fargus more detailed and accurate than that in the *Dictionary of National Biography*, see "Death of Hugh Conway," *Bristol Times and Mirror*, 16 May 1885, 5.

64. The two earlier Arrowsmith Christmas annuals, both priced at a shilling, had been failures; the first, a collection of tales entitled *Thirteen at Dinner and What Came of It* appearing in late 1881, had included Fargus's first published story, "The Daughter of the Stars" (cited by J. W. Arrowsmith in preface to *Called Back* [Bristol: Arrowsmith, 1898], iii).

65. Cited in Arrowsmith, iv.

66. Arrowsmith, iii–iv.

67. Margaret Oliphant, "Three Young Novelists," *Blackwood's Edinburgh Magazine* 136 (Sept. 1884): 312.

68. Fargus has received little modern critical attention, but this position is the one taken by most reference works, from the *Dictionary of National Biography* to John Sutherland's *The Stanford Companion to Victorian Fiction* (Stanford: Stanford Univ. Press, 1989).

69. *Dark Days* proved particularly successful; it was also dramatized and widely translated and inspired a parody in Andrew Lang's *Even Darker Days,* also issued in 1884 under the pseudonym "A. Huge Longway."

70. Collins to A. P. Watt, 14 June 1885, Pembroke College Library.

71. See Gasson, 58, 72.

72. Collins to A. P. Watt, 18 Aug. 1886, Pembroke College Library.

73. Arrowsmith to A. P. Watt, 5 Oct. 1889, Berg Collection.

74. Besant's stories for Arrowsmith were *Katharine Regina* (1887), *The Inner House* (1888), *The Doubts of Dives* (1889), and *The Demoniac* (1890).

75. Simon Cooke, "Reading Landscape: Wilkie Collins, the Pathetic Fallacy, and the Semiotics of the Victorian Wasteland," *Wilkie Collins Society Journal,* n.s. 2 (1999): 21.

76. Arrowsmith, iii.

77. See Collins's letters to Watt, 18 Aug. 1886 and 10 Oct. 1886, Pembroke College Library, and Collins's letter to Harper & Brothers, 6 November 1886, Morris L. Parrish Collection, Princeton Univ. Library.

78. Collins to William Winter, London, 30 July 1887 (*Letters,* 2:542).

79. Wilkie Collins, *Miss or Mrs?, The Haunted Hotel, The Guilty River,* ed. Norman Page (Oxford: Oxford Univ. Press, 1999), 324.

80. Hugh Conway [F. J. Fargus], *Called Back* (Bristol: Arrowsmith, 1894), 22.

81. Bret Harte's *Maruja* (1885), *A Millionaire of Rough-and-Ready* (1886), and *A Phyllis of the Sierras* (1887), for example, all appeared in holiday numbers in *The Illustrated London News,* followed by single volumes from Chatto and Windus. We need to distinguish this pattern from the earlier cases such as those of Collins's *Miss or Mrs?* and *My Lady's Money,* which appeared complete in the Christmas numbers of *The Graphic* in 1871 and *The Illustrated London News* in 1877, respectively. Crucially, although both first appeared as books *overseas* in cheap single-volume format, in Britain the former was eventually bundled with other stories in an 1873 volume from Bentley, and the latter with the longer *The Haunted Hotel* as a triple-decker from Chatto & Windus in 1879 (see Gasson, 105–6, 110–11). Until the abrupt reversal of policy by the circulating libraries in the mid-1890s, however, the serial novels that appeared week by week in the illustrated sixpennies still generally ran for half a year before being issued as triple-deckers.

82. *Serializing Fiction,* 181–91.

83. Collins to A. P. Watt, 4 Jan. 1887 and 29 July 1887, Pembroke College Library.

84. Collins to A. P. Watt, 10 Nov. 1886, Pembroke College Library.

85. Cvetkovich, *Mixed Feelings;* Tamar Heller, *Dead Secrets: Wilkie Collins and the Female Gothic* (New Haven: Yale Univ. Press, 1992); and Nayder, *Wilkie Collins.*

References

Unpublished

Berg Collection, New York Public Library.

Bolton Evening News Archive, Bolton Central Library, Greater Manchester.

The Henry E. Huntington Library, San Marino, Calif.

Letters from Wilkie Collins to A. P. Watt, 1881–89 (LCII 2840-2), Pembroke College Library, Univ. of Cambridge.

Morris L. Parrish Collection, Princeton Univ. Library.

The Harry Ransom Humanities Research Center, Univ. of Texas, Austin.

Published

Arnold, Matthew. "Copyright." *Fortnightly Review,* n.s., 27 (Mar. 1880): 319–34.

A[rrowsmith], J. W. Preface to Hugh Conway [F. J. Fargus]. *Called Back.* Bristol: Arrowsmith, 1898, iii–iv.

Besant, Walter. *The Art of Fiction.* London: Chatto and Windus, 1884.

Braddon, Mary Elizabeth. *The Doctor's Wife.* Ed. Lyn Pykett. Oxford: Oxford Univ. Press, 1998.

———. *An Open Verdict.* London: Simpkin, Marshall, Hamilton, Kent, n.d.

Cave, Richard Allen. *A Study of the Novels of George Moore.* Gerrards Cross, Bucks: Colin Smythe, 1978.

Collins, Wilkie. *Armadale.* Ed. Catherine Peters. Oxford: Oxford Univ. Press, 1989.

———. *The Black Robe.* New York: Collier, 1900.

———. "Bold Words by a Bachelor." *Household Words* 14 (13 Dec. 1856): 505–7.

———. *The Evil Genius.* Ed. Graham Law. Peterborough, Ontario: Broadview Press, 1994.

———. *Jezebel's Daughter.* New York: Collier, 1900.

———. *The Letters of Wilkie Collins.* Ed. William Baker and William M. Clarke. 2 vols. London: Macmillan, 1999.

———. *Miss or Mrs?, The Haunted Hotel, The Guilty River.* Ed. Norman Page. Oxford: Oxford Univ. Press, 1999.

———. "The Unknown Public." *Household Words* 18 (21 Aug. 1858): 217–22.

Conway, Hugh (F. J. Fargus). *Called Back.* Bristol: Arrowsmith, 1894.

Cooke, Simon. "Reading Landscape: Wilkie Collins, the Pathetic Fallacy, and the Semiotics of the Victorian Wasteland." *Wilkie Collins Society Journal*, n.s., 2 (1999): 18–31.

Cvetkovich, Ann. *Mixed Feelings: Feminism, Mass Culture, and Victorian Sensationalism*. New Brunswick: Rutgers Univ. Press, 1992.

"Death of Hugh Conway." *Bristol Times and Mirror*, 16 May 1885, 5.

Farmer, Steve and Graham Law. "'Belt-and-Braces' Serialization: The Case of *Heart and Science*." *Wilkie Collins Society Journal*, n.s., 2 (1999): 62–72.

Flint, Kate. *The Woman Reader, 1837–1914*. Oxford: Clarendon Press, 1993.

Frazier, Adrian. *George Moore: A Biography, 1852–1933*. New Haven: Yale Univ. Press, 2000.

Gasson, Andrew. *Wilkie Collins: An Illustrated Guide*. Oxford: Oxford Univ. Press, 1998.

Griest, Guinevere L. *Mudie's Circulating Library and the Victorian Novel*. Bloomington: Indiana Univ. Press, 1970.

Heller, Tamar. *Dead Secrets: Wilkie Collins and the Female Gothic*. New Haven: Yale Univ. Press, 1992.

Hone, Joseph. *The Life of George Moore*. London: Victor Gollancz, 1936.

Hughes, Winifred. *The Maniac in the Cellar: Sensation Novels of the 1860s*. Princeton: Princeton Univ. Press, 1980.

James, Henry. "The Art of Fiction." *Longman's Magazine* 4 (Sept. 1884): 502–21.

James, Louis. "The Trouble with Betsy: Periodicals and the Common Reader in Mid-Nineteenth-Century England." In *The Victorian Periodical Press: Samplings and Soundings*, ed. J. Shattock and M. Wolff, 349–66. Leicester: Leicester Univ. Press, 1982.

Keating, P. J. *The Haunted Study: A Social History of the English Novel 1875–1914*. London: Secker and Warburg, 1989.

Lang, Andrew. "Émile Zola." *Fortnightly Review*, n.s., 31 (June 1882): 439–52.

Law, Graham. "'Engaged to Messrs. Tillotson and Son': Letters from John Maxwell, 1882–88." *Humanitas* (Waseda University Law Society) 37 (1999): 1–42.

———. *Serializing Fiction in the Victorian Press*. London: Palgrave, 2000.

[Mansel, H. L.]. "Sensation Novels." *Quarterly Review* 113 (Apr. 1863): 481–514.

Moore, George. *A Communication to My Friends*. London: Nonesuch, 1933.

———. *Confessions of a Young Man*. New York: Brentano's, 1906.

———. *Literature at Nurse, or Circulating Morals*. London: Vizetelly, 1885.

———. *A Mummer's Wife*. New York: Brentano's, 1917.

———. "A New Censorship of Literature." *Pall Mall Gazette* 40 (10 Dec. 1884): 1–2.

Muddock, J. E. P. *Pages from an Adventurous Life*. London: T. Werner Laurie, 1907.

Nayder, Lillian. *Wilkie Collins*. New York: Twayne Publishers, 1997.

Oliphant, Margaret. "Three Young Novelists." *Blackwood's Edinburgh Magazine* 136 (Sept. 1884): 296–316.

Peters, Catherine. *The King of Inventors: A Life of Wilkie Collins*. London: Secker and Warburg, 1991.

Pykett, Lyn. *The "Improper" Feminine: The Women's Sensation Novel and the New Woman Writing*. London: Routledge, 1992.

[Rae, W. Fraser]. "Sensation Novelists: Miss Braddon." *North British Review* 43 (Sept. 1865): 180–205.

Review of *A Modern Lover,* by George Moore. *Spectator,* 18 Aug. 1883, 1069.

Review of *The Red Vial,* by Wilkie Collins, at the Olympic Theatre. *The Times,* 12 Oct. 1858, 10.

Stone, Lawrence. *Road to Divorce: England 1530–1987*. Oxford: Oxford Univ. Press, 1990.

Sutherland, John. *The Stanford Companion to Victorian Fiction*. Stanford: Stanford Univ. Press, 1989.

[Wise, J. R.]. "Belles Lettres." *Westminster Review,* n.s., 30 (July 1866): 28–80.

Afterword

Masterpiece Theatre and Ezra Jennings's Hair

Some Reflections on Where We've Been and Where We're Going in Collins Studies

———◆———

Tamar Heller

A CHILD OF THE LATE TWENTIETH CENTURY, I FIRST ENCOUNTERED WILKIE COLLINS THROUGH TELEVISION—A BBC ADAPTA-tion of *The Moonstone* broadcast in the United States on *Masterpiece Theatre* in 1973. Given that my work on Collins would examine his ten-uous status in the canon, it is ironic that my earliest knowledge of his fiction was filtered through such an apotheosis of the canonical as *Masterpiece Theatre*. Each week, the show would open to the stirring strains of the *Masterpiece Theatre* theme with a credit sequence in which the camera would pan over an artfully arranged library of texts adapted for the series. *The Moonstone* was a small volume wedged between more imposingly large—and presumably more canonical—volumes. (How did they find an edition that looked that short? Did it have exceedingly small print, or was it just a mock-up?) While Collins had not been allowed burial in the *Masterpiece Theatre* pantheon of his day—the Poets' Corner of Westminster Abbey—and his work was marginal to the Victorian canon until well into the twentieth century, his inclusion in the BBC production anticipated his shifting critical fortunes, the reevaluation of his literary achievement that started in the 1970s and would accelerate through the 1980s and 1990s.

The production that enthralled me at age thirteen was excellent, but it elided one significant detail of the novel: Ezra Jennings's remarkable hair. Perhaps the screenwriter thought this too excessively Gothic an element, but instead of having the amazing hair of the novel in which "[a]t one place, the white hair ran up into the black; at another, the black hair ran down into the white,"[1] the actor who played Jennings had perfectly ordinary hair. Moreover—and this may be even more significant in terms of a gap or silence in the reading of the text—he appeared unambiguously Anglo-Saxon, with no trace or mention of the mixed racial background that Collins signals by the mingled black-and-white hair ("My father was an Englishman; but my mother—") (*The Moonstone*, 366). Being at the stage of an alienated adolescence when outcasts had a strong appeal, I was fascinated by Jennings (the actor's bland hair notwithstanding) and, when I looked up the book after watching the adaptation, eager to read about him. My fascination with this character, which only intensified when I encountered in print his uncensored Gothic presence, proved prophetic, because my reading of Jennings was central to my book *Dead Secrets: Wilkie Collins and the Female Gothic.*[2] Particularly important to my understanding of this character's significance would be the very aspect buried by the *Masterpiece Theatre* production: Jennings's duality, the mixed Englishness and Otherness that made him a figure both for Collins's sympathy with the oppressed of Victorian culture and his ambivalence about his own identification with them.

The new essays on Collins that make up this volume indicate the extent of the reevaluation that was just taking off when I started to work on him in the 1980s. I see Ezra Jennings's hair, in all its unabashed Gothic Otherness, as a symbol of the new directions in Collins studies. Although the most recent BBC adaptation of *The Moonstone* (1996) chose again to elide Jennings's racial background, it is hard to imagine new critical studies of Collins doing likewise. In fact, one might take Ezra Jennings's hair as an example of the aspects of Collins's work that make him such a compelling author for contemporary Victorian scholars, and the representation of power raised by his fiction so particularly "modern" and relevant. One way of seeing the complexity that recent Collins criticism has discovered, and also to characterize the emphasis of such criticism, is to note the sustained attention it gives to various kinds of hybridity—of race, gender, ideology, class, and even aesthetic value.

In the most obvious sense, the hybridity of Jennings's black and white hair—its dissolution of the boundaries between whiteness and blackness—draws attention to issues of race and power in *The Moonstone*, issues Timothy Carens addresses in his own perceptive comments in this volume: "Those who gaze upon Ezra Jennings confront a symbolic text which graphically illustrates the construction and inevitable confusion of antithetical racial categories."[3] It is not surprising that the efflorescence of new Collins criticism in recent years should have coincided with the critical trend to rewrite the history of imperialism from the perspective of the hitherto silenced racial "Other"; just as, in *The Moonstone,* the doctor/detective Jennings fills in gaps between the fragmented words of delirium, so too has postcolonial theory unearthed a history of racial domination and "Othering" that had long been papered over by hegemonic imperialist discourses. The importance to current Collins criticism of Victorian imperialism and race relations, that historical context symbolized by Jennings's "piebald" hair, is represented here not only in Carens's essay on the ambiguous boundaries between "Englishness" and "Otherness" in *The Moonstone* but also in Audrey Fisch's "Collins, Race, and Slavery," which, significantly, focuses on mixed-race characters in Collins's fiction; Lillian Nayder's "'Blue Like Me': Collins, *Poor Miss Finch*, and the Construction of Racial Identity"; and Gabrielle Ceraldi's "The Crystal Palace, Imperialism, and the 'Struggle for Existence': Victorian Evolutionary Discourse in Collins's *The Woman in White*."[4] Now, too, that Collins's hitherto unpublished first novel *Ioláni* has finally been released, we can expect that scholars will be able to assess the significance of Collins's beginning his career with a fiction about images of the racial Other.

Postcolonial theory helps to illuminate not only Collins's representation of types of hybridity but also what the very category of the hybrid reveals about the ideological tensions surrounding power in Victorian culture. Piya Pal-Lapinski's essay on female poisoners in *Armadale* and *The Legacy of Cain* is an example of how postcolonial theory can inform an essay that is about both race and gender.[5]

Pal-Lapinski uses as a central term Homi Bhabha's definition of hybridity as "a discrimination between the mother culture and its bastards, the self and its doubles . . . [through] a mutation, a hybrid. It is such a partial and double force . . . that disturbs the visibility of the colonial presence and makes the recognition of its authority problematic."[6] While representations such as the *Masterpiece Theatre* production, which elide Jennings's racial origins, erase the traces of these miscegenations at the root of English imperial culture, contemporary criticism of Collins uncovers how a character like Jennings, by being "a mutation, a hybrid," also disturbs "the visibility of the colonial presence and makes the recognition of its authority problematic." It is, indeed, this very disruption of structures of power in Victorian culture—whether in terms of race, class, or gender—that made Collins's work both compelling and disturbing in his own time.

Hybridity is a useful term in Collins studies in regards not only to analyzing race but also to the blurring of gender boundaries in characters such as Jennings, who describes himself as a mixture of the masculine and the feminine: "some men are born with female constitutions—and I am one of them!" (*The Moonstone*, 369). As demonstrated by Richard Collins's essay, "Marian's Moustache: Bearded Ladies, Hermaphrodites, and Intersexual Collage in *The Woman in White*,"[7] the concept of sexual hybridity is crucial to Collins's innovative and (in terms of his culture's values) unsettling, *unheimlich* portrayal of gender roles and their instability in his "mannish" women, such as Marian Halcombe and Magdalen Vanstone, and his feminized men, such as Walter Hartright and Oscar Dubourg. One can point to D. A. Miller's groundbreaking essay, "*Cage aux folles*: Sensation and Gender in Wilkie Collins's *The Woman in White*,"[8] as a significant early examination of sexual hybridity in Collins's work, and one can be certain that, with the current interest in gender studies, the portrayal of gender ambiguities in Collins's fiction will undoubtedly continue to receive attention.

A particularly important type of gender hybridity addressed by Collins's fiction is the permeable divide between the usually dichotomized Victorian categories of the "virgin" and the "whore," the "lady" and the sexual or deviant woman. It is worth remembering that Collins's remarkable portrayal of determinedly un-angelic women—a portrayal in so many ways unique among the male artists of his day—was one of the causes of his reevaluation in the late 1970s and 1980s, which coincided with the rise of feminist criticism; a study such as *Corrupt Relations: Dickens, Thackeray, Trollope, Collins, and the*

Victorian Sexual System (1982)[9] was one of the first to assess Collins's innovative representation of women. Both Karin Jacobson and Martha Stoddard Holmes's essays here address the miscegenation of the lady/whore boundary in particularly innovative and important ways by focusing on the significance of female sexuality to Victorian legal and cultural discourses.[10] Indeed, these essays point to the continuing need to assess Collins's representation of female sexuality in the context of the complex (rather than monologic) discourses—medical, legal, and literary—about that subject in Victorian culture. In these two essays, Collins's portrayal of female sexuality reveals his own ambivalence about female power: his representation of disabled women's sexuality is, according to Holmes, sympathetic, while *The Law and the Lady,* according to Jacobson, eventually contains the subversive energy of female sexuality. Still, as Jacobson says, the novel "present[s] an uncanny view of women as sexual creatures—not women who roam the streets, but Victorian 'ladies.' Finally, [the novel] . . . uncover[s] the multiplicity of female identities."[11]

What the analysis of multiple hybridities in Collins's work has uncovered is thus the *ideological* hybridity of Collins himself, his role as an artist both on the inside and outside of the structures of power in Victorian culture. Retaining a privileged status as gentleman even when most disrupting the rules of respectable society, Collins would typically punish or contain the energy of his most outrageous characters, and he grew more conservative on issues such as gender roles as he grew older.[12] Yet at the same time, his fiction—so "unnecessarily offensive to the middle class," as Dickens put it[13]—persistently interrogated the very structures of power that he himself in many ways upheld. Significantly, studies that have examined such ideological hybridity have seen Collins as epitomizing the ambiguous definition of the figure of the artist in the Victorian literary marketplace. Lillian Nayder's study of the working relationship between Dickens and Collins, for instance, traces not only the ideological tensions and differences between the two men but also examines Collins's strangely dual role as collaborator and employee—as a worker in Dickens's literary mill of the journals *Household Words* and *All the Year Round.*[14] My own work also has suggested a tension between Collins's role as professional man raising the status of literature and Collins the bohemian artist identifying with the revolutionary impulses and lower-class resentment of his day—sentiments that he could, in his own way, share as an artist in the marketplace. Explorations such as these uncover the complex workings of class and economics in Victorian culture—and what one might call *class hybridities*—particularly of the figure of the artist. (Here again it might be helpful to remember that Ezra Jennings, Collins's quintessential figure for the marginalized artist with his "buried writing"—the locked journals he has buried with him in his unmarked grave—is a hybrid of the professional man and the status-deprived drifter.)

The imbrication of economics and ideology in the Victorian literary marketplace is examined in three essays in this volume in especially innovative ways. In "Yesterday's Sensations: Modes of Publication and Narrative Form in Collins's Late Novels," Graham Law makes a sophisticated connection between the ideology of Collins's late fiction and the dynamics of late nineteenth-century publication practices.[15] Dennis Denisoff's "Framed and Hung: Collins and the Economic Beauty of the Manly Artist" examines the tenuous authority of the male, middle-class artist, in the process giving us an important example of how to connect discussions of the writer's class status with his gendered identity.[16] Similarly, Tim Dolin and Lucy Dougan's "Fatal Newness: *Basil,* Art, and the Origins of Sensation Fiction" positions Collins's portrayal of the bourgeoisie amidst the anxieties attendant on the rise of "new money" in the mid-nineteenth century while also comparing Collins's literary work to that of the Pre-Raphaelites and their circle.[17] Like my own work, all recent examinations of Collins's place as an artist in Victorian culture are in some sense indebted to the example of Sue Lonoff's pioneering *Wilkie Collins and His Victorian Readers* (1982)[18]—the first major critical attempt to situate Collins in relation to his audience and their narrative and ideological expectations. At the same time, the most recent work on Collins as an artist in Victorian culture also gestures toward new directions in which Collins studies can continue to develop: examining discourses about class, both in relation to the artist and the status of characters in Collins's work, and what these representations reflect about the complex workings of class in Victorian culture, while also situating Collins's fiction in genuinely interdisciplinary studies of other types of artists and intellectuals of his day.

In many ways, then, the recent reevaluation of Collins's work responds to Fredric Jameson's imperative in *The Political Unconscious*: "always historicize!"[19] Yet could we be approaching a new era in Collins studies, one that rediscovers the pleasure of the text? After all, what made Collins a best-selling writer, and continues to make readers enjoy his work today, was not just his adept manipulation of his culture's most deep-rooted anxieties, but also the sheer, sensational, cliff-hanging genius of his stories. There has been, however, a certain evasion of the categories both of aesthetic pleasure and aesthetic value in recent Collins criticism in favor of the ideological. At some level, one suspects that this is a defense mechanism; after all, what cast Collins out of the canon for so long were negative judgments on the aesthetic value of his work—judgments rooted in a split between the categories of pleasure and value that began with the rise of literary canons of fiction during Collins's own career. Modernism helped reinforce the assumption that "high" literature is less entertaining but more inherently valuable than "low" popular forms such as mystery fiction, with which Collins is associated. Much recent Collins criticism, and criticism of sensation fiction in general, has shown how such aesthetic judgments can be tangled in ideology—how, for instance, the association of sensation fiction with the subversion of gender and class hierarchies helped to contribute to its "low" status in literary canons.[20] In the process of tracing the imbrication of aesthetic judgment and ideology, though, we may also have assumed that the category of "aesthetic value" can only be discussed to the detriment of a "popular" writer such as Collins—and we may continue to feel, despite our new understanding of the historical development of these terms, that there is still a dichotomy between "pleasure" and "value."

My point in making these comments is not to urge us to stop examining the ideological workings of Collins's, or any other, literary texts or to align with criticism of the academy coming from the right that denounces ideological reading as left-wing propaganda designed to obscure the "real" aesthetic value of classic literature. Obviously, such criticism perpetuates the very dichotomies between "value" and "pleasure," the "high" and the "low," that cast Collins out of *Masterpiece Theatre* territory for so long. I would, in fact, like to make the claim that the new ideological positioning of Collins's texts should help us approach the questions both of aesthetic pleasure and value with a greater insight and complexity.

And, indeed, I think it is time for a new look at the pleasure of the text in reading Collins—and the aesthetic as well as the ideological implications of this pleasure. In this context, A. D. Hutter's "Fosco Lives!"[21] in this volume points us in fascinating new directions that I predict are going to become increasingly important in Collins studies. Employing an innovative form of reader-response criticism to the interpretation of *The Woman in White*, Hutter also brings to bear new psychological insights on how our minds respond to texts and their narrative twists and turns. In doing so, he invites us to theorize new ways in which both Victorian audiences responded to Collins and how we ourselves respond to him. In this sense, we may come to see that we can historicize our discussion of the aesthetic pleasures, innovations, and possibilities of Collins's texts. In doing so, moreover, we might come to write the history of our continuing attraction to the Victorians and what that attraction tells us about our own culture.

Notes

1. Wilkie Collins, *The Moonstone*, ed. John Sutherland (Oxford: Oxford Univ. Press, 1999), 319. Hereafter cited in the text as *The Moonstone*.

2. Tamar Heller, *Dead Secrets: Wilkie Collins and the Female Gothic* (New Haven: Yale Univ. Press, 1992).

3. See Carens, "Outlandish English Subjects in *The Moonstone*," this volume.

4. See Fisch, Nayder, and Ceraldi, this volume.

5. See Pal-Lapinski, "Chemical Seductions: Exoticism, Toxicology, and the Female Poisoner in *Armadale* and *The Legacy of Cain*," this volume.

6. Qtd. in Pal-Lapinski.

7. See Collins, this volume.

8. In *The Making of the Modern Body: Sexuality and Society in the Nineteenth Century,* ed. Catherine Gallagher and Thomas Laqueur (Berkeley: Univ. of California Press, 1987), 107–36.

9. Richard Barickman, Susan MacDonald, and Myra Stark, *Corrupt Relations: Dickens, Thackeray, Trollope, Collins and the Victorian Sexual System* (New York: Columbia Univ. Press, 1982).

10. See Jacobson, "Plain Faces, Weird Cases: Domesticating the Law in Collins's *The Law and the Lady* and the Trial of Madeline Smith," and Holmes, "'Bolder with Her Lover in the Dark': Collins and Disabled Women's Sexuality," this volume.

11. Jacobson, this volume.

12. For a further discussion of this ideological hybridity in Collins, see Tamar Heller, Review of *The King of Inventors: A Life of Wilkie Collins,* by Catherine Peters, *Nineteenth-Century Literature* 49, no. 3 (Dec. 1994): 398–92, esp. 391.

13. Dickens to W. H. Wills, Newcastle, 24 Sept. 1858, in *The Letters of Charles Dickens,* ed. Madeline House, Graham Storey, and Kathleen Tillotson (Oxford: Clarendon Press, 1995), 8:669.

14. See Nayder's *Unequal Partners: Charles Dickens, Wilkie Collins, and Victorian Authorship* (Ithaca: Cornell Univ. Press, 2002).

15. See Law, this volume.

16. See Denisoff, this volume.

17. See Dolin and Dougan, this volume.

18. Sue Lonoff, *Wilkie Collins and His Victorian Readers: A Study in the Rhetoric of Authorship* (New York: AMS Press, 1982).

19. Fredric Jameson, *The Political Unconscious: Narrative as a Socially Symbolic Act* (Ithaca: Cornell Univ. Press, 1981), 9.

20. See, for example, Heller, 82–88; Pykett, 30–35; Kate Flint, *The Woman Reader, 1837–1914* (Oxford: Clarendon Press, 1993); and Susan David Bernstein, "Dirty Reading: Sensation Fiction, Women, and Primitivism," *Criticism* 36, no. 2 (spring 1994): 274–78.

21. See Hutter, this volume.

References

Barickman, Richard, Susan MacDonald, and Myra Stark. *Corrupt Relations: Dickens, Thackeray, Trollope, Collins, and the Victorian Sexual System*. New York: Columbia Univ. Press, 1982.

Bernstein, Susan David. "Dirty Reading: Sensation Fiction, Women, and Primitivism." *Criticism* 36, no. 2 (spring 1994): 213–41.

Carens, Timothy. "Outlandish English Subjects in *The Moonstone*." In this volume.

Collins, Wilkie. *The Moonstone*. Ed. John Sutherland. Oxford: Oxford Univ. Press, 1999.

Dickens, Charles. *The Letters of Charles Dickens*. Ed. Madeline House, Graham Storey, and Kathleen Tillotson. Vol. 8. Oxford: Clarendon Press, 1995.

Flint, Kate. *The Woman Reader, 1837–1914*. Oxford: Clarendon Press, 1993.

Heller, Tamar. *Dead Secrets: Wilkie Collins and the Female Gothic*. New Haven: Yale Univ. Press, 1992.

———. Review of Catherine Peters, *The King of Inventors: A Life of Wilkie Collins*. *Nineteenth-Century Literature* 49, no. 3 (Dec. 1994): 389–92.

Jacobson, Karin. "Plain Faces, Weird Cases: Domesticating the Law in Collins's *The Law and the Lady* and the Trial of Madeleine Smith." In this volume.

Jameson, Fredric. *The Political Unconscious: Narrative as a Socially Symbolic Act*. Ithaca: Cornell Univ. Press, 1981.

Lonoff, Sue. *Wilkie Collins and His Victorian Readers: A Study in the Rhetoric of Authorship*. New York: AMS Press, 1982.

Miller, D. A. "*Cage aux folles*: Sensation and Gender in Wilkie Collins's *The Woman in White*." In *The Making of the Modern Body: Sexuality and Society in the Nineteenth Century*, ed. Catherine Gallagher and Thomas Laqueur, 107–36. Berkeley: Univ. of California Press, 1987.

Nayder, Lillian. *Unequal Partners: Charles Dickens, Wilkie Collins, and Victorian Authorship*. Ithaca: Cornell Univ. Press, 2002.

Pal-Lapinski, Piya. "Chemical Seductions: Exoticism, Toxicology and the Female Poisoner in *Armadale* and *The Legacy of Cain*." In this volume.

Pykett, Lyn. *The "Improper" Feminine: The Women's Sensation Novel and the New Woman Writing*. London: Routledge, 1992.

Contributors

MARIA K. BACHMAN is assistant professor of English at Coastal Carolina University. She has published articles on Richardson, Disraeli, Dickens, and Collins. She is currently coediting an edition of Wilkie Collins's *Blind Love* for Broadview Press.

TIMOTHY L. CARENS is assistant professor of English at the College of Charleston. He has published essays on Dickens, Meredith, Stevenson, and Wilde. He is currently working on a book that studies the relationship between colonial discourses and the Victorian domestic novel.

GABRIELLE CERALDI teaches in the Department of English at the University of Western Ontario, where she completed her dissertation on Victorian anti-Catholic fiction. Her research interests include questions of masculinity and domesticity in children's literature and the Victorian novel. She has articles published or forthcoming on L. M. Montgomery and Catherine Sinclair.

RICHARD COLLINS is professor of English at Xavier University of Louisiana, where he is coeditor of the *Xavier Review.* He has published in *Victorian Newsletter,* the *Wilkie Collins Society Journal, Studies in Browning and His Circle,* and the *Gissing Journal.* He is the author of *John Fante: A Literary Portrait* (Guernica, 2000).

DON RICHARD COX is professor of English and associate dean at the University of Tennessee. His books include *Arthur Conan Doyle* (Frederick Ungar, 1985), *Sexuality and Victorian Literature* (University of Tennessee Press, 1984), and *Charles Dickens's* The Mystery of Edwin Drood: *An Annotated Bibliography* (AMS, 1998). He is currently coediting an edition of Wilkie Collins's *Blind Love* for Broadview Press.

DENNIS DENISOFF teaches in the English department at Ryerson University. He is author of *Aestheticism and Sexual Parody: 1840–1940* (Cambridge University Press, 2001). He is currently editing a collection of Victorian short stories for Broadview Press.

TIM DOLIN is research fellow in Australian Studies at Curtin University in Perth, Western Australia. He is the author of *George Eliot in Context* (Oxford Univ. Press, 2002) and *Mistress of the House: Women of Property in the Victorian Novel* (Ashgate, 1998). He has produced editions of *The Hand of Ethelberta* (Penguin, 1998), *Tess of the D'Urbervilles* (Penguin,

1999), *Under the Greenwood Tree* (Penguin, 1999), and *Villette* (Oxford University Press, 2001). He is presently coediting a forthcoming volume, *Thomas Hardy and Contemporary Literary Studies.*

LUCY DOUGAN is an art historian, poet, and editor. She is the author of *Memory Shell* (Five Islands Press, 1998), which won the Mary Gilmore award (2000) for outstanding Australian book of poetry. She is currently assistant editor of *HEAT.*

AUDREY FISCH is associate professor of English at New Jersey City University. She is coeditor of *The Other Mary Shelley: Beyond Frankenstein* (Oxford University Press, 1993) and author of *American Slaves in Victorian England: Abolitionist Politics in Popular Literature and Culture* (Cambridge University Press, 2000).

TAMAR HELLER is assistant professor of English at the University of Cincinnati and assistant editor of *Victorian Literature and Culture.* She is the author of *Dead Secrets: Wilkie Collins and the Female Gothic* (Yale University Press, 1992), as well as articles on Oliphant, Le Fanu, Wharton, and Charlotte Brontë. She has recently coedited two forthcoming essay collections, *Approaches to Teaching Gothic Fiction* (MLA Press) and *Scenes of the Apple: Food and the Female Body in Nineteenth- and Twentieth-Century Women's Writing* (SUNY Press). She is currently working on a book on food and embodiment in narratives by Victorian women and editing Rhoda Broughton's *Cometh Up as a Flower* for Chatto and Windus.

MARTHA STODDARD HOLMES is an assistant professor in the Department of Literature and Writing Studies at California State University–San Marcos. She is also a voluntary clinical assistant professor in the Department of Family and Preventive Medicine at the University of California San Diego Medical School. She has published essays on disability and Victorian culture and is author of *Fictions of Affliction: Physical Disabilities in Victorian Culture* (University of Michigan Press, 2003).

A. D. HUTTER is associate professor of English at UCLA and is a board-certified psychoanalyst. He has published on a variety of subjects from Shakespeare to Collins, as well as contemporary psychoanalytic theory. He has also published a mystery novel and written for television and film. He is currently working on *The Frozen Sea: Myths of Creative Block,* and plans to write a full, new Dickens reading for the actor Patrick Stewart.

KARIN JACOBSON is assistant professor of English and composition at the University of Minnesota–Duluth. Her primary research interests include detective fiction and the Victorian novel. She is currently completing research for a book of creative nonfiction on rock climbing in Yosemite and the Southwest.

GRAHAM LAW is professor of English Studies at Waseda University, Tokyo. He is the author of *Serializing Fiction in the Victorian Press* (Palgrave, 2000). He has edited a number of editions of Victorian novels, including David Pae's *Lucy, the Factory Girl* (Sensation Press, 2001) and Wilkie Collins's *The Evil Genius* (Broadview, 1994). He is coeditor of the *Wilkie Collins Society Journal* and a forthcoming edition of Wilkie Collins's letters.

LILLIAN NAYDER is associate professor of English at Bates College. She is the author of *Wilkie Collins* (Twayne Publishers, 1997) and *Unequal Partners: Charles Dickens, Wilkie Collins, and Victorian Authorship* (Cornell University Press, 2002). She is coeditor of the *Wilkie Collins Society Journal* and is currently writing a biography of Catherine Dickens.

PIYA PAL-LAPINSKI is assistant professor of English at Bowling Green State University. She is currently working on a book that studies the intersections of nineteenth-century fiction, art, medicine, and exoticism.

Index

Clapham Sect, 261

Clarke, William C., xxvi, 25, 125, 166–67, 233, 327, 354

Clément, Catherine, 113–14, 127

Cleopatra, 96, 102–4, 118

Clofullia, Madame (Josephine Boisdechene), 136, 138–40, 142, 164

Codell, Julie F., 42, 54

Colacurcio, Michael, 226

Collins, Charles, 7, 26, 38, 215, 233

Collins, Harriet, 28, 118, 127

Collins, Philip, 138, 163

Collins, Richard, xxi, 169, 364

Collins, Wilkie, *Antonina*, xxvii, 6, 25; *Armadale*, xvii–xviii, xx, xxvii, 94, 97–98, 100, 105–18, 120, 123, 202, 270, 313, 319, 323–27, 331, 341, 354, 363; *Basil*, xi, xv–xvii, xix, xxvi, 1–33, 63, 69, 87, 147–48, 168, 197, 201–2, 230, 330, 366; *Black and White*, xxiv, 268, 280, 313, 315–19, 322, 324–26; *The Black Robe*, 343, 356; *Blind Love*, 351–52; "Bold Words by a Bachelor," 356 ; *The Dead Secret*, 148, 331; *The Evil Genius*, xxiv, 245, 262, 332, 341–43, 345, 347, 349, 355–56; *The Fallen Leaves*, 341; "Give Us Room," 166; *The Guilty River*, xxiv, 313, 319–23, 325–27, 332, 347–49, 351; *The Haunted Hotel*, 357; *Heart and Science*, xvii, 351, 355; *Hide and Seek*, xvii, xx, 26, 37–38, 40, 43–47, 49, 53, 62–72, 77, 87; "Highly Proper!", xxvii; "How I Write My Books," 227; "*I Say No*," 355; *Ioláni*, xxvii, 25, 314, 363; *Jezebel's Daughter*, xxiv, 97, 126, 332, 334–37, 341, 353; "Laid Up in Lodgings," 167; *The Law and the Lady*, xvii, xxiii, 48–52, 55, 97, 107, 126–27, 166, 283–312, 344, 365; *The Legacy of Cain*, xx, 97, 111, 119–22, 127–28, 351–52, 363; *Man and Wife*, xvii, 244, 262, 344; *Memoirs of the Life of William Collins, Esq., R.A.*, 8, 25–26, 41–42, 55; *Miss or Mrs?*, xxiv, 313–15, 317, 325–26, 357; *The Moonstone*, xvi–xvii, xx–xxii, xxiv, xxvi, 30, 62, 69–72, 88–89, 105, 125, 195, 199, 215, 227, 231, 239–65, 267–68, 276, 279, 314, 361–63; *Mr. Wray's Cash-Box*, 25, 28; *My Lady's Money*, 357; *My Miscellanies*, 167; *The New Magdalen*, 341; *No Name*, xv–xvii, xxvi, 107, 149–50, 221–22, 234, 245, 262; "The Peril of Certain English Prisoners," 271, 281, 314–15; *Poor Miss Finch*, xvii, xx, xxii–xxiii, xxvii, 59–60, 72–78, 82–84, 89–90, 266–82, 363; *Rambles Beyond Railways*, 25; *The Red Vial*, 334–35, 353; *A Rogue's Life*, 36, 41, 53; "A Sermon for Sepoys," 260, 271; *Sister Rose*, 214; "A Terribly Strange Bed," 34–35, 52; "The Unknown Public," 352–53; *The Woman in White*, xiv–xv, xix, xxi–xxii, xxiv, xxvi, 40, 43, 45–47, 54, 125, 131–238, 330, 363–64, 367; *The Woman in White* (dramatization), 222–24, 234

Collins, William, 6, 8, 41–42; *Rustic Civility*, 30

Constable, Liz, 53

Contemporary Review, 355

Conway, Hugh. *See* Fargus, Fred

Cook, E. T., 24, 53, 90

Cook, James W., Jr., 162–63

Cooke, Simon, 38, 53, 357

Cooper, Emmanuel, 54

Cooper, James Fenimore, *The Last of the Mohicans*, 314, 327

Cornhill Magazine, 109–10, 115–17, 313

Corson, Richard, 127, 163

Cott, Nancy, 87

Coutts, Angela Burdett, 29

Craig, Jonathan, 328

Reality's Dark Light was designed and typeset on a Macintosh computer system using QuarkXPress software. The body text is set in 10.5/13 Adobe Sabon with display type set in Adobe Galliard and Adobe Initials Bradley and Caxton This book was designed and typeset by Cheryl Carrington and manufactured by Thomson- Shore, Inc.